THE IDEA OF THE AMERICAN SOUTH, 1920-1941

The Idea of the American South

1920-1941

MICHAEL O'BRIEN

THE JOHNS HOPKINS UNIVERSITY PRESS • BALTIMORE AND LONDON

This book has been brought to publication with the generous assistance of the Andrew W. Mellon Foundation.

Manufactured in the United States of America

The Johns Hopkins University Press, Baltimore, Maryland 21218
The Johns Hopkins Press Ltd., London

Library of Congress Catalog Card Number 78-12250
ISBN 0-8018-2166-5

Library of Congress Cataloging in Publication data will be found on the last printed page of this book.

To the memory of
Denys Vernon French

contents

acknowledgments

As a study in recent history, this book has had the advantage and—it must be admitted—discomfort of being aided by the conversation and correspondence of those that lived my subject or knew those that did. Nearly all proved more patient and understanding than I had a right to expect, and many extended me hospitality, wine, bourbon, and steaks beyond the call of duty and the sobriety of historical scholarship. Among these, I must name Robert Penn Warren, Cleanth Brooks, Andrew Lytle, Lambert Davis, Allen Tate, William Couch, Mary Frances Odum Schinhan, Theresa Sherrer Davidson, Charley May Simon Fletcher, Harriet Chappell Owsley, Anne Wade Rittenbury, E. Merton Coulter, Rupert Vance, and, old friends, Catherine and Ella Puryear Mims. For permission to quote from unpublished manuscripts or interviews, I must thank all the above, as well as Mary Bell Davidson, Caroline Gordon, Gerald W. Johnson, Bernice Moore, the estate of John Gould Fletcher, Helen Ransom, Paul Gross, Robert Faris, John F. Cuber, C. Arnold Anderson, Rheba Vance, and Marjorie Lansing. I must single out the staff of the Joint University Library in Nashville and the Southern Historical Collection in Chapel Hill for their help, but others were punctilious: the archives at Duke University, the University of Virginia, Yale University, Atlanta University, the University of Arkansas in Fayetteville, the Library of Congress, the Tennessee State Archives, Princeton University, the University of Georgia at Athens, and the Rockefeller Foundation in Tarrytown. For less specific help, the Cambridge University Library, the British Museum, and the Harlan Hatcher Graduate Library in Ann Arbor were indispensable. For very specific help, I am grateful for money handed over by the Department of Education and Science (especially in sustaining a rickety Chevrolet) and the Michigan Society of Fellows.

Most of this book was read in draft by John Thompson, Jonathan Steinberg, Daniel Singal, Joseph Herzenberg, Mills Thornton, and Richard Lounsbury; all harried me into rectification. Individual chapters were policed by Frank Kermode, Graham Hough, Robert Buffington, and Graham Howes. To Dewey Grantham I owe a long-standing debt for encouragement, often under difficult circumstances. As for my wife, words fail me.

introduction

To undertake a venture into the history of the American South presents an immediate problem. There is no agreement on the meaning of the term "the South." When I first visited the region in 1968, as an innocent English undergraduate, I recall that I asked for a definition of this much-bandied word. It was the year of George Wallace's most formidable challenge for the presidency, and the talk was more insistent than usual. I knew little or nothing about the South and my informants served me with a welter of contradictory suggestions that managed only to bemuse. The South, I was told, is a splendid old European civilization, gentle, leisurely, polite, now somewhat ravaged by time and the contagious acquisitiveness of frantic Northerners. The South, I was told by anxious liberals, is a land of peculiar hypocrisy and oppression to poor whites and blacks alike, its pretensions a sham. Later, on a visit to Harvard, to mention that I had spent the summer in Alabama was to cause looks of amazed horror, as though I had stepped alive from the Orinoco with the toothmarks of piranha fish still on my flesh. The South, I was told, is a quite separate culture. The South, I was further informed, was just like the rest of the United States. The South, it seemed to me by the end of that summer, was anything anyone wanted it to be. But one thing was apparent: it seemed desperately important to Southerners to work out a definition of Southern culture and fix their place in it. Everyone had an opinion on the subject. When I thought of my own relationship to English culture, and that of my contemporaries, the contrast was striking. No one felt the need to define a relation to an entity called "England," least of all to define the nation so as to collapse the distinction between individuality and the society around them.

I offer this small piece of autobiography merely to explain how an outsider became interested in the problem of Southern identity. Later, of course, I discovered that the informal opinions were fragments of an old, if not too ancient, debate about the region and found my way through the writings of C. Vann Woodward, Ulrich Phillips, Howard Zinn, and others who have attempted to distill the essence of Southern distinctiveness from the confused record of the Southern past.[1] But it may be wise to caution the reader, especially if he be a Southerner, that the outsider feels no partisanship on the competing moral claims of these various versions of Southern identity; that is a private debate, on which it would be impertinent to intrude. To him, the debate is an interesting problem in intellectual history rather than a matter of social passion projected into history. To him, it does not matter personally whether Southerners are racist baboons or the true heirs of Aristotle, but he is intrigued by how such opinions should have come to pass. I hope this does not make criticism irrelevant, or incapacitate sympathy.

Since the Second World War, certain changes have occurred in Southern historiography that have made studies of the idea of the South both necessary and plausible. A partial consensus has arisen amongst Southern historians about the relationship between the South and the nation, traditionally and properly a crucial factor in any attempt to understand the region. It has been claimed that the South is and always has been a fundamentally American place, merely a variation on the general norm. Thus racism is not just of Tuscaloosa, it is also of Boston; the politics of the South have been about socioeconomic relationships, like those of the North; the South has had a viable liberal tradition, despite its image as a conservative section. Dewey Grantham is perhaps representative when he holds that "the basic ingredients of Southern politics have been, not doctrines of race, but socioeconomic groupings like those outside the region—business minded conservatives, agrarian radicals, middle class progressives, and the like."[2] The most polemical version of this viewpoint was the collection of essays from a symposium, published in 1960 under the explicit title *The Southerner as American*. It may be significant that these historians came to maturity after the New Deal had impressed anew upon Southerners the value of embracing the American consensus, and the symposium was planned during the 1950s when the struggles over segregation had suggested the inadvisability of not doing so. They were also, to some extent, the Southern wing of consensus historiography: the contention of Louis Hartz that American civilization was peculiarly a liberal culture put these nationalists under an obligation to demonstrate that the South was not exclusively conservative.[3]

At the same time, and not very compatibly, the perspectives of an atomistic sociological tradition had come to inform Southern historiography. Implicitly, sociologists have worked to dismember the concept of a homogeneous region. By close analysis, they have stressed how large and diverse an area the South is. The extent to which Florida with its tourist culture and Atlanta with its corporations, the delta lands of the Mississippi and the clay hills of Alabama, can usefully be grouped under the generic category "the South" is far from clear.[4] As contemporary political scientists have indicated how much political life has varied from state to state, even from county to county, so the assimilation of such methods into a historical discipline eager for new tools of analysis has rendered the leap from the particular to the general, from Macon County to the South, more problematical.

The nationalist perception is not original to our own times: it is strongly reminiscent of the New South movement after the Civil War. But its conjunction with the sociological tradition, not powerful in the South during the 1880s, has mounted a serious challenge to the traditional assumptions of Southern historiography. For it has been a fundamental premise of the discipline that, firstly, the South is different from the rest of the nation and, secondly, areas within the region have shared enough characteristics to make a generalization, "the South," meaningful. Remove these and "Southern history" looks a curiously misconceived exercise. Into the vacuum left by these contrary impulses has tumbled, somewhat dishevelled and unfocused, the historiography of Southern self-consciousness. One is left with the not inconsiderable difficulty that many people, for many years, have been convinced of the South's coherence and reality. Whatever else it may have been, "the South" has been a matter of social perception.

So it is no accident that recent years have seen a growing interest in the "images" that have been entertained about the South since the early nineteenth century: the agrarian South, the states rights' South, the Deep South, the lazy South, the Old South, the New South, and so forth. The nationalist school has acted as the stepfather of Southern intellectual history and its cousin, the history of Southern mythology. George Tindall has had a strategic role in both representing the "nationalist" position and consistently calling for a new approach to Southern mythology. He has even suggested that such studies might yield the final answer to the riddle of the South. "Perhaps by turning to different and untrodden paths," he has written, "we shall encounter the central theme of Southern history at last on the new frontier of mythology."[5]

But shifting the emphasis from social to intellectual history presents its own analytical difficulties. There are great, and complicated, controversies among students of human consciousness and myth that the Southern historian is now obliged to address. Defining what is myth, what is "reality," and where myth can be disentangled from intellectual traditions of perception is not easy. To reduce the difficult to the simple, he is obliged to take up a position in an old dispute: that between philosophical idealism and positivism.[6] In Southern terms, this is a choice between seeing the South itself as an idea, used to organize and comprehend disparate facts of social reality, or viewing the South as a solid and integrated social reality about which there have been disparate ideas.

Given the positivist traditions of American historical writing, it is not surprising that the latter viewpoint has been strongest in the new business of writing Southern intellectual history. In 1964, for example, a symposium was published under the title *The Idea of the South*. Its presumption was to document the ideas held about the South, and to see these as history's imperfect way of describing an underlying positivist reality, "the South." Frank Vandiver put it this way: "Surely there lurks somewhere a South, a tangible, knowable, living South, with traditions and meanings and ideals to serve the present and future as well as the past. . . . The South . . . must be self-defining, self-contained, self-reliant, a section more than a section, a province, or a realm." Most of the authors in *The Idea of the South* would have agreed, one suspects, with a comment by Clement Eaton: the title was a misnomer, for there was no idea *of* the South, merely ideas *about* the South.[7]

It may be the impulse of the outsider, but this study is posited on the contrary assumption. To the author, the South is centrally an intellectual perception, closely tied to the survival of the organicist tradition of Romantic social theory, which has served to comprehend and weld an unintegrated social reality. One of the difficulties of the positivist analysis has been the disconcerting habit of the South to alter its objective realities, without quite changing its subjective perceptions *pari passu*. With each social change since 1800, there have arisen cries that the South must vanish when a particular revolution was complete: the abolition of slavery, the dismemberment of segregation and migration of the race problem to the North, or the spread of industry to the South. Each time, when the dust settled, the South had not consented to vanish with its defining institutions.[8] This perverseness gives rise to the real possibility that "the South" has taken on a psychological reality, not entirely distinct from social reality, but capable of fastening on to successive regimes. It has secured such a hold on the American mind that it is a postulate, to which the facts of American society must be bent, and no longer a deduction. Equally, the reliance of perception on formal intellectual structures—such as the Enlightenment, Romanticism, Victorianism, or modernism—and the fact that ideas migrate across local social boundaries make it hard to explain perception by local social history alone. Naturally, to say this is not to deny the enormous weight of social history in the record of self-consciousness. But, in examining phases in the history of the Southern mind, one comes across systems of perception—Old South, New South, and the as yet unlabelled modern South—that seem essentially local variations on some very old friends: Romanticism, Victorianism, and modernism. The variations are deeply important. The intellectual historian must be interested in the manner of translating these phases into the code of Southernism.

How local social history and intellectual structures have interacted is a chief subject of this inquiry, particularly as the interaction affected the shift from Victorian to modern thought between the two world wars. These years saw a significant intensification in the debate about the region. Ulrich Phillips published most of his pioneer work on antebellum society. *The Virginia Quarterly Review* was established in Charlottesville in 1925, and the *Southern Review* in Baton Rouge ten years later. A whole host of regional organizations for intellectuals appeared: the South Atlantic Modern Language Association in 1928, the Southern Economic Association in 1929, the Southern Historical Association in 1934, the Southern Sociological Society in 1935. Regionalism, especially but not exclusively its Southern variety, was—apart from Marxism—the nearest thing to a central vogue that American literature had in the late 1920s and 1930s. Shops seemed maniacally full of books by and about Southerners. These were the years of the "Southern Literary Renaissance," of William Faulkner, Thomas

Wolfe, Erskine Caldwell, the later works of Ellen Glasgow and James Branch Cabell, the early ones of Eudora Welty and Katherine Anne Porter: a time when Southern intellectuals would chant lists of novelists, poets, and historians, and grin complacently.[9]

It would exceed the grasp and intention of this study to examine all of this. I wish to examine the borderline between the comfort of the nineteenth century with literal definitions of Southern identity and the faltering of such coherent images under the fragmenting influence of modernism. One consequence of this faltering was the growth of symbolic writing on the region, which was partly an attempt to come to terms with the intellectual tension between Romantic sectionalism and modernity of thought by exploiting the fragmented and unliteral images of the novel and poetry. There is much to be said for the argument that this has become the norm for recent Southerners. Some considered herein, such as Allen Tate in *The Fathers,* took this tack in the 1930s. But there is an extensive secondary literature on these aspects of Southern writing, and the reader may readily turn to them to find out what being Southern meant to authors like Warren, Faulkner, and Wolfe; better, he can turn to the novels and poems themselves. So it is prudent to warn him that, although some of my studies deal with figures whose main reputations rest on their literary achievements, this is not an exercise in literary criticism. Consequently, it may seem that I am trying to perform *Hamlet* without the prince. This is illusory, however, for these men hazarded themselves as students of Southern history and society. It is in such moments that I consider them.

There was some agreement before the Second World War that the issues of Southern identity were most cogently focused in the dispute between the liberal sociology of Chapel Hill, led by Howard Washington Odum, and the conservative aestheticism of Nashville. Both groups, relatively indifferent to the general issue of the South in the early 1920s, had come by the 1930s to spend much of their time refining their definitions of the region. In their history can be found many of the themes and tensions that have characterized the modern problem of Southern identity.

This study starts with a discussion of the nineteenth-century origins of the idea of the South, and proceeds by viewing the fragmentation of the Victorian South's consensus into the disparate standpoints of Odum and the Agrarians. Attention is paid to the mutations in the social environment and standing of the post-First World War Southern intellectual. Then individual chapters deal with Odum, who stood at the heart of the Chapel Hill approach and whose intellectual biography is a poignant instance of the ambivalent relationship between Romanticism and modern sociology; John Donald Wade, a man between two camps, who had been a friend to Odum and liberal reform in his youth but turned later, with mixed feelings, towards the Agrarians; John Ransom, whose biography shows how a commitment to modern poetry could both create and destroy a commitment to the South; Allen Tate, the most subtle and self-aware of Southern moderns, who tried to fashion the Southern tradition into a solvent for the dilemma of belief; Frank Owsley, a historian who resurrected a forgotten part of the Southern past, and whose life betrayed the uneasy conjunction between the professional's theory of objectivity and private social passion; and Donald Davidson, who, more than any other Southern intellectual, was left dispossessed by changes in literature, sociology, and society. The final chapter tries both to consider what was happening in these years and to move beyond that to an interpretation of the Southern idea.

It will be clear from this menu that in the dispute between the disciples of Arthur Lovejoy, who hold that the history of ideas can be written without close reference to those who held the ideas, and intellectual historians, my sympathies lie with the latter.[10] To commit oneself to the Southern idea has been a personal decision, one's definition of the region idiosyncratic, and the texture of one's discussion private. The Southern idea has been Janus-faced. In one direction, it has looked towards the "realities" of society; in another, it has reflected the individual's own needs. The idea has sat, uneasily and unstably, poised between the two. Thus these chapters are biographical in form but should not therefore be mistaken simply for biographical essays. The destination of each essay is the idea of the South held by that person, its coming, changing, and going. To get there requires the recovery of the dialectic of personality, ideology, and social environment, but that is not identical with their lives. Men, even professional Southern intellectuals, are much more than what they think about the South.

The sequence of these essays has an internal logic. They run from the least modern mind to the most modern and back again: from Odum to Tate and back to Davidson. A few years ago, I would not have chosen to arrange it in that way. I assumed that Odum, as a student of that most modern of disciplines, sociology, would be the logical culmination of such an analysis. But I rapidly learned that Odum was a proponent of a version of sociology that was relatively insensitive to the breakdown of the Victorian consensus. A little later, I might have arranged the essays in a sequence from the least to the most modern. But I have grown increasingly aware that modernism cannot merely be defined as that which has happened most recently, or that its beliefs are necessarily triumphant. On the contrary, its spread has been uncertain, uneven, and problematical, especially if its presence in different intellectual disciplines and in the perceptions of the public-at-large are considered. The circular motion of the essays stands as a metaphor for this conviction. Modernism undoubtedly came to the South between the world wars, but its success was not thoroughgoing.

By modernism I mean that shift in sensibility that has been closely linked to, but not necessarily sympathetic with, the process of modernization, the growth of industry, cities, secularization, democratization, and a mass bureaucratic society. It has been marked by a heightened awareness of the sharp pace of social change; a sense of intellectual dislocation and doubt in the sufficiency of inherited wisdom; a feeling that change, allied to the individual's greater social mobility and experience, has enlarged the existential obligation of self-definition, whether the resulting definition be idiosyncratic and anarchic or expressed in a self-conscious sinking of individual identity in a social group such as the South; "a weakened sense of objective reality" coupled to a stronger awareness of symbolism and myth; a knowledge that private "freedom" had been coupled to increasingly structured and influential public institutions.[11] Such modernism is not, as I shall argue in my conclusion, a sharp break from the Romantic tradition, but it is undoubtedly a shift in man's sense of confidence in approaching the problems of alienation and progress. Modernism is, in short, a sensibility in dialectic with modernization. It is not, however, a unified sensibility. The professionalization of intellectual trades—sociology, history, poetry, the novel, and so forth—has given each subgroup of the intelligentsia private rules to be obeyed or challenged, and has thereby reduced the community of discourse typical of the mid-Victorian world.

part one:
The Legacy

one:
On the Idea of the South:
Origins, Mutation, and Fragmentation

In his book *The First South,* John R. Alden has demonstrated that there were sectional conflicts during the American Revolution, the Confederation, the formulation and ratification of the 1787 Constitution, and the early years of the republic. Continental political institutions made it likely that the tendency of slavery and the plantation economy to be localized in the South would generate political divisions along sectional lines. From Montesquieu, the American Enlightenment had some notion that character was formed by geography. Alden quotes a striking letter of 1785 from Thomas Jefferson to the Marquis de Chastellux, in which the Virginian set out a table of differences between Northerners and Southerners:

In the North they are	In the South they are
cool	fiery
sober	voluptuary
laborious	indolent
independent	unsteady
jealous of their own liberties, and just to those of others	zealous for their own liberties, but trampling on those of others
interested	generous
chicaning	candid
superstitious and hypocritical in their religion	without attachment or pretentions to any religion but that of the heart

But this observation was not, strictly speaking, sectional, for Jefferson saw a waxing and waning of these qualities in proportion as one moved from North to South. Pennsylvania was a happy medium.[1] Thus climate and environment, and not coherent sectional cultures, were the guiding influences on the formation of a man's character. Nonetheless, this did show the tentative cultural relativism that the Enlightenment had derived from travel books, whose lessons had been driving intellectuals towards a stronger sense of the diversity of man.[2] Jefferson himself, in his *Notes on the State of Virginia,* had been a practicing student of the genre. In Enlightenment thought, however, relativism was a minor theme. David Hume's contention of uniformity in man and nature was more typical: "It is universally acknowledged that there is a great uniformity among the actions of men in all nations and ages and that human nature remains still the same in its principles and operations.... Would you know the sentiments, inclinations, and course of life of the Greeks and Romans? Study well the temper and actions of the French and English: you cannot be much mistaken in transferring to the former *most* of the observations which you have made with regard to the latter. Mankind are so much the same in all times and places that history informs us of nothing new or strange in this particular."[3] From this common lot of human interest and avarice, political arguments in the new nation over the tariff or the role of slaves in fixing ratios of representation were interpreted. With this piecemeal sense of the Southern idea, sectionalism was seen to derive from the fluctuation of interest; interest was not seen as the mirror of a determining cultural sectionalism.

The supersession of Enlightenment ideas by Romantic social theory reversed these sentiments. Romantic nationalism posited very different perspectives. Where the Enlightenment had been cosmopolitan, Romanticism located the wellsprings of man's being in national groups. Where man had been held to be uniform and his experiences similar, the new order decreed that he and they were diverse. No longer could one leap from Greek to Roman and from ancient to recent times without elaborate exegesis on the shifts in cultural context. Mechanistic theories of society were transmuted into organic analogies. Society was not a machine, from which one could subtract or add cogs at one's leisure, but a living thing which might die if the gardener was too cavalier. Rationalism was modified by a mysticism of the *Volk*. Where the Enlightenment had skipped gladly over a superstititous Middle Ages to return to the classics, Herder encouraged a dallying over the folk origins of modern nations. Old folk songs were collected, Ossian celebrated, medieval Christianity reconsidered. Where the Enlightenment had been cosmopolitan about language, Romanticism insisted that language contained the essence of national individuality: Germans, especially German intellectuals, should abandon the parroting of French for their "native" tongue. A skeptical faith in human progress was replaced by a more devious belief, in which men might win progress through a difficult process of self-awareness, alienation, and rediscovery, and in which the recognition of national diversity meant a splitting of universal moral judgments into the separate assessment of right and wrong in particular milieux. Above all, Romantic nationalism taught that man was part of a whole, his individuality defined and expressed through his membership in the group.[4]

Such ideas were to find their way to the United States, and were domesticated in the South. Partly, they came directly from Germany. Herder was read in Charleston; Hugh Swinton Legaré travelled from Brussels to Bonn expressly to meet August Schlegel; one can find in antebellum periodicals articles that betray direct knowledge of German texts, as well as English translations. Partly, they were translated through the mediation of Britain. Few read Kant, but many did understand Coleridge, the popularizer of Kant's disciple, Schelling. Thomas Carlyle, above all, carried the torch of the new German philosophy. Walter Scott helped to establish the new vogue of the Middle Ages and disperse the new faith in historicism. Byron, to be found in the pages of the *Southern Literary Messenger,* brought the *Bildungsroman* south of the Potomac. And the South did not merely imitate. In Edgar Allan Poe, it produced a thinker whose variations on the Romantic theme were sufficiently original that the later heirs of Romanticism, the French Symbolist poets, found in him something new.[5]

It would be unwise to see the novel idea of a coherent Southern *Volk* as just a colonial imitation of European thought.[6] The United States had its own traditions and reasons for moving towards redefinitions of eighteenth-century political theory. Federalism, the struggle over slavery and the territories, the hyperbole of manifest destiny, hardening racial ideology, all contributed towards helping the idea into men's perceptions. Before the Civil War, however, it was a social analysis in competition with others. As the arguments of John C. Calhoun amply demonstrate, the Enlightenment did not die so easily. States rights and Southern nationalism were uncomfortable allies and often fell out. It is unclear, moreover, how far the idea of the South penetrated into the social structure. At one level, to see nationalism as a form of social control—its classic rationale in Europe—can make one argue that the planter class by an ingenious sleight of hand identified itself with "the South," and used the welding emotion of nationalism to support its position, both in Washington and within the democratizing states. But to review the origins and course of the Civil War is to see that such control was imperfect. The record contains too many poorer "Southerners" who prosecuted the struggle for the Confederacy with diffidence, too many Whigs and Unionists who resisted a separate political destiny for the "Southern people." The planters themselves were divided between Whigs and Democrats. For some, being "Southern" was an insult to the antecedent loyalty to Americanism; for others, being "Southern" did not preclude being "American." The confusion was deepest in the 1840s, the heyday of the two party system in the region. But the exigencies of the 1850s diminished the ambiguities in practice, and secession —though most saw it in the light of states rights—helped to affirm the South's allegiance to an undifferentiated cultural identity.[7] Reconstruction did even more, for it touched the whole question of racial equality and not merely the more local question of slavery.

The idea of the South was strengthened, ironically, by the destruction of its political expression, the Confederacy. The war left welding memories and compelling economic realities. By a strange quirk, it left the South as the embodiment of Herder's idea of a nation, for Herder had been insistent that a nation was to be sharply differentiated from the formal mechanisms of the state. Indeed, a nation was weakened by the throttling uniformity of a strong central government: its essence was a free pluralism. Willingly or not, the South no longer had a common political structure.

This left Southernism unembarrassed by the propensity of national governments to act partially in society. Sentiment was left free to roam, and men could define their South without the awkwardness of an administration in Richmond to check their metaphysical freedom.[8]

There was, perhaps, a possibility that in 1865 or 1877 a man might have sat down and reflected that "the South" had been an interesting idea but mistaken. Some came close.[9] In their nationalism, New South thinkers like Henry Watterson could urge that the South was "simply a geographic expression" and the old notion that a different species of person lived below Mason and Dixon's line was a product of "morbid minds."[10] But the assimilation of Whiggery into the Democratic party forced a reconciliation between nationalism and the Southern idea. It was now necessary to have it both ways. One South might be dead, but another was to take its place. The New South was born, which was somehow to be compatible with the Old South while supporting movements that the ancien régime had perished to resist.

The New South helped to make permanent the very idea of a South. The doctrine of temporal continuity, built into a world view based on geography and race, required a reconciliation between New and Old South. Indeed, there was a sense in which men like Henry Grady invented the unitary Old South—a society notoriously disunited—by editing out the aggressiveness of plantation culture.[11] Within the concept of the South, competing ideologies of agrarianism and industrialization reached an accommodation: it seemed that any man could find a warm spot in such an eclectic tradition. In truth, the first success of the New South was ideological. The physical advance of industrialization was so slow that it was to be decades before most Southerners, long accustomed to Mr. Grady's rolling periods, were obliged to see a smokestack.[12]

The reconciliation was not always easy, though it is surprising how readily it came for many—the list of Confederates who ended up peddling railway stock was very long. It was softened because the break between Old and New South was not total. The Old South was never that old: it had lived long enough to see its Romanticism overlaid by Victorianism. *De Bow's Review* had been as strenuous an advocate of industrialization as the *Southern Manufacturers Record.* The ancien régime's religion, manners, racism, historicist sentiment, and ideas of sexuality, as they stood at mid-century, were handed over to the New South, not unscathed but substantially intact. Robert E. Lee, the priggish country gentleman, was equidistant between the deist Jefferson and the solemn Nonconformists of the Southern bourgeoisie who sired the New South.

Before the First World War, the business of mating Old and New South was carried on across a wide spectrum of professions. A poet like Sidney Lanier, a novelist like Thomas Nelson Page, a journalist like Henry Grady, or a politician like General John B. Gordon all played their part.[13] It was not a harmless hobby for intellectuals; in a world in flux, it was a vital process of translating alien ways into Southern terms. Words had to be altered, new connections made within the Southern tradition so that audiences in the South would not bridle at the naked power of the new capitalism. Innovation had to be legitimized. Although the idea of the South was not the only route to a sense of continuity, it helped to integrate the diverse appeals of religion, race, and politics. Such a process handed to later Southern intellectuals a compelling burden of sectional analysis.

There were, indeed, few Southern intellectuals. The war had wiped out most of the educational system and nearly all of the periodicals that had given a fitful patronage to antebellum writers like Poe. If a man had no private income and wished to make thinking his profession, there were few options. By the end of the century, however, things had marginally improved.

The New South may have failed to deliver on its extravagant promises of prosperity by 1900, but if one stretches its term to 1917, one can grant that it did produce the beginnings of a new educational system. Universities and schools, despite the financial burden of segregation and the suspicions of laissez faire state governments, started to provide places for the education of young Southerners and, not insignificantly, employment for Southern intellectuals. In the long run, this was to have its impact on the Southern idea. In the short run, it seemed to make little difference. Even if one defines the term "intellectual" generously, one would have been hard put to find more than a few score, scattered from Virginia to New Orleans. Those that taught in colleges were overworked and underpaid; it was a shade more prudent to find other means of sustenance, such as journalism or lecturing on the circuits. Authorship was not taken very seriously by society. If one bungled the delicate task of treading the line between New and Old South, the penalties could be harsh. William P Trent, founder of the *Sewanee Review* and a critic of slavery, complained in 1898 to a friend of "the fact that at Sewanee what harasses me is not so much lack of books and of city life as it is the fact that a considerable portion of the people around me consider me a traitor and don't like me and only keep quiet because they are afraid of me."[14]

There was little chance of political influence. An occasional state governor might listen to a few intellectuals, but the case was rare. So singular was Charles Aycock of North Carolina that he was repaid with an extravagant devotion from those academics he enlisted in his cause. But even Aycock had little faith in the intellectual as a guide to social reality. He wrote of John Spencer Bassett, the historian who nearly lost his job for breathing the names of Robert E. Lee and Booker T. Washington in the same sentence: "Bassett wrote unwisely, untruly; his view is academic.

He breathes the atmosphere of the cloister. He does not know men."[15]

For what it was worth, these men usually threw their weight behind the New South. Their economic and intellectual position rested on one basic premise, an alliance with the Northeast. The South had no money and little inclination to sustain an intellectual elite. At best, religious groups such as the Methodists or the occasional state government were willing to employ teachers. The Southern liberal was forced to seek help wherever he could. Southern philanthropists were few and far between, though the Duke family did help Trinity College in North Carolina. But Northerners did have money and, if persuaded, the inclination to "do something" for the "backward" region and, not incidentally, for the struggling Southern intelligentsia. The General Education Board was a child of Northern, Rockefeller, finance. Involved in stimulating the board's activities, liberals gained power from helping to administer its largesse. But the power was vicarious.[16]

Outside of the university, and most Southern authors did not depend upon it, the impulse was similar. The great magazines and publishing houses where the writer had to seek a market were in the North. After publication, a book was mostly read by Northerners, for Southerners read little. Walter Hines Page complained that "the southern people don't buy magazines or books.... They have no intellectual curiosity."[17] Whether the latter proposition was true, Page had wearying evidence of the former. It may be that audience expectations in the North influenced the content of Southern literary culture, but the readership may only have reinforced a natural tendency among these nationalists to find an intellectual *modus vivendi* with the North. New England, in the words of George W. Cable, was "the intellectual treasury of the United States," and New South thinkers drew freely upon the capital accumulated there before the Civil War. Emerson could be mentioned in a North Carolina lecture and draw applause. Henry Grady found kind words for Lincoln, the "Black Republican."[18]

This alliance was not without its ambiguities and dangers. It could not be presented nakedly. Both historians and literary critics in the South had to perform the act of cultural translation, to plot a distinctive graph of the Southern past, to trim a fact here, a figure there, and legitimize themselves.

The historians would claim that in 1800 the South dominated the counsels of American liberalism. Virginians like Thomas Jefferson and James Madison helped to define the democratic life of the new nation. With the passing of that generation, the blight of slavery engendered a decline in Southern statesmanship. As Virginius Dabney insisted: "During the three decades immediately preceding the Civil War, openly-avowed liberalism was virtually extinct below Mason and Dixon's Line." William Dodd echoed the theme of a steady recession from the enlightenment of Monticello to the reactionary folly of Calhoun and the secessionist idiocy of Jefferson Davis.[19]

The war was the nadir of Southern history. Woodrow Wilson found more justice in the North's case than in the South's.[20] He was unusual among Southerners in the rigorousness with which he pursued the logic of his position. Most preferred silence on the political righteousness of the war. As Southerners—and they were bent on retaining that title—they could scarcely pour unbridled scorn upon the South's central experience, the Confederacy. They could, however, turn from the politics of the war to the battlefield. The war may have been wrongheaded, but it was bravely done. Robert E. Lee, in particular, benefitted from this: the Lee who hesitated before casting his lot with the Confederacy, who comported himself with dignity in a desperate struggle and then set a model of reconciliation with the Union after the war. Lee had a little something for everyone. Liberals celebrated the manner of his life, while conservatives could relish the fact of his Confederate allegiance. The greatest monument to this phase of Southern liberal historiography—almost an annex to the history of Virginia—was the work of Douglas Southall Freeman. He produced four volumes on Lee, three volumes on Lee's lieutenants, and six volumes on George Washington, with a sense of genealogy that was impeccable.[21]

Southern liberal historians did not believe in racial equality, so Reconstruction was regarded with little enthusiasm. Their special moment, after the wasteland of the years between Jefferson and the Compromise of 1877, came with the New South. They were its heirs, sometimes its instigators. In John Spencer Bassett's eyes, the period after 1877 was the hour of the middle class, which had supplanted an economically and intellectually decadent planter class: "The rise of the middle class has been the most notable thing connected with the white population of the South since the War," he wrote in 1903. In 1926 Bassett's friend Edwin Mims was to publish *The Advancing South*, a book that celebrated that achievement, the arrival of the Southern bourgeoisie.[22]

One phase of the South's history was out of bounds—Populism. Although an account of social reform in his lifetime, Mims's book totally ignored the farmers. Virginius Dabney did mention them and even conceded them some influence on the course of Southern liberalism, but he referred to them with a typical condescension. About South Carolina he explained: "The campaign of 1890 sounded the political knell of the lowland coterie which had been the controlling factor in South Carolina for centuries. The men who had carved for the Palmetto State a place of conspicuous prestige in the annals of the republic and had guided its destinies since its establishment as a British colony, were rudely pushed aside to make way for a raucous band of back-country farmers."[23] Such distaste was clearly the horror of genteel reformers for a blunt, often illiterate, and usually disrespectful company of democrats who tended to wield greater political power than their social betters.

This general viewpoint matured over a span of more than forty years, from the late 1880s to the early 1930s. It might be seen as the Whig interpretation of Southern history, and it is far from dead even now. Though professional historians like Wilson and Dodd played a large part in its articulation, it was as much the work of amateur historians. There was no course in Southern history at a university until William K. Boyd offered one at Trinity College in 1907. There were six such courses by 1913, between thirty and forty during the 1920s, and nearly a hundred by 1940. But the institutional structure of a professional Southern history was slow to develop. There was a Southern History Association, which existed between 1896 and 1907, but it was a collection of nostalgic Southerners living in Washington. Not until James G. de Roulhac Hamilton founded the Southern Historical Collection in the 1920s and gathered up the unconsidered manuscripts of the Southern past, not until the foundation of the Southern Historical Association in 1934 was professionalism entrenched.[24]

The New South produced fewer literary critics. The discrete tradition of American literature was slower to be taught in universities than even American history. Literary study was still bound up with philology and the classics. The number of Southerners who gave serious public thought to the matter of Southern literature before the First World War might almost be counted on the fingers of one hand. Thomas R. Price of Randolph-Macon College published little or nothing himself but had influence over his students, who did. For the rest, one can only count William Baskervill of Vanderbilt, William Trent and John Bell Henneman of Sewanee, Edwin Mims of Trinity College, and Alphonso Smith of the University of Virginia. Of these, only Trent achieved a national reputation, which was recognized by his call to a chair at Columbia University in 1900 and the task of editing the *Cambridge History of American Literature*. Mims acquired some national attention for his biography of Sidney Lanier in the prestigious "American Men of Letters" series, but his standing was provincial.[25]

The line between historian and literary critic was not firmly drawn. Both Trent and Mims contributed freely to the political discussion of the Southern heritage. They did not merely concur in historians' views. Often, they were the historians. It is not surprising that that their theory of Southern literature proceeded *pari passu*.

They had no Jeffersonian golden age to look back upon, though there were occasional efforts to make the political prose of the Founding Fathers a part of Southern literature. The usual starting point was the immediate antebellum period. It was convenient for them that the literature of the Old South was notoriously poor. One could note that certain social forces developing in the New South—urbanization, professionalization—were absent from the ancien régime and then draw a direct line between this vacuum and the lack of an impressive literature. Edwin Mims summed up the matter in his introduction to the literary volume of *The South in the Building of the Nation,* that great compendium of his generation's definition of the South: "In the course of this sketch the main reasons why Southern writers did not achieve greater success in fiction have been suggested. None of them, except Poe, and perhaps Simms, were professional men of letters; their literary work was incidental to what seemed to them more important. Most of them wrote carelessly, even slovenly. Furthermore, the absence of anything like a literary center was a hindrance; there was little of the influence of one writer on another. Slavery, and the feudal system perpetuated thereby, militated against purely literary work." Trent's biography of William Gilmore Simms had dwelt notoriously upon the responsibility of slavery for the weakness of Southern literature. He had claimed that political obsessions had diverted the talented away from literary careers.[26]

The years of the New South, again, were another matter. The novels of "local color" writers like Thomas Nelson Page, George W. Cable, and the young Ellen Glasgow, the short stories of Joel Chandler Harris, the poetry of Sidney Lanier formed a "renaissance" as real to the literary critics of 1900 as the more celebrated "Southern Literary Renaissance" of the 1930s was to become to their more numerous successors. It was the better for offering no substantial challenge to New South nationalism. Mims cheerfully quoted Joel Chandler Harris, a close friend of Henry Grady: "What does it matter whether I am Northerner or Southerner if I am true to truth, and true to that larger truth, my own true self? My idea is that truth is more important than sectionalism, and that literature that can be labelled Northern, Southern, Western, or Eastern, is not worth labelling at all." With his usual puckishness, Trent noted: "We of the South are not so peculiar a people as we suppose ourselves to be, and, fortunately, the more closely we scrutinize ourselves the more we perceive that, save in certain restricted circles of society in restricted areas, our characteristics natural and acquired are those of our fellow-Americans, at least of those who were born in the country." Trent was even struck with doubts about whether it was desirable to write about Southern literature at all, lest the venture be misconstrued as promoting sectionalism.[27]

Literary critics tended to be more forthright than historians about the relative cultural status of the South and the North. Trent asserted that neither "the Old South nor the New can fairly be said to have rivalled New England and the Middle States in contributing to the intellectual development of the nation." The strain of admitting this was relieved somewhat, because they were not overly convinced of the general superiority of

American culture. The well-modulated perspectives of Henry James were in most of them. To admit inferiority to Boston was less onerous when one added, in the same breath, that Boston was a pale shadow of London. In discussing the weakness of universities and libraries in the South, Trent observed: "No great collection of books answering the needs of scholars as well as those of the general public exists south of Washington, and so long as this is the case the South in a sense cannot be intellectually independent." He went on, significantly: "But, as a matter of fact, America as a whole is still, in this sense, more or less dependent upon Europe." This admiration for Europe, especially Britain, was typical. It was common for literary critics to spend most of their time on English authors and write Southern literary history with, as it were, their left hands. This Anglophilia, noticeable in their critique of culture, was also traceable in their politics. Nothing was more representative of the Southern strain in Woodrow Wilson than his admiration for Walter Bagehot and William Gladstone.[28]

In many ways, Mims and Trent were but the Southern arm of the "genteel tradition" in literary criticism.[29] Literature was seen to have a moral function in society: it should be judged for what it taught, not just the elegance of its prose. That gave Walter Hines Page an immediate advantage over the proslavery Simms. Yet it was the genteel tradition with an important difference. The impoverished condition of the Southern intelligentsia drove them towards an economic interpretation of literature long before Vernon Parrington. Trent's contemporaries in New England, men like William Lyon Phelps of Yale or Bliss Perry of Harvard, were several generations removed from the economic revolution that had helped to foster the intellectual supremacy of the North. The ducts down which the industrial income of the mills poured to the endowments of Harvard were well established. One might take a prospective donor to the Faculty Club for lunch, but the privilege was rather for the aspirant giver. Who, after all, would not be flattered to offer his money to the Harvard of Emerson and Lowell? In the South, intellectuals went cap in hand to philanthropists and state legislatures and were soundly disabused of any notion that the gifts flattered the giver more than the receiver. In the circumstance of sowing an industrial revolution and attempting to reap its cultural harvest, the connection was glaringly obvious. To insist that slavery was responsible for the weakness of antebellum literature was to posit an economic basis for literary culture.

The words "intellectual" and "liberal" have been used thus far in this discussion as though they were synonyms in the South. They seemed so to Gunnar Myrdal, when he visited the region in the late 1930s. Southern liberalism seemed unique to him in the close identity between intellectual and liberal communities. The conservative intellectual seemed an extinct species, since the proslavery days when the equation had seemed almost exactly opposite.[30] By 1940, Myrdal was wrong in his diagnosis, for a new breed of conservative Southern thinkers had developed, even though they were in a clear minority. But even before the First World War, there were a few conservatives. Thomas Nelson Page, for example, found Trent's biography of Simms obnoxious for what he thought a pandering to Northern tastes.[31] Even Page, however, though never endorsing industrialism outright, was patronized by New South writers for the plantation idylls he produced for Northern magazines. He was important to them, for his literature of manners in the Old South helped to yoke together the days of Jefferson and the New South: he stopped Southern history snapping irretrievably in the middle and embarrassing the doctrine of continuity.

The old hardline conservatism of the proslavery reaction had died. Journals like Albert Bledsoe's *Southern Review* found it impossible to struggle on after the war; there was no buying public in the South and ideology debarred Northern opinion.[32] When magazines like the *Sewanee Review* and the *South Atlantic Quarterly* were reborn, it was under New South auspices. The Southern reading public had not grown much bigger, though there were the few subscriptions offered by the incipient professional classes. The big difference lay in the access to Northern interest.

When one says that the old conservatism had died, one must be cautious. That represented by organizations like the United Daughters of the Confederacy was, on the contrary, flourishing.[33] But there was very little contact between this sentiment and anything that found its way into the pages of the *South Atlantic Quarterly*. A gulf had opened up between the social conservatism of many Southerners and the liberalism of their discomfited intellectual elite. Occasional fracas would occur when the gulf was too imprudently exposed, as when Bassett linked the names of Lee and a black in terms too flattering to Booker T. Washington and the wrath of North Carolina was loosed upon him. But it is well to note that Bassett survived and did it by exploiting the elite's strongest point, its alliance with the new industrial class. The whole of North Carolina did not sit upon the Board of Trustees at Trinity College in 1903, but members of the Duke family did.

A professional intelligentsia was, socially, a new factor in the equation of the Southern idea. In the short run, it seemed to have made little difference. The new men of the universities may have begun their critique with education and poetry, but they ended up with a call for a sound industrial base. Henry Grady worked in an opposite direction. He had started with industry and concluded with a nonchalant prophecy of a flowering of the Southern mind. The distinction of priorities was obscured, for the result came out the same.

The distinction did matter. The intelligentsia's priority was itself, its diagnosis for survival, its conception of the life of the mind; it had been

acting as an importer and inspector of alien ideas and ways. The Victorian
concepts it was asked to pass had happened to dovetail neatly with the
New South. But in Europe and the North, the old industrial ideologies had
begun to grow doubtful, complex and self-analytical.[34] Some odd notions
started to turn up at the Virginia border and ask for admittance. Southerners
were asked to believe that industrialism did not help the arts, it destroyed
them. They were told that "progress" had died in Flanders. They were even
commanded by new disciplines like psychology and sociology to dismantle
the very Romantic categories of thought built into the idea of the South.
For younger Southern intellectuals, these were to be compelling issues in
the interwar years. It did some very strange things to the "myth" of the
South.

As has been suggested, there was some consensus amongst intellectuals
of the pre-First World War years on matters like race, politics, industrialization, the form of the Southern past. The postwar years saw a breakup of
this, and mutations in the social status of the Southern intellectual.

Notable was a weakening in the enthusiasm for industry. If there was a
central idea in agrarianism, it was an abhorrence of industrialism and
a repudiation of the Victorian faith in progress and science. The 1920s had
seen a particularly lively discussion among American social thinkers about
the benefits that might accrue from the advances of technology. On one
side stood men like Charles Beard, who wrote that the "new drama of
mankind has just opened" and expressed the conviction that "the spirit of
engineering is rationality, a faith in the power of the scientific mind to
undo what should never have been done and to realize whatever human
imagination may suggest in the way of material and social arrangements."[35]
The Agrarian symposium *I'll Take My Stand: The South and the Agrarian
Tradition,* published in 1930, was appalled at this hubris. The Agrarians
were convinced that the vulgarity of industrialism was endemic and the
comforts purchased by the assembly lines of Mr. Ford were gained at too
grave a price. Industrialism was bad for the worker, as it drove him at a
frenetic pace and did not even offer secure employment. For the Agrarians,
factory work was a matter of enduring the necessary, not enjoying the
desirable, as it made labor "mercenary and servile" and no longer "one of
the happy functions of human life". Moreover, industrialism necessarily
generated the evils of overproduction, unemployment, and growing inequi-
ties in the distribution of wealth.[36]

In their hostility to industrialism, the Agrarians lumped together both
capitalist and communist. They objected to the process, not the techniques
of ownership. Both social systems seemed limiting and degrading to

individual freedom. As John Ransom put it: "It must be insisted that the true Sovietists or Communists . . . are the Industrialists themselves. They would have the government set up an economic super-organization, which in turn would become the government. We therefore look upon the Communist menace as a menace indeed, but not as a Red one; because it is simply according to the blind drift of our industrial development to expect in America at last much the same economic system as that imposed by violence upon Russia in 1917."[37]

These were not sentiments that would have made much sense to Henry Grady, and they were not shared by Howard Odum. The sociologist was convinced that science could be beneficent, and industry was necessary. But even Odum worried about the need to keep a balance between industry and agriculture. He had no enthusiasm for the great cities of the North, and was heard to speak of their "artificiality." When the Agrarians offered the alternative of a traditional rural society, Odum dismissed it as an unrealistic alternative. He was too impressed by the debilitating costs of the old ways, the disease, poverty, and provincialism.[38] But, as the Agrarians grew—during the Depression—to modify their utopian vision into an agricultural reformism they came close to Odum's standpoint.[39] While Henry Grady could be enthusiastic about factories when they were but a few looms on the horizon, Odum and the second generation knew a little more, had seen the labor troubles of Gastonia and were more skeptical.

In setting forth these views, the Agrarians were not politicians but dabblers in political ideas. They stood outside political power even more decisively than their predecessors, the New South liberals. An Edwin Alderman or Edwin Mims had existed, at least, within the penumbra of power. They had met and talked with the governors of Virginia, North Carolina, and Tennessee. They had encountered the entrepreneurs of Southern industry at their dining clubs, and extracted endowments for their colleges in exchange for a few talks to the local Rotary Club. Not themselves powerful, they moved in sympathy with power and helped it on its way. The Agrarians, however, shunned such links. They neither sought out the company of the economic establishment nor were much pursued by it. While Edwin Mims crossed the gulf between Vanderbilt University and the downtown business section of Nashville frequently and with ease, the Agrarians found the gap agreeably impassable. They were models of the alienated intellectual in the uncertain years when he had ceased to be a cheerleader for the nineteenth century and did not have the option of becoming a brain truster.

Howard Odum, however, did have that option and exercised it with increasing frequency. Sociologists came to have an assured place in the new order of government, especially during the New Deal. Moreover, he was energetic in the promotion of various nongovernmental reform

activities and in this, as in much else, was a true son of the laissez faire New
South. For the liberal movement in the South before the First World War
had been divided between a neo-Populist wing and a smaller urban middle
class agitation. Its interests had been spread among such issues as public
utility regulation, public education campaigns, child labor legislation, penal
reform, factory regulation, municipal reorganization, and the improvement
of mechanisms of representative government. It had pressed for prohibition
and a more formal version of white supremacy. Like the progressive
movement elsewhere, it had been an uneasy coalition. Local businessmen
joined in the assault on corporate privileges in concert with humanitarian
reformers and "wool hat boys." By the 1920s, it had become clear that this
fragile alliance had fragmented and it was "business progressivism" that
had most effectively stayed the course. The highway had become the
symbol of Southern change. In such a metamorphosis of the reform impulse,
the Agrarians' repudiation of industrialism represented a disillusionment
with the uncertainties of Southern progressivism that had lurched into
conservatism. Odum's cautious continuation of the old ways was a reaffirma-
tion, a desire to put the puzzle back .together, but with the middle class
firmly in control.[40]

The progressive movement had, however, removed one item to the
margin of the agenda—race. All the Agrarians and Odum were racists and
believers in the segregation system. Their relative comfort in such a situation
was a measure of the success of the previous generation in establishing a
new racial status quo. They had all come of age after segregation was well
established. Their education and social training had confirmed the color
bar as a normal and proper state of affairs. None seriously questioned the
inferiority of the Negro. From the perspective of the 1970s, after a decade
in which the formal structure of segregation collapsed with considerable
speed, it is difficult to recall how solid the Jim Crow system looked between
the world wars. As George Tindall has written: "In the 1920's the new
peculiar institution of Negro subordination had reached its apogee as an
established reality in law, politics, economics and folkways—under attack
from certain minorities in the North, to be sure, but not effectively menaced
and indeed virtually taboo among respectable whites as a subject for
serious discussion. The question was settled." In the the 1930s, the position
did begin to slip. The New Deal scarcely mounted a calculated onslaught
on racism, but it did indirectly better the lot of the Southern black. Small
chinks began to appear in the armor of segregation, but the changes were
well below the surface of Southern life. Only in the volumes of sociologists,
mostly from the North, did the coming tide of challenge become explicit.[41]

There were shades of emphasis within this consensus. For most of the
Agrarians, race was an unimportant part of their case. To illustrate this,
one must look at the only occasion in the early days of the movement

when it was seriously discussed. When *I'll Take My Stand* was planned, Robert Penn Warren was accorded a chapter on the Negro as the symposium's "leavings." He wrote it belatedly in Oxford with some diffidence, when his mind was half on writing a novel. It was an essay without passion.[42] When it was sent to the informally appointed "editors" in Nashville, a certain stir ensued. Donald Davidson, in particular, thought it too liberal. He was surprised that Warren had accorded the title "Mrs." to the wife of Paul Robeson and did not much care for the way Warren had talked of equality as a possible, if remote, course of action. Although this incident did touch a raw nerve in Davidson, racism was not the main bone of contention. Davidson's chief objection to the essay was that it wandered from the central lines of the symposium. As he told Allen Tate: "It goes off at a tangent to discuss the negro problem in general (which, I take it, is not our main concern in this book), and it makes only two or three points that bear on our principles at all." He added, a few days later, that "in the kind of lay-out we have chosen, the negro problem, as such, is hardly an issue."[43]

That the Southern racial scene was quiet meant that Davidson could afford relative indifference. When he wrote to Will Alexander, head of the Commission on Interracial Cooperation in Atlanta and a leading racial liberal, in 1929, he listed those items in Southern culture he deemed worthy of preservation. At the top of his agenda, he put "country life—as opposed to complete industrialization." To this he added "Southern manners" and leisure, conservatism in politics, religion, economics, local self-determination, "historical-mindedness . . . in politics and government," religious fundamentalism, Southern architecture, and "the folk arts." At the bottom of the list, he put "the Southern view of the Negro question—I mean the *better* Southern view, not the view of the riff-raff. This means segregation, no social equality, probably economic subjection for a long time to come; it does not mean that the Negro should suffer political injustice, as in the courts, or be the object of any vindictive oppression. I am firmly with the Southern states that keep the vote out of the Negro's hands as far as possible, but that is no real injustice, though it furnishes a convenient focus for agitation, as it did years ago. That is, I sympathize with their point of view. . . . I see no objection to a *qualified* Negro suffrage. . . . Now don't put me down with the 'conventional' Southerners."[44]

Davidson could only have felt reassured when Alexander responded: "I am inclined to think that you and I would be pretty well in agreement on the race question."[45] There was a touch of politeness in this, but not too much. Alexander's views were not dissimilar from his close friend and ally on the Interracial Commission, Howard Odum. Their sense of the time scale for black progress was foreshortened, their positive desire to purge actively the abuses within segregation more aggressive, but the Southern liberal was firmly committed to the system. He spent more of his time, however, preventing and putting out brush fires. Odum himself had a more complex position than the Agrarians. He had, it is true, been no less convinced of the rightness of the Southern way. In his youth, he had published a racist tract in his doctoral dissertation, *Social and Mental Traits of the Negro,* whose gist was that the black had distinctly inferior traits. In later life, he had repudiated that volume and refused to have it republished. He was to be found instructing his publisher on the dust cover of his book *Cold Blue Moon:* "The only further suggestion is my usual one, namely, that the artist do not make a trite stereotyped Negro character, but that what he does have dignity to the general setting and dash to the horsemen. If there is a Negro rider, he ought to show, too, dignity and strength of face."[46] Odum was moved by the new findings of sociologists in ways that left the Agrarians cold. Nonetheless he remained a long way from accepting the equality of the Negro. In 1926, he submitted a proposal to the Rockefeller Foundation for a ten year study on Southern blacks. Its first eleven items showed a continuing passion for the quantification of the racial differences between black and white. He wanted a "comparative study of physical characteristics, including measurement of cephalic indices and other physical traits"; research into "the possibility of devising a valid test of Negro mental ability"; studies of racial differences in singing ability; "emotional testing in relation to the Negro"; comparative studies of Negroes of varying degrees of mixed blood"; research into the psychology of black religious revivals, with special attention being paid to "the swaying, fainting, etc. which often becomes fantastic in the Negro summer revivals"; a look at Negro insanity and "feeblemindedness", black crime, and "the relation of the Negro community to white morality," in which he thought an attempt should be made "to determine what, if any, is the effect of the Negro community upon the morals, achievements, failures, etc. of the white boys of the community." All one can say is that Odum had begun to doubt segregation, but not very much.[47]

The line on religious matters was more clearly drawn between Odum and the Agrarians. They had all been reared in the Church, the Agrarians as Methodists and Odum as a tub-thumping fundamentalist. The latter had experienced great difficulties when forced to reconcile his youthful intoxication at country revivals with the blunt agnosticism of his new profession, sociology. He never came to doubt that it was wise for society to have churches, but he came to care less and less for his private religious beliefs. In later years, he gave up churchgoing for his hobby of rearing prize Jersey cattle. It seemed time better spent to be grubbing in the mud of his farm than sitting, prim and well shaved, in a pew.[48]

The Agrarians, however, belonged to a profession that had less clear feelings on religion. Religion and art had a complicated relationship in literary modernism. Many Agrarians had read and absorbed, with varying enthusiasms, the French Symbolist poets, Ezra Pound, T. S. Eliot, and James Joyce. Allen Tate was to identify himself most thoroughly with the modernism that, appalled at itself, turned to the social and aesthetic conservatism of Eliot.[49] An aspect of this movement was an elevation of the role of religion in both society and literature. Collaterally, it was an attack on Romanticism's expansive faith in the capacity of the individual to challenge and master nature. The attack on Romanticism was led in America most prominently by the literary and social critic Irving Babbitt, by whom Eliot himself had been taught at Harvard.[50] Babbitt had welded together the issues of religion, art and education in a way that the Agrarians tended to find sympathetic. Trained in an educational system that had emphasized the classics, the Agrarians agreed with Babbitt's insistence on the value of the classical curriculum and dislike of its replacement by "utilitarian" subjects, under the aegis of John Dewey's progressive educational theories. Babbitt saw education as a way of encouraging and disciplining man's better "intuition." Although the Agrarians shared Babbitt's view of education as a moral process, they did not share the cool view of his "humanism" towards the Church. Babbitt had written: "The two most notable manifestations of the humanistic spirit that the world has seen, that in ancient Greece and that in Confucian China, did not have the support of Christianity or any other form of revealed religion." To this, Ransom, Tate, and Eliot took public exception. They were far less sanguine about the reliability of man's intuition when unguided by dogma. Without religion, they saw only a decline for morals, manners, and the literature that could flourish only in the context of an "organic" society.[51]

Nonetheless, their devotion varied in intensity. In later life, Tate turned from an indistinct protestantism to a more intense Roman Catholicism. Most could not be regarded as zealots. They talked about religion more than they went to church, and went to church more than they liked. Ransom did publish a volume of eccentric theology and Wade wrote a history of his local Methodist church.[32] But the overall impression of their religious commitment, when contrasted with the previous generation, was of a softening of belief. It was not that they did not render unto God the things that were God's, but that they went through an elaborate process of thinking about it first, whereas the New South had been born into faith and took it for granted. It is true that the Victorian Southerner had had no shortage of challenges to his faith: there had been the crisis of evolution, after all, and hadn't "In Memoriam" been one of his favorite poems? But the challenges had been external. For the Agrarians, the doubts were internal.

Unsurprisingly, they were born and raised in the South. Indeed, they came from a fairly narrow central zone in the region. Their South stretched from the central Georgia of John Wade and Howard Odum northward to the southern middle Tennessee of Ransom and Davidson. Westward, the Owsleys came from Montgomery County, Alabama. Northward, Allen Tate spent his youth divided between Winchester, near Lexington in Kentucky, and the areas in Virginia, close to Washington, of his mother's family. And their Southern roots struck deep. All came of white families that had arrived on the American continent no later than the eighteenth century. Some had ancestors who had been prominent in Southern politics. John Wade was related to the first governor of revolutionary Georgia. The Odums, the Tates, and Owsleys had all had plantation holdings in their recent family past. Only Ransom and Davidson had neither the family memory nor the personal experience of considerable property, but it is not unlikely that, in the recesses of the kinship network, there once lurked a tolerable estate.[53]

The vagaries of Southern economic life had, however, flattened out their fortunes, such that it is not inappropriate to regard their backgrounds as middle class. Only Wade had a youth of conspicuous prosperity. For the rest, their homes were the Southern variation of the Victorian bourgeoisie. John Ransom's father was a Methodist minister; Donald Davidson was the son of a schoolteacher; Allen Tate's father was a lumberman. Only Howard Odum and Frank Owsley grew up outside the small town: their fathers were farmers. These were homes that encouraged a child's education, parlors in which one might find books though not large libraries. A child might sit over a volume and not be thought eccentric. And these were homes untouched by genuine poverty, the barefoot poverty of sharecropping pellagra, though occasional memories of past grandeur might make their modest gentility seem like deprivation.

Relative prosperity is attested by their attendence at universities. Three went to Vanderbilt University in Nashville. Wade and Odum were graduates of the two most prominent Georgia colleges, the University of Georgia and Emory. Owsley went to Alabama Polytechnic Institute, later to become Auburn University. Four had some manner of postgraduate education. Ransom was a Rhodes scholar. Wade and Odum had doctorates from Columbia University; Owsley had one from the University of Chicago. For good measure, Odum had a second Ph.D. from Clark University. Only Odum and Owsley could actually be regarded as one of the new breed of professional scholars who came to inhabit the colleges, the American Historical Association, and the American Sociological Society; but all ended up as college teachers. Tate resisted as a free-lance writer for more than a decade, but he was eventually drawn into its secure web. Wade was granted some detachment by his private income.

It was nothing new for Southern intellectuals to be dependent upon the university, but the scale of dependence was unprecedented, especially for poets and novelists. Once the Southern writer had been a country gentleman, a journalist, or a free lance, living on royalties and the lecture circuit bureaux. The interwar years did not see as complete a movement into the colleges as the record of the Agrarians suggests. William Faulkner, Thomas Wolfe, Erskine Caldwell, and others survived in the old ways. But this was becoming difficult, and by the 1950s the Agrarians' solution was the norm.

The claims of seminar and lecture combined uneasily with the demands of poetry, the novel, and social commentary. The Agrarians were forced to endure an awkward and exhausting moment of transition in Southern education. In the past, college teachers had been jacks-of-all-trades. When William Dodd had gone to Randolph-Macon College in 1900, he found himself teaching fifteen hours a week in five courses: Greek and Roman history, English history from 1265 to the accession of George III, the French Revolution and Napoleonic wars, the history of Virginia to 1828, and European and American government.[54] And he could count himself lucky not to be teaching English and foreign languages, anything and everything remotely related to the humanities. In the future, universities would find not too onerous duties for writers, whose main task was "creative writing." The Agrarians were in the middle. They held their place as ordinary college teachers—though now they had to deal only with one subject—not as adornments to otherwise functional departments.[55]

What they did had to be made to pay. If publications went unrewarded, it was an act of sacrifice. Occasionally, they might benefit from sabbaticals and Guggenheim fellowships. Usually, they were obliged to teach for most of the year: summer schools were a necessary supplement to inadequate salaries. Casting their lot with ill-endowed Southern universities, they were underpaid, spent long hours distracted by irksome administrative tasks, taught courses that were usually uninteresting, struggled with unresponsive bureaucracies for raises, listened to the needs of wife and family, lived under permanent strain, and tried painfully to eke out a few hours of peace in which to write a poem, an essay, or a piece of social criticism. Donald Davidson complained in 1929 that "my life has become quite absurd . . . . It is given up altogether to mercenary pursuits. I teach classes and I edit a book page, both things being done in order to live and to support a family; and, completing the circle, apparently I live and support a family in order to teach classes and edit a book page. In such a scheme of things there has been no room for letters (other than strictly business), for poetry, for thought, for decency."[56]

Tate stood a little aside from this. But the free-lance man of letters had his own problems. Except for a brief boom in the 1920s, the independent writer's lot was also between two happier times. Since Mark Twain's day, the lecture circuits had gone and the royalties shrunk. The aesthetic doctrines of modernism had cut off many authors from a wide public.

In the distance lay the paperback revolution and the rebirth of the lecture circuit, under the more solemn auspices of the university. In between lay Allen Tate's frequent flirtations with debt.[57]

For Odum, the pressures were different. Sociology had always been intimately involved with the university, peculiarly so in the United States. And Odum liked the rush and complexity of the modern university, the unending parade of committees. But sociology was an expensive discipline. Research assistants had to be found and paid. For Odum, the thing that made him run was not freshman English, but the constant search for grants. In his case, the transition lay in the change of emphasis in sociology. No longer did a sociologist sit in his study and draw up abstract schemes of human evolution. He was obliged to collect facts, figures, and people. That cost money, and not usually his own.

For all their troubles with time and money—in Odum's case, because of them—they travelled widely. All but Odum had spent extensive periods in Western Europe, and he compensated with a dizzying rate of movement within the United States. But it would be a mistake to contrast a provincial New South generation with cosmopolitan successors. The older men had as often crossed the Atlantic. There had been a steady flow of Southerners to the German universities, at a time when Southern and most American colleges offered inconsiderable graduate education. The intellectuals of the interwar years were building on the experiences of their predecessors, who had helped to transform Southern country boys into liberal Americans and surrogate Europeans. As a result, the movement in Southern thought was away from cosmopolitanism, towards provincialism, and not vice-versa. Odum knew about the German psychologist Wilhelm Wundt before he discovered George Fitzhugh. Allen Tate read Yeats before he bothered with Sidney Lanier. And this movement gave a distinctive cast to the new provincialism: it offered the resonance of a wider experience.

So there was a witches brew of social tension in the careers of these Southerners, and a variety of social experience to enlist in the formation of an ideology. There were also institutional pressures. The idea of the South was not a private abstraction. It had found its way into the fabric of public life. An adherence to Southern identity was a subtle personal decision, but others had less fussy criteria. Publishers and editors had a vested interest in tapping "local" talent and channeling it into "Southern" modes. Many works were to be semicommissioned. Publishers' agents came trooping through Chapel Hill and Nashville in the late 1920s, looking for "Southern" authors to feed the literary boom in regionalism. John Ransom wrote to Edwin Mims in 1927: "Oxford Press has written to ask me to do a volume for them on [the] History of Southern Literature; they were inspired to this idea specifically by your book on Southern life generally, and by this consideration that there is now a great market for writings about the

South." Davidson confessed in 1929: "One can't resist the publishers. They have hungry scouts in the field, looking for Southern authors. At least three publishers have been after me." H. L. Mencken, amused and impressed by the reaction to his own swingeing attacks on the South, was ever keen to invite Southerners into the pages of the *American Mercury*. Of Odum he was particularly fond. It could, after all, be useful to be a Southerner. It sometimes required an effort of will not to be one.[58]

When they came to look at their region, they shared a certain breadth of interest with their New South predecessors. Odum was a sociologist, but he wrote three novellike volumes of folk literature, history, and occasional pieces of literary criticism. Ransom, Davidson, and Tate were poets, but they hazarded economics, history, the novel, and a little sociology. Wade hovered between history and literary criticism, and turned his hand to a novel and odd pieces of poetry. Even Owsley, the narrowest of the six, once wrote portions of a Civil War novel (unpublished and later destroyed). Nonetheless there was a certain decline of catholicity from the late nineteenth century. It was not that they knew less. On the contrary, they knew much more. But each was a touch more identified with a particular discipline, and that discipline had refined its laws and private logic with the years. One can see the lines of that first allegiance even in their wanderings into other fields. The shades of specialization had not yet closed, but they were closing.

When Donald Davidson had written to Will Alexander of the defining qualities of Southern life, he had spoken of "historical-mindedness." Many observers have shared his belief that this was a peculiar part of the Southern scene. This is doubtful. There is no evidence that the study of history was developed in the South before other regions in the United States. If anywhere, the palm went to New England.[59] That there are more historians or archives or historical works per square mile in the South is questionable. A sense of the past is a run-of-the-mill quality of Western culture, found alike in Paris, Charleston, or Duluth.

It may be true, however, that the South's tradition of social analysis has been more insistent upon historical legitimacy. That historians should have wished to get up genealogies for their social beliefs should surprise no one. That poets, sociologists, and politicians should have shared the same impulse requires more explanation. Davidson himself expressed the interweaving of past and present in the debate of the 1930s: "Since, for better or worse, the Southern habit of mind is historical and retrospective, probably few Southerners . . . would attempt to answer such [social] questions without first committing themselves to some interpretation of Southern history. The historian's question—what the South was?—and the related question —what the South is?—underlie every important literary work or social investigation of the past fifteen years. The discussion of such questions centers in turn upon a strategic problem: how to arrive at Southern policies that will be well founded historically and at the same time applicable to the existing situation."[60]

Although only Frank Owsley could be considered a professional historian, all committed themselves rather haphazardly to a reevaluation of the Southern past. For some, it was a conscious decision. For others, it happened without premeditation. But the Agrarians wanted to do more than dust off the family portraits. They were convinced that an accurate diagnosis of the conservative elements in Southern history would give their contemporary position both consistency and reality. Without it, as Allen Tate remarked, they were "only American liberals offering a new panacea and pretending to a concrete background that doesn't exist."[61]

Odum and the Agrarians disputed most heatedly the relationship of the South to American nationalism. As the New South school had wanted to move the region towards the American "mainstream," so Odum wished that assimilation to continue. The Agrarians desired a reversal. It was a change of direction posited, however, on the political triumph of the American union. No one was suggesting a return to the Confederacy.[62] Where each drew the line between North and South, between nation and section varied importantly. Drawing the ideological Mason-Dixon line was a subtle and crucial piece of metaphysics. Neither Odum nor the Agrarians wanted any part of an Americanism that extinguished Southern distinctiveness. But the Agrarians were the more sweeping historical revisionists, for they focused upon those aspects of the Southern past that the New South intellectuals had spent decades edging towards the margin of the Southern historical consciousness: the agrarianism of Thomas Jefferson, the political thought of John Taylor and John C. Calhoun, the politicians of the Confederacy, the Ku Klux Klan, the critics of Southern industrialization before 1900. Insistent upon the continuity between themselves and a conservative Southern past, they were forced to minimize social change in the region just as the New South school had been—and was—obliged to overestimate it. They needed a static vision of the South's past. As Andrew Lytle saw it: "Southern interests, customs, economics, and problems have been, still are, and will be, fundamentally the same."[63]

Ironically, in scraping away the topsoil of liberalism on the surface of Southern life, the Agrarians often used liberal historiography. As they were not usually thorough analysts of original sources, they had little choice. Any attempt to reinterpret a dominant historical tradition must pick its way through the evidence and assumptions of the old school: fragments of the old perspective will always cling to the new orthodoxy. Odum was much taken with the frontier hypothesis of Frederick Jackson Turner, but the Agrarians went further in a reliance upon the "progressive" historiography of Turner, Charles Beard, and Vernon Parrington. Beard offered an analysis of the Civil War as a struggle between agrarian and industrialist forces, Parrington saw the American mind in sectional terms, and Turner's later work seemed to prove the political and economic permanence of sectionalism. These perspectives, though not strictly compatible, were spliced together and fitted beside the more ancient Southern tradition of regionalism. Southerners did not need, though they welcomed, the approval of a man from Wisconsin to tell them that sectionalism was a real thing, not the paranoia of the politically displaced. William Dodd, who had taught Frank Owsley at the University of Chicago, had been saying it for years.[64]

Although nothing was more common in criticism of the Agrarians —Odum was fond of the charge—than that they were uncritical defenders of the Old South, it is inaccurate.[65] It is true they were protective towards it, but they were very divided in their attitudes towards the ancien régime. Some were glad to honor Jefferson as the philosopher of the yeoman. In this they were in harmony with the sociologist. Others damned the Virginian as a deist. Some saw no fault in the egalitarianism of Andrew Jackson; others agreed with Andrew Lytle that Jackson's hand was in their own predicament, that Jackson "came forward as the defender of the plain man . . . but his defense was that the little man might have an opportunity to grow rich, to exploit the riches of the wilderness as well as the Eastern financier . . . . he must bear his share of the blame for reducing this democracy to a state of landless tenants and helpless workers in mill and office." Embedded in these disputes was a deep ambivalence over the Southern democratic tradition and the question of whether the Old South should be seen as a mature, settled and semiaristocratic society or as a child of the American frontier.[66]

Odum continued the New South tradition of deprecating slavery as a feudal incubus, but the Agrarians had more mixed feelings. Lytle, always a little more thoroughgoing, stated one mood when he suggested that "the personal slavery of [John] Taylor's day had the great virtue of fixing the worker to the soil and defining the relationship between master and man. The loss of this has done farming incalculable damage."[67] But slavery embarrassed most of them and they did not make it central to their view of the Old South. Instead they rested their case on the courtliness of Southern manners, on the principles of self-determination and on strict construction of the Constitution. Convinced that the South was justified in seceding, they saw the Civil War and Reconstruction as the culmination of a Beardian struggle between agrarian and manufacturing interests. Whereas the New South historians had discreetly turned their eyes towards the heroism of the battlefield, the Agrarians divided their critical shafts between both generals and politicians. Convinced that the South came desperately close to winning, they needed to explain the failure. As reasons, they offered the debilitating tactical weakness of states rights feeling in the Confederacy, too great an absorption in the Eastern theatre of war, too many errors in handling its relations with the European powers, and even a certain faltering of will amongst the Southern people. The nationalist school had, after all, been sure that the South was doomed by either providence or the big battalions to failure and responsibility mattered less.[68]

Neither the Agrarians nor Odum changed much in the essential structure of the Southern legend of Reconstruction. New South historians had agreed that carpetbagger corruption had been a terrible experience and racial equality worse. The disciples of William Archibald Dunning were painstakingly insistent on the point. Odum continued the old ways by stressing that Southern truculence was a regrettable short-term necessity, not to be taken as a general standpoint. The Agrarians insisted that resistance was a general and proper principle. Although they had little sympathy with the gimcrack Ku Klux Klan of the 1920s, the Klan of Nathan Bedford Forrest seemed a distillation of the political indomitability of the section.[69]

As might be expected, the gulf between Chapel Hill and Nashville over the heritage of the New South itself was wide. But it was fairly narrow over one of the main challenges to industrialization, the Populist movement. Rupert Vance offered some dissent to Odum's hostility to radical agrarianism, and was to influence the next generation's main celebrant of the Populist tradition, C. Vann Woodward. Odum's own father had been an enthusiast for Tom Watson, but the sociologist had been impressed by the divisiveness Populism had caused in his home town of Bethlehem, Georgia. According to a later report, it had "wrecked the town and divided the school as well as the church, community and families." As for the Agrarians, middle class and the children of landowners, they relished the Jeffersonian challenge to industry but were suspicious of its social radicalism. As Lytle was to observe: "anything I knew about it, I was distrustful. . . . Landed people, which my family was, don't like things like that."[70]

This was the disputed outline of the South's political past, shorn of nuance. But each had his own intellectual specialty, which imposed its own need for defining the past. For Odum, the situation was simple. There was no indigenous tradition of sociology. There were scattered sociologists. Odum himself had been influenced by a young professor of sociology at the University of Mississippi, Thomas P. Bailey. In addition, there was the tradition of rural economics, sometimes stretched to mean sociological study. Odum was to foster its growth at the University of Georgia before he went on to Chapel Hill in 1920. And the sociology department at the University of North Carolina was the offspring of Eugene Branson's Department of Rural Social Economics.[71]

However, there was a living tradition of Southern literary criticism. In the person of Edwin Mims on the Vanderbilt campus, the young Fugitive poets had been vividly reminded of it. Their reaction was decidedly hostile. The New Criticism that Ransom, Tate, and Robert Penn Warren were to found after their Agrarian phase was a continuation of that hostility to such a genteel, historicist, hortatory attitude towards literature. Writing poetry was their essential business, not discoursing on Southern history or economics. Their audience was more than provincial, more even than American. They were read with respect on the other side of the Atlantic. As such, they were too exposed to afford special pleading for their Southern literary heritage. Almost in compensation, they were unsparing in their criticism. Allen Tate said it for most of them when he wrote: "We lack a tradition in the arts; more to the point, we lack a literary tradition. We lack even a literature." In applying this judgment to the Old South, they changed little. In applying it to the New South, the Agrarians buried the reputations of Cable, Murfree, Thomas Nelson Page, and the local color school beneath their indifference. Sidney Lanier, the pride of Edwin Mims, was singled out for a particularly savage demolition job.[72]

A major thrust of the New Criticism was to derogate the Romantic tradition. The Fugitives had admired the metaphysical poets. Cleanth Brooks's *Modern Poetry and the Tradition* had sketched a literary gene-alogy for the Fugitives that ran from John Donne and side-stepped the Romantics.[73] This made them peculiarly unfitted to sympathize with the dominant Romantic tradition of Southern literature. But it is important to note that they were inclined to ignore Romanticism rather than assess their own relationship to it; so they underestimated their own Romantic heritage. They were unaware that their Southernism was a devious legacy of Romantic social thought. The contradiction bred deep tensions in their thinking, and proved crucial to their relationship to the Southern idea.

Even for Howard Odum, less fussy about intellectual origins, the link between Romanticism and sociology was to prove more significant to his success as a student of regionalism than he knew. But, for both poet and sociologist and historian, the Southern myth was an inarticulate stepchild of Romanticism. The years since Herder had masked the intellectual assumptions. Later generations used the idea without knowing why; but the structure of the ideas were still potent. For a time, at least, these men in the interwar years showed a public need for the myth of the South. Some were to continue to do so, others not. They came together, debated and wrote letters to one another, disagreed and went their separate ways. This study attempts a partial explanation of why they felt the need to express themselves in terms of a Southern tradition, how they did it, and why it seems to have failed some of them, but not all: to ask the motives and consequences for Southern intellectuals of the sectional analysis of Ameri-can life.

part two:
The Sociological Vision: Howard Odum

two:
Odum: Sociology in the South

If one had asked most well-read Southerners in the 1930s, Who is making the greatest contribution to the understanding of Southern society? most would have answered "Howard Odum." The Agrarians of Nashville seemed a gesture towards the past, but Odum was the future. If North Carolina was the most progressive of Southern states, its university was near the heart of that advance, and Odum was a leader in Chapel Hill. The liberal could tap Odum's magnum opus, *Southern Regions of the United States,* and indicate a manifesto of the newest New South that seemed to speak with the scientific detachment of the sociologist, no longer the hyperbolic burblings of the mill owner. Edwin Embree of the Rosenwald Fund was only a shade more enthusiastic than most when he told Odum in 1936: "It is a magnificent work, one of the great landmarks in research that will be of inestimable service to students for decades. . . . Now you belong to the ages."[1] Amid the ephemera of journalism and polemic, Howard Odum seemed to be laying down a new and crucial stratum in the history of the South, its modern sociological definition. But the ages have been singularly unwilling to own their possession of him. One must ask, Who now reads an Odum book? Outside the esoteric cabbala of students of the Southern tradition, the answer is "Almost no one."

He was notoriously unreadable, which has proved a hindrance to his intellectual survival. He veered, out of control, between the impenetrable jargon of the sociologist and the declamations of a tipsy bard. He once published three seminovels on a wandering Negro called Black Ulysses. Their staple was a chanting of lists—places, objects, people, remorselessly indiscriminate adjectives—and the dubious proposition that an eccentric grammar was lyrical.[2] A cross between the worst mannerisms of Talcott Parsons and Walt Whitman did not, one feels, have a fair crack at intellectual longevity.

But survival is not all. One could not write a serious history of Southern thought between the world wars without an assessment of Odum. Setting aside the antebellum tradition of a George Fitzhugh, one of the first Americans to use the freshly minted word of Auguste Comte, Odum was the first modern Southern sociologist. The rows of books that issued from the University of North Carolina Press bearing his own name and those of his many students witnessed that he had sired a "school." Several traditions converged on him: the indigenous creed of the New South, the emerging profession of the social worker, modern sociological thought, the new bureaucracy of higher education, the liberal interracial movement, the transforming hand of the New Deal. Out of the synthesis emerged a strange beast, not one of the pedigree Jersey bulls that he loved to rear, but a ramshackle Minotaur, half thinker, half academic politician. From the tension of these halves, there grew the intellectual phenomenon "Southern regionalism." But the route to it was devious.

⊠ Odum was born in 1884, on a small farm near Bethlehem in Georgia. His early youth was far from auspicious. He was a sickly child in a family where ill health and accident claimed a depressing proportion of his parents' large family; partly because of this, he became awkward, shy, and uncertain. His parents wrapped him in love, but his birthright was not an unmixed blessing. For his mother had been born to a substantial slaveholding family, born to expect a comfortable and gracious life. The war had wrecked her life, as she often and freely told her son. It had killed her brother, maimed her father, and destroyed the family wealth. More, it had obliged her to marry far below herself, to a barely literate small farmer of rigidly orthodox and fundamentalist persuasion. In compensation for her losses, she put her energies into her children, a hatred of the North, and a frantic religious zeal.

From his grandparents, with whom he had a close relationship, Odum received equally complex burdens. John Wesley Odum had been a Confederate soldier, who had stuck through many battles, increasingly sickened at it all. As the army was driven back, it came close to his family farm, whereupon he deserted. Thereafter he was conscience-ridden when unable to share in the heroic nostalgia of the war. And he liked to share his grief with his young grandson, who always seemed to like to listen. On the other hand, Philip Thomas, his mother's father, had lost a leg and his affluence in the war, but gained a clear and unalloyed bitterness towards the North. Where John Odum was a confused, unsure if courageous, poor man, Philip Thomas had a certain clarity of aristocratic purpose. His depredations were not his own fault, but they were surely someone else's and he would have his grandson know that. Only from his father did Odum seem to receive a simple love. True, he was a fundamentalist, but he was a kindly man who liked to emphasize love more than guilt in his religion.[3]

And so Odum was reared in a complex moral world. He was told that the war had been an evil thing, in which the South had unjustly suffered, but there was the nagging sight of his grandfather Odum, who reminded him that heroism was fugitive and shame common even in Southern families. And he did not despise his grandfather, but cared for him deeply. More, he was told that it was terrible that the old plantation had been ruined, and saw the price paid by his mother. But his father, though poor, was a good man and his family life a pleasure to him. When he left home and went to teach in Mississippi in 1904, his letters were painfully nostalgic. In later years, he was to remain stubbornly convinced of the moral worth of the small farm and attribute to it all manner of Jeffersonian virtues.

He was always to be sensitive, painfully aware of others' needs and emotions. This was to make him a good diplomat, though it occasionally palsied his capacity for action: everyone had to be placated before he could move forward. But he had an excellent memory, a talent for recitation, and an extraordinary capacity for hard work. In later life, he could make do with only the fewest hours of sleep. He often worked through the night, and would stop only for rumpling naps. Nonetheless he did not do particularly well at high school or at Emory College. He barely made the honor roll at Emory, a traditional Southern Methodist college, not noted for its unorthodox curriculum or its liberalism. In 1902, when Odum was an undergraduate, it dismissed a professor, Andrew Sledd, for the mildest of dissents from the Southern racial ideology. And Odum was majoring in the most traditional of subjects, the classics. He did well enough, but not so brilliantly that he could command a good position. He failed to get a job near his home, and was obliged to resort to an agent. Eventually an indifferent position in an obscure Mississippi high school was found, and Odum found himself unhappily in Toccopola.[4]

It has not been often that Mississippi has offered fresh perspectives to young Southern intellectuals. But it happened that Odum, who decided to do some graduate work at the University of Mississippi and was obliged to ride the twenty-one miles from Toccopola to Oxford, came across one of the few sociologists in the South. Odum began conventionally enough, by writing a master's thesis on "The Religion of Sophocles," a singularly grim topic for a young man's leisure hours. But he met Thomas Bailey, a recently minted doctor in psychology from South Carolina and California. Bailey was working intermittently on the race problem in the South, a venture that was to cause some controversy on the campus. He encouraged Odum's haphazard interest in folklore, especially of the Negroes who were so omnipresent in Mississippi. He told Odum of the new social sciences, a discipline in which Bailey vested great hope for solving the problems of the region. He suggested that picking up the unconsidered trifles of black life in the South might contribute towards a higher degree at one of universities of the North. Odum had read G. Stanley Hall's study *Adolescence* when he was graduating from Emory in 1904 and it had impressed him. Bailey had studied with Hall at Clark, and he knew about William James, Herbert Spencer, Franklin Giddings. He had even dabbled in Hegel. Not a thorough or original mind, Bailey did know a little of what was going on in the intellectual world of the social sciences and told it to an impressionable young man, as yet uncertain of his future. It was natural that in 1909 Odum went north to study with Hall in Worcester, Massachusetts, and took with him the raw material of his research on Negroes.[5]

G. Stanley Hall was the aging *enfant terrible* of American psychology: extremely energetic, unorthodoxly candid, schooled in the best, but yet ill-formed ways of German and American psychology. He seems to have given Odum a measure of confidence in his own ability, and two significant intellectual gifts. He involved the young Southerner in the new discipline of social work, as it intermingled with psychology. Deeper than that, he gave his stamp of authority to the less weighty belief of Bailey in the immense potential of the social sciences. Like most of his scientific generation, but with intoxicating force, Hall had the Comtean vision of a new era when the intellectual elite would order a better world. The psychologist, Hall frequently observed, "is called to-day to be a sort of high priest of souls as in an earlier age the great religious founders, reformers, and creators of cults and laws used to be, for the day of great leadership in these fields seems to have passed. If he is concerned, as he should be, with the education of the race, nation or individuals, he is not content merely to fit for existing institutions as they are to-day but he would develop ever higher powers, which gradually molt old and evolve new and better institutions or improve old ones." Education was the key to this transition, "*the* one and chief hope of the world."[6]

During the late 1870s, Hall had studied in Leipzig under the experimental psychologist Wilhelm Wundt. The main achievement of Wundt had lain in establishing laboratory techniques for exploring psychological reactions. He had made a few faltering steps towards defining a physical basis for the psyche, before Freud turned the new discipline towards more abstract lines of analysis. But Wundt was also a neo-Hegelian social philosopher. Although he broke with the pure idealist doctrine by insisting that philosophy rested upon psychology, and the latter upon physical laws—as Hall put it, "all the secrets of the soul and, therefore, from the position which Wundt assigns psychology we may infer he believes of the universe are wrapped up in nerve cells and fibers"—Wundt subscribed to a modified Hegelian social organicism. According to Hall, Wundt showed "how personality emerged through the interaction of self and others in such a way that the individual himself became 'a special phase of society.'" Ten fat volumes of *Völkerpsychologie,* the psychology of the folk, were produced over many years by the German in a miscellaneous attempt to fuse psychology, social psychology, anthropology, and philosophy. Hall, although he had grave doubts about Wundt's experimental work, was much more enthusiastic about folk psychology. In his autobiography, he was to urge that "Wundt's *Völkerpsychologie,* far too little known by his disciples, should and will some day be seen to be more important for the proper training of professors than his psychological textbook." Elsewhere Hall observed: "As we now conceive the self or ego as made up of many different and partially independent qualities and trends, united in and by an inscrutable something far deeper than consciousness, so the conception of a collective, *Volk*, mass, crowd, mob, group, herd or community soul, which we can never come to know by the study of any number of individuals but which is just as real and even just as unitary as their souls, is now everywhere gaining ground."[7]

It is said that Odum ploughed his way through all of Wundt's ten volumes. From the frequency of his later references to Wundt, it is certain that he read some. As late as 1947, Odum spoke of "the folk psychology of Wilhelm Wundt, a social psychology capable of forming a complete framework for the study of folk sociology." In this, he was cultivating a dying and esoteric intellectual creed, for Wundt had little impact upon the development of social psychology.[8]

Odum stayed only a year at Clark University. In 1910, he moved on to Columbia to take a second doctorate under Franklin Giddings. With Giddings, Odum developed a relationship closer than that with Hall. In later years, he was to plan a biography of his mentor. When a new journal of sociology was founded at Chapel Hill, Odum not only gave it a name, *The Journal of Social Forces,* that echoed a favorite Giddings phrase, but had Giddings write the first article. Giddings was even persuaded to donate his personal library to the University of North Carolina.[9]

Franklin Giddings was a founding father of academic American sociology. As with Hall, Giddings had been deeply influenced by Comte and Spencer. Before 1900, he had developed a typology of social evolution that combined traces of Comte, Hegel, Spencer, William Graham Sumner, and even a touch of Frank Lester Ward. Like Comte, Giddings saw social evolution as a historical succession of three traditions, the theological, the metaphysical, and the scientific. Tribal society had led to tribal feudalism, which had evolved into the "ethnic nation." A developed form of feudalism had produced the "civic nation." But Giddings added an idealist touch by offering "consciousness of kind" as a baseline for defining a society. "A society," Giddings observed, "is a group of like-minded individuals . . . who know and enjoy their like-mindedness and are therefore able to work together for common ends." In short, society was a mental as well as a material organism.

At the heart of civilization, Giddings located a principle of "demogenic association." By this, he meant "social processes, stemming from a people, a 'demos,' with a shared awareness of each other, and of their social unity, going beyond kinship membership." Civilization was "that intercourse, both varied and organized, which develops great civic peoples ever increasing in wealth and in population and ever growing more democratic in mind."

He purported to find three stages in the growth of a culture. The first, and lowest, stage manifested itself in a desire for homogeneity in politics, religion, manners, and habits: this led to national and social unity. The second, and higher, stage came "whenever the nation learns to appreciate the value of unlike-mindedness in the population; the value of doubt, scepticism, and denial in the social mind; the value of individual initiative and voluntary organization; the value, in short, of variation and criticism, as causes of progress." It was characterized by international intercourse, free thought, forms of legality, and the exercise of conscious rational policy. In this way, the early stage, the "Military-Religious" society was supplanted by the "Liberal-Legal" society. It, in turn, would eventually be replaced by an as yet undefined, but "truly democratic" civilization.[10]

When Giddings, in discussing the earlier stages of social evolution, had talked of the bonds of social unity, he had employed many of the notions more comprehensively and darkly stated in Sumner's *Folkways*. From Sumner, via Giddings and cross-fertilized with Wundt, Odum picked the idea of folkways as a basic tool of social analysis. Sumner, however, was more ruthlessly materialist in his interpretation of the origins of social mores. To him, their main source was man's link to his economic environment. When that changed, man's customs changed with it. Meanwhile, folkways that began as unconscious, spontaneous, and uncoordinated sentiments in the social organism, grew to order the running of society by becoming uniform, universal in the social group, and imperative.

Unlike Giddings, Sumner was timid about the chances of ordered rational reform. He did concede that, out of the unthinking mores, "later and more formal differentiation of structure may arise and . . . conscious control (to some extent) may take place." But he was on the conservative wing of Social Darwinism. This caused him some difficulty. For he argued that the mores were absolutes, right for their time and place. Nonetheless, he was a Christian gentleman and was obliged to admit the occasional necessity for moral and social reform; thus he had to find some place for change. But he constantly insisted that any such action had to be based on a profound understanding of the folkways. The social authority of the folkways would crush any ill-conceived tinkering. Sumner's illustrations of this included a pertinent one for the young Odum. "In our southern states," Sumner had written in *Folkways,* "before the civil war, whites and blacks had formed habits of action and feeling towards each other. They lived in peace and concord, and each one grew up in the ways which were traditional and customary. The civil war abolished legal rights and left the two races to learn how to live together under other relations than before. The whites have never been converted from the old mores. Those who still survive look back with regret and affection to the old social usages and customary sentiments and feelings. The two races have not yet made new mores. Vain attempts have been made to control the new order by legislation. The only result is the proof that legislation cannot make mores. We see also that mores do not form under social convulsions and discord."[11]

Odum picked up ideas from all of these men, with no great coherence. Hall and Giddings could be made to coexist, though Hall put more emphasis on the individual psyche in social progress than did the cheerfully Gladstonian Giddings. But the neo-Hegelianism of Wundt and the conservative Social Darwinism of Sumner were ill matched. It was unclear how laissez faire and Auguste Comte could get along. Odum's eclecticism was his lifelong weakness as an intellectual but his strength as a propagator of the new sociological doctrines. For he took back with him to the South notions that, commonplace enough in the intellectual community of the North, were heretical for a Southerner of Black Belt orthodoxy. He imported most of the basic assumptions of the new science of society: its substitution of scientific methodology for metaphysics, its evolutionary perspective, its materialism, its use of classificatory, comparative, and historical methods of study, its groping towards social psychology and its impulse towards purposeful social action. Handled with too much rigor and too little delicacy in a suspicious society like the South, that could have led to a respectable explosion. Occasionally, even the amiable Odum was to tread on a landmine.

Carrying this intellectual mélange to the South, Odum put himself at the forefront of intellectual change in the region. Effecting a peculiar blend of pre-First World War sociology, he made no theoretical advances on it. As his theory grew older, he found little time or inclination for the fresh infusions of later years. Weber, Durkheim, Pareto, Tönnies, adaptations of Marx, played no part in his intellectual biography. Chronologically, Howard Odum was of the second generation of American sociology. Intellectually, he was a survival of the first. Typical of these late Victorian gentlemen, he had some very grand ideas. In time, they were to be turned upon the South and that, as will be seen, did odd things to his sociology.

The nine years between Odum's departure from Columbia and his arrival in Chapel Hill in 1920 were fragmented. He had wanted to return immediately to the South, but frustrated by the absence of posts in either sociology or educational psychology, he accepted a brief job with the Bureau of Municipal Research in Philadelphia. The city was involved in a controversy over the advisability of segregating its school system. The author of *Social and Mental Traits of the Negro,* recently published by Columbia University Press, was hired to make a study of the problem. Unsurprisingly, Odum concluded that segregation would have beneficial consequences. Nonetheless, he had budged a little on the racist theories of his dissertation. At Columbia, through friends if not lectures, he had come into contact with the new theories of Franz Boas, which suggested that environment, not innate racial traits, was most responsible for the cultural and psychological characteristics of ethnic and racial groups. Odum partially assimilated this view. He tried to give as much weight to environment as he could, without actually abandoning his racist assumptions. When he found a problem intractable, or when he was being intellectually lazy, he recurred to the explanation by genes.[12]

The next few years were to deflect his attention from the race problem. In 1913, he accepted an associate professorship in "Educational Sociology and Rural Education" at the University of Georgia. In Athens, Odum entered a program, largely sponsored by Thomas Jackson Woofter, which was dedicated to Southern rural reform, and a city much devoted to the causes of the New South. His Jeffersonian sympathies were quickly and permanently reinforced. Standing on the left wing of the progressive movement in social philosophy, Odum was eager to urge the involvement of the university in social reform and the improvement of rural schools. He joined a campaign, jointly administered by the Athens Chamber of Commerce and the Clarke County Board of Education, to persuade the citizenry to increase school support by higher property taxes. It was successful, and rural school terms leaped from four to nine months. Active in the chamber of commerce, Odum urged that a chautauqua be brought to the city and that the chamber offer its support to the university's summer school. He brought guest lecturers, like Edwin Mims, into town. He sat on the board of education, and was a frequent delegate to various state, Southern, and national educational conferences. Wrapped in the enthusiasm of the Wilson presidency and settled among sympathetic colleagues, Odum was in an optimistic mood.[13]

Then there was the war. His optimism didn't go, but it was chastened. If Sumner represented the gloomy forces of human irrationality, and Giddings the bright side, then the former had rather the better of it for a while. Hating discord, Odum disliked war; but he could identify with the scholarly president and supported the war effort. He was asked by the Red Cross to supervise the home service field work of their Southern Division. Like many an American intellectual, he was obliged to reassess his attitude towards Germany. His verdict was far from lenient.

In 1919, Odum accepted the deanship of the School of Liberal Arts at Emory University. This was a personally ambitious move. The college had recently migrated to Atlanta, it was expanding, and Odum entertained serious hopes of the university's presidency. It was also still a Methodist institution, with powerful trustees bent on keeping it that way.[14] In this new capacity of being charged with reform within a Christian educational tradition, Odum took the opportunity of an address to the "Educational Association of the Methodist Episcopal Church, South" in Memphis to talk about Germany.

He was painfully aware of how much the American educational system owed to Germany. The seminars of Clark and Columbia, his own title of doctor of philosophy had been inspired by the German example. No doubt he remembered how often the efficiency of the German Empire had been touted by progressive reformers before 1917. Perhaps he had done it himself. Certainly he had talked much of efficiency. But the Great War had changed all that. It had made Odum pronouncedly anti-German. He reeled off a formidable indictment. German education, he insisted, had been un-Christian, anti-individualistic, obsessed with efficiency for efficiency's sake, too subordinate to the needs of the state, too specialized, too arrogant, scientific without a leavening of morality, antifeminist. More, its philosophers had been fundamentally misguided. "The erstwhile great philosophers," he had said, "Kant and Ficthe [sic], Schopenhauer and Schelling, Nietchse [sic] and the others, wrought 'well' in philosophy and generalities, but Ah, how poor in life and in their contribution to the Soul of humanity.... Shall we not beware of generalities based on opposite extremes, if out of perspective with the great problems of life or the directing hand of an evolutionary providence in which God's destiny must guide and interpret? Shall we not beware lest we satisfy ourselves with generalities and philosophies insufficiently supported, when before us lie the virgin fields of inquiry and evidence upon which to build our structure of the future?" Although his tone was more pious than was his wont—the audience and his new position dictated that—his message was clear and verging on the anti-intellectual. If general systems of thought had led Germany to this, then the United States was better served by homespun pragmatism. In the long run, immediacy was the best guide.[15]

Whatever practical lessons Odum wished to draw from his recent experience were truncated when he and Emory University parted company under strained circumstances in 1920. It had not been a prudent match. The transformed Emory had been guided by the determined fundamentalist and antimodernist bishop, Chancellor Asa Candler, who had seen Vanderbilt University snatched from the control of the Methodist Church and was not about to see the same happen to Emory. He was against the theory of evolution, an ascetic, an opponent of coeducation, and a believer that religion was an inward theological experience and not a social gospel. Unfortunately, Odum was the reverse of these things. For a while, they cooperated; both wanted to expand the scope of the new university. But the alliance lasted only eighteen months before Odum grew so uncomfortable that he sent distress signals to Chapel Hill for a rescue bid. Mercifully, it was forthcoming.[16]

Howard Odum came to the University of North Carolina in 1920, not as a budding regional sociologist, but as the the founder of a new School of Public Welfare. One might remember that his first doctorate was in psychology, and his first job application had been as an educational psychologist at Peabody College in Nashville. He had no sociological theory of regionalism; he just wanted to study sociology in the South. Chapel Hill offered serious hope that a Wisconsin-like alliance between the university and the state might be brought to bear on social problems. "As you know," Odum told an old friend, Albert Bushnell Hart, "North Carolina has very advanced social legislation and the University is fitting into the state program with commendable service and dispatch. There is every indication that such cooperation will be given the University by certain other agencies, that it will have a real school of social work for the South next year with adequate professional standards, as well as emphasizing government and other social sciences in the regular curriculum, the doing of 'social engineering' work throughout the state, and the promoting of greater research."[17]

North Carolina did not have the first Southern school of social work: by 1918 two had been founded in Richmond and Houston. But as early as 1916, Eugene Branson had recommended to the president, Edward Graham, that Chapel Hill should have its own. The war disrupted its establishment, but in 1919 a council was held, attended by the state governor, to consider the matter further. Soon after the board of trustees set up the school. Its manifesto stated that there was a compelling need for students trained in the task of citizenship. Such a school would "help to train. . .leaders, should offer short courses for workers in service, and should, in cooperation with the State and National agencies, render assistance to the cause of public health, to Superintendents of Public Welfare, Red Cross Workers, Secretaries of Chambers of Commerce and Boards of Trade, to school systems in their social problems, to Bureaus of Community Recreation." The heavy emphasis of Odum's main task can be gauged by a look at the school's ten undergraduate and two graduate courses: in the principles of sociology, social problems, community organization, recreation, community health, family case work, child welfare, juvenile delinquency, statistics, social pathology, immigration, educational sociology, as well as Negro, mill village, and labor problems.[18]

Odum had identified himself closely with the new, and self-conscious, profession of the social worker.[19] This seemed to him the way to get things done. In a letter to the house journal of social workers, the *Survey,* he was to offer a euphoric vision of the representative professional altruist: "Studying facts, making them applicable to folks with human interests and social instincts, utilizing methods, principles, convictions, persistently and almost stubbornly single-minded, he has achieved results, both small and

large in local, state and sectional applications. He has given himself
heedlessly to the work, nevertheless with pride of personality, genius of
foresight, a sort of subtle power and ability to 'put across' his plans, and a
fearless and insatiable ambition for the cause for which he labors. Among
his many other characteristics is his ability to influence leadership in various
fields—the men and women interested in civic endeavor, the capitalist
interested in philanthropy, leaders in labor reform, the law makers of the
land, college professors, university presidents."[20]

This optimistic philosophy of public welfare was to be elaborated in
editorials for his new periodical, the *Journal of Social Forces*. Eagerly,
Odum stressed that the nineteenth-century tradition of "charities and
corrections" was dead. The new public welfare was to be "a regular part of
the organization and technique of government for making democracy
effective in the unequal places." It was to be the twentieth century's main
task, just as public education had been the main contribution of the last
half-century. It was to be a distinct and "perhaps the last of the great stages
of democracy." Mindful of socialism and the excesses of German education,
Odum was careful to emphasize institutional evolution. "There is need," he
wrote in the first number of *Social Forces*, "of a rebuilding and a
restrengthening of the major social institutions, rather than the substitution
for and breaking down of accepted institutional modes of life; but with the
objective being the development of the perfected social individual rather
than the unthinking so-called mass freedom." Six institutions were basic:
the home and family, the school and education, the church and religion,
industry and work, the state and government, the community and association. Social disorders stemmed from human inability to perfect and integrate
these.[21]

Despite opposition to an unrestricted laissez faire, Odum was suspicious
of centralization and bureaucracy. Although he wanted to extend democratic principles far beyond the mechanics of the ballot box, he warned
that "to offer, as a substitute for democratic government, a centralized
bureaucratic service uninformed and unsympathetic; or a dictation by an
intellectual aristocracy; or dictation by a class group; or a 'super legislation'
and censorship is un-American and violates the democratic principle of
community participation in government." Despite his concern for educated
leadership, he cautioned against "the rule of the self-appointed intellectuals
whose arbitrary, isolated and specialized training is mistaken for comprehensive education." For Sumnerian reasons, it was folly to force the
pace with incomprehensible legislation. The people must be offered their
own community organizations to nurse them into the new era. If Howard
Odum was a Comtean, he was a homespun American Comtean.[22]

Southern problems played a prominent part in the new *Social Forces*,
but Odum was insistent that it was not a Southern journal. In his first

editorial, he wrote: "THE JOURNAL, in order to be distinctively complete and adequate, will not be limited to any one section. The south, for instance, wants and needs the best from without as well as from within its own borders. It holds that, in matters of such import as social forces, local and contemporary factors become valuable stepping stones of dead social selves to higher things of progress, rather than ultimate objectives of truth. Provincial dogmatism is no more effective in the realms of truth and thought in Chapel Hill than in New York." Elsewhere he was to comment that "the term 'the South' is not accurate. There are vast differences between states and in many instances these differences are growing."[23]

The contention that social values should be judged by "scientific" criteria was potentially explosive. The 1920s saw many cherished Southern beliefs under strain. Howard Odum and Chapel Hill did not escape the buffeting of these years. Skirmishes with Southern conservatism were not infrequent. A project to study textile mills had to be called off in 1924 because of manufacturers' objections. For years, David Clark of the *Textile Bulletin* was to heap vilification upon Odum's reforming head. In the year of the Dayton trial, an antievolution bill was presented to the state legislature in Raleigh and the university was obliged to throw its weight publicly behind the evolutionists. *Social Forces* itself was to endure the violent censure of ministers for harboring atheists within its pages. Harry Elmer Barnes, in temerity and ignorance of the Southern milieu, once described the Bible as "an alleged sacred book" which was "a product of the folkways and mores of the primitive Hebrews." Worse, he cheerfully announced that two thousand years of religion had produced no definitive ethical system. This was too much for the fundamentalist preachers of Charlotte, North Carolina. They denounced Odum, *Social Forces,* modernity, and the university that bred them in their pulpits for months. Even the newspapers took up the cry. For a while, Odum's future hung in the balance.[24]

That he survived was principally because his position within the university was sound, and the politicians whom the university was obliged to respect did not take up the hue and cry. Moreover, Odum had learned from his headlong mistakes at Emory. Candler had once observed that Odum wanted "to build a university before breakfast—and build it his own way." Now he was all charm and cautious wiliness. When David Clark had begun his criticism, Odum confided to Harry Chase: "I shall...make a personal friend of Mr. Clark and have him working with us. See if I don't?" During the evolution controversy, he invited clerics to Chapel Hill to talk the matter over. No single tactic was more efficacious than the old one of wrapping his heterodoxy in the legitimizing guise of Southernness. In a letter to the press, he once began: "I ought to say at once that I am so Southern that in the old days in our rural community, from vantage point of log cabin and school house and the generations of native folk back of me, we used to think of a person from a neighboring state as a sort of 'foreigner'; and that for all generations of both sides of our house in this country—from the Carolinas and Maryland to Georgia—we have been evangelical protestants of the simple and enthusiastic sort." In private correspondence, he could write in mock innocence: "The bitterness of this whole attack . . . is startlingly amazing to me, an almost professional Southerner and so orthodox that it never occurred to me that we could give offense."[25]

Odum was cautious, but he had been willing to speak out against Southern "backwardness." Again and again, he had condemned the Ku Klux Klan as un-American, undemocratic and un-Christian. Although the Klan was weaker and more "moderate" in North Carolina than elsewhere, that was an act of courage.[26] In 1924 he had accused his section of ignorance, emotionalism, a lack of libraries and writers, laziness, and a stultifying fundamentalism. His indictment was republished as the introduction to essays on Southerners, culled from *Social Forces*. The list of subjects for *Southern Pioneers in Social Interpretation* reminds one, however, that Odum was reiterating the less complacent position of the New South school. Most heroes of the book—Walter Hines Page, Woodrow Wilson, Charles Aycock—stood firmly in that tradition. Odum observed the usual forms: a word of praise for the Old South, a plea for educational change, a panegyric to potential Southern wealth, a call for hard work and less sensitivity to criticism. Mildly revisionist was his talk of race as a social handicap; but he was vague, and meant no more than the usual liberal cry for a just administration of the segregation system.[27]

Nonetheless the buffetings of the mid-1920s softened Odum's boldness. When the crisis of the Southern Intelligentsia broke at Dayton, John Ransom and Donald Davidson were to rally to the fundamentalists. Edwin Mims stuck to the progressive cause. Odum insisted on ambivalence. Partly at the suggestion of H. L. Mencken, with whom he had contracted an unlikely friendship, he went to witness the trial in Tennessee. "On to Dayton!" Mencken had chortled. "The greatest trial since that before Pilate!"[28]

Odum came back, saddened that the issue had ever arisen. He admitted in *Social Forces* that William Jennings Bryan had been accurate to claim that most Americans were fundamentalists. Equally, it was clear that most of the intelligentsia were not. Between lay a "vast, yawning distance." "Now it may be said," Odum argued, "that such distance has always existed between scientist, scholar and common people; and so it has, except that it has not been a conscious distance of antagonism and battle line. Nor has the scholar and scientist in other generations attempted to extend his science and his scholarship into service and democracy, and therefore made contacts so broad and so directly related to the folk. Nor have the taxpayers been so marshalled by visible and invisible agencies against learning and education." Unhappily, Odum was persuaded that this struggle between modernism and the old ways would grow, in religion, in race, in industry. He could only suggest that sociology must learn to bridge these gaps. "May we not therefore propose a truce from duelling, a peace without victory, a generation of social study and research," he hazarded. "Better a decade of research than a cycle of futility."[29]

It was instructive that, while the Agrarians would be driven by Dayton to decide where they stood on the religion and science debate, Odum brushed that aside. He was not so much interested in the intellectual implications of Dayton, as fearful of its social consequences. While his religious commitment had been softened by his observation of fundamentalism, he remained content that he could render both to God and to the Caesar of the sciences without inconsistency.

⬛ In the decade from 1920, Howard Odum was to build up an administrative empire. This interwove intimately with the development of his thought. For Odum was not only the New South turned sociological; he was the Southern intellectual become organization man.

Odum's power rested on three sources: the university, the foundations, and the state of North Carolina. The source of his strength within Chapel Hill was a close personal friendship with Harry Chase, the president of the university. They had been intimates in graduate student days at Clark, and even gone wooing together.[30] It had been Chase's idea that Odum come to North Carolina. The relationship was reciprocally beneficial. Odum's hasty ways made enemies on the campus, as did his commitment to modernization. Chase helped to protect and encourage him. Conversely, Odum the Southerner was serviceable to a university president who, being a New Englander, was subject to the suspicions of both faculty and public. Moreover, Odum brought money in his train.

Links with the New York foundations seem to have been established during Odum's days in Georgia. As early as 1920, he wrote to Chase: "The last of May I shall go to Philadelphia and New York on my own account. I may say that my expenses are paid so that you will not feel disposed to fear too large an expenditure of my funds. I shall make a little skirmish around to discuss with some friends the possibility or probability of finding some moneys for our school." His war experience had forged close links with the American Red Cross, which was to undertake the salaries of two professors and a woman teacher in the new School of Public Welfare.[31]

Looking back in 1954, Odum was to recall that one and a quarter million dollars had flowed through him from the foundations. By the humble standards of academe, this was a great power. He was to become an expert at handling that suspicious man, the foundation executive. Beardsley Ruml of the Rockefeller Foundation was moved to call him a "master manipulator." This was an art that required time and effort to master; there were early mistakes. But he worked at it, to fashion a niche in a notoriously unstable world. His links with New York were occasionally better than those of his own university president. Rupert Vance used to tell of Frank Graham, Chase's successor, cooling his heels in an outer office. Odum breezed in, and was immediately ushered into the inner sanctum.[32] Odum's techniques were simple, but reasonably effective. He kept up a steady stream of correspondence that kept the nabobs involved in his projects. He stressed the social utility of his research. He asked them down to Chapel Hill, where they were installed in the commodious Carolina Inn. One foundation executive was manipulated to impress another. He bombarded them with extravagant plans, and then permitted himself to settle for less. He sat indefatigably on committees, to leave a trail of organizations in his wake. Traditionally, the foundations were interested in starting projects, not keeping them going. And Odum was, par excellence, a man who started something and then moved on to something else.[33]

The third part of Odum's support came from the politicians of North Carolina. Chapel Hill lay within easy driving range of Raleigh, the state capital. Odum came to know and intermittently advise a succession of state governors. In 1921, Cameron Morrison asked him to a conference on race relations. In 1930, O. Max Gardner asked him to investigate prison reform in the state. Later—though this is another story—Odum fitted into the local New Deal by running the North Carolina Civil Works Administration. But most of his dependence on the state government was, naturally, mediated through the university.[34]

On these three resources Odum relied during the 1920s. This was his first empire. That there was a second can be readily explained. The first came down round his ears. And the process of reconstruction helps to explain the emergence of Odum, the regional sociologist.

Odum performed several functions on the Chapel Hill campus. He was the Kenan Professor of Sociology within the small but growing sociology department. He was director of the School of Public Welfare. From 1924, he was deeply involved in the affairs of a new Institute for Research in Social Science. These rested on a complicated system of grants. The Red Cross had provided a three year diminishing grant for the school, which paid the salaries of two professors and a woman field worker. From 1924, the Laura Spelman Rockefeller Foundation gave $60,000 for three years to the school. In addition, the Red Cross had moved its summer training institute for field workers from Emory to Chapel Hill, while the North Carolina Department of Charities and Public Welfare sponsored a six week course for county superintendents of public welfare. Quite separately, the Rockefeller Foundation granted in 1924 a three year grant of $97,000 for the new institute. Thus Odum's time was divided between the particularist social work activities of the school and the more "theoretical" activities of the institute. It fell out that the school was a failure, while the institute secured a modest success.[35]

By his own admission, the debacle of the school was partly Odum's own fault. It had been proposed that it and the state would work in tandem on social welfare problems. The university would train the social workers to staff the new county unit welfare system of the state. In turn, the state would support the school. Neither lived up to its billing. Odum gave only intermittent attention to the school, and next to none to specific advice for county officials. The state never produced the money to make the program effective. Moreover, the school had run into significant opposition within the university community and showed little inclination to supplant the foundation money, due to expire in 1927. Many faculty members were suspicious of the new discipline of sociology, even more of a public welfare approach that smacked of socialism. The Red Cross had insisted that the field work supervisor should be a woman, but the university would not permit a woman to be a faculty member. Moreover, the young ladies who attended the school's courses were inclined to be feminists, unsettling women who could be seen to smoke in public and discourse vociferously on matters that propriety denied them. Chase was a staunch ally, but his budget was limited and he could not blatantly defy faculty opinion.[36]

In lieu of adequate university and state support, Odum was obliged to go back to the Memorial Foundation in 1927 for more money. Not surprisingly, they turned him down. There seemed little point in pouring good money down the drain. Odum was forced to admit to failure. "They were disappointed in the work we did for public welfare," he told his colleague Jesse Steiner. "They saw no cooperation on the part of the county and no promise on the part of the University. Some of the monies which we used . . . did not turn out well. . . . We did not finish the leadership studies and the Chapel Hill study which Dr. Ruml seemed to think so well of. They may have an impression that we think more of what other people think of us than we do about serving our own folks." In April, Odum conceded his "blunders" and started a reappraisal.[37]

The direction he was to take seemed obvious, implicit in the record of the last few years and suggested by New York. While the school had floundered, the institute had flourished. It is true that social research was regarded with suspicion by many faculty, even those on the board of the institute. But this had meant their failure to utilize the resources of the institute. Partly by default, partly by aggrandizement, Odum came to monopolize the institute.[38] It became the research arm of the sociology department. Its research was more abstract, less dependent on the cooperation of state and county governments. And its emphasis on the study of local problems pointed in a direction congenial to the Rockefeller Foundation. When Odum went to New York in May 1927, Ruml cordially but bluntly made his point. "What he said," Odum reported, "as near as I can quote him, was for us to 'forget what other people are doing and start thinking.... In the case of the Institute and the School both, I do not think it is a matter of choice with us whether we make them dynamic in our own region. It has been made very clear in the case of the Institute that if we do not we shall lose out, certainly at home and certainly with the Memorial. And, of course, the lack of appropriation for the School of Public Welfare is testimony of the other."[39]

With typical dispatch, Odum accepted the new mandate. By late May, he was expatiating on the new situation to Steiner: "What I mean by making the Institute and School tie in with its local and regional problems is that most real new movements, new contributions, and new inventions do actually grow out of situations, and, if we study our own folk and our own problems and meet them, the reputation and scientific values will take care of themselves.... I am sure that I could get the money to build up a department of sociology as strong as any in the country if we are sure of its objectives."[40]

Though of crucial importance, this shift to "regional problems" must not be distorted. Odum had had a long-standing interest in the South. But it had been a sociology practiced in the South, not a Southern sociology. He had been skeptical of regional generalization, and more interested in individual states. When Gerald Johnson had written for *Social Forces* in 1922, he had observed to Odum: "The article as it stands relates exclusively to North Carolina...but the change of a sentence here and there, with possibly the addition of a paragraph or two would no doubt make it sufficiently inclusive of the whole South to serve." Odum resisted the temptation to extend the particular to the general with such casualness. His first response to the publication of Edwin Mims's *The Advancing South* in 1926 was to suggest a state-by-state survey of the region. It was this sociological particularism that his experience in the 1920s had begun to weaken. The emphasis had subtly, but decisively, shifted. One thing had been made clear. Of the three possible power bases for the new sociology —the state, the university, and the foundations—the first two had proved unreliable. That left the foundations. If he wanted their support, he needed to broaden his base. If North Carolina alone could not sustain him, perhaps the whole region might.[41]

Over the next decade, Odum reconstructed his empire on the basis of regional research. On sabbatical in late 1928 and early 1929, he spent much of it on the road. He was to travel some ten thousand miles around the region.[42] Out of this grew his first extended foray into the debate about

Southern identity, *An American Epoch: Southern Portraiture in the National Picture.* He encouraged Rupert Vance to develop a "human geography" of the South. The University of North Carolina Press was proffered Rockefeller money to publish a whole range of books on the region.[43] In cooperation with Will Alexander, an old ally in the interracial movement, the Rosenwald Fund was guided into starting a fund for regional research fellowships. Alexander had been persuaded by Odum's new stance that "the regional plan is ultimately the best." The $50,000 fund would be administered by a committee, nominated by the Social Science Research Council. Alexander was its chairman, and Odum was to be prominent in its running. Many of the new fellows would pursue their studies in Chapel Hill. As Alexander indicated, this was a beginning: "It is in fact an effort on the part of the Fund to help out our Regional Research Plans. . . . Now we can quietly use this as the beginning of the regional studies. This money is by way of an experiment. If we make good with it there will be much more available."[44]

At the same time, Odum had persuaded the Social Science Research Council to establish a Southern Regional Committee. Its immediate objective was the organization of regional conferences on social research. Odum was its first chairman, and the committee was chosen largely at his discretion.[45]

There were to be more pieces in the puzzle. That Odum had the standing to put them in place requires a brief detour to explain. While he had been on sabbatical in Florida, he had been surprised to receive a letter from the White House. Herbert Hoover had appointed as his "research and literary secretary" French Strother, the former editor of Walter Hines Page's periodical, *The World's Work.* Strother had been charged with keeping the president "informed upon the broad social currents in this country and to help him formulate ideas for furthering those social movements that are of the most public value." This was bemusing. Having met Odum in Chapel Hill three years earlier, Strother turned to the sociologist for advice. At first, Odum suggested various journals that Strother might read. In time, a more ambitious project was born when Odum conferred with William Ogburn, chairman of the Social Science Research Council's Committee on Problems and Policy. Ogburn chanced to be an old Columbia classmate. More, he was a Georgian. Thus was born the President's Committee on Social Trends. Ogburn became its director, while Odum stepped back to assistant director, with the chief role of persuading the Rockefeller Foundation to fund the venture. Typically, Hoover did not want to expend public money.[46]

In 1933, the committee was to produce two fat volumes on *Recent Social Trends,* which have proved of great value to historians. Politically, it became an embarrassing irrelevance. When Odum and Ogburn were whisked, a little dazed, into the White House for lunches and dinners, Hoover had insisted that research should lead to action. But he gave them no money and obliged them to work quite outside the normal political processes. If this was a brain trust, it was a very remote one. Hoover's contribution amounted to little more than his name and a brief preface to *Recent Social Trends.* And the economic climate changed drastically. It is true that when Odum went to dinner with Hoover on 26 September 1929 the stock market was wobbling. But the president was sanguine that his administration and the economy were sound, and Odum shared that optimism. But 1933, the year the committee reported, was another matter.[47]

Whatever was uncomprehended between politicians and social scientists was further obscured by Hoover's commitment to laissez faire. Most sociologists had a commitment to state action, even the fairly staid collection who authored *Recent Social Trends.* The impasse was fundamental; and it mirrored Odum's own confusions, for knowing Hoover had deepened his own belief in voluntarism. Although he voted for Roosevelt in 1932, much of his sympathy stayed with the Republican. Benjamin Kendrick felt obliged to console Odum: "[I] hope you are not too cup [sic] up about the election."[48] Like many old progressives, Odum had been caught between two forces. Progressivism had not done enough, and the New Deal was to do too much.

All this dabbling in high places enhanced Odum's standing in his profession and in the South. In 1930 he became president of the American Sociological Society. As his own star rose, that of his university did not. The depression had badly hit the University of North Carolina. Ambitious plans for the university to take over the major responsibility for the Institute for Research in Social Science had to be shelved.[49] While Odum found himself flatteringly wooed by Northern universities, he was threatened with a salary cut and a cry from the North Carolina legislature that the university be held more minutely accountable for its expenditures. He grew very concerned that Chapel Hill would be forced to buckle down to business and political interests. During 1931, he thought very hard about leaving.[50]

Andrew Carnegie once remarked that a man was a fool who could not make money in a depression. True to this entrepreneurial tradition, Odum extracted the last piece of his imperial jigsaw from this unpromising situation. At a meeting with Will Alexander in Nashville, he confided his doubts and anxieties. Later Alexander wrote to him: "In view of the facts about the North Carolina situation, I did not feel justified in urging you to stay there. On the other hand, I was not convinced then, and I have been less so since, that the only alternative was to leave the South. . . . I am ready to say now that I don't think you should leave the South, and that I believe an opportunity can be developed somewhere that that will enable you to do the thing that you have so marvelously under way." This opportunity was a fresh grant. In December of 1931, Jackson Davis, the Southern agent of the General Education Board, was conferring industriously with Edmund Day of the Rockefeller Foundation. On the nineteenth of that month, Odum was informed through the secretary of the Social Science Research Council that an appropriation of $45,000 had been approved by the Board for a Southern Regional Study.[51]

Thus armed, Odum was able to announce his relative independence from the University of North Carolina. Frank Graham was told that the money had been granted to Odum personally, and through him to the institute. He promptly asked for a leave of absence, with the concession that he might offer one seminar course. He observed ominously: "My understanding is that prospects for a minimum appropriation for the Institute for five years are good, and that by the time we are through this very comprehensive regional study you will have had time to take stock and work out plans for a more comprehensive financing of all the University's activities." The message was clear: ingenuity had worked this time. It might not do so again. If Chapel Hill wanted Odum indefinitely, the house must be set in order.[52]

Thereby the pattern of Odum's empire had clarified. From the Rockefeller Foundation, he received a basic grant for the institute. From the General Education Board, he had an appropriation for the Southern Regional Study. From the Rosenwald Fund, he shared in the patronage of the Southern fellowships. As an integrating and administrative device, there was the Southern Regional Committee of the Social Science Research Council: occasionally, the council itself disbursed small grants. In the background was the slim financial backing of a weakened university.

This network sounds dispersed and flexible. In fact, it was dangerously reliant on one resource. Both the General Education Board and the Social Science Research Council were financial siblings of the parent Rockefeller Foundation. Although the Rosenwald Fund was independent, there was an overlap of personnel between it and Rockefeller Plaza. Moreover, during the depression the fund was weakened seriously by the fall in stock market values and the Rockefeller Foundation stepped in to prop it up.[53] The crucial nexus in all this was Odum's friendship with Will Alexander.

Step by step, Howard Odum had committed himself to regional research in Southern sociology. He had the money, the bureaucracy, the graduate students and colleagues to gather and process the information. He had come a long way logistically from the tattered days of 1927, when his department had seemed to collapse around him. But the question remained. Where had all this taken him intellectually?

three:
Odum: Southern Sociology

It seemed proper that the mass of data accumulated by the institute during the 1920s should receive a preliminary synthesis by its director. Rupert Vance, Harriet Herring, J. J. Rhyne, Jesse Steiner, Roy Brown, Clarence Heer, Guy Johnson, and Claudius Murchison had looked into many things: the rural economy of cotton, the mill villages, interracial relations, Negro folk songs, Southern income levels, the prison system of North Carolina.[1] These had broken new ground, but their findings had not been brought together. Odum's *An American Epoch,* published in 1930, implicitly was an effort to do this. But it was more, for Odum was deep into his most rhapsodic flirtation with "art." Much of his time in the late 1920s was spent in finishing a trilogy of folk novels on Left Wing Gordon, an itinerant black laborer and teller of tall tales. For several years, Odum would interrupt Gordon's road digging activities in Chapel Hill, lightly grease his palm, and note down the stories that followed. In these, Odum tried to fuse sociology and literature. Many thought he had succeeded, including Mencken and Ulrich Phillips. The first of these, *Rainbow Round My Shoulder,* enjoyed some popular success. In such a mood, Odum approached his first sustained effort to analyze the South.[2]

It was interesting, and not unusual, that Odum used familiar personal experiences to comprehend and integrate his narrative. Understanding the South meant, to some extent, coming to grips with his tangled family history. Throughout *American Epoch,* he used thinly disguised portraits of his grandfathers as metaphors for the divergent democratic and aristocratic traditions of the region. It was clear that, in retrospect, Grandfather Odum had won his greatest sympathy. At the heart of Odum's normative definition of the South lay the old man, a symbol for the honest rural middle class. If Philip Thomas had lost out to his poor relation, it was partly his own fault. He had not argued the case for the ancien régime to his grandson with total conviction. For him, the "aristocracy" had always been but a step from the frontier rudeness that still marked his daughter's father-in-law. "The old Major," Odum recalled, "had often maintained that the whole economic and cultural system of the South, although having many admirable features in it and at times approximating great possibilities, was neither well thought out nor well balanced." Thomas had doubted the value of slavery, though he had been an adamant racist. Like Jefferson, he had deprecated the loose and violent ways of plantation owners, and deplored the hypocrisy that had lauded the sanctity of family life but dallied in the slave quarters and sent blood relations to a dividing auction block. Reduced in later years to a grubbing existence as the local tax receiver, Philip Thomas had maintained a cynical detachment at the "gentle

51

folk" who retired to an isolated and injured pride. With such instruction, it is little wonder that Odum could endorse the lessons of a Darwinian social science and write that the Old South "could not survive an evolutionary world. Its philosophy and religion were not consistent with the development of social justice and democracy."[3]

This idiosyncratic family history impelled Odum to endorse the New South's social theory about its own rise, though Odum's middle class had more mud on its boots. Warmly he wrote of "the millions of middle folk not commonly recorded in the annals of the heroic or in the stories of sub-merged groups." If their fortunes had wavered, not only the war and Reconstruction had been to blame, but the inherent instabilities of the Southern economic and social structure. They themselves had been a stable bedrock for both rural and industrial society. Industrialization had not destroyed their vitality, for the plain folk had just packed their bags and gone to the mill villages. Around this transition, Odum composed the statistical information gathered by his colleagues. Although his narrative was allusive and impressionistic, he buried great quantities of data in its flow. A reference to his grandfather Odum would lead to a mention that one of his grandchildren was "among the commercial boosters of the South." This unleashed figures about the resources and economy of the region: that it was 32 percent of the American land, and 30 percent of its population. Did the reader know that the South had only 14 percent of bank deposits, or 24 percent of developed water power? A description of his grandfather's somewhat wobbly tenor voice led to a chapter on the region's folk music. Reminiscence about the country revivals of his youth started a discussion on regional religion.[4]

In this way, autobiography became sociology. Subjective experience was the core, but it was amplified by more sophisticated information than had been granted to any previous New South critic. And on two issues, the social psychology of sectionalism and the religiosity of Southern politics, Odum came close to breaking fresh conceptual ground.

In his many travels, Odum had been impressed by the variety of opinions expressed about the South. He recalled his graduate school days in the North and "a distinguished man who expressed the opinion that the southern people were so different from the rest of the country that they always would be different and would never really become a part of the Nation. This, he [Odum] thought, was unreasonable. . . . He recalled the earlier beginnings of the South, how its leadership was national in scope, how its population was recruited from all parts of the country and from European sources, even as was the North, and how so few years had intervened that a verdict of permanent differences between two such peoples, ascribed to so brief an evolution, was manifestly absurd." But Odum also remembered that this intellectual conviction was contradicted by the instruction of his youth, "the fact that all he had ever heard, from his childhood up at home, was that the South was different and, please God, would always be different."[5]

This tension had made Odum acutely conscious of the subjective awareness of sectional reality. It loomed enough in his mind to devote three chapters to the North's image of the South, the South's awareness of the North, and the South's view of itself. He was, one ventures, the first Southerner to consider seriously the problem of this particular social psychology.

He paraded all the images he had come across in his many years. Recalling the bitterness towards the North he had learned at his mother's knee, Odum sketched the Southern legend of Reconstruction, the mold in which he insisted its prickly self-consciousness had been formed. But he pointed to the Northern images of the South, which seemed to divide into two contrary versions. The first mirrored the myth of the Old South. The second excoriated or mocked a flawed New South, a Menckenian Sahara, a "Bible Belt, ruled by morons and cowards, manacled by clergymen and politicians, void of intellectual or cultural contributions." Odum took a melancholy pleasure in remembering the visitors to Chapel Hill, who had marvelled at the existence of intelligent men below the Potomac, and those who believed that "a chief pastime in the South was the lynching of Negroes, the massing of night riders, the marching of the K.K.K.'s, the working of women and children, the drinking of moonshine liquor . . . . Or else, again, gentlemen's estates, beautiful women, courtly manners . . ."[6]

Odum identified the subjectivity and assumed that it was the distorted vision of a more complicated reality. The images were rehearsed rather than evaluated, though he was sure that the indigenous school of social critics, exemplified by a Walter Hines Page, would eventually sift truth from fiction. Romance would give way to the hard accuracy of sociological insight. But he remained the American positivist. He had distanced himself from the confusions of social psychology, but he felt obliged to assert his own version. Nowhere was this more clear than in his harping on the election of 1928.

While he had travelled the South on his sabbatical, the scathing presidential election of 1928 had been taking place. The fulminations of Bishop Cannon against Al Smith, the whole outburst of bigotry, xenophobia, and provincialism had appalled him. It weighed on his mind in *American Epoch*. Time and again, in unlikely places, he would recur to it. It was not that Odum was a zealot for Al Smith. On the contrary, he had some prohibitionist sympathies and even acknowledged a certain suspicion of Roman Catholicism. But he hated the hypocrisy of Cannon, just as he had despised the Klan's claims to Christianity and Americanism. The inconsistency of Southern behavior seemed to turn his stomach. "Many southern critics," he was to write, "regretted the fact that the South could not see the inconsistency of its clamoring for states rights with reference to the Negro and child labor, but clamoring for federalism for the enforcement of prohibition . . . of the South's individualism and its well known tradition for rich eating and drinking alongside its extreme damnation of all those who questioned the perfection of the National Prohibition Law. . . . of the churches clamoring for law enforcement and 'righteousness' with reference to prohibition, and silent on injustice to Negroes and mill workers. And southern Protestants recommending that the United States interfere in Mexico to free the Mexicans from ecclesiastical domination!"[7] While Odum had been careful to preserve his neutrality during the Dayton trial, 1928 moved him towards an outright condemnation of the fundamentalist influence on Southern life and unquestionably sharpened his sense of the intimate links between the two. For a while, the sociologist came very close to echoing Mencken's anticlerical theory of Southern decline. It was an uncharacteristic moment.

It was worrying that Odum had joined the growing band who were writing about the region, for he feared the taint of popular polemic. Not wishing to be labelled a professional Southerner, he began to insist that even when he was writing about the South it was the South in a national setting. These were Southern pictures, but American too. Equally, his descriptions of Southern diversity did not undermine the organic unity of the region. "Both the old and the new culture abounded in sharp contrasts and logical paradoxes," he admitted. However, "There were many Souths yet *the* South. It was preeminently national in backgrounds, yet provincial in its processes." This conundrum was not explained, but merely asserted. "The South was different, and it should be different," he announced. "But it was the normal difference of an important region of a great Nation, and should not continue to develop a sectional difference as of one section over against another."[8] This was puzzling, even as it was traditional. The nationality of Southern character was an old New South doctrine. But Odum had extended its lines by a more eclectic sociology and a more skeptical attitude towards the mythology, not only of the Old South but even of the New.

For the moment, he remained unchallenged. He seemed unaware that he might be challenged by anything other than the odd proponent of Mencken's boobocracy. He gathered that a few dabblers in belles-lettres in Nashville had hazarded objections, but *I'll Take My Stand* didn't seem serious. To Mencken, he observed that "what these brethren do not sense . . . is the fact that all of the old southern romanticism has been thoroughly interwoven with a realism, which, even though in the long run may develop a fine culture, is at present a pretty sordid fact, and that even before the War Between the States it was being rotted into from various sources." It was true that Stringfellow Barr, editor of the *Virginia Quarterly Review,* had suggested in a review of *American Epoch* that Southerners should struggle to preserve parts of their culture. "Virginia would be like that, wouldn't it?" Odum complained. "I have emphasized southern qualities as distinctive and powerful contributions to the national fabric so much already that I have almost become an apologist. And how one section can keep on trying to build a wall around itself and be different from the rest of the world is more than I can see."[9]

Neither the Agrarians nor the more indistinct flutterings of Charlottesville unduly bothered Odum. They were publicists; he was a scientist. In material resources, there was no contest between Chapel Hill and Nashville. William Couch, director of the University of North Carolina Press and no friend to Odum, grumbled to Donald Davidson in 1932 about the relative poverty of the humanities. Davidson backed him up, from his own experience at Vanderbilt University: "The sole important instances that I know of in our Division of Humanities where aid has gone to a professor is the case of Ransom, this year on a Guggenheim fellowship. What others have done has been at their own expense, unencouraged by foundation interest. On the [other] hand, I know of several important instances in the field of the natural and social sciences where very generous aid has been given. One professor that I know of has received repeated grants. It is seemingly easy for scientists and social scientists to get help."[10]

Nonetheless, versions of agrarianism were to give him trouble. For Odum was exposed on several flanks. Although he was the most important duct down which foundation money flowed to the Southern intelligentsia, especially in social science, he was not the only one. Nor could he control all the tentacles of his network of organizations. The pell-mell of undisciplined and uncoordinated scholarly research was unnerving, and he liked to restrain it. In 1924, he had complained of the rush of studies on the cotton mills. In 1926, his concern had been a plethora of work on the Negro: "There are so many cross currents and different people wanting to work in the field the situation will soon be literally unbearable."[11] His reasons were understandable. He had learned that sociology was a disrupting new discipline and prudence was more easily attained within a small group of like-minded thinkers, such as he had in the institute. An imprudent stranger could destroy his careful groundwork overnight.

In the event, the disruption came from North Carolina. At the Woman's College of the University of North Carolina at Greensboro, Benjamin Kendrick, late of the historical seminar of William Dunning at Columbia, had proved himself occasionally useful to Odum. This historian had offered detailed and shrewd criticism of the manuscript of *An American Epoch.* When members of the Southern Regional Committee had been selected, Odum had put forward Kendrick's name. Upon Odum's surrender of the position, Kendrick had advanced to chairman of the committee.[12]

In January of 1934, Odum received an official letter from Kendrick under the letterhead of the Southern Regional Committee. Unexpectedly it told him that the recent Gainesville conference of the committee had "voted to go ahead with the organization of a Southern Council for the Advancement of Knowledge," and that Kendrick expected Odum to "give me the benefit of your full cooperation and influence in putting the thing over in the South in general and in North Carolina in particular." It must have been with surprise and trepidation that Odum turned to an enclosed reprint from the *Southwest Review,* in which Kendrick laid forth his views.[13]

Ominously, it began with a questioning of the New South's materialism. A brief account of the New South movement was followed by this remark: "During the past four years a larger and larger number of Southern intellectuals and some few Southern business leaders have begun to wonder if the prophets of the New South were altogether true prophets. Was there not something in the Old South which after all is worth preserving and revivifying? These questions do not point toward a resurgence of the old sectionalism, but toward the creation of a new regionalism."

Kendrick wanted to create a public opinion that would support enlightened change within the region. To this end, he proposed that curricula in Southern colleges be reorganized to make an educational system more socially relevant and less bent on producing professional scholars. In addition, he foresaw a periodical that would provide the Southern undergraduate with discussion of Southern problems. There should be correspondents in each state capitol to report on political and legislative events. This journal would be sponsored by the council or "confederation," as he called it in the article. 1300 charter members would be found, 100 from each Southern state: these would be "socially-minded men and women of intellectual ability, of scholarly attainment, and most important of all, of good will." Colleges would be expected to have an institutional membership in the "confederation's" drive to reorganize and improve graduate education. Kendrick hoped that Southern universities might delegate their degree granting powers to the "confederation," or three divisions of the "confederation." Aspirant scholars would apply, not to individual universities, but to the "confederation," which would organize courses of instruction that combined the facilities of several colleges.

Optimistically, the historian hoped the scheme would be inexpensive. For an executive director and a small staff, a budget of about $25,000 a year was envisaged. However, Kendrick was eager for a central research fund that might promote study, "purposive in character and local in conception." Kendrick did not want scholars too fastidious to enter the arena of public debate.[14]

These proposals had been put to the Gainesville conference and received its cheerful endorsement. It seemed worth exploring. And it was natural that, in trying to implement a controversial policy, Kendrick should have turned to Odum. Foundations had to be cajoled, universities persuaded, founding members located. Moreover, Kendrick was involved with Odum's new regional study. He and a fellow Greensboro historian, Alex Arnett, had been commissioned to write a brief historical preface to Odum's magnum opus.[15] Knowing Odum's views, Kendrick was confident that they were in substantial agreement. Both had doubts about the speed of industrialization. And, although Kendrick had paid his respects to the Agrarians for stimulating a useful debate about the shortcomings of the New South, the extensiveness of the "confederation" barred any Agrarian monopoly.

Odum's response was immediate. He disagreed about the need for a southern periodical and rehearsed his old decision to make *Social Forces* a "national" journal. Kendrick's ideas were "diametrically opposed to the conclusions of the Southern Regional Study," and no action should be taken until its results were available. His help was summarily refused, though he did suggest that the Social Science Research Council might publish Kendrick's views as a minority report or "your and Arnett's little volume might give you a chance to set forth your conclusions."[16]

Kendrick was puzzled and insulted. After all, he had come with the official mandate of a not inconsiderable body, the Southern Regional Committee. Although Odum had been so kind as to say that he didn't mind if Kendrick and his committee "wish to join the Nashville group," Kendrick knew he was no Agrarian. Odum had been cryptic, asserting airily that the scheme was "opposed" to his own regional study, which seemed to have a necessary priority. Incensed, Kendrick wrote back: "I cannot to save my life understand how you can say that the 'New Regionalism' as I described it in my article is contrary to all your group has been standing for for the last ten years.... So far as my article was concerned it was entirely in keeping with the outline in your 'Work Book' which I prepared two years ago and which I understood you approved.... I had been under the unfortunate delusion that in this volume we were laying the historical background for your Southern Regional Study and it had never occurred to me before that it offered any 'diversity of viewpoint.'"[17]

The argument thus joined, Odum decided to check around the Southern intelligentsia to see how matters stood. Through John Wade, whom he had known for many years, he inquired of Donald Davidson whether Kendrick might be considered an Agrarian. The poet thought, on the whole, not. George Fort Milton told Odum that he had attended the Gainesville conference and voted for Kendrick's proposal. It seemed to him "a really useful idea." Moreover, he could not "at all see how Kendrick's background or general organization of ideas can be likened to that of Donald Davidson."[18] Despite these reactions, Odum grew increasingly convinced that Kendrick should be relegated to the "moonlight and magnolias" school of social critics. His characterizations of the historian became more savage. To Sydnor Walker of the Rockefeller Foundation, he was to refer to "this southern confederacy of learning and goodness and the resurgence of a 'new sectionalism' rationalized into the 'new regionalism' and sponsored by sundry charming, eloquent, rosy-cheeked gentlemen and scholars, my over-lords of the Southern Regional Committee." Hyperbolically, he insisted that this was "the most critical situation that the southern so-called intellectuals have faced since the aftermath of the reconstruction period." He was even to draw a sinister parallel, when mentioning Kindrick's interest in the religious basis of Southern society: this "religious zeal . . . comes extraordinarily near the Nazi mode."[19]

In his correspondence, Odum hardened his commitment to the absolute distinction between sectionalism and his own regionalism. He insisted that sectionalism was egocentric, while regionalism was unselfish integration into the national scene. Davidson and Kendrick argued that practice would muddy the theoretical distinction. If one conceded the South's distinctive-ness, as Odum did, and attempted to devise a localized infrastructure of power, as Odum wanted, you could not control the eventual relationship to the nation.[20] It would appear, from the general reaction, that Davidson had rather the better of the argument. Odum was reduced to a shrill dogmatism, determined to separate himself from the old and new sectional traditions. Milton would not accept his case, and even Sydnor Walker puckishly told Odum: "Both Mr. Day and I read the . . . material which makes it evident that there is trouble brewing in the Old South. The worst of it is that if one has not considerable background on this subject, the argument of these gentlemen [Kendrick and Davidson] sounds quite reasonable." Later she was to observe more awkwardly: "I should be inclined to think that you and Mr. Davidson could unite on most practical questions of policy. I have felt from the beginning that your definition made sectionalism and regionalism seem farther apart than they necessarily are, and that some of the individuals concerned in the controversy may not be at all certain of their position in relation to the invisible line."[21]

Even as he lost the intellectual argument, Odum won the institutional battle. With an instinct for the jugular vein, he simply cut Kendrick's hopes of raising money for the scheme. To the Social Science Research Council, to the Rockefeller Foundation, to the General Education Board, to Harry Chase, now President of New York University and influential with both the SSRC and the foundations, Odum dispatched a series of crippling letters. Despite some doubts, the powers listened to Odum and denied Kendrick funds. The project withered. It was significant that the only money Kendrick could lay his hands upon came from the Carnegie Foundation, which lay outside the Odum network.[22]

Seeking an explanation for Odum's agitation, Davidson hazarded this guess to John Wade: "I gather, from direct remarks as well as from reading between the lines, that Odum fears that Kendrick and Pipkin, now suddenly and perhaps strangely talking in tune with some of the 'Agrarians,' are about to commit some form of sociological sabotage, and set awry other plans, perhaps Odum's plans, for fostering the kind of regionalism in which he is interested." And it was true that when Kendrick's first letter dropped on Odum's desk the sociologist had barely finished unsuccessfully scouting in New York for a centralized Southern Institute.[23] The new Confederation posed a threat. There were, in addition, good reasons for opposing Kendrick. Odum knew, better than most, that funds would not likely be forthcoming. It was improbable that universities would be persuaded to yield up their autonomy, and quixotic to challenge the tide of scholarly professionalization. But Odum did not use these arguments extensively. He attacked the rhetoric. For several years, he had been easing himself into the regional movement and grown used to seeing the word "Southern" in his own books and speeches. He had felt secure in the stability of the New South consensus; but the ideological context had begun to change around him. By 1934, "Southern" was a word in the process of being annexed by the Agrarians. Odum was determined not to let it go.

And, in his plans for the Southern Regional Study, the political context was exerting different pressures. The New Deal had begun to transform the relationship between social scientists, government and social planning. While Odum had talked in the 1920s loosely about rationalizing the social order, he had had only reluctant and imperfect political instruments to hand. By 1934, he and his fellow sociologists at Chapel Hill were bound up in the actions of the Roosevelt administration. For Odum, it was a reluctant change. In 1931, he had approved of Hoover's veto of the Muscle Shoals Bill. By 1933, he was confronted with the reality of the Tennessee Valley Authority. He had not changed his views, as he told Sydnor Walker, "but the present bill has passed, it is a law, it is an actual regional-national experiment, and one of the most significant ever proposed.... Mr. Roosevelt has projected this thing on the basis of a human welfare experiment in social planning, whereas Mr. Hoover interpreted it largely as government entering the field of private business."[24] Odum never wasted time on arguing with a *fait accompli*. He was to send T. J. Woofter off to Knoxville to make an emergency study of the Tennessee Valley subregion, and latterly threw in Harriet Herring and Rupert Vance to help. Odum himself accepted from Harry Hopkins the job of North Carolina director of the Civil Works Administration and agreed to sit on the State Planning Board. Woofter was later to move to the Federal Emergency Relief

Administration. Members of the institute were pressed for memoranda by the National Resources Board, the Rural Resettlement Administration, as well as FERA. In due course, they were to have influence on federal policy towards farm tenancy. In all this, however, Odum—unlike his younger colleagues—was a reluctant New Dealer.[25]

The social melting pot of the 1930s put Odum under fresh pressures. He felt that the Southern Regional Study had to serve two masters, sociological description and administrative recommendation. Even as he gathered the material for *Southern Regions of the United States*, his responsibility seemed to deepen. The 1936 publication was nothing scanty. It was a volume to test the stoutest bookshelf: nearly 700 pages, 340 maps, 270 charts and tables, a dizzying compendium of data.[26]

Southern Regions seemed to offer something new. All the old disputes about the region had rendered impressionistic definitions. The South was race, or it was the land, it was manners or it was kinship. Odum presented an apparently scientific system for defining, classifying, and planning for the South. More than that, he split the whole United States up into six neat regions. There was the Southeast consisting of Kentucky, Virginia, Tennessee, North and South Carolina, Georgia, Florida, Alabama, Mississippi, Louisiana, and Arkansas; the Southwest of Oklahoma, Texas, New Mexico, and Arizona; the Northeast of Maryland, Delaware, West Virginia, Pennsylvania, New Jersey, New York, Rhode Island, Connecticut, Massachusetts, Vermont, Maine, and New Hampshire; the Middle States of Ohio, Indiana, Michigan, Illinois, Wisconsin, Minnesota, Iowa, and Missouri; the Northwest of Montana, North and South Dakota, Kansas, Nebraska, Colorado, Wyoming, Idaho, and Utah; and the Far West of California, Nevada, Oregon, and Washington. Around this sixfold division, the book's maps and statistics were grouped.

How had Odum cut the Gordian knot of impressionism? He had a system of indices, listings of statistics that showed the cultural, economic, and social life of individual states. Agricultural production, the numbers of schools and colleges, the lengths of highways, the quantity of insurance policies, the size of libraries, anything and everything that Odum's staff could quantify. As they were the only figures readily available, statistics from states formed the basis. Odum, however, admitted that states were an imperfect reflection of socioeconomic divisions. These indices were correlated and made to produce six comparatively homogeneous regions.[27]

Many contemporaries were puzzled by anomalies. Delaware and Maine, for example, were deemed more alike than Delaware and Virginia. Gerald Johnson, writing from Baltimore, wanted to know why Maryland had been read out of the South. Odum referred to his indices. "I need scarcely call attention," he replied, "to the unreality of Maryland as a southern state when it comes to such items as farm tenancy, the size and nature of farms, nature of crops, percentage of Negro population, bank deposits, savings, purchase of automobiles" and so forth. In short, Maryland was too rich. Odum was obliged to admit that this rubric was slippery. Virginia, after all, was taking the path of Maryland. Florida was going the same way. But Odum could remove Maryland from the Southeast, while he was stuck with Florida, for one of the principles of regionalism was contiguousness. Florida, as Rupert Vance was to admit, was unquestionably "embarrassing." By the same token, Delaware could not be part of the Southeast, because Maryland interposed a barrier.[28]

It was natural that border areas posed Odum's greatest problem. Kentucky and West Virginia had a confusing set of indices. Of West Virginia, Odum observed, "In perhaps forty indices commonly denoting deficiency in culture and institutional standards it tends to rank with the Southeast. Thus in value of farms, lands and property; in horse power per worker, machine farming; in population under twenty years, over fifty years; in wage earners and wages paid; in value of manufactured products; in rank in education and other services. On the other hand, in its industries, its educational institutions of higher learning, its Negro population, its foreign born, its wealth and income, its fertilizer consumption, and many others it ranks with the Northeast." With Kentucky, the dilemma was similar. But they had to be assigned somewhere. So West Virginia went to the Northeast, and Kentucky to the Southeast. Odum offered no explanation for the former decision, but observed that Kentucky's "population, folkways, culture, history, cities, rank it without serious question in the southeastern group."[29]

This was the effect of indices, but he was asked how he evaluated the indices themselves. When Gerald Johnson was asked to write a popular condensation of *Southern Regions*, to be called *The Wasted Land*, he faced this methodological problem. As the journalist put it, "A blind man can see that some of these questions are more important than others. The total population of a State, for example, is more important than the number of illegal distilleries seized in that State." But Johnson was convinced of Odum's scientific credentials and reassured the reader that "the statistics . . . had to be 'weighted' by complicated mathematical operations familiar only to statisticians to balance this varying importance."[30]

One can look through the long pages and many numbers of *Southern Regions* without finding an exposition of this mathematical alchemy. Embarrassingly, Odum had no such technique, though he admitted to wanting one. To G. W. Forster of the State College in Raleigh, a reviewer of *Southern Regions*, Odum wrote: "I agree with your criticism of the statistical technique. I tried hard to get one or two of the statisticians to give us a refined scale of indices. Like the delineation of regions in which we are just beginning, so also the utilization of these indices must be approximate till the time the statisticians will come in and attempt some real methodological study. I need scarcely add that one of the tasks which appears necessary from this study is a series of methodological studies of indices and homogeneity groupings of likenesses and differences." In *Southern Regions* itself, Odum seemed to give away the game. "Like the old fallacies of aggregate figures," he conceded,". . .measures fabricated from arbitrary comparative indices fall short of either scientific accuracy or practical application of living society."[31]

Odum had achieved a circular argument in one respect. He had examined a number of indisputably southern states. From these, he had derived a rough norm in which poverty was an important common denominator. Then he had worked outwards until the levels of wealth grew incongruous. This had obliged him to cut off Maryland. As significantly, it had led him to sever the Southwestern states of Texas and Oklahoma from the Southeast. But this left a worrying question mark. If the economic revolution, in which—despite the Depression—he remained confident, was to be consummated and the affluent edges of the region worked inwards, would the South shrink to a patch of exhausted shrub on the border between Alabama and Mississippi? Odum had tried to nail firm boundaries on a fluid social reality. His Southeast had to be static, or it would have to disappear.

In *An American Epoch,* Odum had cast his lot with the impressionism of social psychology. He had taken historical evidence seriously. In *Southern Regions,* he admitted, "The cultural equipment of the Southeast is not only powerfully conditioned by its geographic factors but can be understood only through a knowledge of historical backgrounds and regional incidence which have played an extraordinarily dominant rôle in the development of the civilization of the South." But the new book made no serious effort to integrate history into the attempt to understand the region. Odum offered only a shallow listing of "crises" that bore little functional relationship to the sociology it was intended to underpin. These had been casually requested of Kendrick a few years earlier, with the remark that research into primary sources was unnecessary, that "it was the 'sweep' that we wanted rather than exhaustive research."[32]

His indices bore only a haphazard relationship to the inscrutable facts of social psychology. Could one measure culture by figures about libraries and universities? In some ways, yes. In others, equally as crucial, no. For planning reasons, Odum needed to distil precise regional boundaries. One cannot draw up blueprints of social change if one doesn't know where a place is. Odum might begin to quantify human activities, but no figures

told him what people felt and no sociology instructed how emotional
identity should weigh in administration.

All these were weaknesses, most apparent in a long retrospect. From the
standpoint of 1936, the book's impact was more striking. Odum's regional
theory, although it was to affect his empirical planning, did not much limit
the reader's ability to use the book with profit. The mass of statistics was
overwhelming and impressive. Although they were grouped into Odum's
six regions, and his maps bore thick lines that divided region from region,
the underlying data was accessible. With *Southern Regions,* the New South
intelligentsia had taken a precise stock of its milieu. It stripped away the
woolly optimism of boosting chambers of commerce, and defined the
immense task that Southern poverty still imposed. All those maps and
charts were to provide the cannon fodder for informed discussion about
the South for decades.

But there was more than figures, there was also a commentary. Here
Odum returned to many of the themes of *An American Epoch,* especially
his emphasis on the middle class and education. For Odum, the non-
slaveholding whites were the backbone of the reconstructed South. "They
illustrated," he insisted, "the Sumner theory that 'the share that the upper
strata (the large middle group) of the masses have in determining the policy
of the masses is therefore often decisive of public welfare. This group
stands out in contrast to the 'planter class,' to which so much attention has
been given. . . . Yet in all the averages and distributions of deficiencies and
lags this group still constitutes the norm around which judgements should
be made and plans developed." This large claim was coupled to another:
"Any region which has the will and capacity to support educational and
scientific institutions of the highest order, because of this desire and capacity
and because of what the institutions achieve in leadership and technology
in economic and political direction, in upraising of standards and in social
guidance, will automatically develop increasingly an adequate culture."
And both claims were linked to the nationalist enthusiasm which the fracas
with Kendrick had strengthened. But now Odum offered a sterner reason
for "integration." Their money was needed: "The evidence would seem to
indicate the inability of the southern regions to develop their capacities
independent of resources, coöperative effort, and conditioning attitudes of
other regions and of the nation as a whole."[33]

"Conditioning attitudes," by which he meant social values, were left
prudently obscure. It raised, for one thing, the prickly issue of race.
Southern Regions did not dwell on the problem, though it said a little. One
courtesy Odum paid to Southern blacks. He did not segregate his figures.
"The Southern Regional Study," he observed, "has been projected and
carried out on the assumption that the Negro is an integral, normal, and

continuing factor in the culture of the Southeast. Consistently the study, whilst recognizing the Negro as one of the chiefest of economic problems, has refused to set up a dichotomous framework in which one set of figures would present the whole southern picture and another would present the picture of what would be if the Negro were not included." Quietly, Odum has dissented from Ulrich Phillips's claim that Southernness consisted in precisely that dichotomy.[34]

Aware of the economic and social cost of segregation, Odum assumed its permanence and believed that the Negro could progress under its aegis. He made a point of repudiating the old notion of inherent racial inferiority, but left untouched the more perplexing issue of an inferiority rooted in cultural conditioning. Instead, he confined himself to endorsing the report that Guy Johnson had made for the Interracial Commission in which the participation of Negroes "in the rights and duties of citizenship in the broadest sense" had been recommended. But he was ominously careful to add: "this step can be taken without destroying the integrity of the races. Negroes and whites have been meeting together in various organizations in the South for years now, and there is no evidence that either race is any the worse for the experience. . . . Furthermore, the increasing race pride among Negroes will act as a conserver of racial integrity." Odum had not, after all, abandoned his substantial respect for the power of genes.[35]

It was most striking that Howard Odum's vision of Southern development was almost as agrarian as Nashville's. When the sharecropper and tenant problem was uncovered during the 1930s, Odum and Rupert Vance, Arthur Raper and T. J. Woofter had gathered the data to feed the New Deal debate. By comparison, the institute's work on race was less influential, despite Guy Johnson's role in helping Gunnar Myrdal to write *An American Dilemma*.[36] Even weaker was the Odum school's grasp of politics: V. O. Key's *Southern Politics in State and Nation* paid little heed to them. On agriculture, however, the institute had deepened and enriched the tradition of rural sociology that had begun in Eugene Branson's days.[37]

"In fine and in sum," Odum wrote, "the agrarian problem is *the region,* for better or for worse, and the agrarian statecraft which is involved." This sounded eminently Nashvillian, and, indeed, Benjamin Kendrick had once told Odum: "Insofar as they [the Agrarians] believe that the farmer should be more nearly self-sufficing than at present is the case I do agree with them and I suspect you do also." For Odum did put together passages of skepticism about industrialization. "This region," he said in *Southern Regions,* "need not lag, on the one hand, nor, on the other, follow blindly the paths of a hectic, urban, technological, transitional period of civilization."[38] Partly Odum was repeating the old New South theory of the "belated section" that could learn from the mistakes of its industrializing predecessors, but it ran deeper than this. For a Henry Grady, this meant little more than the inconvenience of labor disputes and grim working conditions so notable in New England. Odum's sense of industrialism's abuses was richer. And while the Agrarians attacked industrialism from without the assumptions of scientific theory, Odum was a fifth column that peppered it from a hiding place in the sociology of a William Graham Sumner.[39]

Odum had dabbled intermittently in a grand theory of social change that might fuse the viewpoints of Sumner, Wundt, and Giddings. In his presidential address to the American Sociological Society in 1930, he had suggested that Sumner's distinction between the folkways and the state was still a fundamental premise. But it no longer served to restrict the meaning of a "folk" to rural classes. New York City had its folkways: the world of the "cultivated classes" was not apart. A folk society was, for Odum, present "in any stage of culture or civilization whenever the major conditioning factors are extra-organizational or when a synergy of conflicting forces and processes results in an integrated transitional society." The proper study of sociology was the conflict between the homogeneous world of the folk and technological change.[40]

In a 1937 article, Odum was to elaborate the point. As he saw it, from the basic Wundtian folk society developed "stateways," the formal legal structures that regulated the informal ways of the folk. With the inruption of scientific technology, there came "technicways." These were not the technology itself, but the ways of adjustment to the technology. These "arise from the pressure of technological forces and procedures to impel conformity of individual and group to quick-changing patterns, regardless of empirical considerations or of mass sanction. Thus," Odum explained, "'fashions' superimposed through the technics of advertising do not represent the tastes of individuals or groups, nor do they reflect the gradual evolution from one style to another. Such fashions are not folkways to meet needs but *technicways* to fall in line with pressure or gadgets of the market place."[41]

There is no doubt that Odum regarded the technicways with profound distaste. Paradoxically for a bureaucrat and social planner, he feared bureaucracy and imprudent social engineering. Man was not plastic, to be molded at will. If ill-considered change outran the folk society, the folk would turn upon it and crush the good with the bad. The sociologists's job was to find the middle way, to establish an "orderly transitional democracy."[42]

This perspective informed Odum's thinking in *Southern Regions*. He complained that material technicways were speeding up evolution in a helter-skelter way. The South had to look for a "balanced economy which is also primarily a 'culture' which will serve as a medium for the continuing sweep of science and technology which in turn can be made to serve mankind rather than exploit it." For Odum, American society was dangerously imbalanced by the preponderance of urban industrialism over "the natural agrarian elements". City and country needed to succor each other, not vie to destroy the best in each. Thus it was vitally important that a palsied Southern agriculture be restored to health.[43]

With his feeling for the underlying strength of the nonplantation South, Odum saw a Southern history, not where a decaying plantation world was being replaced by industry, but where a white frontier society, lately shackled by the plantation, retained the capacity for great development. As he frequently put it, "southern culture is immature rather than decadent." Often he pointed to the demographic strength of an area, whose birth rate was the highest in the nation and which exported many of its offspring. Odum's South was "rich in folk reserves, where resides a great seed bed of population for renewing the national stream . . . . rich in the sheer organic vitality of the folk life and society which has always been a definitive force in the rise of new cultures." This sentiment echoed Odum's interest in the cyclical historical theory of Oswald Spengler. Like the German, Odum felt that cultures tended to degenerate into mere civilization, whose most destructive agent was the megapolis. The South was yet a culture.[44]

One must stress that, despite Odum's prudent regard for the brutal censorship in Southern society, he retained a deep faith in the common man. Even in the evolution controversy of 1926, he had confided to Harry Chase: "The bulwark of this State and America is the great integrity of the mass of the people. We may exclude, of course, the socially deficient and the demagogues. Likewise the people are, contrary to some opinions, open and eager to hear the truth if presented before they have been driven into emotional states and if and when presented in terms of truth and not shibboleths."[45]

But who were the folk? Odum was vague on this point. In 1930, he had adapted Sumner in this way: "The after-war society of the South was pre-eminently folk society in that this region, although conquered and outwardly controlled by organized stateways and state force to the nth degree, had its culture and its future primarily conditioned by a folk society which was organic, natural, and material, such that its mastery was almost complete." This implied that the whole South was a single folk, with the exception of the blacks who formed a folk group of their own. But a footnote made the position opaque: "For the purpose of this discussion 'region' is not an entirely separate concept but an extension and attribute to the 'folk.' . . . 'the South' as a section would comprise the technical, geographic, and political 'Confederate States of America'; as a region it would vary, with subdivisions according to the fusion of culture and geography—the Piedmont mountain folk, the Piedmont mill folk, Saint Helena Island, the Black Belt, the Southwest, etc."[46] This was confusing. Was the folk the small social group, such as the Piedmont, and the region a congregation of folks? Or was the region the folk, and the smaller groups but subdivisions? Was the South a section, with smaller regions? If so, why did Odum call the post-Civil War South both a region and a folk?

Southern Regions dispelled a little of the fog. He was careful to insist that differentiating evidence about the Appalachians made it clear, "just as there is no longer a 'South,' so any blanket classification, 'southern people,' no longer constitutes an authentic characterization." Elsewhere he re-iterated the paradox that "the South not only differs from the rest of the country, but also, and radically, within its former bounds. . . . There is no longer 'the South' but many Souths." So it was that his book was titled *Southern Regions,* not *The Southern Region.* However, this clarification introduced an instability into Odum's case. If the South was dismembered, why was it proper to analyze it as an entity? His answer was "folkways." But he had still not defined the boundaries of his folk group.[47]

Believing that this was an essentially vital folk society, Odum's planning proposals were directed at unshackling the South. Agriculture must be restored to health, with aims such as these: the reform of the tenancy system; the development of an adequate credit system for farmers; the readjustment of crop land uses, especially by the promotion of more food and feed crops; the raising of commodity consumption in the region; the improvement of the comforts and conveniences of farm life by electrifica-tion; a method for the redistribution of submarginal lands and people within the present submarginal areas rather than the wholesale retirement of such land and the relocation of its population; the increase of agricultural exports; the pooling of rural labor and farm machinery in cooperative ventures; the development of small industries to serve agricultural needs; reforestation and erosion work; the promotion of livestock and dairy industries; the reparation of housing deficiencies; the equalization of facilities for blacks.[48]

If all this could have been done, it would have wrought a minor social revolution. But this was not a revolutionary program, so much as an attempt to make a platonic agrarian ideal workable and eliminate the immense waste in Southern society. It was the old progressive message of efficiency, echoing with a chastened Jeffersonianism. For Odum was noticeably silent on urbanization and heavy industry. These plans were aimed at putting industry back to work for agriculture, and at reversing the historic trend of agriculture becoming the handmaiden of industry.

It was obvious to Odum that none of this was possible in the existing Southern political structure. Candidly, he admitted that "modification of the political culture of the region. . .lies at the base of any planning approach." Knowing this, he had no convincing solution save for a few technical suggestions about public administration and the bold, if quixotic, suggestion that the Theodore Bilbos might be simply bypassed. Education might be the answer. Thus Odum wanted a series of strong centers of education, in which social research, technological development, and training for public administration might be concentrated. These institutions would agree upon and cooperate in projects of social change. More than this, Odum wanted an extended system of adult education. "There can be no success without an extraordinary effort in adult education," he insisted, "carrying to the people the power of fact and thinking." Thereby the strain of the technicways might be eased. One might produce "a powerful regional motivation and also a spontaneous folk movement". In this way, one could sneak behind the political intertia of the Eugene Talmadges and give the people "the truth," before they had been "driven into emotional states."

All this would require a high degree of coordination. To this end, Odum proposed a series of planning councils, funded by Washington, state governments, and private philanthropy. A national planning council and regional planning councils would be superimposed on the existing state planning boards. The myriad of regional divisions employed by federal agencies would have to be standardized around his own sixfold division. On the Southeastern Planning Council, there would be twelve members, of which eleven would come from each state and the twelfth would be an ex-officio representative of the Tennessee Valley Authority. In addition, Odum foresaw "certain national-regional advisory councils in which private agencies and institutions can formulate programs." These would cooperate with the government boards. Lest all of this should produce an immense and unresponsive bureaucracy, Odum suggested a progressive touch. There should be provision for referenda on proposed reforms. And, out of all this, Odum wanted two six-year plans to be fashioned.[49]

This was the vision. It contained elements of nearly all the instruments of social planning he had ever experienced; the university, the foundations, the state planning board, the New Deal agencies. This Comtean blueprint was mated to his intellectual conviction of the social reality of regionalism. He was confident that his data proved scientifically that regions were a firm basis upon which to rest a superstructure.

Southern Regions was widely publicized and enthusiastically received. Copies went to Franklin Roosevelt, Herbert Hoover, Senator Josiah Bailey of North Carolina, Maury Maverick of Texas, Rexford Tugwell, Governor O. Max Gardner of North Carolina, Arthur Morgan of the Tennessee Valley Authority, Louis Brandeis, and David Lilienthal. Brandeis was very pleased. George Foster Peabody was sure that the president ought to read it, and duly sent a copy to his old friend in the White House. Odum got polite notes from the president's secretaries, though it is doubtful that Roosevelt ever read it.[50]

The intellectual community took it well. Only Donald Davidson, from Odum's right, and Broadus Mitchell, from his left, offered substantial dissents. Most reviewers were overwhelmed by a large and complicated book. Gratefully, they praised it. It is doubtful that many actually read it with thoroughness. As a study of the South, it was never to receive a substantial assessment. Its theory of regionalism had to wait several years for real criticism, when Odum extended his ideas to the whole nation in 1938.[51]

Southern Regions was a hybrid of planning and description. As such, Odum awaited two verdicts on the study. Was it intellectually convincing? Could any of its plans be put into effect? In the years between 1936 and the Second World War, Odum was to receive judgments on both.

four:
Odum: The Failure of Regionalism

⊠ To enact the whole program of *Southern Regions* would have required an immense effort and many powerful allies. To manage a fragment was more practical, especially if it was the most familiar of ambitions, the rationalization of the infrastructure of the Southern intelligentsia by means of foundation money. And changes in the world of New York philanthropy made the task more urgent, for they were threatening the very existence of the Institute for Research in Social Science.

Odum's ability to practice sociology in the South, and to continue the development of a Southern sociology, rested on the Rockefeller Foundation. For more than a decade the foundation had supported the social sciences. Odum's slice was only part of a much bigger pie, in which diverse organizations like the Social Science Research Council, the Institute of Human Relations at Yale, the London School of Economics, and others had shared. But the trustees, in the inner sanctum of the foundation, had always been a little skeptical of a wholesale commitment to an imprecise and controversial "science." One of the most skeptical was the foundation's later historian, Raymond Fosdick. He was to remember in 1952 that sociology was "a new field and it involved serious possibility of public misunderstanding. Still vivid in the minds of some of the trustees was the recollection of the Congressional investigation and the bitter criticism which had followed the Foundation's attempt...[in 1914] to make some approach to the problem of industrial relations." In helping Odum, the foundation had been careful to walk softly and carry no stick at all. When Odum had sought financial support for the University of North Carolina Press and *Social Forces* in 1925, one foundation executive had scribbled on Odum's request as advice to his colleagues: "Don't let either Memorial or any other foundation give one penny *directly* to their press or the Journal of Social Forces. That would arouse another kind of fundamentalism that would be fatal and set their whole publishing activity back."[1]

The charter for the foundation's involvement was a 1924 memorandum. Under its aegis, Odum had prospered. Four points are especially pertinent. The memorandum advised that no money be given to organizations "whose purposes and activities are centered largely in the procurement of legislation"; no attempt should be made directly "to secure any social, economic or political reform" or "contribute more than a conservative proportion toward the current expense of organizations engaged in direct activity for social welfare"; no influence should be exerted on research findings "through the designation of either personnel, specific problems to be attacked, or methods of enquiry to be adopted." This was hard to sustain, as Odum's experience with Beardsley Ruml in 1927 had indicated. But it

70

tended to make the foundation emphasize the training of social scientists in university centers and the accumulation of raw data.[2]

In 1934, a new committee chaired by Fosdick recommended a change. With some complacency, it judged that the intention to train social scientists had been largely fulfilled. Moreover, it expressed a disillusionment with the sterile quantity of research the old mandate had generated. Fosdick was eager that there be more emphasis on ends, and less on means. "This would not mean, of course, the relinquishment of research as a method," the committee report remarked. "It would mean that we have no interest in the promotion of research as an end in itself. . . . The mere accumulation of facts, untested by practical application, is in danger of becoming a substitute rather than a basis for collective action."[3]

Immediately this affected Odum. The foundation's support for the institute was reconsidered. In 1935, he was offered a five year grant that would fall each year by five thousand dollars from $25,000 to $5,000. The understanding was express that this marked the beginning of the end.[4] This presaged a large hole in the Odum empire. As usual, he had a plan to plug it.

Odum had long wanted a Southern Institute, an Institute for Research in Social Science writ large for the whole region. The new situation seemed to demand that this was not only desirable, but necessary. In 1932, he had confided to Louis Round Wilson that, after "excellent conferences lately with some important people," he was hopeful of a "pool endowment for the Southern Region." In 1933, some foundation executives came to Chapel Hill for a visit and Odum raised the possibility of making the Southern Regional Study into a permanent "Southern Regional Institute instead of a local, state and regional one." Edmund Day discouraged the idea, without closing the door on it.[5]

Early in 1934, just before the Kendrick fracas, Odum had begun to feel the cold wind of the new foundation policies. As he told Wilson, "the foundations are seemingly very critical of us now." While Odum had corresponded with Charles W. Eliot of the National Planning Board, a division of the Public Works Administration, to suggest that "our state planning boards might need to be enlarged," Edmund Day had lectured Odum severely in New York on the dangers of spreading himself too thin. It seemed prudent to abandon the project for a while.[6]

During the next few years, Odum intermittently kept the idea before the Rockefeller Foundation without receiving substantial encouragement. The publication of *Southern Regions,* however, helped him to recover some impetus. During 1936, three "Institutes on Regional Development" were held at Chapel Hill, Charlottesville, and Nashville to discuss his findings. In April, he mentioned to Frank Graham the need for a "unified Southern policy group." Not until late in 1937, however, did Odum decide to act on a new approach.[7]

During 1935, Will Alexander had become increasingly involved in managing agricultural policies in Washington. This had detracted from his attentions to the Interracial Commission. As a surrogate, he had asked Odum to make suggestions for the commission's future. From this germ, Odum took the chance of realizing his thwarted ambition for a centralized Southern Institute. In October 1937, Odum wrote to Alexander: "If I am asked for a recommendation, it would be that the Commission on Interracial Cooperation merge with a Southeastern People's Institute, or something of its kind, in which the four corners of emphasis would be interracial relations, agricultural reconstruction and farm tenancy, labor and industrial relations, and public administration." Feeling that the fate of the Negro and interracial work was no longer an isolated or separable issue, he was persuaded that carrying on the commission's old approach would yield diminishing returns. To this, Alexander returned a prompt, encouraging, and purposeful reply. "At the Board meeting we had a full discussion of your suggestion," he told Odum. "The idea was new, but the members of the Board were openminded. They were quite ready to accept the approach which you had in mind. . . . We all decided that the way to work it out was to ask you to become President of the Commission." Odum accepted.[8]

Things began to happen quickly. On 1 November, Odum was urging the new concept on Jackson Davis of the General Education Board. This was a shrewd move, for Davis, as Southern representative of the board, was more amenable to such an approach than the parent foundation in New York.[9] This time Odum was careful to make New York his last stopping place, not his first. If he could not persuade the Rockefeller Foundation to aid in organizing the South, perhaps he might have more luck in organizing the South himself and presenting a *fait accompli* in New York. Could they then turn him away, unfunded?

On 22 November, Odum's new position as president of the Interracial Commission secured his election to the board of trustees of the Rosenwald Fund. On 13 December, he found his way on to the Advisory Committee on Southern Education for the General Education Board. On 15 January 1938, he made his bid for organizing the Southern intelligentsia by convening an "Interim Southeastern Regional Advisory Committee" in Atlanta, in the stolid surroundings of the Biltmore Hotel.[10]

The list of attendants was impressive, if uncomfortably confined to Odum's familiar allies. There was Charles S. Johnson of Fisk University, the leading Southern black sociologist; Oliver Carmichael, the new chancellor of Vanderbilt University; Wilson Gee of the University of Virginia, who had labored long for the Southern Regional Committee; David Coker, a pioneer of scientific agriculture; Virginius Dabney, Jonathan Daniels, Mark Ethridge, and John Temple Graves, all liberal editors of considerable influence; Edwin Embree, Arthur Mann, and Jackson Davis, representatives of the Rosenwald Fund and the General Education Board; Herman Nixon of the Southern Policy Committee and a contributor to *I'll Take My Stand;* and Charles C. Spaulding, the black insurance magnate from Durham, North Carolina. With these came a number of lesser figures.

To this group, Odum made his proposal for a Southern Institute. He made much of the inability of the universities to carry the burden of social reform. Their resources were badly overextended and, like the foundations, peculiarly subject to reprisals if they should promote specific measures. But this new approach might serve by the consolidation of the Interracial Commission, the Southern Policy Committees, and liaison work with the Congress of Industrial Organizations, the American Federation of Labor, and the National Association for the Advancement of Colored People. Odum wanted the institute to undertake the adult education program that he had suggested in *Southern Regions:* "an effective set-up for new service to the public, broader adult education and promotion in the main fields of interest and special contact with public administration and political groups." And he wanted the institute to formulate a twelve-year plan.[11]

Without difficulty, Odum secured the backing of this meeting. This was not too surprising, as he had handpicked the members. But he had been given a mandate by a certain spectrum of Southern leadership, a rough blueprint and a call for "about two million dollars." Things looked hopeful, for he had the backing of the Interracial Commission, the Southern Policy Committee seemed to be leaning towards amalgamation with the institute, and the foundation executives in Atlanta had seemed sympathetic. Moreover, Odum had an important promise from Will Alexander that the latter would return from Washington in 1940 to head the new institute. Meanwhile Odum engaged himself in a widespread and largely successful canvass for Southerners and non-Southerners willing to attach their names to the new project. In time, Odum was to send a thick folder of acceptances to the General Education Board. And it included some weighty names, such as Thurman Arnold, Stuart Chase, James H. Dillard, Clark Foreman, O. Max Gardner, James Weldon Johnson, Walter Lippmann, Dumas Malone, Maury Maverick, S. C. Mitchell, George Fort Milton, Lewis Mumford, William F. Ogburn, William Alexander Percy, Carl Sauer, Beardsley Ruml, T. S. Stribling, Jerry Voorhis, and W. D. Weatherford.[12]

All this took time. In the meantime he could not act, because Will Alexander took a well earned rest in Europe during the summer of 1938. On his outward voyage, however, Alexander had been encouraging. "The time is ripe," he had written from the Cunarder *Antonia,* "for this sort of non-governmental approach to southern problems. This point should be stressed with our prospective supporters." And Alexander offered some modest influence mongering through Edward Lowry, a Georgian and ex-political correspondent for the *New York Evening Post*. Lowry was glad to help the Odum scheme and try to open a few doors in New York. "I count strongly on his help being effective," Alexander said.[13]

The strategy relied heavily upon the marshalling of a united front in the South. The January conference in Atlanta had, however, betrayed disquieting signs of disagreement. There was a consensus about general objectives, but each had seemed to place the emphasis differently. David Coker, for example, had insisted that the first priority was to establish the health of tenant farmers. "It is impossible," he had said, "to build character or a farm setup made with sick people. Ought we not to start with such problems and with the education of illiterates on farms before going into interracial and other problems?" For Virginius Dabney, a journalist, the priority was an enlargement of the reading public in the South. As for Thomas Staples of Hendrix College in Arkansas, he thought that a general improvement in the quality of education, from the elementary school upwards, was essential.

While there had been some feeling that agriculture and race relations were the main problems, there had been disagreement over their relationship. Harvey Couch of Arkansas had stuck with the Booker T. Washington tradition in thinking Negro education a sufficient lever of progress, while another even denied that there was a special race problem. From the standpoint of the black bourgeoisie, Charles Spaulding had criticized the functioning of the Jim Crow system. In his opinion, the facilities for Negroes in places such as railroad stations were such that "no decent Negro" would want to use them. Both he and Edgar Stern of New Orleans had urged greater openness in talking about racial matters. But Spaulding could scarcely have been happy at Stern's way of expressing support. The Negro problem, he had said, had been too much hushed up in the South. It should be brought out in the open, along with such issues as the elimination of syphilis.

Charles Johnson echoed Odum in stressing that race was no longer a problem separable from other issues. Mark Ethridge had already made this point. However, the journalist had been most insistent that the institute be a direct action group. He was interested on no other terms, for he saw the crucial issue as a bypassing of a corrupt and unresponsive political system. Johnson, on the contrary, had seen no serious hope of securing agreement in such a diverse group. "At this stage," the black sociologist had commented, "a common denominator on a great many issues would be rather meaningless." John Temple Graves had also seen the institute as a clearing house or forum. Pessimistically, he had said that "the organization could not agree on so many questions."

Around this issue had hung the unresolved question of the institute's organization. There had been some sympathy with Odum's idea of a fourfold division, with each segment concentrating on either race, industrial relations, administration, or agricultural matters. But it was unclear how integrated the leadership or direction of the institute should be. Walter Matherly of Florida had suggested a large "federate with a fairly large board of advisers, maybe 100, coming from two or three groups, such as one-third from federate agencies, one-third from each State and one-third from the public at large." But Wilson Gee, with a certain Virginian elitism, had wanted a small directorate, deciding policy and handing it out to the separate groups.

These were significant, but not yet grave dissensions. The discussion had been even-tempered, with the feeling general that social reform was a shared objective and Odum's plan would be a suitable vehicle for change. Nonetheless, O. C. Carmichael, summing up in an evening session, had felt it necessary to address himself to the "great divergence of views." An observer might have felt that these small cracks would have widened into substantial fissures, if the organization had been established.[14]

This had been a gathering of fairly like-minded liberals. In the world outside, differences were more profound and were to crowd in upon Odum's delicate planning. Things started to go sour in the summer of 1938. Even in February, scarcely back from Atlanta, Odum had received a tentative program for the Southern States Industrial Council. This had been established in 1933 as a response to the National Recovery Administration; it had wanted to preserve wage differentials and keep Southern wages low, lest their improvement attract foreign labor and affect the South's "racial purity." It seems that in 1938 it was seeking to revive its impetus. To Arthur Mann, Odum had expressed his concern that there might "continue to rise up groups that are mere advocates for economic or industrial development or for special pleadings."[15]

The probability of this was increased during the summer, when the political climate warmed up with the weather. In July, the President's Report on Economic Conditions in the South was published. In itself, the document was harmless. Indeed, it was largely a précis of research done at Chapel Hill. But Franklin Roosevelt had seen fit to hang around the South's neck the contentious label, the "Nation's Number One Economic Problem." This started a furor below the Potomac that was only intensified by Roosevelt's linking of the report with his attempted purge of conservative Southerners from Congress. The feeling rapidly grew that the Administration's policy towards the South was in the melting pot and it was imperative to move quickly to influence it. This cut clean across Odum's desire to move with only deliberate speed.[16]

It seemed as though pressure groups were crawling out from the woodwork with the summer's cockroaches. The Progressive Education Association started to plan a series of regional conferences. A Louisiana group had in mind a Southern Conference in Public Welfare. Most importantly, the Alabama branch of the Southern Policy Committee moved to call a major conference of reform groups in Birmingham. This was to be the Southern Conference for Human Welfare. With not very mock excitement, Odum grumbled in August 1938: "Between the Right Honorable FD, the Southern Conference for Human Welfare, and twenty other groups that are literally taking the lead to do what the Council ought to do, I think I'll presently go heat-wave hay-wire!!!"[17]

It was worrying for Odum that many of his Southern Council supporters offered their backing to the Southern Conference, and that it seemed to attract the political and labor union contacts he so noticeably lacked. Eleanor Roosevelt was to come to the Birmingham meeting. William Dodd, the ambassador to Germany, threw in his support. And one could find on the list of sponsors people like Lister Hill, Bibb Graves, Luther Patrick, Brooks Hays, and H. L. Mitchell of the Southern Tenant Farmers' Union. Odum was concerned, but Charles Johnson reassured him: "Looking over the list of sponsors of the Southern Conference for Human Welfare, I believe it has possibilities for constructive projection into the future, and can help rather than injure the chances for establishing our Council . . . on a sound foundation. . . . Not only should this Conference have before it a statement about our Council, but I believe the fact of the growing frequency of these south-wide service groups might have some weight with the General Education Board or the Rockefeller Foundation in deciding to help support a substantial Council." Without great conviction, Odum came around to repeating Johnson's analysis.[18]

In October, Odum was asked by the SCHW's field agent, Herman Nixon, to join the organization and preside over a race relations panel at the Birmingham meeting. After canvassing friends, Odum returned an ambivalent reply. He suggested he might present his council plan to the conference, if it had "matured sufficiently." This was a probably intentionally crippling proviso. With the conference but six weeks away, he must have known that he had little chance of securing backing by then. Part of Odum's view of the SCHW was offered by Wilson Gee: "I do not know that it will prove to be as significant as the old Southern Sociological Congress was but I rather look for it to follow a somewhat similar course. It will stir up a great deal of enthusiasm and do some good work over a period of a few years and, as is true of so many organizations of that nature, it will likely dwindle and pass off the stage . . . . you and I both have watched many organizations appear on the horizon and vanish off the scene." Such sentiments encouraged Odum's stand-offish attitude. He held to the point he had made at the preliminary meeting of the council in January: "The difference between the agency and the conference is fundamental; namely, the agency is a permanent, full-time functioning organization, well endowed and with its staff composed of men everywhere comparable to our university presidents and faculty members."[19]

In late October, Francis Miller made it clear that he was unwilling to merge his Southern Policy Committee with the Southern Council. This weakened Odum's hand with the foundations, who had indicated that unanimity was important in determining their attitude. The only encouraging moment was a November trustee meeting of the Rosenwald Fund in Atlanta, when Odum talked Edwin Embree into presenting his scheme to the next board meeting in Chicago in April. Moreover, a Rosenwald trustee had hinted that the Rockefeller Foundation was in the mood to acquiesce.[20]

Meanwhile the conference in Birmingham had begun, with Odum purposely absent. After the heated imbroglio over segregated seating in the auditorium and the confused, if stimulating, proceedings, Charles Johnson and Mark Ethridge reported back to Odum that the Southern Conference need not inhibit the Southern Council. But the racial tensions that Odum had been diligently downplaying had been violently exposed in Birmingham. Disharmony was further stressed when the Southern States Industrial Council decided to meet in Atlanta and answer the "radical" Southern Conference. And the conference did not plan to go away, as Odum devoutly hoped. Herman Nixon was eager to carry on and was backed by the conference's new president, Frank Graham. It was embarrassing enough to have Odum's own university president as the head of a "rival," but it was worse when Franklin Roosevelt himself warmly commended Graham. As usual, Odum and Graham had diametrically opposed views of social reform. While Odum wanted a controlled planning organization, Graham with his customary optimism believed that democracy should run its course, that the more pressure groups the merrier. While Odum twitched anxiously at every sign of independent initiatives, Graham was benign.[21]

Will Alexander continued to do his best, mainly through Edward Lowry. A protege of Lowry's had assumed an editorial post with the *New York Times,* and offered publicity and an endorsement for the council. But it was becoming clear that Raymond Fosdick was a major stumbling block within the Rockefeller Foundation. Lowry volunteered to go to New York, but he was unsure how to get at Fosdick himself. Alexander had gathered from Jackson Davis that a holding grant might be recommended, "unless our friend Fosdick steps on the whole thing".[22]

Through the spring of 1939, Odum remained stubbornly optimistic. He would have been less so, if he could have read the reports that the General Education Board itself had been gathering from the South. The Board had not been idle, or been content to take Odum's word for what Southerners were thinking. Some twenty interviews were conducted.

They were not markedly against Odum's proposed council, but very few were unreservedly in favor. When it was endorsed, too often it was thought that a legislative pressure group was neither practical nor desirable. It might be tried for a few years, on a limited research basis, but in time it would be best replaced by having its policies assimilated by existing state and federal agencies. A few were not too keen on Will Alexander, who had become identified with the New Deal. Several were unsure how the "public administration" division of the council could be made to work. Even Alexander himself, interviewed in Washington in March 1939, was unclear about the "labor and industrial relations" division.[23]

Before the interviewing, the board had had serious reservations. As early as May 1938, Arthur Mann had cautioned Odum that it was not the board's practice to "assist in enterprises which may contain a considerable element of reform or controversy," and this might be fatally inhibiting. In March 1939, an interoffice memorandum with the board had questioned the wisdom of Odum's application. As was so often the case, Odum suffered from wording his proposals with sweeping vagueness. "The listing of a variety of efforts without indication of why such a council as is envisaged would be particularly fitted to perform the several tasks or how or through what agencies it would work to perform them seems to me to leave much to be desired," the memo continued. To this a more fundamental criticism was added: "The inherent weakness of the program lies in the conception of assembling an unofficial group that will develop wise programs of action with the expectation that those who control policy will accept such a self-constituted group's recommendations. There is a further weakness as I see it of organizing a group to represent a very broad region when there is no official machinery for dealing with the problems of that region when it might be more effective to organize the research agencies upon the basis of much smaller units." It was to become apparent that many Southerners shared this latter doubt. Wilson Gee, when interviewed, was to question the practicability of such a comprehensive proposal, and rather thought that existing agencies were "safer bets." Paul Gross, professor of chemistry at Duke University, echoed this sentiment. The council, he thought, might be useful in three or four states for a few years but "it could not possibly serve the entire southeast." The president of the University of Virginia, John Newcomb, was to express the strong opinion that the only practical course was on the basis of state and local units, not regional.[24]

As important as these criticisms was the board's realization that Odum did not have the mandate of the South. One of the first interviews was with LeRoy Hodges, the state comptroller of Virginia. Hodges had attended Odum's Atlanta meeting in January 1938, and was listed as a supporter of the council by Odum. Hodges, however, voiced a similar skepticism to that in the board's memo. The South was not quite so homogeneous.

He had said, the memo observed, "there would be little use for instance of preaching the lessons of a cotton economy to Virginians because they would not know what the discussion meant." Just as damaging was Hodges's remembrance of the Atlanta meeting: "Hodges said that he had started to voice his skepticism but had commenced by asking whether there was real reason to believe that funds upon such a scale as $200,000 for ten years would be available. He said that Odum had given assurance that if the plan could be broadly endorsed the funds would be forthcoming from founda-tions and others. At this point Hodges said he dropped further questioning. Here was a plan drawn out in great detail for which funds which Hodges understood to be outside funds seemed to be committed. Research in general was good. Surely the endeavor would do no harm even if it proved to be not very effectual and Hodges said that he did not see why he should throw monkey wrenches. Therefore he and the others at the conference approved although Hodges stated that from conversations that he had afterwards he was certain that some of the members of the conference shared his skepticism." With this in mind, it was unsurprising that the board memo concluded: This "raises sharply the question of just how much is meant by the endorsements offered in Odum's document."[25]

It was even less surprising that Odum was summoned to New York early in May to receive the final dismissive word. He was always resilient: for the next several years, he refused to give up. When the Tennessee Valley Authority was thinking of setting up a research institute, Odum tried to revive the project. And, indeed, in due course, a body called the Southern Regional Council did appear. But it was little more than a revamped Interracial Commission. The grand design had failed.[26]

The year 1939 was not, after all, a good one in which to pursue regional interests. The coming war in Europe seemed to dwarf them. Long interested in international affairs, the Rockefeller Foundation had grown more and more absorbed by the war. Odum, in a letter to Will Alexander twenty-one days after the German invasion of Poland, remarked that "the war seems to demoralize New York." Howard Odum's lack of interest in the other side of the Atlantic—he never went there—was limiting. When Gerald Johnson, brooding on the deteriorating situation, wrote to the sociologist that "for the first time I begin to think that perhaps it is a swell idea not to be a young man any longer; if we are heading for the Dark Ages again, at least I shall never know it," Odum replied with a chirpy indifference. "With reference to the world situation," he said, "you may recall that I have always said that I am an optimist in general on everything except to areas of association. I always know before hand that neighbors if in too intimate contact and competition will not get along together; ditto for nations! So what? Why not, looking at it from the larger viewpoint of 'God and freedom' or historical evolution in the grand manner, let the nations of Europe go into eclipse, from which we start the eternal process of the common man coming back up and up and up."[27]

In this manner, Odum had received the practical judgment on *Southern Regions*. Its intellectual assessment had to wait a little longer. In the meantime, he had set about extending his analysis of regionalism to the whole nation. His formulations in *Southern Regions* had been national, and to see their implementation required a wider persuasion of informed opinion than just that of the South. If the whole South had been convinced and banging at Roosevelt's door for a regional planning council, Odum's regionalism would have been incomplete. It was logical, therefore, that he set about writing *American Regionalism: A Cultural-Historical Approach to National Integration,* which was published in 1938. Its fate proceeded with a discomfiting precision alongside his endeavors for a Southern Council.

It was not written without help, as was true of many of Odum works. Behind him had always been the staff of the Institute for Research in Social Science. But this time a young sociologist, Harry Estill Moore, was asked to collaborate directly with Odum. By 1937 teaching in Texas, Moore had done a brief doctoral dissertation at Chapel Hill on "Theories of Regionalism." It seemed sensible that Moore's perspective be included in Odum's general survey. With minor interpolations, Moore was to write part 2 of the three-part book: a study of the intellectual growth of regionalist thought in six major disciplines—geography, anthropology, ecology, economics, political science, and sociology. Odum contributed most of part 1 on the rise and nature of American regions: natural geographical regions, determined by such things as soil, climate, rivers and mountains; "culture regions," built upon but altering the natural configurations. To this, Moore added two chapters on "service regions," by which was meant the organizational growth of regionalism in government administration and private business. Part 3 was entirely Odum's: a survey of the six regions. Interspersed were chapters pleading the cause of regional planning.

It was inevitable that Odum should repeat himself, but a few things had changed. The experience of the 1930s was digested into his views on regionalism. He had been uncomfortable with the centralizing trend of the New Deal. And, like many American intellectuals, he feared that the totalitarian movements of Fascism and Communism posed a cruel dilemma for the American future. For Odum, a simple patriot, America was "the hope of western civilization." Naturally, he wished to unite his belief in regionalism with these fears by arguing that regionalism offered "a medium and technique of decentralization and redistribution in an age now

characterized as moving toward over-centralization, urbanism and totali-
tarianism." Like Frederick Jackson Turner, Odum was concerned that
urbanization would make America a class society. Regionalism might hold
the line, or even reverse the trend, by pitching institutions of geographical
control against class divisions. It was, he wrote, "a symbol of America's
geographic as opposed to occupational representation; of popular as
opposed to class control." Odum wanted the South to defy and moderate
modernity by drawing together.[28]

It was sometimes suggested that regionalism was the idle musing of
sociologists with nothing better to do on warm Southern evenings. *American
Regionalism* was eager to belie that impression. And its evidence was
cumulatively impressive. Odum was able to point to the development of
metropolitan regional planning. Both St. Louis and New York had organized
planning commissions that went far beyond traditional municipal boundaries.
There were, Odum claimed, 506 metropolitan planning agencies at the end
of 1936 that included territory beyond city limits. And he could point to the
evidence gathered by the Chicago school of sociology, led by Robert E.
Park, which demonstrated the necessary influence exercised by cities on
their hinterland. To this, Harry Moore added a survey of governmental
and corporate regionalism. More than a hundred government bureaux and
agencies were divided into regions of administrative convenience. But they
were of varying sizes and extents, following no consistent pattern. Seven
agencies had divided the country into either four or nine regions. Nine
bureaux had set up twelve areas. Four agencies had split the country into
only two parts, while another had no less than eighty-three divisions. Some
used state boundaries, others did not. The heterogeneity of these arrangements, Moore argued, was sometimes beneficial and functional. At other
moments, it led to extreme difficulty in coordinating government policy
in particular areas. Moreover, as agencies transcended state boundaries, it
had become difficult for states to control them. Interstate compacts helped,
but these—although growing in number—dealt with political, rather than
social problems.[29]

In this way, Moore linked these heterogeneous administrative divisions
to Odum's case that a homogeneously defined regionalism would help to
combat centralization. For the patchwork had made it difficult for the
states to control not only the federal agencies, but even to master the
burgeoning city within its borders. Squeezed between the city and the
federal government, the state had become an administrative bankrupt. As
Moore put it, "The traditional guardian of local initiative in our governmental machinery has become impotent in at least some of its functions."
It was logical and necessary, therefore, to replace it with a regional unit
that could effectively challenge both the cities and Washington.[30]

The growth of such regional arrangements was both a help and a hindrance to Odum. It was useful to be able to point to existing regionalism as evidence of a growing trend. But the complexity presented entrenched agencies that would yield most unwillingly to his proposed sixfold standardization. And they left him vulnerable to the argument that their very diversity was proof of a necessary functional flexibility.

Harry Moore, dealing with the theoretical underpinnings of regionalism, had even greater problems. Theory seemed to be volatile. While Odum casually liked to see regionalism as just "the most natural thing in the world," Moore had grasped that modern thought was divided and ambivalent.[31]

The bedrock of Moore's position was the old Montesquieuan perception that man was defined by his environment, the pattern of rivers, mountains, snow, and sun. But it was clear that this eighteenth-century determinism was no longer adequate. With the development of "social geography" or "ecology"—the name varied, but the standpoint was similar—it had to be recognized that man's intelligence and social organization was a partially independent variable in cultural formation. Separate disciplines were wont to stress different starting points: geographers started with landscape, anthropologists with the culture of tribes, ecologists with the links between man and his environment, both organic and nonorganic. Interconnections, however, were evident to all. It seemed to Moore that specialization had bred an inward-looking caution. Each discipline was cagey about extending its theoretical assumptions and absorbed in internal disputes. Anthropologists doubted that one could transfer lessons from simple tribal societies to the modern world. Economists were divided between macro- and microeconomics. Historians were dubious about the concept of "culture areas," for they inadequately accommodated temporal change.[32]

All this was worrying to Moore. Not without quavering, however, he stuck to his guns. "Empirically and impressionistically," he insisted, "it seems undeniable that, making all possible allowances for class differences, there are commonly recognized regions the essence of which is awareness by observers of the region as a whole of a general 'spirit' or *Weltanschauung*." This seemed sound, but it was a worryingly imprecise criterion. The approach from social psychology was a shade woolly, as Moore admitted to Robert McKenzie of the Chicago school of sociology who had taxed him with the unconvincing nature of the sectional/regional distinction. "I am inclined to agree with you," he wrote, "that the distinction is somewhat vague and is not supported by objective data as it should be to carry statistical conviction. But, so far I have not been able to work out objective measures of this difference." Earlier Moore had fretted to Odum: "I quite agree that the region is a function of the problem or use, but am sure also, that those problems and uses cluster sufficiently to make a region a relatively stable and permanent element in national structure. If this is not true," he added, uneasily, "we have been wasting a hell of a lot of time and a considerable amount of work—on your part at least." This disquiet was to find its way into Moore's pages in *American Regionalism*. "The boundaries of culture areas are vague zones," he was to say, "or if a definite limit is set by statistical methods there remains an indefiniteness indicated by lack of homogeneity of the traits used as criteria. The center also is often vague." The region did seem to crumble in one's hand. How did one escape this problem of intellectual atomism?[33]

Moore came up with an ingenious solution. He turned to one of the foremost antiatomistic theories in modern thought, gestalt psychology. If the argument seemed to drive one back upon psychology, it was necessary to find one that allowed one to hold the crumbling pieces together. It was ironic, but gestalt had begun as a revolt in 1912 against the dominant influence in German psychology, Odum's old enthusiasm, Wilhelm Wundt. Three young Berlin psychologists, Kurt Koffka, Max Wertheimer, and Wolfgang Kohler, had been discontented with Wundt's residual associationism, his "bricks and mortar" approach to the new science. While they accepted his neo-Hegelian emphasis on the study of conscious experience as psychology's proper focus and his belief that understanding was the synthesis of assorted responses, they were philosophically unhappy at the direction of Wundt's logic. They refused to believe that life, and psychology, could be understood or endured by the dismemberment of meaningful experiences into meaningless elements. Problems should be analyzed, not from the bottom up, but from the top down. More, they asserted this to be the normal and necessary human process. Man was not only able to organize experience with his perception, but it was in his nature for him to do so. Parts were meaningful only as segments of a whole. Taken in isolation, they meant nothing.[34]

Gestalt had some basis in empirical observation, but its motive force was a philosophical distaste for the disintegrative tendency of modern thought. Wertheimer put it like this: "To live in a fog...is for many people an unbearable state of affairs. There is a tendency to structural clearness, surveyability, to truth as against petty views." Koffka, however, made the point clearest at the end of his 1935 volume, *The Principles of Gestalt Psychology:* "If there is any polemical spirit in this book," he admitted candidly, "it is directed not against persons but against a strong cultural force in our present civilization for which I have chosen the name positivism. If positivism can be regarded as an integrative philosophy, its integration rests on the dogma that all events are equally unintelligible, irrational, meaningless, purely factual. Such an integration is, however, to my way of thinking, identical with a complete disintegration. Being convinced that such a view is utterly inadequate in face of facts, I had to attack it, and that the more since its hold over our generation is strong."[35]

If Odum and Moore's intellectual discomfort had a root, it was this same positivism. Gratefully, Moore had taken the idea of gestalt, the German word for a form, configuration, or structure, and applied it to the region. It, they claimed, was intelligible only in its entirety. It too was rendered superfluously meaningless by atomistic analysis. And, in truth, this was an interesting approach to the intractable difficulties of keeping analysis as coherent as the common perception of Southern regional character.

But there were difficulties. This idea wandered, an orphan, through a few scattered pages of *American Regionalism*. It seems probable that the concept had been Moore's, rather than Odum's, though each politely attributed it to the other.[36] But gestalt surfaces nowhere else in Odum's work, and he was never one not to repeat himself. In the confusion of coauthorship, with the younger man eager to agree with his senior partner, much was left unreconciled or hastily hammered together. For it was not clear that gestalt and Odum's folk sociology were compatible. Odum had rested his case on Wundt's extension of his psychological theories to society, but the gestaltists had repudiated that basis. Moreover, his borrowing from William Graham Sumner had emphasized the irrational human response to environment, while gestalt had insisted upon the clarity of human understanding. Moore, with Odum's apparent approval, tried to reconcile the viewpoints but with no great success.

After a description of gestalt psychology, Moore hazarded a summary: "This is tantamount to saying that all the factors are mutually conditioning, at once cause and effect," he wrote. This seemed sound, hinting at the Hegelianism that the gestalt school shared with Wundt. But Moore's next step was debatable: "In still other words, regionalism points to cultural determinism in that the tools by which man has surrounded himself, both physical and mental, and by which he seeks his well-being, direct and affect his response to the physical area in which he finds himself. For both the individual and the social group, the pre-existing culture is largely determinative of the present organization. The older strata of this culture . . . . form the valuable heritage of 'the folk,' and it is through the study of the folk that the significance of these elements becomes clear." This was bold, leaping from gestalt to folk sociology in one fell swoop, but it was very dubious. The jump from gestalt to cultural determinism was too long, for it underestimated the anti-Wundtian revolt in gestalt. The deterministic hand of social mores was precisely what gestalt was not about, but rather the necessity of human rationality. A psychological theory had been hastily transmuted by Moore into a sociological one, one commensurate with Odum's older line of thinking. In retrospect, the high promise of gestalt in the 1930s that it might be applicable to the wider scope of the social sciences has not borne fruit. But Moore had written in the first glimmer of hope, and snatched at it to resolve his doubts. At the last, his uncertainty clashed with Odum's sanguine faith in the "naturalness" of regionalism. For Moore, gestalt was an important mode of reconciliation in an unsure venture. For Odum, it was an amiable bonus in an assured intellectual assertion.[37]

After this intriguing diversion, part 3 of *American Regionalism* was bathos. Odum turned to a description of his six regions. Like his maps and statistics, these were less descriptions of homogeneous units, but more accumulated sketches of meaningful social divisions within these regions. One could not describe a unified Middle West, but one could add together paragraphs on Chicago or the Corn Belt, Detroit or the river culture of Missouri. In the South, at least, Odum had the binding force of social consciousness. The further his pen travelled, the less that worked. In truth, Odum was trapped by the old logic of the New South school. He had been taught that sectionalism and nationalism, South and nation, were intrinsically compatible. It followed that what was true of the South's relationship to the center was true of other parts. The New South had not wanted a special relationship. But it *was* special, so it had become necessary to upgrade the coherence of other regions to diminish the South's peculiarity. Thus Odum had to grant the Middle West and the Far West, the Northeast and the Southwest the same shared coherence that a troublesome and welding history had granted the South. Without it, the South did, after all, bear a peculiar burden; and for Odum, that was intolerable. It diminished the region's Americanism. And no word was used with greater frequency and more normative enthusiasm than "American" in his tumbling portraits.[38]

American Regionalism was not substantially criticized upon its publication. It did not become the talking point that Odum's strategy required, nor create the stir of *Southern Regions*. Indeed, it was to be 1942 before a verdict came in and, even then, Odum had to promote the discussion personally. He published in *Social Forces* an article entitled "A Sociological Approach to the Study and Practice of American Regionalism: A Factorial Syllabus." Reprints were dispatched to various members of the profession and criticism requested. And Odum got it, enough that he was moved to remark: "I have never had any series of letters or critiques so important." Taken together, these responses constituted the judgment of his peers on Howard Odum, the theorist of regionalism.[39]

Much criticism centered on his empirical divisions of American society. Were not his regions arbitrary, mistaken, or conceptually untenable? George Renner, for instance, puzzled over Odum's "success in wishing out of existence the region of which I happen to be a native—viz the Shortgrass Country or Great Plains. . . . You are able to slice it up and attach the two halves to other regions to which it bears no organic relation." And Read Bain, well acquainted with the Far West, could not understand why Odum thought California, Washington, and Oregon could be lumped together.

Equally, he thought it arbitrary to assimilate southeastern New Hampshire to the rest of the state, or eastern to western Massachusetts, or western to eastern Texas. Otis Duncan, in addition, felt that Oklahoma was culturally more like North Dakota than Mississippi, despite its cotton growing and its Southern settlers. Even on the score of the South, he was unsure: "I have been in all the southern states, but I have never been in one that does not contend, in reference to most specific points, that it is different from all the rest, and I agree.... There is as much variation within the region as between it and other regions."[40]

The feeling was general that Odum had been wrong to use states as a statistical basis. Renner hazarded that Odum had been inconsistent in arguing that social phenomena should be studied with all possible accuracy and then that such results be abandoned for the practical convenience of group-of-states administration. "Aren't you really up against a situation like this," he asked. "We have pies; but we want cakes; so let's get cakes by re-combining our pies? I'm vastly interested in regionalism, but I for one, don't readily accept the premise that a re-grouping of our pies will yield the pragmatic equivalent of cakes, and I don't believe anyone will find the alchemist formula for effecting such transmutation." Woundingly, he added that Franklin Giddings would have frowned upon the attempt. In this, Read Bain agreed with Renner, but with more bluntness: "If region can be defined, I'm sure it must dispense with state boundaries."[41]

As for social change, that was a disturbing factor. Both Maurice Davie and C. Arnold Anderson felt that even if you could devise satisfactory regional boundaries time would unfix them. Floyd House insisted that "regions as determined by cultural and commercial facts are *not* necessarily fixed; they may, and in cases do, expand or shrink." Moreover, Logan Wilson was bothered by the unevenness of the regional hypothesis in different areas. "Special problems," he told Odum, "are presented by borderline areas having heterogeneous cultures and by those lacking any highly indigenous developments. Within even the sub-divisions there are likely to be large 'islands' (often metropolitan centers) that depart considerably in their characteristics from the surrounding territory, and which share more in common with islands similarly situated in other regions."[42]

As for statistics, there was concern at the bias in Odum's methodology. J. F. Cuber cautioned that an intention to find homogeneity obliged the statistician to underestimate the evidence of heterogeneity. Svend Reimer, in an article for *Social Forces,* put it more strongly. Noting that indices were not infinite but selected, he observed that "the whole process of index construction and that of the composite indices is guided by the attempts to verify empirically the existence of such regions as the theory of regionalism was decided upon in advance of statistical procedures." To illustrate the dilemma, Otis Duncan offered a slice of his own experience: "I have observed that I can block Oklahoma off into groups of counties on the map according to my own fancy. Then if I get averages for these groups, almost invariably they will show significant differences when compared to each other. I would almost wager that the same thing would happen if I grouped the counties shown red, blue, green, and yellow on an ordinary political map."[43]

In his *Social Forces* piece, Odum had made a few suggestions for national and regional planning. He wanted a national planning council, authorized and paid for by Congress, with the power of referendum. Although it would have no coercive power, he envisaged a status "analogous to the Supreme Court." There would be nine members of the council, six from each region and a few members-at-large. Regional representation was to be a fundamental principle. The council would have three objectives: "first, to insure a continuous scientific inventory of the state of the nation and to provide essential information for the President, the Congress, the Supreme Court and special needs; to coordinate research and approximate a clearing house; to reduce overlapping and economize on congressional committee organizations; second, to act as a buffer between the President and the other branches of government and to provide a safe-guard against over-centralization and power through government by persons to serve in emergency situations; third, to act as buffer and democratic interpreter between the national government and the states and regions, and the necessary federal centralization." Below this national level, there would be similar regional and state councils.[44]

Few were persuaded of this scheme. Robert Faris was unsure that social problems were sensibly divisible into regions. Even if they were, they were not as well handled "by a group representing districts, as by a group representing scientific disciplines relative to the question, and such groups would have to have different compositions for each matter to be studied." Moreover, Faris saw no way or hope of a national council acting as a buffer between different branches of government: "It has taken a desperate war to make even a small crack in the states' determination to raise trade barriers against one another, and I don't see how an agency without power could get far against such forces." As for F. E. Lumley, he gagged at the very thought of trying to persuade Congress of such a council, especially without the improbable pressure of public opinion.[45]

Lawrence Frank wondered if it might not be easier to use existing organizations, like the National Planning Board. Edgar Schuler made the same suggestion, but went on to ask if the principle of regional representation implied that "the regions, in general, are supposed to be of equivalence in significance, in nature and complexity or difficulty of problems, or that planning decisions would eventually come down to majority vote." If so, he thought the notion misguided. It might be well to adopt planning methods from totalitarian societies, but the people must decide policy directions. Committees, he indicated, were a recipe for paralysis.[46]

Such methodological and practical objections were disturbing. Even more striking was the consistent rejection of Odum's theoretical framework. Many puzzled over his application of the "folk" idea. "Do we have any 'folks,' in the original sense of that term, in this country?" Lumley asked. "Isn't that something yet to be shown rather than to be accepted?" Robert Park doubted that there were any folks in the United States, outside of New England and the South. And he saw more than one folk in the South. There were Negroes, Cajuns, the mountaineers of the Ozarks, as well as the whites.[47]

While many correspondents criticized Odum's mingling of social planning and social science, they were divided over its general wisdom. Maurice Davie was sure that the combination was unwholesome. Edwin Sutherland took a different tack. "Regionalism . . . ," he suggested, "does not seem to me to be sociology or science of any other kind. Although you make statements about the science of regionalism, your interest and elaborations are definitely along the line of social control or practical planning. Your regionalism impresses me as analogous to social work or to communism, in that it is concerned primarily with social control and regards the accumulation of knowledge as concerned primarily with the techniques by which objectives can be realized." This sentiment was echoed by Edgar Schuler. To him, Odum's regionalism "was more of a philosophy, a religion, a faith, than simply an approach to science . . . . In fact, I was reminded of Auguste Comte . . . . there still is . . . something reminiscent about Comte in the entire treatment which, in a way, merges science with belief, research with prescription, and even includes a panel of sociological (?) high priests to run the whole show."[48]

Otis Duncan, however, was pleased with Odum's contention that science was a mix of "the discovery of truth and the attainment of mastery." Edwin Sutherland concurred in this instrumentalism. "I believe thoroughly in Dewey's proposition that efforts at control are useful in the development of scientific knowledge," he said. "I believe that regionalism, even if it is concerned primarily with social control, may have an ultimate value in the development of scientific knowledge." Ellsworth Faris, for his part, was happy to give Odum a breezy endorsement, but by dumping Odum's sociological claims overboard. "I greatly admire both you and the effort and the program. But does it need all this elaborate pseudo-sociological dressing?" he politely inquired. "As a Southerner you have a passionate devotion to the south and as a man of vision and energy you are working on a program that ought to improve conditions, not only in the South but over the whole nation. In that effort, no one could wish you anything but success.... But...you weaken your case and do not strengthen it by the verbose and confusing argument."[49]

Ambivalent support was offered by Logan Wilson to this position: "You state that an objective of regionalism is to *discover* 'the new balance and equilibrium between supercivilization and American culture in the balance between men and machines, between men and resources. If ever there was a new frontier this is one.' This logical position represents a Baconian view of science, taking for granted that the balance is just beyond some horizon waiting to be discovered. My own view is that the way out must be *invented*, not discovered. Consistent with this view of science as something more than fact-finding, I should say that classification is largely a matter of convenience." This was shrewd, but it must have been hard for Odum to be accused of being a Baconian and a Comtean, all in the same week.[50]

There was a widespread consensus that geography was an antiquated theoretical basis for any modern sociology. Robert Faris, Otis Duncan, and Pitrim Sorokin concurred on this. Sorokin summarized the objection by writing to Odum: "your regionalism assumes a paramount importance of territory and territorial basis of groups and communities. This basis—all important in the past—seems to me to have lost its importance and is losing it rapidly. Territorial adjacency, proximity or remoteness becomes less and less important factor in uniting individuals into one social unity, in making them solidary [sic] body, in creating and destroying real communities or social systems. Its place has been taken by other cultural factors (religion, nationality, economic interests, political party, state, class and caste interests, character of culture etc.) At the present time, 'regional' factor is only one among many and far from being most important. Therefore, for planning any rational division of mankind into some social units, it has to be reckoned with, but only as one among many other factors and interests and bases."[51]

Implied in such criticism, both methodological and theoretical, was the impression that social psychology had been slighted in the pursuit of instrumentalism. H. C. Brearley thought that regions existed more in men's minds, and less in "reality." And J. F. Cuber was sure that "the identification of the person with the regional culture is important to the definition of the region." But Lawrence Frank assembled the objections most acutely, especially by adding a few observations on the historical roots of Odum's difficulties: "If you have to resort to factor analysis to delineate regions," he observed, "is it because you are trying to force the stubborn and recalcitrant diversity of people in to a few hard statistical concepts or factors? I feel that Thurstone uses factor analysis to escape recognition of the complex diversity and individuality of personality, preferring a more or less spurious simplicity and homogeneity.... If I had time and energy I'd elaborate a bit on the handover of 19th century scientific concepts of order, regularity and uniformity, etc. which are obsolete nowadays in their original form and must be reformulated in terms of the admitted disorder, lack of uniformity (except statistical probability) discontinuity and relativity of all measures and data. Such regional studies must accept 'social relativity,' and acknowledge that every measurement or data must be ordered to the field (region) in which observed where it may be enhanced or attenuated, so that its absolute quantitative significance disappears."[52]

To telescope these criticisms is unfair to Odum. Doubts were scattered through several minds, not concentrated in one. Many sociologists, even when they expressed skepticism, were interested in the possibilities of regionalism. Almost none, however, endorsed his peculiarly rigid version. After noting lengthy objections to Odum's case, Otis Duncan had pondered the apparent contradiction. "On the other hand," he admitted, "I am on several regional committees which are conducting research of one kind or another. I attempt to justify this apparent inconsistency with the argument that a geographical division of labor is necessary because it is impossible to study the whole country.... Regionalization.... is mainly a mechanical expedient." Logan Wilson, equally, thought there was some point to organizations like the Southern Sociological Society, but "for most purposes ...the functional principle of organization is better than the territorial." And the latter might become obsolete if transportation should become sufficiently fast and inexpensive. Regionalism, Robert Faris surmised, was useful, but it was "much more efficient to have a different set of regions for each purpose, without attempt to make them coincide. Cultural homogeneity does not coincide with necessities which are answered by such arrangements as TVA, Port of New York Authority, seaboard gasoline rationing area, and the like."[53]

Those sociologists and geographers who answered Odum's inquiry came mostly from outside the South, and were thus beyond his sphere of influence. To Raymond Bellamy of the Florida State College for Women in Tallahassee, Odum's sociology loomed more immense on the horizon. Bellamy was deeply concerned that Odum's dominance over Southern sociology was unhealthy. The intellectual structure of regionalism was part of the problem, and Bellamy illustrated his complaint with an anecdote: "Some few years ago I sent one of our graduates to Chapel Hill to do graduate work in sociology. She was a bright girl, unusually bright, and had the capacity for almost unlimited work.... But after one term she came back and reported that she could not get any general sociology at N.C.... She went over the catalogue with me and I believe she was right.... I have the feeling that the strong development of Regionalism is rather directly the cause." When Odum protested the point, Bellamy insisted: "The quarrel I have with the Regionalists is that they seem more and more to be crowding out the general sociology. I consider this a fatal blunder and think that in the long run it will work disaster.[54]

Bellamy might have discounted Odum's protest with more alacrity, if he had seen a long 1942 letter from a disillusioned Northern graduate student to Odum. John Lansing had come from Columbia University, fresh from the influence of Robert Lynd and Herbert Marcuse, and eager to see sociologists appreciate and cultivate the element of "value judgments" in their "science." The University of North Carolina had been a disappointment. Rupert Vance did offer a course on social theory, but he was not deeply interested in it: most of his time was given to regionalism and demography. "Subconsciously I expected to find a university in the South," Lansing told Odum, "instead I found a Southern university. I thought the atmosphere would be one of a university which thought of itself primarily as an intellectual institution, a national and international center of learning in the great tradition. Instead Carolina is primarily a Southern institution." The sociology department was staffed almost exclusively by Southerners. Naturally it was making great contributions to research on Southern problems, but it thereby placed "limits on what the University and the department have to offer a Northerner not primarily interested in the South for its own sake." The message was clear. In turning from a sociology in the South to a Southern sociology, Odum had surrendered valuable perspectives for his gains.[55]

Odum could only have been wounded by these accusations. Had he not proved the foolishness of the distinction between Southern regionalism and nationalism? That he had not was testified with depressing regularity by his 1942 correspondents. Two Southerners, Brearley and Bellamy, refused to acknowledge his fundamental distinction between regionalism and sectionalism. Brearley even thought that Odum's discussion of regional rights was "quite reminiscent of 1860 and the demand for 'states' rights.' ... like the sectionalism of Thomas R. Dew and Thomas Cooper." Bellamy dismissed Odum's cherished belief that regionalism was for the national good: "The deepest dyed old sectionalist that ever got up in Washington and bellowed for high tariff on manufactured articles or stormed because Cuban tomatoes and other truck goods were allowed into the country would have insisted vehemently and possibly even profanely that he was interested in the good of the country as a whole, and he would have thought he was, too. A very large percent of Regionalism seems to me unmistakably the same thing. I am tempted to think that its very foundation is the same." A non-Southerner endorsed this viewpoint, as he puzzled: "How prevent regions becoming sections? So long as interest groups are self-conscious and our culture permits them to apply pressure, why should they be less harmful as regions than as states...? Regionalism is very valuable; but I can't see that it really offers an escape from localistic autarchic tendencies."[56]

Odum remained sanguine under this bombardment. The criticisms were noted, but dismissed as "misunderstanding" of his meaning. But the mainspring was broken. It was not that he ever ceased his constant running after change and understanding; books continued to emerge from his scrawling midnight pen, trains were still taken to meet foundation executives, stewardship was exercised over Southern academic liberalism. And he never ceased to plead the regionalist cause, but fewer and fewer listened. When he went back to the General Education Board in 1949 to finance a revised edition of *Southern Regions,* the private comments within the foundation office were dismissively the opinions of a new generation. "The original volume," one observed, unkindly, "was essentially a cut-and-paste job which did not make an important contribution to science." And today the Institute for Research in Social Science, blessed with the financial backing of a much wealthier state of North Carolina, the backing that was unobtainable for Odum, has scarcely any interest in regionalism. Only one member of its large staff has any interest in the South, and he deals with the social psychology of sectional perception, the perspective that always just eluded Odum.[57]

Howard Odum had come at a peculiar moment in the history of American sociology and that of the South. He had inherited from Wundt, Giddings and "progressive" sociology the neo-Hegelian theory that society was a "whole of closely related and interdependent parts." For Odum, such an integration was natural and basic. No amount of atomistic analysis could fragment these wholes. The assumption of organicism was fundamental. On this perspective was piled the burden of the Southern idea. But the New South version of this idea transmitted an ambivalence to him. It gave him two candidates for his natural organic unit of analysis, the South and the nation. And it told him that they were substantially identical. This imposed strains that he boldly, but unconvincingly, tried to resolve by his distinction between regionalism and sectionalism.

At the same time, Odum was an ambitious empire builder for a new and contentious discipline. His region was not sure it wanted him, and his state was positive that it couldn't afford him. As in the old days, he was driven into reliance on outside sources. But, more than this, he chose to spread the load of support to the whole region and make the South his bailiwick. This strengthened his hand in New York, and it increased the chances of survival. And, as in the old days, he needed to legitimize himself and make the new seem old.

However, the step from practical necessity to theoretical respectability was a long and straining one. By the late 1930s, the comforting theory hastily absorbed in his youth had been challenged by a changing profession of sociologists. His peers and juniors were less interested in social involvement and more involved in particularist scholarly investigation. Grand theory was no longer very respectable, unless it came marked with a European label. The new temper was strenuously positivist, the instinct was to take one thing at a time, the mood was skeptical of the old Hegelian assumptions. The mold into which Odum, with little thought, had poured his mass of statistics and plans, was broken. Few seemed to mind if the pieces were left on the floor. The old obsessions of Darwinian theory with nature, conflict, and geography were deemed less germane than the internal mechanisms of advanced social organization. Odum's nostalgic faith in the inherent strength of the farm began to make little sense to a generation raised on city blocks.

All this helped to determine Odum's fate, but he was little aware of it. He had told his colleagues that regionalism was merely natural, so fundamental that it scarcely needed a theory. He had been puzzled when the General Education Board had not found it equally obvious and refused to fund his Southern Council. He had not understood that the shifting terms of thought implied in the uncertain relativism of modernism were potentially hostile to his thought, his vision of the South. He had been sure that he was on the side of the future, but the future seemed disinclined to sustain him. Others in the South, working in other fields, writing poetry or history, understood the quagmire of intellectual modernity better. They did not necessarily like it more, but they were not to be surprised when it dealt with them harshly.

entr'acte:
A Still Point: John Wade

five:
Wade: A Turning Inward

It is a truism, long attested, that Southerners are rooted in "place." This has, no doubt, been an unjust differentiation against the settled townspeople of New England, the robust enthusiasts for the Lower East Side of New York, the convinced loyalists of Colorado. It has gently distorted the vulnerability of modern Southerners to the vagaries of social mobility. Few Southern intellectuals of recent times have lived in their family home, the town, or country area in which they were born. Caroline Gordon once remembered that her "grandmother used to call Allen and me 'the free niggers' because she said we were always on the road just the way niggers were right after they were freed."[1] To be sure, links were maintained. Howard Odum went often back to Covington in Georgia, Frank Owsley returned to Montgomery County in Alabama. But universities did not sprout in the backyards of villages, and too often the decision to pursue an intellectual life meant severance. It is well to remember that the definitive American statement on exile was made by Thomas Wolfe, a Southerner.

John Donald Wade was an exception. His family had lived in Marshallville, a middle Georgia village, since the early nineteenth century. He was born there. He lived there for most of his life. He died there. Friends would visit Wade and come away declaring that he could be defined by the white-columned mansion and the rich peach orchards. He seemed almost a caricature of the Southern squire: tall, urbane, affluent, paternalistic towards his Negro servants, comfortable in ancestral estates overflowing with remote cousins and scuppernongs, sitting down occasionally to compose an elegant essay in defense of the South. He seemed remote from tense intellectualizing, fixed in an old pattern, an outcropping from an older South long since worn away.

It was not that he didn't travel. But new environments seemed to offer no challenge to his identity. He would enjoy a place—Harvard, New York, Washington, London—or not, and then go home. One day in 1917, when a young man of twenty-five, he went with friends to examine some family land. Later he noted in his diary: "Standing on ground which had so long been in the hands of my people, I marvelled at the wide divergence of outlook between myself and...[a] well meaning friend, who enquired so blandly—Lord save the lady,—whether or not I meant to settle here. As if any other settling of mine could be much more than a sojourn!"[2]

Or so it seemed. In fact, the story of his rootedness was more tangled. The apparently comfortable equation between John Wade, Marshallville, and the South had its tensions and complexities. Even the most fixed of men approached himself through the ambivalences of modernity. To sketch this process helps to explain the transition from Odum to the Agrarians, from liberalism to conservatism, from conviction in the firmness of modern thought to doubt about its fixity.

Wade's father had been, as well as a landowner, a country doctor. His death in 1905 had damaged the family's fortunes and left John Wade to be raised by a mother of enormous drive and uncertain business acumen. Ida Wade liked to dabble in the speculations of the New South. Sometimes she was lucky, as when she gambled on cotton futures during the First World War and made a fast thousand dollars. More often she was not prudent, as when she nearly wrecked the family income with injudicious investment in the Florida land boom of the 1920s. Fortunately, behind Ida Wade was the remote but steadying hand of a genuine entrepreneur. John Wade's uncle, D. E. Frederick, had left the depressed area of middle Georgia after the Civil War to seek his fortune in the West. He had founded a large retail store in Seattle and become a millionaire. It was Frederick who paid for the young Wade's education and preserved Mrs. Wade from the misfortunes of ill-directed acquisitiveness.[3]

The education to which Wade was treated was unexceptional in its early stages: a few of the better preparatory schools in Georgia, a private tutor who drilled him in Cicero, and then the state university in Athens. It was a comfortable ascension up a familiar ladder, which stood in marked contrast to the parvenu uncertainty of that other young Georgian, Howard Odum. Wade could belong to the best clubs, Odum had no place in them. But the new ways of the South exerted their pressure even on Wade. It was the opinion of D. E. Frederick that Wade should become a businessman. In the booster enthusiasm of Athens, this might have seemed a laudable ambition. Upon this hint, Wade registered at the Harvard Business School in 1914. As "Uncle Edward" had cautioned Ida Wade: "It appears to me that you should let John Donald follow his bent, unless he should want to paint pictures or write poetry or trim windows, and in that case I should certainly do all in my power to talk him out of it."[4]

Unfortunately, Wade did have such a disreputable enthusiasm for literature. Rapidly he became bored with economic studies and switched to the intermittent scrutiny of English and American literature. This brought him under the influence of Bliss Perry, famed for his love of Browning and Tennyson, and Barrett Wendell, a severe and eccentric pedagogue who celebrated, above all else, the New England tradition of Emerson. This was the Northern root of the New South creed, viewed with great immediacy.[5]

Wade himself had some interest in his own region, though there is no evidence that he was a truculent Southerner. He seems seldom to have frequented the Southern Club at Harvard. But the loyalty was indistinctly there. On his trip North, he had written that "it seemed like severing a close tie to get out of reach of Pennsylvania Station, where all the Southern trains run in." In the May of 1915, he travelled to New York to see Woodrow Wilson pass by in a parade. They played "Dixie" and he cheered with the rest.[6]

Nonetheless, he cared enough to begin research on Southern literature. He was to recall the incident: "I had told Barrett Wendell that I was interested in 'Southern literature.' Poe, perhaps? Lanier? Who knew? Not I. Wendell thought, then, he said, that I had better go down to New York and work with Professor Trent, who knew more about Southern literature than *he* knew." For it was to be said of Wendell's *Literary History of America,* it should have been entitled, "A Literary History of Harvard University, With Incidental Glimpses of the Minor Writers of America." In 530 pages, Wendell had given twenty to the South.[7]

So Wade transferred to Columbia University, where Odum had been four years earlier, and there studied with the foremost literary critic of the New South persuasion. To Trent's influence was added that of the young Carl Van Doren. Van Doren's lectures and personal guidance appear to have emphasized the South more than might have been expected of a Northern critic teaching in New York City in 1915. Wade's lecture notes contain discussions of Edgar Allan Poe, of whom even Wendell had heard, but also John Esten Cooke, William Gilmore Simms, William Garrott Brown, Augustus Baldwin Longstreet, and George W. Cable. Van Doren was especially interested in the indigenous tradition of Southern humor that grew from Longstreet and was consummated in Mark Twain.[8] But it was Trent who suggested to Wade that in Longstreet, the antebellum humorist, politician, and university president, there was a natural subject for a young Georgian. For the next seven years, Wade was intermittently to collect material for a biography.

Rumination was interrupted by war. The United States entered the European conflict just before Wade took his examinations for the Ph.D. In solemn mood, he began to keep a diary. Feeling himself in the midst of great events, he was inspired partly by an analogy with the Civil War. "Up till a year or so back," he wrote, "I had wondered earnestly how some people could ever have come to think the War of 1861-5 at all necessary; and consequently of late...I have wondered whether this would ever become as dim and foolish-seeming to the young creature of 1967 as that other war did to me in 1912." The impulse was, alas, a shade priggish. He dreamed extravagantly of going to war and sharing in the catharsis of the trenches. But Wade was not a William Alexander Percy, who had headed towards the sound of gunfire and Herbert Hoover's Commission for Relief in Belgium.[9] The diary turned into a chronicle of Wade's social activities in Marshallville, a cheerful round of fried chicken dinners and motoring, punctuated with the occasional reverie on the war. "I could probably sit here throughout the war's length, occupying some little teaching job, or even farming, and running meantime a good automobile which I am sure Mama would buy with small urging," he morosely noted. "But this war, it seems to me, is the great experience of this age, and to be so far off from it, not to be with in the huge vibration, even, of its pulse beat, seems to me like voluntarily abscenting [*sic*] ones self from the one agency capable of developing his soul as every soul of this time should develop." But he missed his chance. In the lottery for conscription, his number came very low. A medical examination showed that he had a hernia. And his mother had little inclination to let her only son develop his soul in so sanguinary a fashion. By her intervention, he ended up in nothing more heroic than a desk job in Washington with the Motor Transport Division of the Marine Corps.[10]

In comparison with the graceful and ironic John Wade of the 1930s, the young John Wade was an obvious snob. He was given to lecturing his friends on their duty to their country, on their morals and manners. Quite convinced of his powers, he remarked during rumors of a Negro insurrection: "Trouble in that quarter is the least of my worries. I do not pride myself much as an orator, but I could muster up tears enough and enough sincere emotionalism to control a goodly number of brothers-in-black, especially when the object is, like this, distinctly negative." Occasionally, however, he would pause and wonder about his own weakness, especially a disturbing proclivity for the pleasant amenities of Marshallville.[11]

Marshallville did not suffer much from the war. It lost only one of its sons, and he died not in France but in Mississippi. The price of peaches rose and the Wade family did quite nicely. Wade was altered, indeed, not by the force of the war but by its lack of impact. He had thought before 1914 that wars were an anachronism. He had been shocked to discover that they were not. He was, in turn, discouraged to find out that, either way, it didn't seem to matter to him. He lamented: "This complete reversal in the scale of progress, has had on me no appreciable effect whatever. While millions suffered and died in Europe, my food has continued to seem good to me, sleep has in nowise forsaken me, and I am sad or merry on occasion just as beforehand." With this insight, he gathered a melancholy feeling for the gulf between the rhetoric of human aspiration and its mundane reality.[12]

His war diary offers only intermittent clues to his appreciation of the South. It is more striking for its nationalism. Throughout he was a devoted admirer of Woodrow Wilson and registered not a single dissent from administration policy in the whole course from the declaration of war in 1917 to the fight over the League of Nations. When the *New Republic* ran a contest in 1919, Wade composed a poem in honor of the President. Even before the war, he had been belligerently anti-German and scornful of those who saw any merit in the German position. When war came, nativist scruples about conscription surfaced: "Southern members of congress who vote against it [conscription] must not realize the proportion of non-native people through the north and east; to my mind, there is no reason why these people should not, just the same as anybody, bear the burden of this war. They will never do so except by conscription. So may the future race of this nation become less and less like what we who have been here longest would most like it." Much of Wade's sense of North and South appeared to rest upon these genteel class scruples and xenophobia. He thought, for example, that Tennesseans were "instinctively more gentle-manly and more agreeable to deal with than the 'slum-boys' from the big northern cities."[13]

This vein of feeling had paradoxical consequences. When the news of the Bolshevik Revolution came, he was oddly impressed. Communism might, he thought, eventually triumph in the United States. Having little truck with Marxism, he did share its sense of the deep malaise in the Western democracies. "I should be eager to embrace some theory which would bring justice more universally into the world," he mused. "My present judgement, from what I can read, is that Bolshevism does not do this at all, or at least without violating more principles than it observes." If social excellence was being undermined, perhaps democracy had done it. Barrett Wendell had been insistent on that point, and Wade was inclined to agree. Nativism, gentility, and the masculine prerogative persuaded him that the suffrage, far from being extended to women, ought to be restricted to those over twenty-five and capable of passing stringent educational tests.[14]

After the war, Wade went to the University of Georgia and taught English and American literature. At the same time, he finished his biography of Augustus Baldwin Longstreet. The research had naturally deepened his involvement with the South and Georgia. Subtitled "A Study in the Development of Culture in the South," his *Longstreet* was the first major biography of a Southern literary figure since Mims's *Sidney Lanier* in 1905 and the first to be produced by the second generation of Southern literary critics. And yet, considering the subtitle, it did not quite live up to its billing. Not for the last time, Wade proved himself more interested in the state of Georgia than "the South." Unwilling to subsume the character of his home state beneath the title "Southern," Wade twice borrowed Trent's description of the Georgian as "the Southerner who comes the nearest of all the inhabitants of his section to being a normal American." As Trent had seen it, "The various elements that compose the population seem to have fused . . . rather than to have preserved their individuality; and the result is the typical Georgian, energetic, shrewd, thrifty, brave, religious, patriotic, tending on the extremes of society to become narrow and hard, or self-assertive and pushing." For Wade, Longstreet had to be understood as a Georgian. "A Middle Georgia villager this man remained always in sentiment," Wade insisted, despite the fact that Longstreet had lived in several Southern states and underwent a change of political opinions from nationalism to sectionalism parallel to his friend and mentor, John C. Calhoun. This eminently New South definition of the Georgian-as-American was augmented by Wade's admission of New England influence on the state in the migration of New England Puritans in the eighteenth century. And so Wade's feelings about the sectional conflict were much less partisan than those of the old judge. He did not doubt that the South had had a position of integrity, but he did regret that matters should have fallen out with such bitterness.[15]

A Southern bishop was to marvel at the book's tone: "He writes with an air of the utmost detachment from all the things Longstreet was most interested in—the Methodist Church; the cause of Secession; the life of the South. Indeed, with more than an air of detachment, with a touch of scorn." The bishop was near the mark. In 1924, Wade was undecided about his South. Half of him looked to William Trent and the *New Republic* when he criticized the shortcomings of antebellum Southern literature or the region's complacent immunity to self-doubt. He was repelled by the crudity of frontier Georgian life, and went even further than Trent in distancing himself from the mythology of the Old South. Wade realized that there was more to antebellum life than Virginia, and more than the measured pace of the oldest plantations. Yet he was attracted by the neighborly boisterousness of the Georgia frontier. Whilst he regretted the South's commitment to slavery, he forced himself to acknowledge that Longstreet had been an honorable man, "typical of the best thought of the South toward the Negro."[16]

In granting the South both sin and virtue, Wade began to turn social thought into style, to convert his priggishness into a very personal voice of ironic ambivalence that might serve as a mode of accommodation. He had read *The Education of Henry Adams* and passages in his Longstreet biography were strongly reminiscent of both the *fin-de-siècle* mood and the ironic intention of the New Englander. "Later, Gus Longstreet found that he understood it all, but [George] McDuffie never did grasp it, went to his grave in fact, broken, almost an imbecile, still wondering. Just before his death, Gus Longstreet came to him at his home to explain it all, but for all Gus could do, the matter was still vague to him, past any hope of his ever grasping it." This is pure Adams, if not yet vintage Wade.[17]

Such undertones were, no doubt, lost upon his audience. The book was received gratefully by Southern progressives, who did not catch the phrases that indicated Wade's doubts about the New South. That he deprecated the Old South was more readily apparent. Gerald Johnson in the *Greensboro* (N.C.) *Daily News* offered the praise, which seemed to confirm its status.

Wade, he wrote, "has done a piece of work immensely creditable to the south, but one wonders if he will receive credit for it in the south."[18]

Indeed, that Wade was not yet the Southern quietist of later years can be seen in his academic career in the mid-1920s. Like Odum, he was to gain a few honorable scars. Wade taught at the University of Georgia with mixed credentials. True, he was a son of Georgia made good, his biography praised by all. But he was a friend of men like Carl Van Doren and had been praised by the South-baiting Mencken. He knew and was liked by Odum. And there was a clear tension between this perceived John Wade and certain sectors of the university administration, who disliked such "liberal" influence on the impressionable youth of Athens. In these years, the effective ruler of the university was not the chancellor, but an entity called the "Prudential Committee," which consisted of those university trustees who resided within the town of Athens. Wade had been injudiciously outspoken in his demands that the faculty have greater say in the university's affairs.[19]

In 1924, the *Nation* ran a series of articles on the states of the Union. Wade composed a critical piece on Georgia, called "Georgia Shell-Shocked." It was not taken by the *Nation,* but Odum came to hear of it and asked to consider it for the *Journal of Social Forces.* Liking it, he asked if Wade was willing to see its publication, considering that "it will bring you some criticism." The younger man got cold feet and asked Odum to postpone matters until he could think it over. Odum, understanding caution, agreed. "I hope the time will come when one can speak the truth without involving the welfare of the whole university," the sociologist observed. "That, in my judgement, is the most discouraging thing about our beloved Georgia."[20]

Wade continued to equivocate. In the autumn of 1924, there was an incident that only worsened his dilemma. A new member, Howell Erwin, was appointed to the Prudential Committee. Professor Robert Park, a friend of Wade in the English department, took it upon himself to test the attitude of the new man. "The other night," Wade reported to Odum, "Professor Park read him [Erwin] Georgia Shell-Shocked, by way of learning how he thought it would be received. He learned all right, emphatically, conclusively. It would be held a dangerous, traitorous work, and perhaps, Professor Park gathered, would be held so justly.... It was a mistake to show it to Erwin, I suppose, but he has the reputation of being such an anti-Klucker that we thought he might approve of the work of some fellow 'antis.'" Again the article was postponed, and eventually abandoned. Wade had reasoned that he would do better by the university to stay, even though mildly gagged, than to publish, be damned, and leave. But his position remained uneasy.[21]

The summer of 1927 was a troublesome one for the University of Georgia. There were incidents involving swirling coalitions of students, alumni, a new chancellor and the Prudential Committee. A young assistant secretary of the university YMCA was dismissed for arranging group meetings between undergraduates and members of "a colored institute": the editor of the *Athens Banner-Herald* muttered darkly that the offender had been in the pay of Moscow. Undergraduates associated with Wade had started a sprightly and irreverent magazine called *The Iconoclast*. Their Menckenian *jeu d'esprit* was not appreciated and they were expelled. During this, Wade was away in England on a Guggenheim fellowship. He thought it prudent to test his position by asking the new chancellor for promotion to a full professorship. The chancellor agreed, then hesitated, then declined. Wade resigned. "I had the highest hopes of Col. Snelling," he confided to Odum with disappointment, "he had given me intimations to justify such hope. I knew the Prudential Committee wished me in limbo, and it seemed to me that now was as good a time as ever to see whether the Chancellor would defy those gentlemen by urging my promotion."[22]

In his absence, a controversy ensued in Georgia over Wade's departure. Students wrote in protest to the newspapers, alumni meetings gathered to deprecate the decision and sundry sins of the administration. Under this pressure, the chancellor and the Prudential Committee wavered, but did not break. Regretfully, Wade reconciled himself to exile. He wrote again to Odum, who knew about the regrettable tendency of Georgian colleges to expel their dissidents: "The outlook there now seems bad to me. You are encouraging about Emory, and perhaps you are right. Perhaps in a thousand years Mercer [University] also will be commendable—I don't know. The most tangible present hope seemed to me to be in Athens. . . . The outlook *is* bad, isn't it? I remember that you told me that it was."[23]

His Guggenheim fellowship turned into a stopgap, while he decided his future. The trip had been designed to collect material for a biography of John Wesley, and to enjoy a little of Europe. For a genial epicurean, the emphasis was a shade on the latter. The choice of Wesley as a subject had not been uninfluenced by the rule that Guggenheim fellowships had to be spent abroad. But it was an opportunity to take his mother with him as he pottered around England, dined as visiting Americans did with Lady Astor and travelled on to the Middle East and Jerusalem. In the meantime, he was offered an editorial post with the new *Dictionary of American Biography* in Washington.[24]

Depressed, he went to Washington. "It seemed to me," he wrote to his mother in September 1927, "that night before last I was really more despondent than I had ever been previously, so old I seemed and so very very little accomplished." He was an easygoing man, and the mood would pass, but an undercurrent of discontent was to stay with him as long as he was away from Marshallville and Georgia. He could not imagine a life permanently outside Georgia. Recent events made it hard to picture one within it.[25]

The job with the *Dictionary of American Biography* proved, however, unexpectedly valuable. The necessity of composing brief biographical entries pruned the prolixity that had marred his study of Longstreet. It helped to turn Wade into a miniaturist that made comparisons with Lytton Strachey far from inappropriate.[26] And the refinement was directed into Southern modes, for he was often set to work upon Georgians and Southerners. His erudition about the obscure crannies of Southern history was miscellaneously increased. As he noted of Timothy Bloodworth, a North Carolina politician: "Almost all his life he stood against the main trend of history, and sixty years after his death even a newspaper editor in the North Carolina state capital was obliged to admit that he had never heard of him."[27]

In this year, Wade began to harden his feelings about the South and industrialism. In reviewing the generation of Southerners who survived the Civil War and condemned the raucous New South, he grew in sympathy with them. Of Robert Lewis Dabney, he wrote: "He was a blind, groping old man, championing with dogmatism a waning creed; but he was none the less majestic—and those who listened to him felt that he embodied learning and benevolence and romantic honor." Of Virginius Dabney the elder and his novel, *The Story of Don Miff,* Wade observed: "Regarded at the time of its appearance as exceedingly profound, it in some degree justifies such an estimate. It is conventional at base, but in many important matters its author is revealed as a whimsical, shrewd, and wise critic of the social order he saw making itself paramount in America." In letters to his mother, there is evidence that he was brooding on the problem of man's adjustment to the factory system, the relationship between business and Christianity, Mammon and God. But the thoughts were quite private, surfacing only in a turn of phrase in his work for the dictionary.[28]

In 1928, Edwin Mims asked Wade to come to Vanderbilt University and direct a new graduate program in English. Wade agreed, although the University of Georgia was making overtures, inadequate, that the hatchet be buried. So, at a time when his mind was beginning to run along more conservative Southern lines, he went to an English department little disposed to alter his course. Institutional pressures, in the shape of graduate students eager to study Southern literature, gathered to deepen his engagement with the region.[29] Later he was to be asked to give a summer school course on the New South at Duke University. But the ambivalence of his ideological position can be gauged by the fact that Odum, when he was entering the lists for the Agrarians, was keen to bring him to Chapel Hill as a "Professor of Southern Culture."[30]

In the short run, however, he had to discharge the unfinished business of his Wesley biography. The task was uncongenial, depressing enough to require the aid of an old friend from Athens to help. For Wade's motive in undertaking the project had been flimsy. Technically, his preface claimed that he wished to probe the gulf between Wesley's intentions and the Methodism that resulted and cited, as motive, not his own religion, but "the Methodist preoccupation of certain members of my family."[31] Without compelling interest, he compensated by an absorption in style. He decimated the paraphernalia of scholarship and lightened his irony to the degree that the reader moved through a mist. Detachment, paradox, and irony became indiscriminate when Wade cared little about the actors of a remote morality play. The style was refined, but the subject matter was far from his genuine sympathies. Style awaited engagement.

The South became a natural focus. From the ambivalence of his "liberal" youth, Wade turned more and more with affectionate nostalgia towards the settled South of his Marshallville childhood. Although Nashville was regarded as "Southern" by many, for a man with such particular attachments, it was exile. He was homesick for his Georgia. He constantly made telephone calls to his mother. The letters of his colleagues were full of references to his moroseness. "John Wade is depressed about something," Robert Penn Warren observed. "What nobody knows, but it's a great topic of speculation for idle hours." Andrew Lytle concurred that Wade, returning from a visit to Marshallville, had "a touch of melancholy and a hardened skepticism." In addition, the evangelical earnestness of the Southern Agrarians was never quite to Wade's taste.[32]

He was cajoled into contributing to *I'll Take My Stand,* and concurred as much from politeness as passion. Lyle Lanier informed Allen Tate that "Wade was more or less coerced by R. [Ransom] and D. [Davidson] into contributing. He has—or had at first—no real insight into the problem, protested at great length that he feared the jeers of friends about the possibility of his returning to the farm. . . . His essay is good, I suppose, although I have to confess that I am unable to see as much in it as Don tells me is there." When the controversy over the symposium led to a public debate between Ransom and Stringfellow Barr in Richmond, Wade stayed playfully aloof. "Mighty rumblings of war, or something or other, reach me from time to time from you on the one hand and Davidson and Ransom on the other," he told Barr. "It troubles me a good deal not to understand the whole business as fully as I think it appropriate I should, and I wish you would come out this way and set me clear about it."[33]

His essay, "The Life and Death of Cousin Lucius," stood apart in the symposium in the way that Wade's background and lack of explicit intellectual intensity separated him from the other Agrarians. It was the gentle parable of a Southern gentleman, born in the old world and living to see, bemused, the New South. It was based quite firmly upon his uncle in Marshallville, Jacob Walter Frederick. Mere description seemed to suffice for Wade. He appreciated, no less than his colleagues, the theoretical burdens of modernism, burdens that they spent their time expounding in their own essays. But he simply absorbed the ambivalence of such perceptions into his style. The most brusque of the Agrarians was puzzled by this. "I don't see much point to Wade's," Tate confided to John Gould Fletcher, and later added, "Wade is a timid man, a very fine prose stylist, who thinks it ungentlemanly to agitate; some of our opponents have as nice manners as we have, therefore we should not hurt their feelings."[34]

Wade never made friendships in Nashville that were to equal those he had in Marshallville and Athens. Only Donald Davidson became a permanent friend. It came as a source of regret, but scarcely of surprise, to the Agrarians when he returned to the University of Georgia in March 1934. This was soon after the Prudential Committee had been abolished and replaced by a new board of regents. He could return without loss of honor.[35]

Nonetheless his flirtation with agrarianism was important. The Agrarians put him under some intellectual stress and prodded his diffidence. Without them, his pieces for *I'll Take My Stand*, the *American Review*, the *Southern Review*, and *Who Owns America?* might have gone unwritten. For he never wrote very much in his mature years. The student of the Southern idea need only notice some six essays and two reviews, produced between 1929 and 1937. The quantity is slight beside the quality. Taken together, they constituted a reassessment of Southern and Georgian history between the Civil War and his own time. He dealt largely with Georgians: Henry Grady, Tom Watson, Joel Chandler Harris, Charles Colcock Jones, Longstreet. The South was never far from his mind, but he was aware that it was not an ineluctable framework. He remembered how as a child he had learned the word "Southern." "I know still," he added, "how to look at a book and without reading it to be aware, somehow, of every word on the pages that remotely looks like *southern*. I conceived it as my duty, once, over many years, to inspect that word every time it occurred on a page and to ascertain the veracity or falsehood of the sentence containing it."[36]

Despite his trip to Europe and his biography of Wesley, Wade had little interest in the cosmopolitan neurosis of Henry James or T. S. Eliot. His context for understanding the South was simply American. He thought of Europe, as he had treated the North in his Harvard days, as interesting but not his. "Shall American culture be indigenous or derived?" he asked the Macon Writers' Club in May 1932. "The answer, I believe, is that it should be both. . . . We should be indigenous—quite ourselves—we should be Georgians aware of how people do in Vienna. We should be, however, primarily Georgians and develop things in full as Georgians would develop them. The indigenous thing is quite wholesome." Wade himself was an undemonstrative example of the moral. One is startled, and then unsurprised, to notice an echo of a Dylan Thomas poem in a 1960 essay on a reissue of Longstreet's *Georgia Scenes*. With quiet ease, he had thrown off the cultural inferiority complex of the New South liberal. For Wade, imitation was "a doctrine of tears and unreality."[37]

He was drawn to the problem of the New South tradition by temperament as well as inheritance. Georgia was not solely responsible for the industrialist creed, but she did have Atlanta, its symbol, and Henry Grady, its prophet. In distancing himself from the alienating burden of his liberal youth, Wade chose to distance himself from the mythology of the New South. In the years between Reconstruction and the new century, it seemed to Wade that something had happened to which the rest, including himself, was postscript. For all his amiability, Wade's vision of the South was bleak. Things seemed to by dying around him, slowly but inexorably. And it came from no specific piece of fireworks, no single group of abolitionist deeds, but the simple flawed nature of man rendered worse by the pressures of modernity. In Wade's regretful opinion, Southerners were men like any others. "It is as well to concede everything at once," he confessed, "and to say that the mass of the people in the South have been, always, in certain regards, not merely worldlings, but American worldlings. As such, they grew weary of and quickly discarded the hard doctrine of a group of native prophets that the South must continue odd and peculiar, because of some abstruse ethics."[38]

It was peculiarly Wade's achievement to resurrect the memory of three Southern intellectuals who continued to defend the ways of the Old South after the spiritual divide of Appomattox. Wade regarded them as "prophets . . . actuated by regrets and fears of a cosmic order, [who] executed figures too intricate to be widely understood or valued." The Virginians, Albert T. Bledsoe and Robert Lewis Dabney, and the Georgian historian, Charles Colcock Jones, had seen the Civil War as a struggle between a spiritual and a materialistic philosophy of life. As Wade saw it, "They felt that more-and-more and not better-and-better was the inevitable motto of the new order, and they believed that such a premise was compatible only with the standardized and un-polite, the essentially un-human." They drew on cosmopolitan sources for their thought in Burke, Cobbett, Carlyle, Ruskin, as well as the locals, Jefferson, Calhoun, even the "better" sides of Lincoln and Emerson. They echoed old Judge Longstreet's belief that the war had been a conflict between a "Christ-taught band" and a "science-taught band." Unpopular aristocrats, they stood apart from the crescent New South creed and hurled their unheeded anathemas at it. As conservatives, they embodied a doctrine too little powerful in America. For it had been weakened by the process of migration to the New World, by the detection of the Loyalists during the Revolution and by the defeat of the South. Wade saw the Southerners as "the only substantial and organized group, who, in spite of pioneer handicaps, were determined to keep constantly in mind the values of a proven immemorial tradition." Tragically, the "sporadic natural-allies" of the South in distrust of a headlong industrialization, men like Emerson and Lincoln, the Romantic individualists, were diverted from coalition by the "comparatively minor and irrelevant (because it was surely doomed) issue of slavery."[39]

Henry Grady was taken as the central figure of the New South. The portrait was drawn with affectionate sorrow: "He was irresistible. He was completely earnest in his patriotism; and he was a superb orator.... He felt toward the South as a lover feels for his lady—he wished her so extremely well that he wished she would abandon being herself and try to be another lady, more robust, more practical." Wade's Grady was eloquent, but a little innocent and well-meaning. The image of the capitalist entrepreneur was impeccable, but the practice was ramshackle: too many of Grady's ventures went astray for him to appear as anything but a poor cousin of Jay Gould. But he did succeed in tapping the acquisitive desires of a Southern people wearied by war, Reconstruction and poverty.[40]

More than this—and Wade was the first to understand this fully: it was the measure of his disentanglement from the New South creed—Grady embraced the legend of the Old South. There was a symbolism in the fact that Grady and Joel Chandler Harris shared the same editorial office in Atlanta. As Wade put it, the New South's thesis was "a mixed one, and so, likely to fare far. It was that Southern men before 1860 were the finest men ever seen anywhere, but unfortunately quite wrong in all their conceptions except that of private virtue.... Its program was, while speaking reverently, always, of the past, to repudiate that past as rapidly as ever one might—with one exception, that the nigger be kept in his place." And Wade was not dull to the fact that this was a creation, not only of a dispirited South, but a North in need of nostalgia in the midst of its own, more hectic, industrial transformation.[41]

To the New South, Wade identified only two major challenges, Populism and the institutionalized nostalgia represented by organizations like the United Daughters of the Confederacy. In a biographical sketch of Tom Watson, "Jefferson: New Style," he interpreted the agrarian revolt as a protest against the drift of the nineteenth century. "If a choice were necessary," Wade wrote of Watson, "he preferred poverty, which patently is within endurance, to a prosperity founded on assumptions he thought fatal to all dignity and completeness of living." In this, Watson stood with the surviving ideologues of the ancien régime. But Wade thought Populism a vulgar outburst, and the rough company that Watson kept betrayed him. Watson's "army took on the appearance of a mob generalled by an autocrat, who, to retain his power, was capable of expedient concession to the mood of his supporters." Such Populists seemed too guided by blind opposition to the unfamiliar, and too little by reasoned dissent from industrialism. Watson's demand for a South "prosperous without being unmechanized" was "ordering out the moon for a pancake". For all his good motives, it seemed to Wade that Watson had left little permanent mark on Georgia, save to disrupt the pattern of her politics: "It begins to seem that his most enduring monument is the truly excellent watermelon hawked by his name through the revolving Summers."[42]

From the standpoint of the 1930s, Wade thus ironically sketched the failure of reasoned intellect and vulgar politics to deflect the New South's push for standardization. And he took little comfort in what had seemed to hold back enough of the Old South for him to enjoy. "Only inertia was left," he noted, "that great bog, spreading through the whole South—to be deprecated by all right thinking men. Grady had said drain it; Page had said drain it. It, only, prevented the South from looking like the rest of America; it only, said the liberals (always amiable and sometimes sensible), remained to hold us from the course followed by the rest of our countrymen with such conspicuous success." There was inertia, and there was the Negro. For, without the black, Wade thought that the Americanization of the South would have proceeded more rapidly.[43]

If Wade's South had been surrendered in its essentials long before his own time, it seemed to him that one eked out an existence in its scattered remnants and paused only to mock not too intolerantly the discomfiture of the brave new American world in the slough of the Depression. This was the rationale for his style. Where Wade found most comfort was in chronicling and expressing in his own prose the tradition of Southern humor. He was, indeed, reluctant to put too fine a definition to the word "Southern." "In my mind there is a body of notions that hold their hands up and answer present when one says southern," he confessed, "yet to define these notions (since in definition one must be definite) is more than I can do . . ., or more than anybody could do, I judge, except by implications and overtones and suggestions that nobody in this swift-moving time would trouble to follow, or, indeed, would trouble in the first place to set down."[44]

For the Chapel Hill symposium *Culture in the South,* Wade developed in 1934 his own philosophy of Southern humor, though the whole corpus of his style might be taken as those "implications and overtones and suggestions" that defined "Southern" for him. He suggested that, in the antebellum period, both North and South had had a humor that fed on the contrast of social groups: Southern, Yankee, immigrant, and Negro. Judge Longstreet was a prime exponent. But it survived the war with Joel Chandler Harris. Its essential strategy was ridicule of the simple hayseed. As a child of a rural society, it necessarily dwindled in the North with the dehumanizing process of industrialization. As this transformation proceeded more slowly in the South, so the old humor persisted. In Harris and Mark Twain it found its consummation. "They were the court-jesters of a homogeneous culture," Wade remarked, "and they are extinct now not because the culture they represented has crumbled utterly, but because it has grown self-conscious and ashamed, wistful to be cosmopolitan." The essence of Southern humor was its dependence upon community, upon the teller of the yarn knowing the listener, and upon the invocation of resonances, superficially extraneous to his story. Thus the Negro dialect joke illustrated the point: "For the initiated understand well enough that the teller, in the telling, is himself the main point of his story. They know that the southerner is in many ways bi-lingual, bi-mental, bi- (if I may say so) attituded; he speaks his own language and the dialect, his own thoughts and the Negro's thoughts. . . . It is the interplay of all these traits that makes the yarn worth listening to." And Wade held that this humor, largely oral, persisted in the South. It had even found its way into the urban sophistication of a James Branch Cabell or an Ellen Glasgow.[45]

There is little doubt that Wade believed himself to be an exponent of the old art. If one takes the comparison between him and Lytton Strachey offered by his contemporaries, one stylistic difference is apparent. While Strachey's prose was orthodox if irreverent, Wade often indulged in folksy whimsicality. One can find snatches of popular songs, fictional dialogues between assorted Southerners, reminiscences of what ancient cousins once said to one another, liberally scattered through ostensibly solemn subjects. Wade could not arrest the decline of his South, but he could laugh at it.

At least, he could try. Sometimes the seriousness of his bleak vision broke through. One detects a growing willingness to pass by the dissimulation of irony and speak out directly in his later essays. A piece in 1937, "What the South Figured: 1865-1914," was more dogged than a similar essay for the *Virginia Quarterly Review* in 1935. In his contribution to *Who Owns America?*, he sounded almost bitter. He concluded his comments on the tendency of the countryside to ape the manners of the city with severity: "That is not the way of improvement, but of degeneration. It entails, whatever all the literary henchmen of the metropolis may say, be they novelists, dramatists or 'critics,' an active going out after spuriousness and vulgarity. It implies, more basically, the spectacle of independence doing obeisance before parasitism, of sanity turning presumptuous in the face of nature, and of humanity turning infidel to loving-kindness."[46]

In stepping out of the indecisive liberalism of his youth, Wade could sound the reformed rake. He wrote to Howard Odum in 1934, in summary of his transformation: "Until five or six years ago, instructed as I was so largely by the Nation and the New Republic, I had an impression. . . that however wrong the world might be at large, the specific part of it called the South was some million or so times more wrong. I repudiate that impression now with my whole conviction. I deeply suspect that the shoe is on precisely the other foot. In this definitely 'backward' community there are many people who are pretty badly off, but I do not hear any of them talking as if they had sooner renounce life than live it. In the 'better-type' communities that I have had opportunity to sample, there are enough people calling life nauseous to make it seem so, even to stout-stomached huskies like me who might otherwise even fancy that it is sometimes as agreeable as it is disagreeable."[47]

After his resignation from Vanderbilt, Wade took to Marshallville with all the zeal of a convert. The friends who came to see him in the late 1930s found a man freshly revelling in his rural tradition. Assuming the mantle of his village's natural aristocrat, he cared for its mental and physical health. He founded a reading club, that might persuade his own fellows of the wisdom of their ancestral ways. "All that these people have heard from acknowledged highbrow sources these forty years tends to the conclusion that they should try to emulate Ohio," he instructed Donald Davidson, about to address the club. "They should perhaps in many things; but in some cases they shouldn't. What are those things?... The club is new, as you know, and I am anxious for it to keep going. If you can manage to send the members home feeling 'improved,' I think you will have taken a good hand in the Lord's work." He gave his villagers a library, a boy's club, a bridge, and a foundation to make the town more beautiful. Trees and flowers were planted. He became Marshallville's Capability Brown and Squire Allworthy. And, as he became more absorbed in the village, so he wrote less and less. The confusions of modernity seemed finally to get him down. "I can't make up my mind...about 'intellectualizing,'" he told Davidson in 1938. "I hardly know *how* in the present state of Life. I remember how Chesterton grumbled for some *limits* to do his thinking in. There seem to be so few limits in our time; and thought is always so likely to turn purely volatile! And the Bridge and the boys club have been comfortingly tangible."[48]

It would be a neat piece of intellectual history, if one could record that Wade lived happily ever after and never wrote another line. It is true that he did not write very much more: a history of his local Methodist church, a section on culture for a Georgia state history, and a historical novel that remained unpublished at his death in 1963.[49] But he did found the *Georgia Review* in 1948. It represented the final victory of his particularism over his sense of a wider "South." The review was to be by and for Georgians, as well as edited in Georgia. To a correspondent, he explained that "in planning for the Georgia Review I felt that we needed to avoid the sort of thing undertaken by the Yale Review and by the Virginia Quarterly, the latter of which calls itself, I believe, a National Magazine published in the South. As things go I feel myself often somewhat beyond my depth in implying that the Georgia Review speaks in a way for this state. I should feel more hesitancy in the implication of speaking for the South at large." As he put it in the first editorial of the new journal: "The *Review* will exist particularly to be of use to Georgians. . . . Unless the import of a composition is clearly universal in its nature, everything that is published in the *Review* should be of special interest to Georgians. All else being equal, an article about the Okefenokee Swamp would be more acceptable than an article about Yellowstone Park, and an article by the mayor of Ball Ground, Georgia, more acceptable than an article by the mayor of Tacoma, Washington."[50]

Wade's hold upon a conception of the South had always been tenuous. He had always felt that it meant something, but never precisely what. The older he grew, the more he withdrew from its volatile nebulousness to the more modest fiction of the state. He retreated to the firm ground of localism, which kept him sane, happy, and of little moment to the outside world. From this vantage point, he could afford an unusual detachment. In 1954, he characterized the South to Davidson as "one of the really great abstractions of our race."[51] For Wade was unusual. He really could go home. He could be self-consciously Southern or not, even intellectual or not, as the mood and the times took him. He had not been forced to live by ideas, when he had his peach orchards. He could afford to be casual about Southern identity, when he had an identity of his own.

part three:
The Reaction to Modernism:
The Southern Agrarians

six:
John Ransom: The Cycle of Commitment

No one man dominated the symposium *I'll Take My Stand.* Each Agrarian was jealous of intellectual prerogative. John Crowe Ransom, however, was the nearest thing to a leader the group ever acknowledged. Though the old *Fugitive* never had a single editor, Ransom had set the tone of meetings.[1] An established poetic reputation, an air of authority, a detached and ironic manner, a metaphysical subtlety and foresight that made younger men seem constantly to turn the corner of a thought and find the urbane Mr. Ransom already there, all combined to generate deference towards the senior member of the Vanderbilt literary set. His draft of a "Statement of Principles" formed the basis for discussion in 1930. His essay "Reconstructed but Unregenerate" stood first in the symposium and left its stamp upon the hasty reader's impression. It was he who articulated the volume's boldest assertion: "The South is unique on this continent for having founded and defended a culture which was according to the European principles of culture; and the European principles had better look to the South if they are to be perpetuated in this country."[2]

That contention about the "European" quality of the South was the core of Ransom's perception about the region in 1930. His road to it was, however, a devious and idiosyncratic one. The episode of John Ransom, the Southern Agrarian, was a strange detour in the broad course of his intellectual life. One needs to delve into his pre-Agrarian years to understand the force of that deviation.

That he was an Anglophile in 1930 was little doubted and significant. In explaining this sentiment, it is logical to point to the three years spent by the young Ransom as a Rhodes scholar at Christ Church, Oxford, from 1910 to 1913. It was assumed by most that Ransom's courtly ways derived as much from Oxford as from the reserved atmosphere of his family home: his father was a Methodist preacher and something of a scholar. Despite local opinion to the contrary, good manners are not confined to the immediate vicinity of the Isis, but still the impression lingered. Students could look at Ransom and remark, upon later reflection, that "there was something there that was not quite native . . . which I didn't recognize until I knew something about Oxford myself."[3]

Hence one is surprised to find that, when the matter of Oxford was raised in conversation in later years, Ransom would deny that the place influenced him unduly: "I didn't come out an Oxford man, quite, I think."[4] Were it not for the accident that the Rhodes scholar wrote to his Tennessee family and the correspondence survives, one would be inclined to dismiss that belief as a trick of the memory. These confirm, however, that Ransom stopped far short of Anglicization, though he didn't spend his time in an agony of resentment against Oxford's un-American ways. He enjoyed himself, as well he might. Oxford in those few years before the Great War looked, in the warming summers, at her best, and few vantage points were more peaceful than Ransom's spacious rooms in Peckwater Quadrangle.[5]

It is true that he picked up some incidental mannerisms. On a visit to Britanny in 1912, he was surprised when an American tourist "could not detect the American in my accent." He took up golf, spent some of his vacations at Hawarden, a genteel country retreat populated mainly by Anglican vicars, and went in for Oxford literary clubs with enthusiasm. But he remained convinced that Tennessee was the best place he had ever seen and sure that "no American could ever be content in England." On a summer trip to Germany in 1912, he was to meet a young American lady, overwhelmed by Europe and diffident about her control of the English language. Ransom was not pleased, and observed, "I think it is evidence of great moral weakness to become so easily ashamed of one's own speech and ways of life, but it is often to be observed among travelling American ladies." One would not have found Henry James adding, "I have been trying to impress on her that the reason Americans speak with less pains and precision than the English is that they are interested more completely in the things of life that matter, and that the English people devote a disproportionate degree of attention to the more irrelevant things, like etiquette and accents."[6]

Ransom could, indeed, sound like the Woodrow Wilson for whom he would have voted if the 1912 elections had found him in America. The United States seemed to him a healthier country, both practical and idealistic. Her foreign policy, alone among the nations, seemed fair and just. And, in keeping with this, Ransom was keen when president of Oxford's American Club to discourage the boisterousness of his fellow Rhodes scholars. Pranks were, no doubt, "the fashion of the English clubs, but I think the American Club ought to be somewhat more serious and digni-fied."[7]

Nor did he abandon himself to the quasi-aristocratic theories of social conservatism that he found in the junior common room. Not that he didn't appreciate the value of conservatives in providing a useful restraining force and in "steering the safe course that will not endanger the public loyalty to the common society, knowing that a general disintegration follows upon its loss." But laissez faire did not seem an adequate prescription for that more American preoccupation, social progress. The contention that society should refrain from helping the weak would, Ransom thought, "paralyze all compulsory legislation, and reduce the state to that aggregate of anarchy from which we have so painfully emerged." And he did not shrink from compulsion, for he saw, like Frank Lester Ward, the character of political progress as "the extension of compulsory equality to new provinces of activity hitherto dominated by competition." He even offered some consideration to the claims of socialism, though they seemed to him premature. It was not the dispossessed of society who brought change, but the pressure of a developing national conscience. Believing this, he was not surprisingly irritated by the Oxford obsession with history. Texts on Roman history bored him. He was glad to turn in his "Greats" course from such matters to philosophy, but even there he found a stumbling block. For Oxford went about philosophy as though it were history, and the place was cluttered with neo-Hegelians. Ransom himself preferred the new American philosophy of pragmatism, especially as represented by John Dewey's *Studies in Logical Theory.*[8]

Upon leaving England, Ransom taught for a year at the Hotchkiss School in Connecticut, despite a prejudice against private schools, for the very reason that they aped the snobberies of Eton and Harrow. A letter to his father in 1913 offers firm evidence that he was then neither very conservative, very interested in being called a Southerner nor enthusiastic about agrarianism. Life in Tennessee seemed to him markedly inferior to that offered by an urban existence. "Country conditions," he hazarded, "operate to produce in country people the qualities of stolidity, conformity, mental and spiritual inertia, callousness and monotony." Tennessee's ideal of humanity was too fixed and very narrow. New York, on the other hand, produced more interesting people and ideas, because its life was inherently dramatic. The artist in the big city did not have to await the accumulation of years, for urban time was compressed. But Ransom's fundamental objection to agrarianism was moral. "Morality, if it has any meaning at all, means the subjection of the natural man with its animal cravings into conformity to some ideal standard that is different from the natural man," Ransom believed. "When it is identical, it ceases to be a moral standard at all, there is no moral ideal and no moral struggle."

He still liked Tennessee, its climate, landscape, even its cooking. But he was uneasy at the vain boastfulness and provincialism of his home state. Admittedly, he saw some progress there, but gave most of the credit to the missionary efforts of journalism. He himself had toyed with becoming a reporter. In many ways, John Ransom sounded like a typical American progressive, and it is doubtful that he found much to quarrel with in the "New South" opinions of Edwin Mims, who summoned him to teach English at Vanderbilt University in 1914.[9]

Mims would, however, have looked askance at Ransom's even-handed attitude to the war in Europe. In its early days, Ransom thought that the German and English cases were equally just. He even published an article in the *Yale Review* to explain his viewpoint. In his opinion, Germany had been obliged by the pressure of a large population and legitimate imperial aspirations to push outwards, while Britain was equally bound to defend a status quo amiable to itself. The problem was not culpability, but the inadequacies of an international system that still tolerated the unrestricted competition increasingly outlawed in domestic society. "A body of articulated opinion" was needed to devise "for a permanent constitution some socialistic scheme of internationalism, wherein the periodic clash of natural and static justice might be tempered and adjusted." For Ransom, the United States was the natural author of such a movement. Unfortunately, the outburst of anti-German feeling had incapacitated any such American initiative.[10]

However, the fact of war changed such detachment. Ransom himself went to fight in France and became more anti-German the longer he stayed on the front. His deep fear was that a prolongation of the war would drain the energies of the United States just as it had weakened, depressed, and coarsened the life of France. Like Odum, he began to abandon the enthusiasm for German civic efficiency that had been his first impression on a visit to Heidelberg, and emphasized a secondary thought that had come to him on his journey back to Oxford: "I have not seen in either English or American faces, though possibly in France, anything like the great proportion of coarse and brutal expressions that strike one very forcibly when travelling in Germany."[11]

That he fought in a Southern regiment made him slightly more conscious of his Southern heritage. He was amused, when at his training camp in Chattanooga, he was berated by "Union" generals who had fought at Chickamauga on the inferiority of the Confederate effort. Many of his companions found it hard to become "Union soldiers," but he himself found it no strain and was content to describe himself as just "an American in France."[12]

These were small steps in the evolution from the John Ransom of 1915 to the convinced Southern agrarian of 1930. The greatest one lay in a matter far from his opinions on public affairs. Ransom had begun to write poetry, and this absorbed his energies for some ten years after he diffidently showed to Donald Davidson in 1916 a poem called "Sunset."[13]

The history of *The Fugitive* and Ransom's involvement in it has been well told elsewhere. One need only note that Ransom wrote his best poetry in the early 1920s by mastering an ironic style to supersede the sentimentality of his first volume of verse, *Poems About God*. What is less often observed is that Ransom wrote virtually his only poetry in those years. After 1926, he was to strive for a new kind of creative activity but was to write little more verse. Of the 168 poems in the Ransom canon, just seven were written or published after the issuing of *Two Gentlemen in Bonds* in early 1927.[14] Perhaps it was in the nature of Ransom's poetry, even at its best, to be short-lived. It was about texture, the ironic stance adopted in the poem: poetry written about poetry, and not the subjects external to the style of the verse. It needed "objective" events only as incidence. As such, the style perfected and polished, it rapidly became redundant. He himself felt this, and was to strive for an escape route from the conundrum.

His reaction to the Scopes trial must be seen partially against this background. For some years his doctrine of aesthetics had taken strength from a perceived conflict between science and the humanities. In Ransom's mind, art and religion were intimately related. In the euphoria of the 1920s about the potentiality of science, he had been uneasy and had begun to write in 1926 a formal philosophical volume, to be called "The Third Moment." As he wrote to James Southall Wilson, the editor of the new *Virginia Quarterly Review:* "My subject is the relation of science to art, and I am quite positively on the side of art. I have felt that science occupies now a too dominating position in our life, and that all the 'humanities' ought to make common cause in self-defense." Thus the Scopes trial cut firmly across this conflict and unexpectedly, by linking the struggle between science and religion to the South, conjoined his aesthetic worries with his region. In 1924, Ransom had been musing on art and science in abstract Kantian terms. By 1926, the furor at Dayton and its impact on the Vanderbilt campus had localized the metaphysic. It seemed natural that in offering an article to Wilson, Ransom should have added: "I would greatly like to find my expression in a Southern journal, because I feel my position is one peculiarly for the Conservative South to lead." This was a step away from the Ransom who had penned the first editorial of the *Fugitive,* with its whimsical declaration of the death of Southern literature and abhorrence of the "high-caste Brahmins of the Old South."[15]

Two things ran in tandem in Ransom's mind for the next several years: the development of an aesthetic theory and an interest in the South. Aesthetics, however, came first by a considerable margin. This was best expressed in letters sent to Allen Tate during 1927. Tate had reviewed Ransom's *Two Gentlemen in Bonds* for the *Nation* and suggested an intimate connection between its qualities and the South. "Mr. Ransom is the last pure manifestation of the culture of the eighteenth century South," Tate had written. It seemed to Tate that both rationalism and noblesse oblige, so important in the old Southern order, were basic elements in the Ransom style. With this, Ransom was pleased and thanked his younger friend. He confessed, however, that he did not write consciously as a Southerner or a non-Southerner. In the next breath, he went on to discuss his own creative problems as a poet: "It is perhaps for that reason that I am not willing as yet to confess that I shall not write any more poetry, or that when I do it will be a redundancy along the old lines." He admitted that he wanted to write more, for "that way lies health and sanity; but I have a notion that it will become more and more radical and fundamental and less and less local."[16]

Considering that, at the same time, Ransom was becoming absorbed in a local matter, the South, this seemed a paradox. In April 1927, Ransom began to resolve it. Poetry, he now insisted, was the action of an adult mind: "It must do more than one thing at the same time; its basis is a prose or logical substrata, but that must consist with a rhythmical development of sounded words and with one or more, often many, secondary and 'associational' meanings . . . . Poetry is more than prose, but it must first be prose, that is my thesis." He denied Tate's contention that a poem could be an absolute: "I think your insistence that we mustn't psychologize the finished poem, but that it is an ultimate, finished, absolute is a species of idolatry." The swirl of relativity around the poem was too great for anyone to fix its position.

The act of writing poetry required thought: "The obligation to be aesthetic is the obligation to open your eyes very wide." Poetry was simply another way of thinking, and thought went on in many different ways. For poetry was a function of life and, before one's poetry could be "major," one's life must become "adult." "The vision, as a matter of fact," Ransom suggested, "doesn't amount to much unless it handles *values* . . . terms which count in practical and ethical life by daily repetition. The exquisite pain and joy of art depends on exhibiting and then surrendering these values." And the basic end of art was tragedy or nostalgia, "the destruction of dear and familiar values." Genuine poetic stature could not be extracted simply from the external world, for "its index is the amount of turnover produced in our gray stuff. The size of the values depends on how much we use them, govern our practical lives by them; our schemes and desires and passions which have dominated us and will do it again."

Only at this point did Ransom raise the issue of the South. Tate had suggested a symposium, perhaps of criticism on Southern literature. Ransom was mildly enthusiastic, though he was bothered that the literature was too feeble. But he reflected that such might not be a fatal problem, for it helped to point up his moral: "I subordinate always art to the aesthetic of life; its function is to initiate us into the aesthetic life, it is not for us the final end. In the Old South the life aesthetic was actually realized and there are the fewer object lessons in its specific art."[17] The line of the argument was running from aesthetics to the South. Ransom's apparent abandonment of poetry was merely tactical, an attempt to move back to a more mature muse through the mediation of "life." He was later to write of his impulse to write "The Third Moment" that it was "a kind of Prolegomena to Any Future Poetic" and added, "I suppose I was rationalizing my own history."[18]

So John Ransom had consciously determined to raise his eyes to life, to become involved in it, and it is not curious that he should have noticed the South. The Dayton trial had intimated at its possible relevance to his aesthetic position. He had always had a fondness for the place. The mellow landscape of middle Tennessee had found its way into his verse. "The more I think about it," he mused to Tate, "the more I am convinced of the excellence and enduring vitality of our common cause. . . . I like my own people, or rather I respect them intensely. I also walk a great deal and throw fits over the physical beauty of this place." He wanted especially, in his search for values dying and tragic, to use something not merely invented but organic. "I believe in universals. . . . But I object to universals which are constructed and not found," he had said. The South was eminently to hand, the embodiment of a "natural" universal.[19]

He was not unaffected by the new insistence on the South which his friends were making, and impressed that both Tate and Andrew Lytle had been unable to make themselves at home in the North. "This fact, many times repeated within my own knowledge, argues something ineradicable in Southern culture," he thought. Moreover, he had his eye on Europe: "Croce . . . appears to have inspired a genuine and powerful revival of Italianism (in a most advanced aesthetic sense) among the younger genera-tion of Italians. Why can't we?" But before he could put his weight upon the Southern tradition, old ideas, long dormant, had to be jettisoned. The moral sloth of country communities was no longer to be condemned. By September 1927, he was admitting to Tate: "I have to acknowledge a personal bias: of late years (it was beginning during your latter days in Nashville) I have become somewhat soft and easy in my assessments of human nature; I am particularly taken, on the positive side, with the idea that provincial life is the best; this was my idea before Spengler reinforced me." His internationalism and endorsement of social compulsion were never entirely to vanish, but for the moment they became inconspicuous.[20]

In 1927, Ransom sent an article on the South to Tate as part of this debate. He apologetically called it "rather emulsified into pap for popular consumption." In due course, it went to the *Nation* where Carl Van Doren, John Wade's old mentor, rejected it with the observation that one editor didn't believe the South had ever had much of a culture, and all of them doubted its chances of survival. "There is bad abolitionist blood in the Nation personnel," Ransom, not entirely inaccurately, consoled himself. In 1928, it was published in the *Sewanee Review* as "The South—Old or New." A year later a second piece, "The South Defends Its Heritage," was to find wider circulation in *Harper's*. These two articles, contracted and welded together, were to form his essay for *I'll Take My Stand.*[21]

"Reconstructed but Unregenerate" is the fundamental document of the early formulation of Southern agrarianism. Its starting point was an assertion about the separate characters of European and American culture, in which Ransom was inclined to make England do service for the whole continent. England, he wrote, had a conservative culture, that is, she "did her pioneering an indefinite number of centuries ago, did it well enough, and has been living pretty tranquilly on her establishment ever since." But America was still adolescent, dreaming youthful materialistic dreams. The South, however, was an extension of Europe's conservative ways for she had had her pioneer days, and then settled back to enjoy herself: "The South took life easy, which is itself a tolerably comprehensive art." Whilst other American communities had done the same, it chanced that the South had been almost exclusively composed of such a society before the Civil War, and so became solid. It was not a great society, but it was "a way of life that had been considered and authorized" into a squirearchy, rather than an aristocracy. It had been inferior to Europe, but it had been young and might have matured.

The Civil War had destroyed the influence of Southern conservatism and released industrialism, "the latest form of pioneering and the worst." Poor, the South declined. Only now, Ransom thought, was the industrialization of the region a serious threat, and the farmer, too weak to resist, was the first victim. Progressives, trying to make farming a part of the industrial system, were bent upon breaking the agrarian's attachment to the soil. As the urban South had already capitulated, only the rural South offered a serious hope of resistance. There were, no doubt, several modes of resistance. The most familiar was the ancient cry of havoc against the carpetbagger. That was efficacious, but open to demagogic abuse. The most difficult, but statesmanlike, alternative was to fight through the ordinary political system. The South must unite with any or all agrarian and conservative elements in American society, especially the "very belligerent if somewhat uninformed Western agrarian party." Such a coalition might try to make the American world safe for farmers and render a convincing critique of the twin doctrines of progress and industrialism. The nineteenth-century experiment with industry should be rejected as a failure and the Democratic party, the traditional instrument of Southern politics, wooed to principles, "agrarian, conservative, anti-industrial."[22]

Such was Ransom's position. It was stated with grace, which helped to ease the reader over its uncertain sociology and worse history. In his haste to put together a social theory, Ransom had incorporated parts of New South mythology, while tinkering with its polarities. The perception of the South as peculiarly English had been transmitted from the "Cavalier" school of antebellum authors to the postwar years. It had been inaccurate before the war, for it had only been weakly relevant to Tidewater areas, only imitatively pertinent to the South settled after the eighteenth century, and never appropriate to nonplantation culture. But it had meshed conveniently with postwar Social Darwinism, used by Southerners against the horrors of the new immigration in Northern cities and pertinent to the defense of segregation. Its logic, though Ransom was indifferent to this, was racial. One was English, apparently, if one's forebears were once

English. Moreover, Ransom had absorbed the New South fascination with Europe, an assumption that the Old World was better. Whereas it had been the custom to try to bring South, North, and Europe into an equivalence, Ransom deleted the North and industrialism from the New South equation. This left him with the daring assertion that the South was the old Europe.

That his history was uncertain did not bother him unduly, for the essay was a conscious exercise in the manipulation of social myth.[23] And Ransom's tactics were sound when he used familiar pieces of mythology, but subtly transmuted them. It is striking how commonplace are its assertions: Europe is conservative, old, and superior; America is progressive, young, and inferior; the South is leisurely; the farmer is attached to the soil. Allen Tate once remarked to John Gould Fletcher upon this talent of Ransom's: the ability to make the ordinary seem unusual.[24]

Ransom's experience as a poet had accustomed him to a certain distance between image and belief. Indeed, his philosophical musings on the abandoned "The Third Moment" had elaborated the intellectual underpinnings of his 1930 position in *I'll Take My Stand,* but obliquely. "The Third Moment" had been what can only be described as an eccentric Hegelian dialectic, left with the dualist assumptions of Kant. There are, Ransom had told Tate in 1926, "three moments in the historical order of experience." The first was the original experience, "pure of all intellectual content, unreflective, concrete and singular." The second moment was the beginning of cognition, in which "the record must be taken of the first moment." Cognition leads to concepts, which divide into abstractions both unconscious and practical: "experience becomes History, conceptualized knowledge, in respect to a part, and Unconscious Knowledge, lost knowledge, in respect to the vast residue of the unconceptual." For Ransom, the scientific habit was associated with this second moment: its impulse was to rationalize understanding for the purposes of action. The third moment came with recognition that the second moment had been an inadequate awareness of experience. "All our concepts," Ransom had told Tate, "and all our histories put together cannot add up into the wholeness with which we started out." Philosophical synthesis, such as that practiced by Absolutists—by this, Ransom probably meant the severe Hegelians whom he might have encountered in Oxford—was not adequate to its recovery. Only one route was sufficient—imagery. And even that was not enough. "The Imagination is the faculty of Pure Memory, or unconscious mind; it brings out the original experiences from the dark storeroom, where we dwell upon them with a joy proportionate to our previous despair. And therefore, when we make images, we are regressive; we are trying to reconstitute an experience which we once had, only to handle and mutilate. Only, we cannot quite reconstitute them. Association is too strong for us; the habit of cognition is too strong. The images come out much mixed and adulterated with concepts." As Ransom saw it, there were various works of the third moment, which he presented in ascending order of consciousness: dreams, fancies, religion, morals, and art. And poetry was the highest form of art, in which the mixed nature of experience and cognition were held in a dualistic tension.[25]

This was a phenomenological position, something novel in the Southern mind. It had been implied in John Wade's irony, but Ransom had made it intellectually manifest. In this mood, he had published a study of one aspect of the third moment, his *God Without Thunder: An Unorthodox Defense of Orthodoxy,* in 1930. Here Ransom had tried to use his phenomenology to run the gauntlet between his religious instinct and the disintegrating philosophy of modernism of which he was as aware as any T. S. Eliot or Gertrude Stein. Pondering the scientific principles raised during the Scopes trial, Ransom tried to use the mythic reconstitution of religion to oppose its inadequate rendering of reality. He was driven to defend a fundamentalist position and rally to the old thundering God of the Israelites, because he felt science had taken the very premise of "wholeness," God, and tried to distort it to a pale and practical concept.[26]

There is some evidence that he cared more deeply for this theology than he cared to admit. He told Tate in 1930 that his main interests were "literary and religious matters, which ultimately are about the only interests I have." He was to be unexpectedly angry when *God Without Thunder* was criticized for showing how far his intellectualism was from the earthy religion of the Tennessee hills. Friends in Nashville were surprised to see passion in this diffident man. One noted: "I've a notion he [the reviewer] proved by the degree of fury that he aroused in Ransom that the book was more sincerely an expression of fundamental religious belief than any of us realized."[27]

It is testimony to how much Ransom's irony was assumed by those about him that they were surprised at an unreserved commitment. And passion in John Ransom during 1930 was noticeable. When it was proposed that the Agrarians found and run a country newspaper, Ransom was its most energetic proponent. When there was a dispute over the symposium's title, he sided with Donald Davidson for a "Southern" emphasis to the book.[28]

This reversed the usual line of cleavage within the group. One source of this passion is to be found in Ransom's position as a university teacher. He had concluded that teaching was a dead end. For a man of forty-two, whose life had been spent in the university, that was an unsettling insight. Vanderbilt University had begun to move away from the classical curriculum towards a more "progressive" education. Ransom confessed in January 1930 that he was "very discouraged about the good of academic employment, on the ground stated in my Article 9—the one that is most personal of them all to myself." If one turns to the ninth item in Ransom's draft statement of principles for *I'll Take My Stand,* one finds this: "The trouble with our life patterns is to be located at its economic base, and we cannot rebuild it by pouring in soft materials from the top. The young men and women in colleges...cannot make more than an inconsequential acquaintance with the arts and humanities transmitted to them from the happier periods.... Industrial technique is the things [*sic*] that can be admirably communicated to the students of the colleges. The effort to communicate the so-called 'cultures' is mostly a vanity."[29]

True to this, Ransom's concurrent involvement in the humanist controversy centered on the charge that Babbitt's humanists were "an Association of Schoolmasters, trying rather helplessly by an academic discipline to communicate to the younger generation a schoolmaster's taste." "It is pitiable," Ransom said, "to reflect upon the petulance of us, the embittered schoolmasters, trying to instruct them by the examples of a day that is gone. As Mr. Tate wrote to me recently: 'Teaching is obviously a lost cause.'"[30]

Life for John Ransom in 1930 was very out of joint. He was not writing poetry. He had abandoned his study of philosophy. The activity which absorbed most of his energy, teaching, seemed futile. In his early forties, he had reached a crossroads, an intellectual menopause. And, if one looks at his language in *I'll Take My Stand,* it is striking how much it revolved around age. America was "adolescent," the exponents of progressivism were "immature." The South and Europe were "adult." It was the same language he had developed for his aesthetic theory: poetry was the exercise of an adult mind.

His argument about the South had three major dimensions: historical, philosophical, and economic. He knew no history, and was not inclined to pursue that aspect. The philosophical had been handled obliquely in other writings, albeit unpublished. He knew as little economics as he did history, but he made the brave decision to follow that where it took him. For the problem of education seemed to revolve around economics, in that the university was being forced to adjust to the ways of industry. As long as the necessity of industrialization was unchallenged, nothing would check the drift from a humanist education. English teachers, Ransom had observed, "must become teachers of economics.... I do not mean the technique of modern industry and commerce, but something much more radical and philosophical.... [teachers] have to propose a sensible way of life as a substitute for the industrial. Perhaps they will even feel obliged to live it, and that may be the occasion of some personal embarrassment."[31]

One might justly enquire why he picked on an agrarian society as that most conducive to the humanities. Part of the reason lay in his starting point, poetry. Ransom had lain within the tradition of the English pastoral, and his own verse had been richly informed with a pastoral vision. But it was literary, not practical, for he had never been a farmer. He was not even the son of a farmer. In Andrew Lytle's phrase, "he had a garden."[32]

Much of his attempt to produce a volume of agrarian economics was done on a Guggenheim fellowship in England during 1931-32. This was a pleasant relief for Ransom. His cottage in Devon was congenial. He taught a little, not too much, at the nearby university in Exeter and met old friends from Oxford. Christopher Dawson, the Roman Catholic medieval historian, lived down the road and gave encouragement to Ransom's religious views. But his daily copy of *The Times* gave him alarming news of the Depression in the United States. "Seems to me," he wrote to Donald Davidson ". . . that the 3rd of the Hoover Christmases in America is not going to be a great popular success. Or are the English papers just jibing when they report the Depression in such evil colors?"[33] This put his book under stress. It had been begun after the Wall Street Crash, but its inspiration had been the headlong prosperity of the 1920s, not industry's failure in the 1930s. Economic events were moving very quickly, and it was difficult to keep pace.

He wrote his book, but with diffidence. By October of 1932, back in Tennessee, he confessed that his "poor book is nearly a total loss—I don't like it. It would have been a passable book published a year ago. Several publishers nearly took it. Within these next ten days, I will have kicked it into the incinerator or else taken a grand new start."[34] The fire was to claim it, but one can pick out its lines from various articles, published by Ransom in the early 1930s. In *Harper's* during 1932, he hazarded "Land! An Answer to the Unemployment Problem." In it, he tried to adjust his defense of agrarianism to the new constraints of the Depression. A return to the land was both necessary and desirable, Ransom suggested. The farm had been a traditional refuge for those dispossessed by the vagaries of industrialism, and it should be again. The difficulty, as he saw it, was the involvement of farming itself in the commercial economy. Therefore it was necessary to reestablish self-sufficiency as the economy of the American farm, thus saving the present agricultural population and putting people back on the land. In a second piece, "Happy Farmers," published in the *American Review* during 1933, he made more play with the inherent Jeffersonian virtues of the agrarian life. But he added the assertion that the First World War, by transforming America's foreign debt situation, had made it easier for her to repudiate an expanding economy. Self-sufficiency was easier if the country did not need to export. To this end, the government should encourage the farmer's independence by levying taxes on commercial fertilizers and tractors, by reducing land taxes and increasing the income tax, by introducing a graduated system of taxation that might penalize the large producer, and by having agricultural colleges that disseminated the arts of self-sufficiency rather than the techniques of commercial farming.[35]

For the moment, Ransom was very interested in practicality, as two 1933 articles attest. The first, "A Capital for the New Deal," was the result of a chance conversation with a Nashville friend on the welter of proposals brought forth by the New Deal. This friend had his own idea. Why not stimulate the economy with a huge public works program? Why not get the federal government to build an immense new capital city on the banks of the Mississippi, far away from the Eastern seaboard in the heartland of America? Ransom was taken with the notion, and went imprudently into print with it. A city more modern, larger, more beautiful than any other should be erected. It might house 15 million people, with museums, theatres, libraries, and a national university "to which collegians from all over the nation, according to some principle, are to win their admission by competition; and in which they are not to be instructed in the technique of business ...but...in the more timeless, and less utilitarian branches of art and science, in order that our citizens, like the European citizens of a few centuries ago, may have within them the dignity of citizenship and the matter of culture." It was, in short, to be an enormous Welwyn Garden City, with Oxford transplanted to its midst.[36]

In the same year, Ransom had another idea. He had been following in England the controversy over the unpaid debts of the First World War. Correctly he judged that there was little hope of payment. Instead of cancelling the debts outright, he suggested turning war credits into a fund for higher education, from which Americans might be sent to Europe to receive a university education. If Hannibal, Missouri, could not be transformed into Oxford, then perhaps Oxford itself was the next best thing.[37]

Unlike the first, this second notion was not monstrously unsound. It was to be another Southerner and Rhodes scholar, J. William Fulbright, who was to mimic Ransom's idea to clear up the war debts legacy of a later European war. But Ransom had an alarming tendency—alarming for some of his Agrarian friends—to be eclectic and inconsistent. An agrarian who proclaimed in one place the evils of the city and the virtues of a yeoman existence looked curious when he popped up elsewhere to suggest a megalopolis. Economics and aesthetics conjoined uneasily. His allies looked askance at him, especially when in contradiction of all Southern tradition, he recommended a high tariff and proclaimed, in the pages of *The Times* itself, that he was a very Republican on the issue. Tate wrote to Warren: "if what you say is true about the tariff maybe he [Ransom] isn't an agrarian: or maybe he is, and all the rest of us are merely heroes." And Frank Owsley, as Warren reported, was not "by God, going to be convinced by anybody that a high tariff is anything but the work of the adversary."[38]

Part of Ransom's problem was a confusion of frameworks. He had made the equation in 1930 between the South and agrarianism. Certain notions about the South—its conservatism, its religion, its continuity with England

—were matched to more general social beliefs in the value of rural life. But the two were only synonymous as long as he could sustain the vital connection by stressing that the South was composed exclusively of such agrarian communities. Moreover, he had inched away from his aesthetic image of the country gentlemen, under the pressure of the Depression, towards the more rudimentary concept of self-sufficiency. The history of the South put constraints upon Ransom's speculative freedom that mere agrarianism did not. An agrarian might approve a high tariff, at a pinch. A Southerner had more difficulty.

For the three years after 1930, Ransom had absorbed himself in the agrarian side of his Southern/agrarian equation. By this, the Southern side had grown unstable in his mind. For one thing, the experience of living abroad had diminished his sectional consciousness by renewing his awareness of the whole United States. "In England last year," he told Tate, "I got so used to defending America that I forgot there were two or half a dozen Americas: I'm trying to see if we can't save the whole business." And he observed to a skeptical Davidson: "The value of my year abroad was to cleanse my mind of the *idola* of restricted intercourse and take a new start."[39]

This distancing effect was enlarged by spending a summer within the United States but outside the South. In 1933, he took his family to New Mexico and went, like all tourists, to look at a few American Indians. He was deeply impressed by the simplicity of their life. But so profound was the confusion in his mind between where his agrarianism stopped and his regionalism started that he began to refer to the Pueblo Indians as "regionalists." Upon his return, he went down to Baton Rouge to talk to the Graduates Club of Louisiana State University and took the opportunity to refine his doctrine of regionalism.

He began by inquiring how a regionalism came to exist. Its root was a physical area. In the pioneering stage of development, the economic motive predominated, but, in time, patterns "meant for efficiency...survive for enjoyment." As with the Navajos, necessity became art. This was true of regionalisms both in Europe and the United States. Insofar as regionalism was the growth of many generations, Europe was superior to America. But the disparity was diminished, because "what we have in this country...is not so much a regionalism *de novo* as a transplanted regionalism. The Fathers of the Republic were not savages.... They were European regionalists." Thus the differentiation between American regions was not just the response to local physical conditions, but equally an accretion from varying settlement patterns.

This was the case for the South. But there was a difficulty, as Ransom had now begun to realize. In recent years the wide diversity of the South had become apparent to him, and he had been reminded of it on his trip south from Nashville to Louisiana. He had been "startled equally by the distinctness and by the unassimilatedness of the regions entered and crossed, finally marvelling at the power of that interregional but sympathetic symbol, the South." This was puzzling, and Ransom resolved it in a traditional manner. Slavery had separated the South from the rest of the nation, but more than that it had gathered up the different parts of the South itself. Slavery, he said, had given "a spiritual continuity to its many regions, and strengthened them under the reinforcement of 'sectionalism,' which is regionalism on a somewhat extended scale." Ransom, in other words, despite an indifference to the race issue, had argued himself around to the position of Ulrich Phillips. "The darkey," he said, "is one of the bonds that make a South out of all the Southern regions. Another is the climate."[40]

This was unsettling to the comfortable equation between agrarianism and the South, the notion of a unitary South, that Ransom had asserted in 1930. But his difficulties were growing piecemeal. For at the same time he was writing on Southern literature with the dogmatism of 1930. He was keen, however, to take aspects of the Southern tradition with a pinch of salt. When a new biographer of Sidney Lanier claimed that the nineteenth-century poet was a forerunner of the Agrarians themselves, Ransom was moved to issue a rejoinder. "It fits in with something I've wanted to do," he explained to Tate, "dissociate myself from certain aspects of Southernism by defining those which I believe in." Much of the resulting essay was an onslaught on Lanier: his sentimental poetry, nationalism, deficient understanding of the ways of industrialism, weak personality, feeble emphasis on the capacity of love to heal the wounds of the Civil War, and unwise rapture for the potential of science. But Ransom's root objection to Lanier was the latter's insensitivity to the contemporary needs of the South during Reconstruction. "The plainest duty of the South happened to be the one which was humanly the easiest," Ransom insisted, "to offer contumacious resistance." If the artist must be political, it was as well that he chose the right politics. For if industry undercut the artist's position, the artist had no business to encourage industry.[41]

This was severe. If his earlier essay on regionalism had betrayed difficulties in his relationship to the South, this demonstrated continuity. But it was a slight shift, from the wider arena of economics and politics to the narrower focus of literature. It was an argument from the artist to society, not the society to the artist. And, indeed, this was Ransom's mood. An important element in forcing a breach with the South and agrarianism was his growing resignation towards both teaching and the loss of his poetic creativity. When John Gould Fletcher protested to him in 1934 that the Agrarians were having no practical influence, Ransom was sanguine. He stressed that they were being read, that "we are probably doing about as much writing and talking as our time and abilities permit." In 1930, he had been deeply worried that mere publication was futile. Now he was content to observe: "As for myself, I am primarily a teacher of literature, therefore a professional man, and you must not judge me as an independent like Tate and yourself. That is to say, I have a profession not only by economic necessity but by choice, and I do not propose to quit it. My writing, whether on the subject of Agrarianism or sometimes something more creative, comes second, and will continue to come second." Ransom's jitters at the menopause had settled down. His need for the South started to die with them.[42]

In 1935, an invitation to write for the tenth anniversary issue of the *Virginia Quarterly Review* allowed him to reconsider his views on Southern literature. It exposed how tenuous his position had become, when he addressed the problem of modernism in the South and tried to arrive at a satisfactory definition of "Southern" as it applied to literature.

After the manner of Joseph Krutch's popular study, *The Modern Temper,* Ransom took modernism to be "skepticism and disillusionment...[which] ends in despair. We come to such a degree of self-consciousness that we question our natural motives of action and our inherited patterns of thought...we commit a spiritual suicide." Such modernism had gained ground in the South, Ransom acknowledged, but the pace of its advance had been slow. Those who opposed it had preferred "to go down under standards which, if tattered and disreputable, may still be technically said to fly."

Just as he had moved to see the South as an "interregional but sympathetic symbol" rather than the immediate outgrowth of physical area, so Ransom dismissed the aesthetic validity of "local color" writers like DuBose Heyward and Julia Peterkin of Charleston. Even more radically, he denied them the title of "Southern." As he insisted, "a Southern literature...will never be constituted by a local color, for its essence is a spirit." Neither could the extreme literary modernism of stream-of-consciousness writing be accorded a place in Southern literature. The resistant irony of Ellen Glasgow or James Branch Cabell exemplified the modern Southern way more precisely: to note the philosophy of modernism and to spurn it.

The reader might wonder what axiom could exclude Charleston from the South. It was this: "A writer may evidently have the juridical status of a Southerner without having the temper of one; for the South cannot now be construed, under the legend, as a unified, powerful, ubiquitous spirit who imposes one habit of mind upon all her children...some writers must impress us as having Southern quality, or something like it, who are not physically of the South." Having thus detached the spirit of antimodern localism from place itself, Ransom was able to suggest that the younger Henry James, Edith Wharton, or Willa Cather might qualify for their insistence upon the value of formal societies. But Hemingway, "the inclusive realism, which aims at volume in the objective detail," T. S. Stribling, for his militant liberalism, Erskine Caldwell, and his "proletarian fiction," lay beyond the bounds. As for "juridical" Southerners, Stark Young, Caroline Gordon, and Elizabeth Madox Robers were within them.[43]

This was curious, but it had a perverse logic. Later in his life, Ransom was to use a similarly odd argument to argue that John Donne was a better sonneteer than William Shakespeare. As Donald Davidson was to observe of this later aberration of dialectic: "He is always building his argument on too narrow a base—he looks at details & forgets other things.... What I say applies...to John only when he is on one of his tremendous excursions that end, almost, in fantasy, for all their logical brilliance."[44]

In such conundrums, John Ransom began to lose his hold upon the Southern tradition. Gradually his allegiance to Southern Agrarianism tapered away. His energies were shifted to more purely aesthetic matters, as he began to marshal the critical arguments that formed *The World's Body* in 1938.[45] His involvement in Tate's symposium, *Who Owns America?* was incidental and apologetic. His contribution, "What Does the South Want?" showed little desire either to stick to a firm definition of the South or to speak for the South's ambitions. To the question "which is the real South?" he refused in 1936 to put up an answer. "So various," he wrote, "are the attitudes taken by Southerners toward Southern history, so various the views held about Southern policy, and so uncertain the future. The unitary South has passed." He was willing to make his old recommendations about the virtues of agrarianism, but even they were tempered by a rapprochement with industrialism. Elsewhere old calls for Southern-Western congressional alliance were issued, but he prefaced them with phrases like "If I try, I can imagine legislatures and Congresses for years to come whittling away at that special instrument of big business, the corporation." But he really didn't want to try any more. When he sent the text of this essay to the *Virginia Quarterly Review* to be republished, he remarked to Lambert Davis: "I feel the thing was all right in substance, without a bit of literary quality to it. I have sworn not to commit myself to any other print in the field of economics, but to stick to my trade henceforth. My ideas are too limited, and I have been repeating myself."[46]

Aesthetics had taken him into the debate about the South, and aesthetics were to take him out. In 1927, he had hoped that society and politics might serve as a moral sounding board which might enrich his sensibility. It was obvious, however, that whatever agrarianism may have done, it had not succeeded in reviving or improving his poetry. And he still wanted to write it. In February 1935, he confessed to Warren: "I yearn to settle down in peace and see if I can poetize again." Society, unfortunately, had proved resistant to being used for poetry's ends.[47]

Ransom had published in September 1936 a review of Tate's new book,

The Mediterranean and Other Poems. In an emotional letter, he turned to Tate to explain the new direction of his thoughts: "I say there in one place that *patriotism* is eating at *lyricism.* What is true in part for you (though a part that is ominously increasing) is true nearly in full for me: *patriotism* has nearly eaten me up, and I've got to get out of it." To this end, he proposed a new departure "to counteract the Agrarian-Distributist Movement in our minds." An American Academy of Letters should be established to embody "an objective literary standard." He had mused about a Southern academy, but feared that it was too close to the ideological perils from which he was fleeing. Such an American academy might be catholic in its membership, and Ransom offered a tentative list of names—of Southerners: Cabell, William Dodd, Fletcher, Douglas Southall Freeman, Ellen Glasgow, Tate, Wade, and Stark Young; of non-Southerners: Willa Cather, Theodore Dreiser, Robert Frost, Sinclair Lewis, Ezra Pound, George Santayana, and a few others. Its purpose was to fight two main literary ineptitudes: "(1) the kind of writing which is merely specialized and lacks implications and background; (2) the ostensible pure art which is hired out to causes . . . . Our intentions would be two, and they would look contradictory: to have our literature created by persons of philosophical capacity; to have its pure forms without taint of explicit philosophy."[48]

Thus, after ten years, John Ransom abandoned his flirtation with a social theory of literature and turned exclusively to the internal dialogue of the New Criticism. It seems that he wrote a recantation of Southern Agrarianism for the *American Review,* but it was never published. "Perhaps this one had better never been written," he wrote, "because it will seem to Don like treason and unfriendship. It's been on my conscience a long time." In the event, it was to be 1945 before Ransom formerly issued a *mea culpa.* He sent the relevant copy of the *Kenyon Review* pointedly to Davidson. Yet the younger man had seen the movement of Ransom's thought at the time. He understood that Ransom was given to these sudden lurches. In 1937, Davidson had reminded Tate that "in the 20-odd years that I have known John, I've seen him break out many a new sail—and flag." Ransom's controversial departure from Vanderbilt in 1937 was not without a measure of relief for both men.[49]

The political opinions of the young Ransom began to reemerge. Again he became an unexceptional American liberal, smiling upon the necessity of industrialization while regarding with distaste some of its manifestations. His internationalism had never entirely died out. But now a sense of place evaporated from his writing, as though it had never been, and the South with it. The region became the indistinct object of sentiment it had been for him at Oxford. He missed it mildly and toyed with joining Tate when the latter was teaching in North Carolina. Ransom admitted that "Greensboro is South . . . and it's three times as comfortable in the South, for a Southerner."

But Tate himself was to give the most damning comment on Ransom, the Southern Agrarian, in a letter to Andrew Lytle in 1939: "Of course, John is never bothered by environments."[50]

By his own admission, John Ransom's attempt at a social theory of literature was not a success. His need for the South had been genuine and, briefly, intense. But it was short-lived; only four years from his first publication of an essay on the South to the year in England that started his reversal, only eleven years from the Scopes trial to his scheme for an American academy. In a life of eighty-six years, it was a brief episode. It lasted about as long as his active span as a poet and should properly be seen as its curious postscript. One is not surprised to learn that when historians went to Ohio in John Ransom's last years they found him disinclined to talk about agrarianism and the South. He was interested, in his dotage, only in his poetry.

seven:
Allen Tate: "The Punctilious Abyss"

At first glance, the early career of Allen Tate seems to conform to the legend of literature in the American 1920s: the flight from a tedious provincial society to New York, hard times and book reviewing for the metropolitan journals, late nights of discussion, journeys to Paris, retreats to the countryside around New York. There is a photograph of Tate taken in the 1930s. The high domed brow, the small moustache, the frown, the casual cigarette just lit, might almost be a caricature of the bright young author. Only the suit and tie, the pocket handkerchief not too neatly folded, suggest an unwonted formality. One is not surprised to learn that some of Malcolm Cowley's *Exile's Return* was written in Tennessee, on a visit to Tate.[1]

Such jauntings in New York and Paris set Tate aside from the experiences of his fellow Agrarians. It was not that Davidson, Wade, Ransom, or Owsley had not been out of the South, but they had never been so involved in the intellectual implications of such travel. Moreover, they were provincial figures. They had little to do with New York, and it had less to do with them. Tate, however, was between two cultures: he was provincial and metropolitan. This was to have echoes in his conception of the South.

He had been the self-conscious modern among the Fugitive poets, coming to Baudelaire through the critical writing of Arthur Symons and ending with the "demi-god T. S. Eliot," of whose virtues he attempted to persuade his reluctant elders. It was Tate who trotted around the Vanderbilt campus as an undergraduate with the *American Mercury* under his arm and championed the brash new poetry magazine, *Secession,* to Davidson with the words: "I can see the back of your neck bristling now. In many ways I feel the same way, checked only by an opposite tendency to sympathize with almost anything revolutionary, sensible or not, and at the same time to derogate conservatism of all kinds." And true to this, his views about the South upon his graduation in 1923 were not dissimilar from Mencken's. One finds him speaking of the "damnably barbaric Southern mind." But he didn't seem to care much for the region: the topic occupies a miniscule proportion of his collected correspondence with Donald Davidson in the years before 1927.[2]

He went to New York in 1924, at the age of twenty-five, when it seemed the natural course for a young man of great ambition. Settling there with some ease, he found a hack editorial post to keep him alive, picked up some reviewing jobs, made friends with the likes of Hart Crane, Malcolm Cowley, and Kenneth Burke. "I didn't come to New York to conquer it," he told Davidson in 1924, "merely to live as a civilized being in a place where it isn't important whether you drink liquor or are a virgin, and to see

136

a few congenial people when I care to; and thus to concentrate my energies on my own work." It was fun to dine alone in cheap Italian restaurants, to go to the theatre, to ride the subway, to meet an actress who graciously told one that she was a lesbian and no one was bothered by it. In the flush of enthusiasm, he seemed to be putting his provincial Fugitive days behind him. Davidson was urged to give up on Nashville and come north to teach at Columbia University. Almost in obituary, he wrote to Davidson: "I can never forget you all. But really I shall never return to Nashville; so you must come up here when you can."[3]

That his lot seemed cast with cosmopolitanism was confirmed by an esay on Southern literature for the *Nation* in 1925. From its title, "Last Days of the Charming Lady," to its theme, it rehearsed the typical act of intellectual dissociation from the Romantic tradition of Southern literature. Little in Southern culture, Tate suggested, whether old or new, was of any use to the contemporary author. There had been no conditions for a literature before the Civil War, and the Old South had transmitted to the New South "no tradition of ideas, no consciousness of moral and spiritual values." Without any critical awareness, no Matthew Arnold, no groundwork had been laid to produce a Henry James. Indeed, the task had to wait long for an outsider in the shape of Mencken, to do it. Indigenous critics of the New South, like Edwin Mims, had been handicapped by "unrealized moral and social values" which prevented them from detecting the errors of the "local color" school. They had blundered into the "ingenuous opinion that a particular setting is intrinsically more 'poetic' than another." Thus, unlike the New Englander, the young Southern author could find nothing in his native tradition. In this, however, lay a small grain of hope. For the Southern writer "may be capable, through an empiricism which is his only alternative to intellectual suicide, of a cosmopolitan culture to which his contemporary in the East is emotionally barred." It was the burden of the Southerner to realize himself through the eyes of others: "he of all Americans is privy to the emotions founded in the state of knowing oneself to be a foreigner at home." The Southerner, having no culture, might be free.[4]

The month of May 1925 saw the completion of this severe essay. It also saw Tate trying to get the *Nation* to send him to cover the Dayton trial. It seems unlikely that he would have cheered either Clarence Darrow or Bryan, but the trial did stimulate him to ponder Ransom's concern, the problem of science and religion. By the spring of 1926, he was planning an essay on fundamentalism. Like Ransom, he had become convinced that "science has very little to say for itself." Science might be an admirable system of classifying the fabric of reality, but it could bring no judgment upon ethics. Only philosophy could bear such a responsibility. However, it seemed to Tate that the errors and presumption of science did not, ipso facto, demonstrate the virtue of the Church. "Those who attack science from the rightness of the Church aren't likely to shake it; they should attack science from principle, philosophically. This is my thesis," he told Davidson. By 1926, Tate had decided that he disapproved of science, but not yet resolved that he approved of religion.[5]

Indeed, his reaction to that other spin-off of the Dayton trial, Edwin Mims's *The Advancing South,* showed that he placed a low value on moral judgments. Mims was accused of refusing to acknowledge that a society was judged, not for producing a liberal culture, but for fostering "first class minds, liberal or illiberal." But Tate had changed his mind on the function of criticism. In 1925, he had suggested that the Old South had had no Henry James because it had been insufficiently self-critical. Now he insisted that literature preceded criticism: "It is the literature itself that creates the state of mind for its acceptance."[6]

Tate had maintained his interest in T. S. Eliot at a time when Eliot was moving from the bleak existentialism of *The Waste Land* towards Anglo-Catholicism and social conservatism. For Tate had shared Eliot's instinctive diagnosis of a disordered time. In the April 1924 issue of *The Fugitive,* Tate had pronounced: "An individualistic intellectualism is the mood of our age. There is no common-to-all truth; poetry has no longer back of it, ready for use momently, a harmonious firmament of stage-properties and sentiments which it was the pious office of the poets to set up at the dictation of a mysterious *afflatus*—Heaven, Hell, Duty, Olympus, Immortality, as the providential array of 'themes': the Modern poet of this generation has had no experience of these things, he has seen nothing even vaguely resembling them."

In 1921, Eliot had announced a singular doctrine, the notion of a "dissociation of sensibility" in modern times. Eliot's essay on "The Metaphysical Poets" had argued that there had been, in Elizabethan and early Jacobean dramatic verse, "a degree of development of sensibility" that had evaporated by the time of Tennyson and Browning. "The difference," Eliot had contended, "is not a simple difference of degree between poets. It is something which had happened to the mind of England between the time of Donne or Lord Herbert of Cherbury and the time of Tennyson and Browning; it is the difference between the intellectual poet and the reflective poet. Tennyson and Browning are poets, and they think; but they do not feel their thought as immediately as the odour of a rose. A thought to Donne was an experience; it modified his sensibility. When a poet's mind is perfectly equipped for its work, it is constantly amalgamating disparate experience; the ordinary man's experience is chaotic, irregular, fragmentary. . . . We may express the difference by the following theory: The poets of the seventeenth century, the successors of the dramatists of the sixteenth, possessed a mechanism of sensibility which could devour any kind of experience. . . . In the seventeenth century a dissociation of sensibility set in, from which we have never recovered."[7]

That Tate subscribed to this doctrine is clear from his review of Eliot's *Poems: 1909-1925.* "Mr. Eliot's poetry," Tate commented, "has attempted with considerable success to bring back the total sensibility as a constantly available material, deeper and richer in connotations than any substance yielded by the main course of English poetry since the seventeenth century." And he diagnosed and approved the movement in Eliot towards an attempt to impose order on the chaos, "the anarchy which he has subsequently rationalized."[8]

Accepting such a doctrine, Tate was more concerned in 1926 with pondering the dissociation than evading it. In this mood, he wrote his "Ode to the Confederate Dead." That it was woven around a Southern theme was not too important to him. He was writing about himself, not the Civil War. Davidson pointed this out: "The Confederate dead become a peg on which you hang an argument whose lines, however sonorous and beautiful in a strict proud way, leave me wondering why you wrote a poem on that subject at all. . . . Your *Elegy* is not for the Confederate dead, but for your own dead emotion. . . . Where, O Allen Tate, are the dead?" Tate's answer was succinct. "Was Keats's Nightingale Ode *about* Nightingales?"[9]

But the poem had an unexpected consequence. The ode had contained the lines:

> Turn your eyes into the immoderate past,
> Find there the inscrutable infantry rising,
> The demons out of the earth—they will not last.
> Stonewall, Stonewall, and the sunken fields of hemp,
> Shiloh, Antietam, Malvern Hill, Bull Run . . .

As later Tate recalled to Davidson: "That passage came out of God-knows-where (as most poems do); and after it was on paper it served to bring up a whole stream of associations and memories, suppressed, at least on the emotional plane, since my childhood." For there had been much in Tate's childhood to merit suppression. In his own words, "since the Civil War my family has scattered to the four winds, and no longer exists as a social unit." His father had been an incompetent businessman, migrating around the region in search of economic stability and once involved in a mild scandal that enforced his resignation from a gentleman's club. His mother was a strong figure, but neurotic and unhappy under the strain. So Tate's early education had been haphazard and unsettled. In an appropriately ironic comment on the legend of the Southerner rooted in "place," he did not know accurately until he was thirty where he was born. His mother, a Virginian nostalgic for the old days, let him believe that he was a Virginian. In fact, he came from Kentucky.[10] Thus Tate's emphasis upon the lack of a usable tradition for Southerners in 1925 had been mostly a comment upon his unstable background. New York was a way of cutting himself off. But New York, his marriage to Caroline Gordon, the birth of a daughter, the recognition by both New York critical circles and even Eliot himself, was a steadying influence. He was never to be settled, but he had managed some kind of equilibrium. With this, he could begin to come to terms with his own past and, as part of its baggage, the South.

Intermittently he started to read Southern history. Barely two weeks after Davidson had commented on his ode, Tate was writing: "I've attacked the South for the last time, except in so far as it may be necessary to point out that the chief defect the Old South had was that in it which produced, through whatever cause, the New South." And he tied the South to his new sympathy for Eliot's social conservatism and the issue of "right values." In these same months, he was corresponding with Ransom over the problem of values in poetry and toying with the idea of a symposium on Southern literature. In March 1927 he wrote to Andrew Lytle: "Interesting things are, I believe, at last stirring in the South, and in that part of the South which we cannot help taking about with us forever, wherever we may go." In May, he was asking the editor of the *Virginia Quarterly Review* to put him in the list of contributors as "Allen Tate (1899-)...a Southern poet and essayist living in New York." At the end of April, he had signed a contract with Minton, Balch, and Company to write a biography of Stonewall Jackson and had a cash advance in his needy hand.[11]

It would be idle to deny the impulse that financial expediency gave to the new interest. That royalty advance was enticing. Biographies were, in his own words, "commercial magic." Malcolm Cowley was to recall: "About that time it became possible for young men of promise to support themselves by writing novels and biographies. The book trade was prospering, new publishers were competing for new authors, and suddenly it seemed that everybody you knew was living on publishers' advances." Minton, Balch were very much in the hunt for authors, especially for their popular "American Biographies" series, and it was convenient for Tate that interest coincided with profit. As he remarked to Davidson: "I must make my pleasures pay."[12]

While he was beginning the hectic research for the book, Vernon Parrington's *Main Currents in American Thought* was published. His reaction, contrasted to his feeling about Mims's *The Advancing South,* showed how much he was groping for a moral standpoint. Parrington "lacks any real values," he told John Gould Fletcher. "It is a very enlightened Liberalism—as enlightened as any Liberalism can ever be. I can't understand contemporary Liberalism at all; although I can sympathize with Liberalism in Jefferson's day; then it was only a differentiation within a single attitude, which kept the balance exact. But I think that Jefferson would be something like a conservative today; I say 'something like' because the agrarian parties are today so conservative that they are radical." While Parrington encouraged a sectional approach to the American mind, Tate was resistant. As he wrote to Davidson, on the same day: "Our best cause is not of our place and time."[13]

Writing about the Civil War and Jackson seemed to reconcile Tate to his family history. He went to Virginia on a tour of the battlefields in the summer of 1927. He visited Manassas, "a romantic spot to me since childhood. My grandfather fought there; and my great-grandfather was four miles away, on his farm, an old man, listening to the roar of the battle." In Woodstock, he called upon an old lady cousin, poor but proud of a family home built in 1794. In every town, he seemed to find those who remembered the war. The Civil War past was palpable, when one could walk into a field near Port Republic, kick up some dirt, and find a squashed minié ball. Along the Shenandoah Valley, it was still easy to follow the marks of Jackson's trail. All this renewed a bond with his family's past, the stability beyond the fragility of the last generation, as well as with his own. In his childhood, his mother used to take him to the ruins of "Pleasant Hill" in Fairfax County and make him ponder the stones and gaunt chimneys of a family estate, burnt in the Union march to Manassas in 1861.[14]

The war came to fascinate him, and he tended to pour into its brief span almost the entire burden of Southern history. But he was ever the pessimist, the detached figure at the gate of the Confederate cemetery. He had no faith that enough of the old tradition survived for him to live off. Thus he agreed with Fletcher: "You are right; the battle was lost long before we enlisted for the war. The stupidity of our people turns me in rage against them, and I wheel in greater rage against their enemies. In this state of mind it is hard to be coherent." He was irritated with critics like Van Wyck Brooks and Lewis Mumford, who seemed to imagine that America was a land east of the Hudson River. Yet he had little confidence that the Southern people might be wooed back from liberal values and the New South.[15]

While Tate was writing the *Stonewall Jackson,* Fletcher had sent from England a volume by a young English Catholic, Christopher Hollis. *The American Heresy* was a curious mélange of American history, seen from the standpoint of an Etonian, Oxonian, Roman Catholic, polemically talented Englishman. It started from the premise "here is a Continent gone wrong"—a familiar premise in the Oxford Union—and attempted to explain why, in four essays on Jefferson, Calhoun, Lincoln, and Woodrow Wilson. The thesis was that "there went into the Civil War two politically minded nations. There emerged from it, or rather from the period of Reconstruction, one nonpolitically minded nation, content, and even anxious, to allow the rich to order its life to the smallest detail." For Hollis, Calhoun was the unsung hero of American history. Jefferson was amiable and intelligent, but pagan; Lincoln was tragic, a noble warrior for the wrong causes; Wilson was a misguided academic, servile to industrialism and ignorant of Europe's needs. Calhoun alone had stood against the rising spirit of capitalism. As Hollis put it: "A people, he [Calhoun] thought, must live upon its traditions or perish, and industrial capitalism, whose very advertisement was that it was daily changing men's material condition of life, was the enemy."[16]

This impressed Tate. "The value I set upon this book...is perhaps, at the moment, beyond reason," he told Fletcher. "...I have had an idea for my Jackson that Hollis gives me the courage to use, in giving me further intellectual conviction of its truth. (I have long had the emotional conviction.)" This idea was to see the North as the revolutionary aggressor and the South as the conservative status quo. By his own admission, however, *The American Heresy* left a good deal to be desired: it was "incomplete and inaccurately documented." But still Tate flattered the book as "the first effort to comprehend the supposedly mixed forces of American history under a single idea."[17]

This volume had a double significance for Tate. Its standpoint was religious, and Tate was moving away from his atheism. At the end of 1928, he described himself as "an enforced atheist, who differs from an agnostic in that the atheist is willing to be convinced." Hollis had damned the United States partly because it had "heretically" deduced its political philosophy from secular ideas, and not religious dogma. Moreover, Hollis was a European. Although Tate was never an Anglophile, his adverse judgment on American civilization inevitably involved a certain appraisal of European culture. It was not that he wanted to become a European, like T. S. Eliot. As Tate remarked to the expatriate Fletcher, "I will always believe that one's nationality is never eradicated, and it's suicide to try to eradicate it." Rather, he wished to run the South as a culture parallel to the mature civilizations of Europe.[18]

As soon as the *Stonewall Jackson* was finished in early 1928, Tate began a biography of Jefferson Davis during the war years. Both books were haunted by the feeling that the South could have won the war. Tate took satisfaction in dwelling upon the incidents that, if reversed, might have produced an independent South: the dilatory defensiveness of Davis in 1861, the failure of Longstreet to attack at Gettysburg until late in the day, the inability of Davis to see the importance of the Western theatre of war, the death of Jackson. The sighs in the prose were audible. As he put in the *Jefferson Davis:* "In spite of the mistakes of leaders, of the dissension among the people, of the lack of grand strategy in the field, the Confederacy came within a hair of success; its entire history is a mosaic of tremendous *ifs. If* any one set of unfavorable circumstances had been warded off, the South would doubtless have won."[19]

Taking his cue from Hollis, Tate hinted in the *Stonewall Jackson* that the South should properly be seen as conservative, but forced into revolution by Northern trespass on the Constitution. The point was not developed, for the rest of the book was a straightforward analysis of Jackson's campaigns, competently if not impressively sketched. By the time of the second biography, Tate had grown in confidence and knowledge. He had acquired a greater feel for the social diversity of the South. To write of a Mississippian like Davis was to note differences between the Upper and Deep Souths, the seaboard and trans-Appalachian Souths. Tate portrayed the Lower South as "new and expansive, unbound by strong local tradition . . . agricultural, slaveowning, aristocratic," as the heart of the secession movement. Confederate politicians were, par excellence, victims of a paradox: they were conservative revolutionaries. And the paradox was crippling: "Because that document [the Constitution] had been their best defense within the old Union, they imagined it to be the government best suited to a new social order; and they were wrong." Davis himself, Tate suggested, did not understand the nature of the sectional struggle. He imagined he was an American, with no suspicion that he was ever "the leader of a profoundly anti-scientific society." No more did he grasp that the South was making "the last stand, they were the forlorn hope, of conservative Fundamentalist Christianity and of civilization, based on agrarian, class rule, in the European sense. . . . The issue was class rule and religion *versus* democracy and science." As Tate saw it, the war was the final struggle between America and Europe, and in the victory of the Union, America finally won. "The South was the last stronghold of European civilization in the western hemisphere," he insisted, with an echo of Ransom's sentiments. Though the Old South might be quite dead, the Southerner had one satisfaction. He had not been hoist by his own petard.[20]

This view of the Civil War was the mirror image of the warfare in Tate's mind between a religious temperament and an atheist mind, a conservative view of culture and a modernist training. Tate was as divided against himself in 1928 as had been the Union in 1861. The Confederacy stood for what he wanted to be, the Union for a pessimistic diagnosis of what he feared he was. In his family's terms, it was a division between the old Virginia and the new Kentucky. For Tate was both an elitist and a democrat. "I believe as you do in an aristocracy," he had told Fletcher, yet he shrank from its exclusiveness. He found Stark Young distasteful for his "cotton snobbery," and resisted John Wade's "genteel scruples." Moreover, he was reluctant to identify the South merely with aristocracy. "It is absurd to suppose that only the quality people were Southern. In my view the poor whites and the negroes were as Southern as any other people. I fear that [Jefferson] Davis was intimidated by this Virginian belief. . . . That sort of snobbery is utterly offensive."[21]

During the tenure of a Guggenheim fellowship in 1928 and 1929, Tate had lived in England and France. In London, he finally met Eliot, with whom he had begun an intermittent correspondence in 1926. And he became involved in the skirmish between Eliot and Irving Babbitt over humanism. This impelled his movement towards Southernism, so inter-twined had the issue of religion become. Eliot had asked him to contribute an article on humanism to the *Criterion*.[22] Tate explained his views on the humanists to Fletcher: "The fault I find with them . . . is that they actually do separate art and morals, ignoring the former entirely; you will look in vain in [Paul Elmer] More and Babbitt for a single remark pertaining to the means of expression. They are concerned entirely with the moral results." For Tate, it seemed that a new inventory of ideas was needed that might recognize the "dissociation of sensibility" doctrine: "we have got to go over the surface of our minds to see if it is really what we think it is . . . . We must go beyond the moral plane to the philosophical support beneath it. Down to the time of Milton, if not later, a moral system might be identical with the attitude of the mind holding it; but now that is not necessarily the case . . . . we have got to *create* the attitude that will be really their equivalent." Despite a sympathy with humanism, Tate disliked its eclec-ticism and deplored Babbitt's inability to see that "the discrepancy between the terms of thought and the supporting attitude is the modern problem *par excellence* . . . . It is our job to create a foundation for thought; not to move to France and give up the ghost with Gertrude Stein."[23]

Thus far, Tate could go along with Eliot. But he drew the line at Eliot's Anglo-Catholicism. That could only work if one tried, like Eliot, to assimilate England into your life and thought. Tate himself was leaning towards Roman Catholicism. "Babbitt is right," he reflected, "in pointing to the most universal church of all, because into it all varieties of national feeling may be assimilated." A skeptical Donald Davidson was informed in February 1929: "I am more and more heading towards Catholicism. We have reached a condition of the spirit where no further compromise is possible." And yet he was not yet willing to enter the Church. Where could he look for that philosophy to resolve the dissociating problems of modernism?[24]

The South seemed a kind of answer. Tate told James Southall Wilson in April 1929, "I wish we could have a counter movement in the South toward Humanism; we are historically much closer to its true meaning than a man in the New England tradition can ever be." But he wanted the South to serve his own special purposes. He was interested in "permanent forms of truth which, under the varying conditions of time and place, may be made pertinent." The impulse was not dissimilar from Ransom's, and Tate was quick to see a parallel between his own *Criterion* essay on humanism and Ransom's 1929 *Harper's* piece on the South.[25] Thus he insisted in the discussions that led up to *I'll Take My Stand* that religion was the crux of the agitation. "We need a stable order," he insisted. "I don't care how we get it or what it looks like." Keenly aware that the South, unlike Ireland, had no common religious faith, he was to daydream that it might be possible to demonstrate the influence of Catholicism on the Old South. Prudently, he abandoned the speculation.[26]

Such thoughts were forming in France, and the location was not without its influence. Tate was sufficiently Francophile to read the *Action française* regularly, and it was this model he urged upon his friends. A mere symposium would not be enough, he insisted. They needed an organization that could help to *"create an intellectual situation interior to the South."* There should be a society, complete with a constitution, which should be dedicated to setting forth "a complete social, philosophical, literary, economic and religious system." Tate was conscious that his situation differed from that of Charles Maurras, even from that of the Anglophile Eliot, one of Maurras's admirers. As Tate put it, "Maurras had a body of ready-made, non-secular doctrine at hand for re-interpretation to the needs of his time." The Southern past was only partly usable. Still, it was all there was, and it would have to be bent to their purposes. It could be used "not in what it actually performed, but in its possible perfection." Such a Southern organization might have organs of publicity, such as the *Action française* itself. By defining their common position and suppressing their differences, the Agrarians could force their progressive opponents to define their own. If action was to result, lines would have to be clearly drawn. *"Organization and discipline are indispensable,"* he told Davidson. It seemed to Tate that ideological disunity had destroyed the Confederacy, and the mistake should not be repeated. In this mood, it was unsurprising that Tate strenuously emphasized that the proper model for the South was not the deist Jefferson, but Calhoun and the "South Carolina idea."[27]

It was a headlong scheme; but he had little faith in its practical success, and his confused modernism made him feel a certain admiration for lost causes, be they his own Southernism or Eliot's Anglo-Catholicism. My skepticism, he said, "is one of hoping to be convinced, not by standing aside to watch the spectacle, but by exerting myself . . . .since I see the value, I am morally obliged to affirm it."[28]

By a leap of imagination, Tate had fitted the South into Eliot's schema for the "dissociation of sensibility" doctrine. He had to tinker with the chronology. Eliot had put the point of "dissociation" in the early seventeenth century, before Milton. Tate had modified that to "the time of Milton, if not later." And by seeing the Old South as a type of the old European civilization, surviving the destruction of the original, he contrived to extend the life of undissociated sensibility in the Southern United States to the Civil War. "We must be the last Europeans," he told Davidson, "there being no Europeans in Europe at present." Thus armed, he chided the humanists with ignoring the only "classical and humanistic society that America has ever had."[29]

It must be recalled that the rationale for Eliot's theory was finally not historical but aesthetic. Its destination was the recovery of that lost immediacy, that fresh smell of the rose, in poetry. So Tate had to adjust his own relationship to one of the villains in the history of aesthetic dissociation, literary Romanticism. For Eliot had been taking a firm stand against Romanticism. The most immediate product of Tate's desire to apply these ideas to the Southern literary heritage was an attack upon the ironic Mr. James Branch Cabell and his dream world of Poictesme. Cabell was especially pertinent to Tate because the author of *Jurgen* was a Virginian and, as Tate dubbed him in a review of *The Way of Ecben* in early 1930, "our first novelist of stature to mold an American mind to something of the attitude of French romantic rationalism from Voltaire to Anatole France."[30]

In Tate's eyes, the most fundamental influence upon Cabell was the transformation from the Old to the New South, "from God to Mammon." "In Mr. Cabell's generation," he suggested, "this change of religious impulse must have worked unconsciously . . . . it permitted the values of his Southernism to support unconsciously his creative faculty. And he wrote a couple of distinguished books." According to Tate, however, Cabell began to misread the influence of these values and to imagine they came from elsewhere: "Mr. Cabell has evidently not been aware of the moral origin of Poictesme in the Old South: he has tried to escape from the Old South by making Poictesme a place of his own creation." Thus, Tate suggested, Poictesme was "not a way of escape *into* the Old South but an escape *from* it into a world that Mr. Cabell both dislikes and needs." As Romantic literature, Cabell's novels had evaded the issues by neglecting the root of its dilemma. In a letter to Davidson, with a copy of this review, Tate elaborated: "Isn't the point about Cabell and Glasgow this: that *because* they have a mixed thesis—i.e. mixed of old Southism and Progress—*because* their intelligences are split into contradictory values, they are bad novelists . . . . their social attitude, because it is muddled, distracts the creative mind into mere propaganda and ruins the work of art. This could almost be made into a principle—that all great, or really good writers, must have a simple homogeneous sense of values, which incidentally are the kinds of values we wish to restore."[31]

If his ambivalent schemes for the restoration of such values were to be realized, Tate could scarcely live in France or even in New York. Upon his return to the United States in January 1930, he boldly decided to attempt the life of an independent man of letters in the South. But his income was to remain basically non-Southern, with advances from his publishers and fees from his reviewing in New York. Even his house near Clarksville, bought by his brother, was purchased with funds culled in Cincinnati.[32]

His first task was to write an essay for *I'll Take My Stand,* and it was natural that he chose the topic of religion in the Old South. Despite, or because of, his brooding on the subject for several years, he found it hard to compose. His self-division on the subject, combined with its amorphousness, made the production of a disciplined essay difficult. But he was eager to stress, in the discussions among the Agrarians, that the symposium be explicitly related to the humanist volume *Humanism and America: Essays on the Outlook of Modern America,* also published in 1930. And he was keen to deplore the Confederate particularity displayed in the title *I'll Take My Stand,* so much so that he insisted on placing before his essay the following note: "The general title of this book is not quite true to its aims. It emphasizes the fact of exclusiveness rather than its benefits; it points to a particular house but omits to say that it was the home of a spirit that may also have lived elsewhere and that this mansion, in short, was incidentally made with hands." True to this, the piece was ten pages gone before the word "South" appeared.[33]

"Remarks on the Southern Religion" began with a discussion of religion and the modern mind. Like Ransom, Tate found little value in the God offered by the "cult of efficiency." For, in its optimistic immaturity, it was incapable of dealing with human failure. It could only predict success. No more could Tate find satisfaction in "the religion of the Symbolist poets, and of M. Henri Bergson," in their belief that nothing is predictable.

Abruptly, Tate's argument jumped to the philosophy of history. There were, he suggested, two ways of examining history: the "Long View," which seeks out abstract continuity, and the "Short View," which reestablishes the contingency in which finite events took place. The former was "the cosmopolitan destroyer of Tradition," because it reduced traditions to a type whose functions were interchangeable. Christ and Adonis were equal in both standing for religion. Moreover, it was abstract and defeated tradition because, as Eliot had suggested in his essay "Tradition and the Individual Talent," traditions must be automatically operative. As soon as choice was admitted into religion, religion was defeated. Then, as Tate wrote, "we are at the verge of committing ourselves to the half-religions that are no religions at all, but quite simply a decision passed on the utility, the workableness, of the religious objects with respect to the practical aims of society."

Religion, defended by reason, seemed to Tate the peculiar quality of the Western approach to tradition. And it had been transmitted by the Renaissance, which consummated the religious argument from reason and utility. This was a paradox, but one built into the modern's cultural inheritance. Nowhere was the confusion greater than in America, where the medieval faith in faith itself was weakest.

In the South, Tate argued, it was more complicated. There one found once a feudal society, but without a feudal religion. For the region was founded at a time when European religion was disintegrating, and so the South had been "Protestant, aggressive and materialistic." For reasons of soil and climate, the area developed an agrarian culture distinct from the North. But it did not develop its own theology. In Tate's opinion, presumably adapted from Max Weber or R. H. Tawney, Protestantism was the religion of traders and nonagrarians. Thus the South was at odds with itself. With a world view that gave its own social structure no close sanction, its ideological resources failed it during the struggle with the North. "The South shows signs of defeat," Tate wrote, "and this is due to its lack of a religion which would make her special secular system the inevitable and permanently valuable one. We have been inferior to the Irish in this virtue, though much less than the Irish have we ever been beaten in war."

Tate saw the difference between the South and New England in the nineteenth century partly in terms of Europe. In reduplicating European society, the South did not need Europe. But New England "was one of those abstract-minded, sharp-witted trading societies that must be parasites in two ways: They must live economically on some agrarian class or country, and they must live spiritually likewise. New England lived economically on the South, culturally on England." Thus it was natural that Boston should have produced cultural émigrés like Henry James and Henry Adams. The South was European in the sense that it had "taken root in a native soil." In such a context, intellectualism had been redundant. As a society, the Old South had known little of the Long View.

In conclusion, Tate recurred to the religious deficiencies of the ancien régime. Under Jefferson's influence, the South had believed too much in science and practicality. After Hollis, Tate reiterated the absence of religious tradition in Jefferson's influence and the secularity of the vision he offered the South. The modern Southerner was the heir of this heresy, "that the ends of man may be established by political means." Since the Southerner cannot conjure up an inarticulate religious tradition without articulating it, he was left with the unsatisfactory Jeffersonian program. "How," Tate asked, "may the Southerner take hold of his Tradition? The answer is, by violence." He could only turn to political reaction. But the pursuit was quixotic, the game long since lost. For, as Tate concluded: "The Southerner is faced with the paradox: He must use an instrument, which is political, and so unrealistic and pretentious that he cannot believe in it, to re-establish a private, self-contained, and essentially spiritual life. I say that he must do this; but that remains to be seen."[34]

This was scarcely a confident rallying call, but the mournful speculation of a confused atheist. As the opening pages of the essay demonstrated, Tate was the spectator of religion. In later years, near or within the Roman Catholic Church, he was to delete those phrases that marked the gulf between himself and religious faith, the distance that in 1930 was a source of "deep regret" to him.[35] It was a long way from the immediacy of a rose in a poem to political reaction, and Tate knew it. Crucially, he failed to make the connection between religion and the South that he wished. The result was the essay's sterility. And it is only just to Tate to acknowledge that this was a product of his honesty. In his biography of Jefferson Davis, he had struggled with his subject's alarming tendency to look like an American. Now he confronted this Southern proclivity on the religious plane, and he admitted that the region had an American religion and, in Jefferson, the prime author of the "American heresy." So he was forced to make a gulf between Southern society and his desired version of religious tradition. Into that gulf, he poured all the failure of the South to give him an operative tradition.

If he had been more cavalier with his history, like Ransom, or less inclined to grant the primacy of Roman Catholicism, Tate's paradox would have been lessened. As it was, there was a curious irony in one of the South's more formidable intellectuals offering his allegiance to an Old South whose mind was, by his own description, "simple, not top-heavy with learning it had no need of, unintellectual and composed . . . personal and dramatic, rather than abstract and metaphysical," possessed, indeed, of the qualities Allen Tate lacked. The essay had the mark of a profound self-contempt.[36]

Despite his failure to secure a Southern religious tradition, Tate did lay hold of a version of Southern social history. And that was crucial for offering him genuine involvement in the region. As he wrote to John Gould Fletcher: "Our entire program is based on the assumed fact that the tradition is there to work on; otherwise we are only American liberals offering a new panacea and pretending to a concrete background that doesn't exist." And yet that was not quite what he wanted from the South. It was something, but not enough.[37]

Pessimism was an old instinct with Tate, and he turned it most consistently towards John Gould Fletcher. It may be significant that Fletcher was an émigré Southerner, living in London, and a founder of the Imagist movement. Moreover, he stood close to Eliot, though not without a jealousy that was to intensify as Fletcher's reputation waned and Eliot's grew beyond bounds. Tate's letters to Fletcher are full of observations, such as this on the 1928 presidential elections: "I believe that you are a little more shocked at the turn of affairs in America than I am. You are older and have some memory of the better days. In my time there's never been anything but what there is now, except of course it is now much worse." Though Tate had been too young to fight in the First World War, he seemed to have fully absorbed its gloomy and numbing lessons. It was not surprising that Fletcher, in his memoirs, should remember most keenly this bleakness.

He recalled in Tate "some terrible remnant of a world-blasting medieval Catholicism . . . reducing to ashes not only everything in his own day and time, but all human experience itself. . . . The last historic hope of America had faded in 1860. Since then one could only contrast the fruitless activity of a degraded democracy with the ultimate eternal quietude of complete death."[38]

✒ The first task after the publication of *I'll Take My Stand* was to fulfill a contract with Earle Balch for a new biography, this time of Robert E. Lee. In it, Tate was to approach the ark of several Southern covenants, and he did it with distaste. He was bored with hack biographies, written for the money. Just as the move to New York had prompted a burst of poetic energy, so the shift to Tennessee had turned his mind back to verse. It was irksome to dabble in Confederate military affairs, when he found he could write twelve poems in a week.[39]

But it ran deeper. Tate found Robert E. Lee abhorrent. He confided to Andrew Lytle: "The longer I've contemplated the venerable features of Lee, the more I've hated him. It is as if I had married a beautiful girl, perfect in figure, pure in all those physical attributes that seem to clothe purity of character, and then had found when she had undressed that the hidden places were corrupt and diseased." With this, Tate abandoned the book and had to ask Lytle to see Balch and break the contract. But fragments remain in Tate's papers, and there one can trace the measure of his distaste.[40]

Lee seemed too perfect. As Tate put it: "Lee had no parts, from the day he was born: he was born a perfect specimen of human integration . . . . A man so self-contained may, in a sense, be said to be without ambition, yet in another sense, a more realistic one, his ambition is inexhaustible. No worldly reward can satisfy it; it feeds upon its own perfection, and drops its participation in affairs the moment this inner integrity is threatened. That is the theme of this book." This judgment on the central figure of Confederate mythology was a savage break with tradition, and Tate knew it. "Can any man alive write this way about Lee?" he asked Lytle. At the last, he could not bring himself to it. He saw in Lee "an abyss, and it is to this that I do not want to give a name." It was left to Lytle to draw out the lessons of Tate's objections in a review of Douglas Southall Freeman's biography of Lee in 1935. In this, Lytle suggested that Lee had put his own honor above the military needs of the Confederacy. By adhering strictly to a belief in the subordination of the military to the civilian government, he allowed Davis to bind him to an irrelevant defense of Richmond. And, after the war, Lee had failed to see that Reconstruction was the continuation of the war by other means. Fortunately, wrote the biographer of Nathan Bedford Forrest, "the leadership changed to the middle South, to those who led the Ku Klux Klan, that society which made survival possible."[41]

In Lytle's case, the objection to Lee was that of a trans-Appalachian resentful of the annexation of the Southern legend by Virginia. As he was to remember, "I was very conscious of the fact that Virginia was a special kind of thing, and more Eastern than Southern." Lytle's biography of Forrest had insisted that, if Virginia had been less disdainful of the western theatre of war and less concerned with the defense of Richmond, the war might have been won. For Tate, with half a foot in Virginia and half in a Kentucky that never seceded, the issue was less clear-cut. He had registered his dislike for the modern Virginia of Ellen Glasgow and the consciously moderate mediation of the *Virginia Quarterly Review* between North and South. He deplored Virginia's snobbish combination of old Southern graces with New South industrialism, and was sure that Stringfellow Barr's belief that such graces could civilize the factories was unrealistic. "I am afraid," he had written in 1930, "that Barr has a rather typically modern Virginian attitude—he thinks if the South gets rich again, it will be the South still. But the South is not a section of geography, it is an economy setting forth a certain kind of life."[42]

The Virginia of the Old South was a different matter. One finds in the early pages of Tate's "Lee" a defense of its aristocratic ways. His description of Lee, the Christian gentleman, was an echo of his grief for the integrated sensibility that Eliot insisted had passed away. One sees in Lytle's review the same diagnosis: "Lee's code was strict. It extended into all his relationships, his duty to himself, to his family, to the army, to the Confederacy and its civil authority. It was complete as no code can be today." As Tate himself wrote, "Lee . . . was a finished product, a man whose views were bounded and fixed within an already old society."[43] It was unsettling for Tate to confront the fullest expression of his "classical and humanist" Old South and find that the sight turned his stomach. It was as well not to write the book. And so he left it alone.

In the autumn of 1931, he went to Charlottesville and participated in the Southern Writers' Conference, organized by Ellen Glasgow and James Southall Wilson. He was pleased at a gathering of authors, far from the pressures of New York, on the first occasion that the literary elite of the region had been gathered in one place. It seemed an opportunity for the Agrarians to proselytize. But their attempt to "politicize" the conference was balked by a coalition of Virginians and South Carolinians. The incident did, however, raise with clarity the issue of the relationship between politics and literature. Wilson had remarked to Tate that he believed in regionalism, but not sectionalism. In a subsequent letter, Tate took him up on the point: "I believe we should have regionalism for literature, but sectionalism in politics." With sectional policies, it might be possible to recover the conditions under which a writer might work. This was the point to be reiterated by Ransom, in an essay upon Sidney Lanier three years later. "The leading question before Southern literature," Tate suggested, "is the nature of its peculiar genius, and perhaps it will some time be appropriate for Southern writers, in the lack of political leadership, to point out certain features of the question that do not ordinarily pertain to the literary problem."[44]

In an article for the *New Republic* in November 1931, Tate tried to settle the matter further in his mind. He reiterated his view that regionalism—"the immediate, organic sense of life in which a fine artist works"—was healthy for literature. But sectionalism—"a doctrine, philosophical at its rare best, at its worst boastful propaganda"—was a form of political action. For Tate, regionalism was not quite identical with tradition. It was too self-conscious. At its worst, regionalism could destroy tradition "with its perpetual discovery of it." At its best, it could offer an assumed ambience, which saved the author the labor of defining social and moral fundamentals. The danger was that politics could infect art. As far as Tate was concerned, the distinction between literature and propaganda was absolute.

Or was it? After all, Tate had just come from a Charlottesville conference, where he had made a definite effort to import political perspectives into a literary gathering. What was his defense? It was this: "If tradition is the best condition of literature, then sectionalism, or a preoccupation with the interests of one's community, is the starting point of political philosophy. And it is here that tradition and politics join; each has its invaluable place and each is subversive of order when out of place. They are finally identical in their purposes.... Sectionalism, or politics, is public tradition, and tradition is private, or unconscious sectionalism." In practice, the two were not absolutely separable, although the artist must keep the difference firmly in mind. Otherwise, he could write propaganda under the impression that it was literature. But, if there is no proper political leadership, a man of letters must be forgiven for indulging in social criticism. Yet it troubled Tate, as all self-consciousness did for its apparent testimony to the death of tradition. And so he confessed: "To defend tradition . . . is to violate it; only temporary emergency would justify it."[45]

What was this emergency? On this his case rested. It was not the Depression, for his involvement in politics had preceded it. In that his basic theory was the "dissociation of sensibility" notion, this emergency was either Southern history since 1861, English history since the seventeenth century, or European history since the Renaissance. It was a broad canvas on which to spread even the elastic word "temporary."

This distinction between art and propaganda was at issue between Tate and Malcolm Cowley, who edited this piece for the *New Republic.* It took its place in the wider discussion over Marxist literature that another friend, Edmund Wilson, was helping to foster. Less obviously, it was the beginnings of a rebuff to Donald Davidson. As Tate was to write to Ellen Glasgow more than a year later: "I fear that some of us may hold out too strongly for literal Southernism. . . . One of the baleful effects of Americanism in letters is the lowering of the creative impulse to the level of propaganda. If we become mere propagandists in turn, we shall betray our position. . . . As economists and political writers we may agitate: but as artists we must prove the value of the agitation by keeping the modes distinct, and writing literature."[46] As yet, Davidson was moving only hesitantly towards what Tate regarded as "literal Southernism." With a few years, a gulf was to open between the two men on this score. And they were to differ, not on the theoretical validity of the distinction between art and propaganda, but on a judgment of Davidson's literary performance.

The year 1931 had not gone well with Tate. Although he produced some of his best poetry, his biography of Lee had come to nothing. Moreover, he felt that agrarianism was making little headway. An attempt to apply to the Guggenheim foundation for money to fund a country newspaper had foundered on Davidson's reluctance.[47] And again Davidson had disliked to act, when a labor strike in Harlan, Kentucky, brought a prosecution against certain New York writers on a charge of "criminal syndicalism." Tate had urged the Agrarians to dissociate themselves from this violation of free speech.[48] In November 1931, Tate was lamenting to Bernard Bandler, editor of the *Hound and Horn:* "I fear there are no signs here of a movement in action. We are all grinding our own axes. Last year I gave about six months to the Cause—with the result that I am being sued for debt." In December, he confided to Davidson his belief that agrarianism was dying fast.[49]

The year 1932 was a little better. Tate became "southern editor" for the *Hound and Horn.* In this capacity, he was able to place many of his fellow Agrarians in the pages of one of the more persuasive, and aesthetically progressive, of New York magazines. At Tate's behest, Davidson, Lytle, and Owsley were all invited to review or write articles. In this way, Tate helped to bridge the gap between the collapse of Davidson's syndicated book page for Tennessee newspapers and the establishment of the *American Review.* In the spring, he was asked to edit a "Southern number" for *Poetry.* In June, he gave to the *Richmond News-Leader* his poem "To the Lacedaemonians," in celebration of a Confederate soldiers' reunion in that city.[50] Despite his doubts, he seemed to be holding to his commitment to the South. In succession to the aborted biography of Lee, he was planning a study of family genealogy, to be called "Ancestors of Exile."[51]

For all that, it was a relief to be away from America again and back to France. In June 1932, he went with his wife, Caroline Gordon, when she took up her own Guggenheim Fellowship. They were to stay for nine months. For the first time, he saw more of France than just Paris. They travelled south to Provence. Early in the trip, they were accompanied by Frank and Harriet Owsley, as well as Lyle Lanier and his wife. Neither the Owsleys nor the Laniers, by Tate's testimony, took well to French life. Some tension developed, as Tate complained to Andrew Lytle: "The newcomers to France couldn't at first resist the notion that the novelties of a foreign country were there as criticism of them. This was very trying." Tate himself continued to resist the idea of cultural exile, but he did see in rural France a confirmation of his Southern agrarian ideas. About him was a country in which 57 per cent of the people remained on the land, and in which the traditional culture of the French peasantry remained intact. Tate felt that France should be taken as a model for the South: "I intend to study this subject in order to write about it effectively; their idea here is the same as ours—the land not for profit but for enjoyment of civilized life." He told Davidson that if he could find out what had kept the French "pure of modern contamination," it might be a useful lesson for Southerners.[52]

This experience strengthened his feeling that *I'll Take My Stand* had been sacrificed to Ransom's Anglophilia. More than that, it turned him away from seeing the South in terms of intellectual tradition, towards the practical aspect of agrarianism. "We should have stood flatly on the immediately possible in the South," he insisted to Davidson. Anglo-nostalgia had vitiated the concrete and indigenous facts of Southern rural life. In this Tate showed a fresh consciousness of the Depression. And, like Ransom, it had come to him abroad. He had been impressed that France seemed to be faring better than the industrial United States. Unenthusiastically, he was a supporter of Franklin Roosevelt, but remarked, "I fear that no one is at hand for the crisis, yet it is true that money power is everywhere declining, and the only alternative is land; in that lies our hope."[53]

But the economic crisis cut embarrassingly two ways. It may have been crippling industrialism, but it also hurt industrialism's employees, the Agrarians. Tate was painfully conscious of this. "There's no denying that an army marches on its stomach," he admitted to Davidson. And to Warren, he confessed that "while I find it comparatively easy to be heroic in poverty, I find it impossible to be effective." The return from France put him back into the financial slough. In October 1933, he was chafing at the strains of free-lancing: "The daily financial pressure is demoralizing. Ten years ago such anxieties didn't oppress me; but now they devour me." In this mood, he greeted the establishment of the *American Review* with enthusiasm. Here was a publication in which his agrarian pleasures could be made to pay. It was the more convenient because editorial changes at the *Hound and Horn* had jeopardized his position as its "southern editor."[54]

His writing for the new journal had an unwonted truculence. Briefly, he assumed a sectional belligerence that gave the impression of being influenced by Davidson's and Owsley's writings in 1933. His long review of the Chapel Hill symposium, *Culture in the South,* in early 1934, was severe. He made a point of damning racial liberalism. For him, social equality was not worth attention, as "there has never been social equality anywhere, there never will be, nor ought there to be." The race problem, he charged, was insoluble. "I argue it this way," he wrote, "the white race seems determined to rule the Negro race in its midst; I belong to the white race; therefore I intend to support white rule. Lynching is a symptom of weak, inefficient rule; but you can't destroy lynching by *fiat* or social agitation; lynching will disappear when the white race is satisfied that its supremacy will not be questioned in social crises." Beginning a litany of cuts, Tate damned the social scientists of Chapel Hill for naivety in believing that a committee of academics would ever be appointed to decide the political and economic fate of the South. He was angry at the industrialists of the New South. He jibed at the indistinct definition of the word "culture" employed in the book. He was severe towards the economic determinism that he thought underlay the volume's philosophy. He mocked it for ignoring the world economic crisis. What, he asked, was the point of imitating a bankrupt North? He dismissed George Fort Milton's chapter on politics and its contention that the chief issue was the Solid South. For Tate, the failure of political philosophy was the problem: "We get opposition opposing opposition, while the money power rules. . . . The donkey, political thought, starves to death between the bales of hay, doing justice to them both, and hoping for the best." Tate gave his approval only to those chapters written by Agrarians—Wade, Davidson, and Edd Winfield Parks had wandered reluctantly into the book—or those which offered a neutral précis of aspects of Southern life.[55]

For the first time in public print, Tate had stood by the "agrarian" side of the Southern-agrarian equation. In 1930 he had groaned at the prospect of assuming the name "agrarian"; now he wrote in defense of *I'll Take My Stand:* "It was nowhere said that Southern agriculture at this moment affords an ideal society to set off against the depravity of industrialism: we said that Southern agriculture might be made into a system in which security and stability could be won in a measure impossible so long as the farmer, fixed in the commercial scheme, remains in economic vassalage to his local merchants and bankers and . . . to the whole industrial system." For the first time, he urged practical measures towards the revival of agrarianism: offering land to the Negro, stopping the growth of industrialism, the end of aping the North. Even so, his instincts remained abstract, for his most urgent recommendation was the development of a Southern political philosophy, a "plain program for the South . . . [in which] either by legislation or by revolution, in those regions where the land supports most of the people, the power must pass to those people." He seemed, in echoing Davidson and Owsley, even Ransom, to be abandoning his elitist concern for "culture" and democratizing his perception of the region. He wrote to a friend: "The people must decide what they want to be, not what they want to let the drift of economics make them." When R. P. Blackmur criticized Tate for the unsoundness of sectionalism, Tate replied that it was idle to charge him thus: "Blue eyes and black hair are not unsound; they are facts. The existence of a civilization here different from yours is not unsound; it is a fact. Our purpose is to see what it might and ought to be."[56]

In time, his drift towards "practical" agrarianism was to diminish his sectionalism; but before examining this it is necessary to describe a change in his social condition. In 1934, Tate finally gave up the long struggle of free-lancing and took a teaching job in Memphis. He was to find that a professor's lot was as onerous and benumbing, and he had scarcely made the move before he was seeking ways back to his independence.[57] A new friendship offered some prospect of that. In September 1933, Tate had read Herbert Agar's new short history of the United States, *The People's Choice.* "It is the most brilliant short history of the United States ever written," Tate had enthused. Agar had portrayed American history as the slow conquest of the country by a plutocracy, masquerading behind the name of democracy. Tate had written to Agar, then the London correspondent of the *Louisville Courier-Journal,* and invited him to join a projected second symposium, that he might help "our case for a Conservative Revolution."[58]

Agar was an ambitious man, on the fringes of power. He had a patron, in the form of Robert W. Bingham, wealthy proprietor of the *Courier-Journal* and ambassador to the Court of St. James's. Returning to the United States in 1935, Agar had turned his extensive energies to journalism, lecturing in political affairs and trying to form a movement to lobby the New Deal. To this end, he had hatched the scheme of founding a weekly newspaper to be funded by wealthy Middle Western patrons. Tate and Lytle were invited to join in the drive for money. Trips were made to Cincinnati, speeches were delivered to entrepreneurs. Tate's brother Ben was suggested as a possible backer. Members of the Taft family, deans of Ohio politics, were mentioned. This project foundered, but, in its place, a New York based journal was established, to be called *Free America.*[59]

There was a dispute over the location of the magazine. The Agrarians wanted it to be run from Tennessee, just as they had wished Seward Collins to move to Nashville and there edit the *American Review.* Meanwhile, Agar had added to the core of Agrarian support a motley crew of reformers: Ralph Borsodi and his "back to the land" movement, the English Distributists led by G. K. Chesterton and Hilaire Belloc, the Cooperative movement, the Catholic Land movement, the National Committee on Small Farm Ownership. Some of these the Agrarians were willing to stomach. There was, indeed, a conference held in Nashville in 1936 to coordinate matters and a joint Agrarian-Distributist Committee was established. But the project was doomed, partly because the attempt to broaden the coalition meant a dilution of its sectional aspect.[60] For Davidson and Owsley, that was to miss the whole point. For Ransom in 1936, economics were failing to hold his interest. Lytle was ambivalent; Warren had never shown much interest in such matters. Only Tate seemed willing to sacrifice the local note of Agrarianism, its absorption in the South, for the national issue. Even during the furor over *Free America,* New York, and reformist eclecticism, he quietly asked Agar to consider him as an editor for the new journal. His discomfort at teaching was not an irrelevant consideration.[61]

When plans for a successor volume to *I'll Take My Stand* had been drawn up in 1933, they had been pronouncedly Southern. Of twelve contributors, ten were to be Southern: only Agar and T. S. Eliot were not. Nonetheless, its thrust was less exclusively Southern than the 1930 volume. Agar's involvement impelled the dilution. By the time the symposium saw the light of day in 1936, as *Who Owns America? A New Declaration of Independence,* nine out of twenty-one contributors were non-Southerners, and only three of its chapters could be said to be about the South directly. Tate described it, in September, 1935, as "primarily economic in approach and non-sectional."[62]

In beginning to focus on the practical problem of agrarianism, Tate had, like Ransom, been impelled beyond the exclusive bounds of the South. In his case, social and economic ties outside the region had helped the movement. For years, he had acted as a liaison agent between his friends in Nashville and New York. But it was a delicate balancing act, and the apparent inability of the South to offer him a living that he might enjoy inclined his eyes northward.

In a brooding mood on the problem of the Southern writer and economics—his own problem for the last five years—he wrote his piece for the tenth anniversary of the *Virginia Quarterly Review.* It was an obituary for his free-lance years. As he told Lambert Davis in October 1934, he had been reading "most of the literature of the South, Old and New, and I should like to say something about our lack of the professional instinct in literature." It had been a chastening experience. In its way, "The Profession of Letters in the South" was as much a leave-taking of the region as Ransom's essay in the same issue.[63]

Tate began with a bitter description of the writer's status in American society. He belonged, Tate well knew, to "a sweated class," tied to the tyranny of publisher and book market. To survive, swift turnover was essential. Under such pressure, shoddy goods were the natural result. As usual, Tate traced the origins of the situation to the rise of capitalism and its erasure of an organic society, where the writer had had a natural place. With the crumbling of a patron aristocracy, the writer had become a social fugitive. This was a problem common to both Europe and America, save that in America it was worse. Having said that, Tate turned to the problem of the South. Here was a society that had once had aristocracy on the European model. Should it not have produced the United States' most distinguished literature?

Tate was blunt: it had produced, in the nineteenth century, the nation's least distinguished literature. Only Poe stood out. Why should this be, in a region which Tate now insisted was so similar to France? "In religious and social feeling I should stake everything on the greater resemblance to France," he wrote. "The South clings blindly to forms of European feeling and conduct that were crushed by the French Revolution and that, in England at any rate, are barely memories." Where else, Tate asked, could one find a society where the Code of Honor was taken seriously? Where else had the patriarchal family, the "ancient land-society," the resistance to change, the persistence of a "convinced supernaturalism...nearer to Aquinas than to Calvin, Wesley or Knox" existed? And yet still there was no literature worth reading.

Tate dismissed certain kinds of explanation for this poverty. Not surprisingly, he set aside Trent's old contention that slavery and a tyrannical class system had prevented "the essential faith in American democracy" that nourished literature. Tate was confident that societies could produce good writing amid a good deal of social corruption. But he half accepted Trent's contention that slavery had been part of the reason, by arguing that slavery had prevented the development of a class system in the South. Moreover, black chattel slavery had interposed a barrier between the white man and his own soil. Without that, no literature could flourish. Politics, however, was his basic explanation. The Old South had been "hag-ridden" with politics. The need for the Southern aristocracy to hold its place in a hostile American world had drained talent from the arts: "The South was a fairly good place for the arts, as good possibly as any other aristocratic country; only its inherent passion for politics was inflamed by the furious contentions that threatened its life. Every gifted person went into politics, not merely the majority."

Tate was at pains to emphasize that the poverty of the literature should not be glossed because one found the society attractive. It was a great temptation, and he himself had succumbed on occasion. For the Southern writer, one thing had not changed since the antebellum period. Poe had lived under a commercial aristocracy; the modern writer had to come to terms with a plutocracy. Each was a system of class rule. Both had failed to provide a place for the creative writer. There had not been, nor was there in 1935, a profession of letters in the South or, indeed, in the United States. In his own time, the lack of a Southern publishing system and of a Southern city where writers might naturally gather had driven Southerners to New York.

Such a flight had its dangers, as Tate was aware. But he was careful to resist Ransom's charge that the consequent exposure to modernist influences from Europe was debilitating. He admitted that a "Southern writer should if possible be a Southerner in the South." But, things being what they were, that was not always possible. And it was not always bad to go away, for "the arts everywhere spring from a mysterious union of indigenous materials and foreign influences: there is no great art or literature that does not bear the marks of this fusion." The problem for the Southern writer in the North was not the alien influence, but the feebleness of the literary tradition he took with him.

Willing to grant that modern Southern literature had achieved more than that of the antebellum period, Tate cautioned that the phenomenon was quite temporary, merely the moment of insight offerred at the point of transition between two Southern societies. At such a moment, as in the South, politics was a beckoning siren. "There is no escape from it," he lamented. "The political mind always finds itself in an emergency. And the emergency, this time real enough, becomes a pretext for ignoring the arts. We live in the sort of age that Abraham Cowley complained of—a good age to write about but a poor age to write in."[64]

This article was a break with the New South tradition, but less savage than Tate imagined. Its central call for a profession of letters had been made by Edwin Mims, Tate's *bête noire,* thirty years earlier. Its lament for the absence of a Southern literary capital was the common currency of writers like Trent. Ironically, his call for a Southern publishing system was being half met, even as he wrote. By the end of the 1930s, the region was surprisingly well endowed with magazines and presses: the *Southern Review,* through the dubious largesse of Huey Long, the *Virginia Quarterly Review,* the *Sewanee Review,* and the limping, committee-run *South Atlantic Quarterly;* the University of North Carolina Press, which dominated indigenous regional publishing, and three new university presses in Georgia, Louisiana, and Vanderbilt itself. But these developments were posited on the alliance with the university that Tate disliked and assumed academe's patronage for writers. The periodicals and presses paid little or nothing.

Nonetheless, his image of the Southern writer's fate in the postwar world was a mirror image of his own career. "The Southern writer, of my generation at least, went to New York," he had written.[65] In fact, very few did. The novels of Thomas Wolfe had only fed a legend that had grown, by extension, from the common 1920s myth about the struggling author in the great city. Whatever the truth about other regions, the South kept a remarkable number of its writers within its bounds. Of the "Twelve Southerners" of *I'll Take My Stand,* only two—Tate himself and Stark Young—had serious links with New York. If one looks at major Southern authors in the interwar years, one finds that, aside from the Agrarians, the likes of Ellen Glasgow and James Branch Cabell, the Charleston group of DuBose Heyward, the Mississippi set of Faulkner, William Alexander Percy, and Eudora Welty, the North Carolina set of Paul Green, all remained substantially within the region. There was something of a symbol in John Gould Fletcher, the exile, coming back to Arkansas in 1933.

Clearly Tate's pessimism had deepened with the frustrations of his Agrarian venture. In 1930, he had seemed to cut himself off from the South on the grounds of religion. Now he severed himself from nearly all of the Southern literary tradition, save the Edgar Allan Poe whom he had wished, in his youth, to emulate. He gave himself only the narrow ground of a temporary crossroads in the Southern experience to stand upon, and he could find no economic means that could adequately, and permanently, set him upon that ground. Once again, he was driven back for his sense of Southern identity upon the few characteristics of the Southern society he thought he saw about it—its manners, most of all.[66] And, once again, he feared that the politics of a deranged society would corrupt his art.

Unlike Ransom, Tate took no sudden leave of the South. His involvement had been tentative and racked with doubt. He had carried within him the nagging fear that agrarianism would be the ruin of his literary talent, and it was with sympathy that he greeted Ransom's recantation, the cry that patriotism was the maggot of art. But Tate had a greater need than Ransom for a social context. Ransom seemed, in all but his most energetic agrarian years, to be able to exist without discomfort in a metaphysical vacuum. Tate has continued to need reminders of his origin. Ransom stayed in Ohio after his retirement, but Tate returned to the South. After the publication of *The Fathers* in 1938, he retreated to the intermittent role of a critic of Southern literature and left its society alone.

Tate had needed the South, as he seemed to need many things, as a way of escaping from the burden of a limiting self into a homogeneous society, a world that might satisfy his thirst for an authoritative context of ideas. It failed him, as well it might. The South was too modern, too heterogeneous. In the long run, he chose a more conventional path towards ideological authority. In 1952, he joined the Roman Catholic Church. From that perspective, he looked back upon his agrarian phase as idolatry. In 1954, he wrote: "What I had in mind twenty years ago, not too distinctly, I think I see more clearly now; that is, the possibility of the humane life presupposes, with us, a prior order, the order of a unified Christendom. The Old South perpetuated many of the virtues of such an order; but to try to 'revive' the Old South, and to build a wall around it, would be a kind of idolatry; it would prefer the accident to the substance."[67]

eight:
Frank Owsley: "The Immoderate Past"

On his mother's side, Frank Owsley was a McGehee. For those who know the intricate genealogy of the Highland clans, that will seem no mean burden. These McGehees had changed their name from Mac-Gregor, after James VI had issued Letters of Fire and Sword against the clan in 1603. For sins against the crown of Scotland, it was commanded that the clan be exterminated, its lands confiscate to any strong enough to seize them, its women to be branded and transported. Any outlaw might earn his pardon by bringing the head of a recalcitrant MacGregor before the justices. The remnants of the embittered clan were driven to fugitive banditry upon Rannoch Moor, where they were to be spectators of the Massacre of Glencoe. Others, more prudent, fled their native hills and went to the American colonies. One branch of the McGehees set itself up on a rich plantation in Montgomery County, Alabama, in due time.[1]

On his father's side, Owsley's family history was no less violent. In the 1850s, his great-grandfather had been murdered in Alabama by a gang of outlaws. The shooting had taken place in the family home, to be witnessed by the man's wife and his youngest son. In the spirit of the clans, the child had vowed that he would seek out the criminals and systematically destroy them. And he did so. His long life was divided between an ordinary family life in a remote Alabama valley and errands of vengeance. In his old age, "Uncle Dink" had summoned Frank Owsley's father to his lair. Explaining that he could no longer carry on the vendetta, he asked his nephew, as the male heir, to assume the unfinished task. There were not many left, two or three, not too much work for a young man. The honor was declined. But the story had an unexpected sequel. Several years later, Owsley's father went to teach in Pike County, Alabama. Upon arrival, he was told of a strange old man who would permit no tree or bush near his home, nor let a light be seen from his window at night. It was said that this was the man who, long ago, had fired the shot that killed Uncle Dink's father. And it is said that, when the murderer heard that an Owsley had come to town, he had a heart attack and died clean away.[2]

Such yarns were the commonplace of the Owsley fireside. With such a twofold heritage converging on the youthful Frank Owsley, it is not surprising that he was inclined to see dark shadows in men's motives. When Andrew Lytle turned the tale of Uncle Dink into a novel, *The Long Night,* he made the avenger seem a trifle psychotic. Owsley objected to the interpretation. To him, such a man may not have been normal, but he was not mad. For people were capable of such things.[3] It is well to keep this elemental vision of human nature in mind when considering Frank Owsley, the Southern historian.

Abner McGehee had founded a substantial plantation in Alabama which by the time of Owsley's birth in 1890 had been divided between his heirs. Owsley's mother had secured a corner, which formed a still adequate farm. The boy went to the one room schoolhouse that catered to the children of the plantation. Later, at the Alabama Polytechnic Institute, he had wanted to train as a farm demonstration agent, a new profession made fashionable by the recent pioneer work of Seaman A. Knapp. But a professor of history had other ideas. George Petrie, late of the Johns Hopkins seminar and proud owner of a "historical laboratory," cajoled the young man into historical research. It is likely he instilled into Owsley a respect for the German tradition of historical scholarship, dominant at the Baltimore graduate school. From William Dodd at the University of Chicago, to which Owsley later went, the doctrine was less pure. Despite a doctorate from Leipzig, Dodd scarcely bothered to expunge his Jeffersonianism and partisan enthusiasm for the Democratic party from his writing or from his teaching. Under the tutelage of such a Virginian, Owsley did not find Chicago a cultural shock. Indeed, the two most important Northern centers of historical research were both offering pro-Southern interpretations. When Owsley ran into trouble with a few Chicago professors, he contemplated decamping to Columbia University and the seminar of William Archibald Dunning.[4]

As early as there are records, one finds that Owsley had a deep love for his South and an abiding resentment against the North. He had been weaned on the legend of Reconstruction, and the steady stream of monographs from the Dunning school only confirmed the impression. Owsley liked to tell the story of a fellow lodger in his Chicago rooming house. This man was virulent in his hatred for the South, and hazarded the opinion that a steamroller should have been run over the region during Reconstruction. In all serious rebuttal, Owsley replied that it had been.[5]

But Owsley was singular in placing his affection for the South over a love for his home state, Alabama. The primacy of that emotion was the guiding impulse of his doctoral dissertation, *States Rights in the Confederacy*. The idea for the study was Dodd's, but it meshed with Owsley's own views. Owsley held that the pertinacity of certain Confederate politicians, like Zebulon Vance of North Carolina and Joseph Brown of Georgia, in upholding states rights during the Civil War crucially sabotaged the South's chances of success. Squabbles over the surrender of arms to a needy Confederate army, over conscription and the writ of habeas corpus were neatly laid out. Like Tate, Owsley assumed that the South could have won, if this or that had gone differently. As he put it: "If the leaders had been able to bury their differences as to the theory of government, if they had allowed the Confederate government the same freedom as that of the federal (harassed though the federal government was by internal strife) during the space of the war, it would have been almost an impossibility for the South to suffer defeat." This was a contentious assumption, proud in explaining failure by internal villains; it slighted the not inconsiderable role of the federal army in bringing about Appomattox. Nonetheless, *States Rights in the Confederacy* was an interesting documentation of various aspects of Confederate dissension and foreshadowed Owsley's own political theory, emphasizing sectionalism as a superior alternative to the traditional Southern doctrine of states rights.[6]

Walter L. Fleming, an old pupil of both Petrie and Dunning, secured Owsley a job at Vanderbilt in 1920. Though he was on the campus during the heyday of the *Fugitive* and was a subscriber to the magazine, Owsley's links with the poets were small. Like most of the historical profession, he did not know of, care for, or understand the relevance of literary modernism for the historian. As a discipline, history was the most perfectly preserved of nineteenth century intellectual pursuits, as yet only indifferently impressed by the worrying arguments over relativism that absorbed novelists, poets, and physicists. In aesthetic matters, Owsley was a traditionalist. In Paris during 1927, he wrote home to Davidson: "When I look around over here and see all these 'contemporary artists' in *revolt* against the old masters, not because the old masters were not good, but because it is believed these old fellows painted everything worth while, it seems pathetic in view of the fact that these rebels are without subject, technique or philosophy, but merely are *'revolting'* for the sake of being different."[7] It is doubtful that he lingered before a Picasso on the Left Bank.

With his Jeffersonianism and antipathy to modernism, it is not too surprising that his first visit to Europe was no pilgrimage. In pursuit of reasons for the Confederate failure, he had planned a study of the foreign relations of the Confederacy. Like Wade, he had fancied a trip to Europe under the auspices of the Guggenheim Foundation. With his wife as research assistant and amanuensis, he went to the Public Record Office and the British Museum in London, and to the Bibliothèque Nationale in Paris. Despite his gory heritage as a McGehee, he came to Britain full of enthusiasm for the old country.[8]

He came away profoundly disillusioned. Sitting in a hired car in the grounds of Blenheim Palace, he jotted down his distaste in a notebook. It is a remarkable document of Anglophobia. Owsley had been unlucky in meeting a steady succession of Englishmen cut in the fashion of Mrs. Trollope. They patronized him. They lectured him on the American attitude towards the war debt problem. They told him to eat his peas with an inverted fork, held in the left hand. He endured the clammy English climate and the indifferent menus of English hotels with less humor than a Caroline Gordon, who once wrote to Andrew Lytle from London:

"It has rained every single day since we have been here . . . . The sun shines a few minutes every day, and then our fellow lodgers look at each other and say 'A lovely day, isn't it?' Sometimes they go about panting and exclaiming 'How hawt it it is! I can hardly get my breath.'" The severity of the class system appalled Owsley. He didn't like thatched cottages any more than the drab housing estates of the 1920s building boom. Too many centuries of power had made the English disdainful and insular, he thought, and anyone but a "Rhodes Scholar who begins his career by putting his face on the floor and England's foot on his head in obeisance" could see it. "With only one exception," he wrote, "during our four months sojourn in England, we found them all patronizing, insulting and ill-mannered."[9]

Such a reaction contrasted vividly with the Anglophilia of Ransom's "Statement of Principles" in *I'll Take My Stand*. Equally, it marked off Owsley from Tate's love of France. When Tate and the Owsleys travelled together in France during 1932, Tate was driven to moan: "I got so tired of Frank Owsley complaining about the parsimony of the French . . . that I could have doused him with a glass of bad French beer." For Owsley was the convinced American democrat. When Davidson sent him in Paris a copy of *The Tall Men,* he responded nostalgically: "Over here where Tennessee and Pioneer history are as remote as an undiscovered planet your words were music singing to my heart and making me realize just how 'Tall' the men were who used bullets for words and who did things Europe can never understand."[10]

This antipathy found its way into *King Cotton Diplomacy*. The book, begun in 1927 and finished in 1931, was a great advance upon the sketchiness of his dissertation. For the most, it was a reliable documentation of the dispatches that passed between Richmond, London, and Paris. But the concluding chapter was sharply etched with his social beliefs. As France had refused during the Civil War to act without England, Owsley concentrated his attention upon the latter in "Why Europe Did Not Intervene." The central assumption of Jefferson Davis's diplomatic strategy had been that the Confederate embargo on cotton and the destruction of crops would so cripple the British economy that intervention would be enforced. As it was true that there was severe hardship in the cotton mill towns of Northern England, the problem occurred. Why did not Palmerston's government act? Owsley discounted the popular theory that the idealism of the cotton operatives made them support the North against their own economic interests. The working class proved as ready to listen to Confederate propaganda as to Union pleas. As Owsley saw it: "The population of Lancashire and of all industrial England was politically apathetic, sodden, ignorant and docile, with the exception of a few intelligent and earnest leaders." Moreover, as the government was undemocratic, their opinions had little influence upon Westminster's decisions. Equally, Owsley could not accept the theory that Britain feared a shortage of wheat supplies from the North: American wheat was only slightly cheaper than that from Eastern Europe and the change would have occasioned only slight inconvenience.

Owsley assumed that there had to have been an economic motive for British inactivity, and he found it in war profits. He saw that Britain had made money from the sale of arms and ships, and noted that the destruction of the American mercantile marine had been welcome to a British merchant fleet severely challenged by the Americans before the war. Britain had even made money from a cotton famine that had driven up cotton prices. In this perspective, Owsley was deeply influenced by the popular theory that the United States had been forced into the First World War by profiteers. He admitted as much by writing: "Those who are at all familiar with the war profits in the last war ought not to have any great difficulty in grasping the rôle England played of war profiteer, and the powerful influence upon government of her war profiteers especially when all, even the small fish, were prosperous as a result of the war."[11]

In giving primacy to economics, Owsley showed the same reliance upon Charles Beard that was to mark his later writings. The concluding pages of *King Cotton Diplomacy* lay open to all the caveats that have been entered against a crude economic determinism. It was the more noticeable, because of a collateral failure of historical imagination. Owsley did not much understand British social and political life, nor did he much want to. When he wrote of the English working classes, he was insensitive to the nature of their culture. In his 1927 notebook, he had spoken of the "empty-headed 'yokels' [who] flock to swill the cheap beer and ale vended at these places [pubs] by the barrels." Equally, he did not grasp the ambience of British government. As one reviewer pointed out: "His Englishmen and Frenchmen are hardly ever more than names." As an outsider, he had the worst of both worlds. He saw the working class as a Jeffersonian property owner, and the elite as a democrat. More worrying in *King Cotton Diplomacy,* emphasizing an undercurrent in *States Rights in the Confederacy,* was Owsley's tendency to use his facts to search out the unsavory motive, the conspiracy, the Uncle Dink in everyone. His analysis of British motives and, not incidentally, Northern diplomacy, was less a documentation than an accusation.[12]

Owsley had advised the movement on the Vanderbilt campus that led to *I'll Take My Stand,* without being a major instigator. Wrapped in his robes of the objective historian, he had made suggestions on reading in Southern history. The perspective of *States Rights in the Confederacy* underlay much of Tate's thinking on the war.[13] But his intellectual discipline was separate from that of Wade, Ransom, Davidson, or Tate. In explaining his view of the South, one must move in a different world from that of

T. S. Eliot or Ellen Glasgow. His was a quite separate Southern Renaissance. Owsley was self-consciously a part of the rebirth of Southern historical studies that boasted Ulrich Phillips, William Dodd, William Archibald Dunning, and the spreading network of their students. They represented a determination to redress the balance for the South, a resolve that found its consummation in Avery Craven's *The Coming of the Civil War*. And it was a remarkably successful movement. By the Second World War, it had supplanted the pro-Union studies of James Ford Rhodes's generation with its own pro-Southern perspective.

Owsley was enthusiastic about the proposed symposium. In the spring of 1930, he gave a paper to the Tennessee Historical Society on the causes of the Civil War. This was the basis of his essay, "The Irrepressible Conflict," for *I'll Take My Stand*. It is significant that the piece began with Reconstruction, not the origins of the sectional conflict. Owsley's inspiration was the aftermath of the war, and he gave primacy to an exegesis of the traditional Southern myth of Reconstruction. In this manner, he described the postwar years as uniquely savage, in which the South was delivered to ex-slaves, "some of whom could still remember the taste of human flesh and the bulk of them hardly three generations removed from cannibalism." After the physical devastation came the spiritual conquest, in which Northerners wrote Southern history and Southerners were forced to read it. Not until the Dunning school was "the holiness of the Northern legend" challenged. For Owsley, this was a significant shift amongst the intellectuals, but did not yet touch the masses. As he saw it, the purpose of the symposium was "to aid the South in its reorientation and in a return to its true philosophy."

From this, Owsley moved to an idiosyncratic explication of the Beardian thesis on the Civil War: "Complex though the factors were which finally caused war, they all grew out of two fundamental differences which existed between the two sections: the North was commercial and industrial, and the South was agrarian." Owsley's Beardianism was pure in its emphasis upon economic motivation, but deviant when he insisted that sectionalism was more than an accident of geography, feeding into a fundamental conflict between agrarianism and capitalism. Owsley took sectionalism more seriously than Beard, who assumed it would pass with the transmission of industrial capital to the South. For Owsley, sectionalism was not accident but substance.[14]

Owsley dwelt with affection upon the virtues of the agrarian life and foresaw for the Old South, if untouched by war, a future as dizzy as any prophesied by liberals for the New South. But Owsley differed from Ulrich Phillips in seeing the root of Southern agrarianism, not in the plantation, but in the yeoman farm. For shifting the emphasis from the plantation was a major aim of the essay. With it, he played down slavery. "Slavery . . . ," he wrote, "was part of the agrarian system, but only one element and not an essential one." Without slavery, the economic and social life of the South would not have been radically different. In Owsley's opinion, the proslavery reaction was not about slavery per se but the race question. Race united the differing strands of the Southern economy, and states rights was but the defense mechanism of a decentralized laissez faire economy that embraced both plantation and farm. Thus the war was not a struggle between slavery and freedom, but a fight over economic interests in which the North had taken the initiative. Owsley did not see the South as an undifferentiated whole. Indeed, he viewed its system of local government as necessary for an agrarian society that required decentralization. Localism was antecedent to the strenuous use of states rights during the slavery controversy. It was a system of personal liberty that embodied the "Anglo-Saxon principles expressed in the Magna Carta, bill of rights, habeas corpus act, supported in the American Revolution, and engrafted finally in every state constitution of the independent states, as 'bills of rights.'" It was a tradition whose spokesmen were Jefferson, Madison, John Taylor, and John Randolph.

The last note of the essay was a stern assertion of the permanent gulf between the sections. The economies, political and social philosophies of North and South "were as two elements in deadly combat. What was food for the one was poison for the other." Nature required that the North should wish to crush a South alien to its existence.[15]

This analysis was not revolutionary. Owsley had put together several historical traditions: Beard, Dunning, even ironically Rhodes, who had popularized the notion that the regions were irreconcilable. But he did clarify with peculiar force how much the tide had turned against the nationalist historians of the late nineteenth century. A more distinctive contribution was to point away from the plantation towards the small Southern farm. This insight was undeveloped in 1930. For the moment, Owsley was more concerned with the negative task of destroying the nationalist interpretation of the war. In this, Owsley was strictly *au courant* as a professional historian. But the subject was close to his heart and his language responded accordingly. Blacks were "barbarians." Reconstruction leaders were "savage." Garrison "knew no moderation...no balance or sense of consequence." Owsley's problem with the historical guild was never the character of his views. Perusing the Owsley correspondence, one is struck by how often his positions were applauded by his fellow historians. Avery Craven agreed in 1934 that the coming generation of Northern writers had no case and were best met by ridicule. Thomas P. Abernethy was to read an Owsley article on the Scottsboro case in 1933 to his Charlottesville students. "It has things in it which are good for them to hear," he told the author. "In the name of Jove and all the gods, why has the South so long taken the interference and sneers of the Yankees lying down? I wish that I might have been the author of your article, as it expresses my own sentiments so fully." The difference was that such men left their bluntness in private letters and between the lines of their work. Owsley was bent upon bringing it out into the open.[16]

He was candid about his intentions to friends. Feeling the gulf between the confidence of his historiographical position and an insecurity, engendered by the sense that his kind of South was slipping away, Owsley tried a reconciliation by suggesting that the intellectual eventually influenced the public. *I'll Take My Stand* was academic, for intellectuals; but its doctrines would find their way slowly among the less intellectual. To Tate, he laid down his credo: "I believe that the spiritual and intellectual conquest of the South, which Dodd laments, is superficial. . . . The purpose of my life is to undermine by 'careful' and 'detached,' 'well documented,' 'objective' writing, the entire Northern myth from 1820 to 1876. My books will not interest the general reader. Only the historians will read them, but it is the historians who teach history classes and write text books and they will gradually and without their own knowledge be forced into our position. There are numerous Southerners sapping and mining the Northern position by objective, detached books and Dodd is certainly one of the leaders."[17]

This was an awkward ambition, by the canons of the historical profession. On one level, it was straightforward. Owsley believed that the Southern position was the objective truth, so there was no problem. But a professional historian was obliged to rest his case upon evidence. For a John Ransom, history was myth. It did not matter too much what counter-evidence was thrown at him: the final appeal was to an intuitive judgment about the nature of man. As a committed "scientific" historian, Owsley could not merely practice his own prejudices. He was on a knife edge of historiographical change.

In viewing Owsley's attitude towards historical objectivity, it is instructive to note an exchange of letters between him and Robert Penn Warren in 1938. The former had written an unfavorable review of Robert McElroy's *Jefferson Davis* for the *Southern Review*. In manuscript, Owsley had commented in this fashion upon McElroy's condemnation of Davis's proslavery views: "After all is it the business of the historian to pass ethical judgments? Is it not rather the duty of the historian to explain why individuals and peoples have conducted themselves in a certain fashion or have thought as they have?" Warren was puzzled by this, and asked if it did not contradict Owsley's own known propensity for passing ethical judgments. The historian's reply was a mirror of his own analytical confusion, and it is worth quoting at length: "I am sure that you treed me: what I seem to mean is that Mr. McElroy had no right to pass an ethical judgement, but that I reserve that right for myself. I find that I was being holy on that particular occasion. I still feel holy: Mr. McElroy obviously does not have the proper ethical values, therefore he should not be permitted to express an opinion. No it is probably not quite so intolerant as that—I mean my position. I still insist that the true historian has no right to say whether a thing is morally right or wrong—not as a historian, though he may do it as a moral or immoral being. On the other hand a historian must say, frequently, that a thing, judged from accepted economic and social standards, has had a good or bad effect—your 'value judgements,' I think. For instance, the Civil War had a bad effect upon the South because (1) it destroyed the economic and social institutions of the South without putting anything in their places (2) it killed and maimed several hundred thousand men (3) it sterilized the intellectual life of that section for nearly thirty years (4) it enabled the East to lay a protective tariff which has been detrimental to agriculture (4) [sic] it made reconstruction possible and this created animosities between the negro and white people of the South and deepened the sectional bitterness already existing between North and South (5) It gave rise to the intellectual scalawag who makes a living out of mis-representing the South in the North. Leaving the latter category of bad effects out, I would not consider any of these ethical judgements—not necessarily." This was unclear. Significantly, he agreed to the deletion of the passage from his review.[18]

These difficulties were compounded by the imperfect match of institu-tions with the regionalism of the American historical mind. It was impossible to match the tone of his prose to the character of his audience, when the audience was never predictable. The readers of the *American Historical Review,* the *Journal of Southern History,* the *American Review,* or the *Virginia Quarterly Review* were not identical, nor were they totally dis-similar. The tone appropriate to one was unwise in another, if one wished to have designs upon the beliefs of one's audience. In moving outside professional circles, as he did fully in the *American Review* or partly in the *Southern Review,* Owsley could gain a certain stature from the mantle of objectivity. The young Cleanth Brooks, for example, although he wondered if the tone of "The Irrepressible Conflict" was not too militant, was happy to add: "I have no reason to believe that all of his allegations can't be proved up to the hilt." Inside the magic circle of historians, Owsley was to be regarded with suspicion by many for his excursions into the partisanship of agrarianism.[19]

It was a difficult game to play, and he did it badly. The Scottsboro case tipped his hand more than anything. This was one of the few occasions during the 1930s when the three issues of race, intersectional relations, and communism came together. On all three, Owsley was sensitive. When he had been a student in Chicago, he had joined a discussion group called the Current Events Club. Discovering it was left wing, he had resigned.

But, for many years, he had remained on its mailing list and, by the 1930s, they were sending him down from the waste lands of the North a succession of communist pamphlets. Some related to the American Communist Party's position on the race problem, which called for the establishment of black states in the Deep South. Naively, Owsley was shocked by the proposals and got the idea that he was gaining, through the party's blundering, access to their deepest secrets. In fact, one could buy them in any New York bookstore.[20]

Reading *The Communist Position on the Negro Question* coincided with the opening of the Scottsboro trial. The accused black "rapists" were being defended by the International Labor Defense, an adjunct of the Communist party. Owsley thought he saw a conspiracy. "I am exceedingly anxious and seriously alarmed over the present agitation," he wrote. In this mood, he delivered the essay "Scottsboro: The Third Crusade" to the new *American Review* in 1933.[21]

He tried to put Scottsboro into historical perspective by claiming that there had been two concerted attacks on the South by the North, which used the Negro problem as an excuse for capitalist imperialism: the abolitionist crusade and Reconstruction. In Owsley's opinion, Scottsboro was the spearhead of a third crusade. For abolitionism, he insisted, "the industrialists, carefully coached by their lawyers and statesmen and 'intellectual' aides, realized the bad strategy of waging a frank struggle for sectional power; they must pitch the struggle upon a moral plane, else many of the intelligentsia and the good people generally might become squeamish and refuse to fight." Slavery offered the perfect excuse, even though industrialism itself was ridden with abuses. As far as Owsley could see, slavery was a paternalistic system, at least, while the factories provided appalling conditions and sired dubious sexual mores.

To emancipation, Owsley thought, was added the crime of Reconstruction, which consolidated the industrial regime. Again the blacks were pawns in an insincere game. This time the relationships of Southern whites and blacks were fatally poisoned: "The slave-holder of former days was more tolerant of the Negro's irresponsible acts, for he regarded the Negro as a juvenile race badly advised; but being human, he came to distrust and in many cases to hate the Negro." Thus the whites disciplined the presumption of blacks. But Owsley dwelled upon the psychological scars of Reconstruction: "too bitter to be soon forgotten. It has formed and will continue for many years to form the background of Southern society and political attitudes."

Scottsboro was a third move against the South. "The method is familiar," Owsley wrote. "Holding the South up to ridicule as backward, ignorant, unprogressive; waving the bloody shirt during political campaigns . . . and giving wide currency to race conflicts and lynchings in the South, while ignoring such difficulties in the North as the Chicago and St. Louis race riots." Again the intelligentsia were put into an attack on the validity of Southern justice. Now, however, the industrialists were split between capitalists and communists. By an uncomfortable analogy, Owsley tried to say that the former, in control of the Republican Party, wished to recover power after the defeat of 1932 by the old methods of "Negro governments and Republican control of the South." Understandably, he did not press the point. The communist attack seemed more clear. He outlined four groups in the crusade: the industrialists, whether capitalist or communist, "with their smart lawyers and publicity advisers"; the intellectuals paid to be propagandists; the actual victims of Southern "outrages"; and the public itself, "ready because of its inherited dislike of the South to believe the worst of that section." Thus, lastly, he explained the communist position on the Negro question. As in Reconstruction, he saw the blacks as being tempted by empty promises of land. Once more, he thought it was insincere and impractical. For the arbiter of the Negro fate was not the North, but the Southern white. As long as whites outnumbered blacks in the South by three to one, the power of veto remained.[22]

Clearly this was no stealthy smuggling of the Southern case into the court of public opinion, but a reprise of the proslavery argument, mixed with Charles Beard and Uncle Dink. To elevate Scottsboro to the dignity of a full-dress onslaught on the South was an ill-considered judgment. The intemperateness of his language, the accusations of conspiracy, seemed a dress rehearsal for the radical right literature of the 1950s. From the viewpoint of tactics, Owsley, if he wished to maintain his standing in the historical profession, would have been well advised simply to bury the essay quietly in the *American Review.* Instead, he took it with him to the annual convention of the American Historical Association in Illinois at the end of 1933. Ironically, it was the gathering to which Charles Beard gave his presidential address, considering the analytical difficulties of relativism. Tartly, the managing editor of the *American Historical Review,* in the subsequent report, relegated Owsley's paper to a footnote. Nonetheless, and interestingly, Owsley reported enthusiastic responses from his fellow Southerners. Davidson passed the news to Wade:"He said he got quite a favorable reception. The Southerners shed tears of joy: the Westerners were quite impressed. As for Easterners, they were not there in any numbers. It is the complaint of the Westerners that the Easterners don't come to Western meetings, and their antagonism toward the East (which Frank Owsley reports as enormous) is accordingly increased."[23]

The mood of Owsley was bitter, almost desperate. He talked of a student organization that might proselytize militant agrarianism. John Gould Fletcher picked up the idea on a visit to Nashville and elaborated it enthusiastically: "The movement should begin not by declaring any bold political program, but only with the ostensible object of keeping alive the memory of the Battles and Leaders of the Civil War." He suggested a name, the "Grey Jackets." They might march with pomp on Confederate anniversaries. Perhaps they might even "threaten" chambers of commerce who pursued too strenuously Southern industrialization.[24]

To this, Owsley responded promptly. He and Davidson had decided to organize the group after Christmas 1933 from sympathetic students at Vanderbilt. They were to draw up a credo, "based upon the framework of the apostles creed," which members would have to commit to memory. They would keep up a stream of correspondence to the press. "Open debates and forums will be scheduled, and our opponents invited to enter on occasion so that we may slaughter them in the presence of the multitudes — the multitudes usually being hand picked by ourselves," Owsley suggested, almost waggishly. Appropriate reading would be assigned: Howard K. Beale's study of Reconstruction, *The Critical Year*, J. T. Carpenter's *The South as a Conscious Minority*, Avery Craven's biography of Edmund Ruffin and Tate's life of Jefferson Davis. In the spring, the group could visit the Confederate cemetery at Franklin, Tennessee. If the idea was a success, other Southern universities might take it up. As Owsley saw it: "They should be dignified, restrained, but grim in the purpose of renewing the spirit and self respect of the South."[25]

In his letter Fletcher had half apologized for writing with emotion. Owsley replied: "You do not have to excuse yourself for being emotional on such subjects—the angels must weep at the arrogance, complacency, conceit and success of the Northern Industrialists. I am bitter to the marrow, clear through to the marrow. So bitter that I feel that I am losing my poise as a historian." This was written a few weeks before Owsley went to the convention in Illinois. Bitterness and a fear of violating the discreet canons of the historical profession vied in his feelings. Later he would admit to Warren that he had "stepped outside the limits of history" in his Scottsboro article. For the moment, bitterness held the upper hand.[26]

So was born the student organization, called Phalanx. At first it was secret. But in the spring of 1934, it was forced into the open. Vanderbilt University had a regular radio show on a local station, WSM. Owsley gave a talk on "Communism and the Southern Negro." There seems little doubt that it carried the same message as his Scottsboro article. He had shown it to Chancellor Kirkland of Vanderbilt, who had cleared it for transmission. After Owsley had spoken, however, WSM abruptly cancelled the series. In the ensuing controversy, the existence of Phalanx came to light. Much to Davidson's surprise, the stiff New South liberal of a chancellor didn't mind: "He is positively friendly—is glad 'there's *some* organization to speak out on such matters.'"[27]

Benjamin Kendrick, fresh from his row with Howard Odum, came to speak to the group. Seward Collins was invited. The organization would appear to have survived until the autumn of 1934, as Owsley then asked Wade if the latter was interested in a chapter of Phalanx at the University of Georgia. But it did not run as smoothly as he had hoped, for he toyed with changing its membership basis. "Only a half dozen or so serious thinkers should be admitted. Let the others go and join the K.K.K. or the Southern Manufacturers' Association," he grumbled. Perhaps its seriousness was diminished by undergraduate flippancy and Owsley disbanded it: after 1934, one finds no more reference to Phalanx.[28]

As late as 1936, Owsley was bent on his assault upon the Northern "legend" and wished to write a study of the "irrepressible conflict" between 1820 and 1876. As he outlined the plan, "It is my object in particular to examine the papers of as many abolitionists as possible—particularly *political* abolitionists like Charles Sumner—to see what motives besides religion or humanitarianism . . . lay behind the Anti-Slavery Movement." He saw his conspiracy and he would have it out. But he had scarcely articulated his intention, before he allowed the project to die. By the summer of 1936, he had changed direction. To explain this, one must retrace steps a few years.[29]

For reasons of ill health, Owsley had not been active in the agrarian movement immediately after *I'll Take My Stand.* In fact, his wife was obliged to put *King Cotton Diplomacy* through its final stages with the University of Chicago Press in 1931 for him.[30] Despite his youthful farming experience, he had been slow to interest himself in the practical side of agrarianism. But, like Tate, he was impressed on a visit to France in 1932 with the ability of an agricultural nation to withstand the Depression. As an enthusiastic Democrat, he was to be given much hope by the New Deal. By August 1933, he felt that Roosevelt was a great leader: "He aims, I am convinced, to reduce the plutocrats to ranks as far as control of government goes." And he thought, correctly, that he saw in the new administration an inclination to restore people to the land.[31] In 1935, he decided to put his thoughts on the land movement into print. "The Pillars of Agrarianism" was an attempt to "restate and elaborate the fundamental economic and political principles on which an agrarian society will probably have to rest in the United States, and most particularly in the South."[32]

Like the North Carolina liberals, for whom Denmark had held a certain fascination in the 1920s, Owsley saw a useful analogy in the agricultural-industrial balance of Scandinavia and France.[33] Restoring the strength of agriculture would not only help to solve the Depression, but it would have ideological benefits. It would create a profoundly anticommunist society; for Owsley identified the enemy as "a system which allows a relatively few men to control most of the nation's wealth and to regiment virtually the whole population under their anonymous holding companies and corporations, and to control government by bribery or intimidation." But, if economic power were decentralized, a proletariat would be rendered ineffective and communism made impossible. How could this be done?

Owsley's strategy was sectional, his prime concern to offer "a fundamental program for the South." The first priority was to take land from absentee owners, the insurance companies, and banks, and give it in fee simple to smallholders. Tenancy should be abolished, with the government buying and redistributing land. It should give "every landless tenant who can qualify, eighty acres of land, build him a substantial hewn log house and barn, fence him off twenty acres for a pasture, give him two mules and two milk cows and advance him $300 for his living expenses for one year." Such land should be assigned on the condition that, if any attempt be made to mortgage or sell it, the state would reclaim it. The unemployed might be brought from the cities to the country; those with agrarian experience could go straight to a farm, while the others might serve an apprenticeship on a plantation. Owsley also saw a need for rehabilitating soil long abused by wasteful methods, and suggested a system of fines for those who damaged the land.

Subsistence crops should be given priority. This would not eliminate the need for cash, so commercial agriculture would still be needed. Unlike most commentators, Owsley saw a bright future for the South's two staples, cotton and tobacco. Protective tariffs should be lowered and a subsidy on cotton exports established, based on the differential between domestic and world prices. In this way, the natural superiority of Southern short staple cotton would enable it to restore its primacy in world trade. Moreover, he demanded that "in order that foreign countries shall have sufficient American exchange with which to purchase our staple farm products we further insist that all farm products and raw material shipped into the United States be used in creating foreign exchange with which cotton and tobacco may be purchased and exported."

This was not too different a program from Odum's, and it faced similar difficulties of implementation. Unencumbered by Odum's nationalism, however, Owsley turned to simpler solutions. It was clear to him that none of this was possible in a government dominated by the sectional imperialism of Northern industry. It was necessary to bypass it by fundamental constitutional reform, in which the American constitution would finally recognize the reality of sectionalism. Regional governments must be established to embody the fact that the United States was not a nation, but "an empire made up of a congeries of regions marked off by geographic, climatic and racial characteristics." In this demand, Owsley was echoing a recent study by William Yandell Elliott, *The Need for Constitutional Reform*. Although a Harvard political scientist, Elliott had been at Vanderbilt in the 1920s and had even written poetry for the *Fugitive*. Under such a scheme, the federal government would retain control over matters of war and peace, interregional and interstate commerce, banking and currency matters. Sections would be equally represented in Congress, the Cabinet, and in the process of electing presidents. Congress itself would be unicameral and dominated by regional legislatures. Each region would control its own tariff or, at least, a national tariff would be the product of intersectional bargaining, "somewhat in the fashion of the late Austro-Hungarian tariff treaties." The Supreme Court would have regional seats, determined upon the nomination of individual sections. In these ways, sectional imperialism would be contained.

If this were done, Owsley saw the prospect of an agrarian renaissance. "The old communities, the old churches, the old songs would arise from their moribund slumbers," he imagined. "Art, music, and literature could emerge into the sunlight from the dark cramped holes where industrial insecurity and industrial insensitiveness have often driven them. There would be a sound basis for statesmanship to take the place of demagoguery and corrupt politics. Leisure, good manners, and the good way of life might again become ours."[34]

This was Frank Owsley's vision of an agrarian America, more thoroughly sectional than anything John Ransom ever proposed. When Ransom had dabbled in agrarian reform, he had found it weakening his sectionalism. In Owsley, the sectional instinct was more basic and showed in this daring attempt to slice through the old tension between states rights, sectionalism, and nationalism. Nothing better illustrated his indifference to states rights and devotion to the South. As a set of proposals, "The Pillars of Agrarianism" bore the mark of several influences: traces of Populism in the cry against absentee owners; progressive conservation policies as old as Owsley's ambition to be a farm demonstration agent, though purged of the implications of "efficiency"; a demand for a sectional voice in the federal government as old as Calhoun.[35]

It would be easy to dismiss this essay as daydreaming. If so, it was of a species all too common during the flexible days of the New Deal. Indeed, those interested in influencing the Roosevelt administration were to react to its publication. The essay fell into the hands of Francis Miller, chairman of the Southern Policy Committee. The committee had been founded to promote debate amongst Southerners, to hold conferences and distribute pamphlets, and to act as a lobby in Washington. The Agrarians themselves were interested and involved in the committee's activities, which formed a bridge to Odum's North Carolina group. Miller was enthusiastic about Owsley's suggestions and ordered a hundred copies of the article to be distributed among the "Southern Policy Groups" into which his organization was divided. It seems likely that, through Miller, a copy passed to the hands of Senator John H. Bankhead of Alabama.[36]

The senator had proposed a bill in Congress that would establish a subsistence homestead program. By 1937, it was to pass as the Bankhead-

Jones Farm Tenancy Act, which created the Farm Security Administration. Owsley liked to think that he had influenced the course of events. It is true that Bankhead had written to him in praise of "The Pillars of Agrarianism." But, in fact, the chief inspiration for the Bankhead act was Frank Tannenbaum of Columbia University, a specialist in Latin American history who had been impressed by agrarian revolution in Mexico. Tannenbaum's scheme had been hatched in concert with the Rosenwald Fund and certain Southerners, such as Will Alexander, who had intimate contacts with the Chapel Hill group. Owsley's correspondence with Bankhead came in March 1935, a month before the Congress established the Resettlement Administration, the Farm Security Administration's immediate predecessor. The former had been brewing as an Agriculture project for some time.[37]

Nevertheless, Owsley's article ended up as part of the general Southern pressure for the Bankhead-Jones bill, a lobby that united both Nashville and Chapel Hill. In late April 1935, Owsley, Davidson, Lyle Lanier, and others forming the "Nashville Policy Group" went down to Atlanta to participate in the Southern Policy Committee's conference that endorsed the bill. And Owsley found himself beguilingly in the midst of a buzz of interest. William Dodd, now American ambassador to Germany, congratulated him on the article: "What you say about the way to recovery represents what I pressed upon the President before inauguration." Hugo Black, the junior Senator from Alabama, responded to an Owsley reprint with a more than perfunctory answer. Apart from echoing the historian's call for tariff reform, his criticism of too much power being concentrated in too few hands, he added: "Many of the ideas included in this article have been advanced in 'I'll Take My Stand.' Perhaps with most of the arguments present[ed] by you I am in thorough accord."[38]

There was a wide consensus among Southerners in 1935 that some measure of land reform was necessary. Chapel Hill, Nashville, Washington, all concurred on that. On details, consensus failed. Some wished to establish peasant proprietorship, some to break the power of the landlords. Owsley himself was particularly virulent against absentee ownership. In his eyes, landlords themselves were not villains for they had long since lost their power to mortgage holders. In this, he was influenced by his own family history. As he told William Couch: "My father died two years ago with about 1,000 acres of land, a warehouse and a large ginnery. He had mortgaged it all to keep going during the depression which really set down in the cotton belt about 1924, and the Metropolitan Insurance Company and a couple of banks took it all over for the indebtedness which none of his heirs were able to take up because they too were in as bad a plight."[39]

From Chapel Hill itself, Owsley received encouraging letters. The foremost student of the cotton economy, Rupert Vance, expressed sympathy with the thrust of Owsley's arguments but doubted that Southern agricultural interests were sufficiently united to back even the Bankhead bill: "Areas of disorganization and poor land may welcome such a measure, but certainly not the richer areas where landlords make money occasionally by the aid of government bounties." Moreover, Vance could see little advantage in fixing people to the land "in a world of mobility."[40] William Couch, who had published his own "agrarian program for the South" a year earlier, was inclined to look benignly upon Owsley's proposals, though his own designs were more collectivist. Couch had called for farm villages, not unlike the Russian *zemstvo* of the late nineteenth century, in which the title of all village business property would be vested in the village itself: private enterprise would be limited, to prevent the growth of monopolies, and investments possibly restricted to government bonds.[41]

That Owsley was resistant to collectivism was unsurprising in that the intertwined concerns of racism and communism had impelled much of his thinking about land reform. He was keen to deny Couch's belief that economic rivalry lay at the base of racial antagonism. "There is considerable doubt in my mind," he wrote to the North Carolina editor, "whether the homesteading and general economic betterment of the negro would remove the negroes' chief grievance against the whites: the desire of the white man to maintain his social and political supremacy for the purpose of preserving the integrity of the white race." While Owsley was willing to take certain neo-Populist steps towards socialism in the form of public ownership of railroads, power companies, gas companies, steel corporations, and public utilities, he was oppressed by the fear that America might have to choose between fascism and communism. In that event, the race issue was decisive in driving him away from Marxism. As he put it to Couch: "The jargon of Marxianism . . . is the wrong language for a land with a bi-racial population. . . . .The moment violence starts the tenant white farmer and the industrial worker will become a fascist rather than a communist."[42]

In all this, Owsley had found himself drawn into contemporary political discussion. As a professional historian, he was painfully aware that he was paying a price. At the last, he got cold feet. When Tate and Agar were planning *Who Owns America?*, Owsley in an abrupt change of policy refused to join the symposium. "I am strictly an amateur in social criticism," Agar was informed, "and I feel that I am weakening myself professionally by taking too prominent a part in affairs in which I have no great knowledge." Too much time was being lost from historical research and "the kind of writing and thinking in which my training and my taste—and the means of my livelihood—lie." To Tate, he announced that he was "irrevocably out of the picture." Agar came back with a conciliatory letter, pleading that New Deal affairs were at a critical moment and all influence needed to be brought to bear on Washington: the group in the administration, sympathetic to agrarian ideas, must be helped in their struggle against the "planners" from New York. Because Owsley had been offended at the way Tate and Agar had planned the symposium without much help from Nashville, Agar made efforts to sooth Owsley's wounded pride. Briefly placated, the historian agreed to try and find time for an essay.[43] Partisanship could not be abandoned so abruptly. He continued to find himself in the middle of the correspondence between the Agrarians and the miscellaneous land reform groups who were to come to Nashville for the Agrarian-Distributist Conference in 1936. Catholic priests from the Middle West took to praising him and pointing out the sympathy between agrarianism and Benedictine feudalism. It was all getting to be too much. Agrarianism had a way of turning to strange forms, many of them speaking in accents decidedly non-Southern.[44]

But the long term decision remained. "For years I have personally and through my students, been digging at the abolition roots of American history and its writing," he had told Agar. "Until recently, I have got mighty far under some of these roots without being distrusted or accused of bias or motive . . . but I detect a certain suspicion which has without doubt arisen out of my partisan writings in the American Review and elsewhere." As he saw it, in his essay on Scottsboro and in *I'll Take My Stand,* "I not only stuck my knife in the enemy's belly, but I turned it." Inconveniently, the enemy had noticed.[45]

His essay for *Who Owns America?* was a more systematic attempt to wed his Beardianism to his sectionalism. By taking a Beardian analysis of the Constitution of 1787, he argued that the natural rights philosophy of the Founding Fathers had been modified in Philadelphia and subsequently diminished by the power of judicial review, exercised by the Supreme Court. Thereby Hamiltonianism had come to dominate the governmental process. It seemed to Owsley that it was imperative to return to first principles, especially Jeffersonian ideas, and apply them afresh to the problem of political structure. Without the philosophy of natural rights, among which he counted those of life, liberty, property, the pursuit of happiness and self-government, he saw no hope of escaping "the communist or fascist totalitarian State." In Owsley's opinion, states rights, as seen by Jefferson, was not a fundamental doctrine but a strategic improvisation to meet the needs of Jefferson's day. In the 1930s, a comparable strategy in defense of self-government would be the establishment of regional governments. Moreover, Jeffersonian laissez-faire had been so appropriated by the monied interests that Owsley thought a measure of government intervention was now necessary to protect natural rights. Most importantly, the right to personal, but not corporate, property had to be restored, for property was the basis of all other rights. Without property, a man could have no control over his fate and the American people would lose both its inheritance and its instinct for freedom.[46]

This essay showed, even more than the "The Pillars of Agrarianism," that Owsley had added Frederick Jackson Turner on sectionalism to the influence of Charles Beard. Pessimistic observations on the decline of individual property holding were not far from Turner's gloomy fears for American democracy upon the demise of the supply of free land. Owsley had reviewed Turner's posthumous volume, *The United States, 1830-1850,* in the summer of 1935 and given partial approval to the frontier thesis, though he preferred to see Turner's later work on sectionalism as a more mature synthesis than his earlier frontier hypothesis. As Owsley put it: "Turner finally realized that frontier conditions were transitory while regional and sectional factors were permanent elements and hence of more importance." And it is not idle to see in Turner's essay "The Significance of the Section in American History," with its comparison of American sections to European nations, the shadow of Owsley's call for regional regimes. In Turner's words: "The thing to be avoided, if the lessons of history are followed, is the insistence upon the particular interests and ideals of the section in which we live, without sympathetic comprehension of the ideals, the interests, and the rights of other sections. We must shape our national action to the fact of a vast and varied Union of unlike sections."[47]

So it was no accident that Owsley permitted his project for a study of abolitionist motives to die. By the summer of 1936, he was planning research into the role of the "yeoman" in the Old South, a subject at which he had barely hinted in *I'll Take My Stand.* Polemical interest in land reform had deepened his engagement with the topic. Save for the writing of a textbook, this was to engage his energies for the next twelve years. No less an expression of his agrarianism, it was crucially less suspect. For it removed him from the contentious area of intersectional relations, where he had difficulty in controlling his emotions. With an issue interior to the history of the South, he was safer.

As a student of Southern history per se, Owsley was markedly less iconoclastic than many of his fellow Agrarians. He shared their disgust with the New South, even deepened it, but he was sanguine about the democratic credentials of the ancien régime. He shared none of Tate's doubts about Jefferson's deism or Davis's self-perception of Americanism, none of Lytle's brooding on the entrepreneurial aspects of Jacksonian democracy. He was as uncritical as Douglas Southall Freeman on Robert E. Lee.[48] Sensitive on the issues of race and industrialization, Owsley was indifferent to the wider issues of social conservatism that Ransom and Tate had urged. Where they saw a contradiction between the South and the liberal democratic tradition, he saw none. In the terms employed by Louis Hartz in *The Liberal Tradition in America,* where they wished to supplant a Lockean philosophy construed as Burkean with Burke pure and simple, Owsley was happy with the mingled status quo. In Owsley's case, however, racism drove him into desperate stratagems in his interpretation of the progressive heritage.

Owsley's research on the "plain folk," despite long and hard work for himself, his wife, and his students, was to remain inconclusive. In the days before computers, it was a tedious and exhausting business to collate and assess the scattered evidence of censuses, county records, and reminiscences.[49] His main achievement, the recovery of the nonplantation Southern middle class, was very important if swiftly accomplished. The point scarcely needed to be asserted, before it was proved. Only the ideological myopia of the generation of New South historians, too bent on coping with the awkward heritage of slave plantation culture, too busy with shying away from its agrarian culture towards their own urban bourgeois society to spend time exploring the niceties of social structure in the countryside, had prevented its discovery. For too long, nonplantation whites had meant "poor whites." Owsley sometimes got his precise figures wrong, as Fabian Linden indicated in a devastating review in 1948, and was prone to over-estimate the political weight of the yeoman class, but his central argument was important and inarguable. What he did with the society he had uncovered was more contentious.[50]

Like Odum's, Owsley's feeling about the "plain folk" was Herderian in its emphasis upon "folkways" and nationalism. As he wrote in *Plain Folk in the Old South:* "It may be contended with much force that there can be no true nationalism where the population does not constitute a folk. The Southern people . . . were a genuine folk long before the Civil War." With such a premise, he was obliged to be rather cavalier with ethnic anomalies in his folk. He took as his norm the Scotch-Irish and the English and merged them into a unified folk with a nonchalance that, though traditional, would have been impenetrable to a citizen of Wiltshire or Londonderry or Glasgow in the eighteenth century. Southerners were "predominantly British, being a mixture of English and Scotch, with here and there a dash of German, French, or Irish." Nor was it clear that the Salzburgers of Georgia or the Creoles of Louisiana would have been unjustified, in protesting their dismissal as just so much seasoning in an Anglo-Saxon stew. And Herderian was Owsley's emphasis upon a Southern language. "The spoken English of the South," he wrote, "was as distinctive a characteristic of the Southern folk as corn bread, turnip greens, and sweet potatoes."[51]

The impulse to recover the past of the nonplantation white was to broaden and complicate the vision of Southern social structure. But Owsley was unwilling, unlike his contemporary Roger Shugg, to deal with the corollary of social conflict.[52] For his Herderian historicism led him to merge the problem of social conflict into the issue of class struggle, and the latter was anathema. In this he was similar, ironically, to Ulrich Phillips. Whereas Phillips had ignored the small farm, on the grounds that it was the shadow of the plantation, Owsley ignored the plantation because he saw it as the cultural cousin of the farm.[53] Thus on language he wrote that "the speech of the plain folk and that of the more cultivated Southern people was basically the same, except, of course, that the well educated would not customarily use archaic word forms." Owsley's animosity to Marxism and his related devotion to the group loyalty of Southernism required this emphasis upon Southern cultural unity. "The Southern folk," his study insisted, ". . . were not class-conscious in the Marxian sense, for with rare exceptions they did not regard the planters and men of wealth as their oppressors." Later one finds this: "Such were the association of rich and poor in all religious activities and in the schools, the frequent ties of blood kinship between them, and the generally folkish and democratic bearing of the aristocracy. This sense of unity between all social and economic groups cannot be stressed too much, in view of the strongly and widely held opinion to the contrary. Indeed, when the entire social and economic structure of the Old South is placed in perspective, rather than viewing each segment as a separate thing, all parts will be seen as bearing a relation to the whole." Not for nothing has Herder been seen as one of the intellectual progenitors of gestalt psychology.[54]

Once again, Owsley had shown how deeply he was committed to a sectional view of American social structure. That he was himself an offspring of the "plain folk" had both qualified him to be a prime author in its historiography and disqualified him from being its dispassionate historian. As his enthusiastic and nostalgic reveries on barn raising, corn shucking, and revival meetings abundantly showed, he cared a little too much. To be in the thralls of one analytical presumption, the idea of the South, was a severe handicap, though a common one. To be caught by a second, an Arcadian vision of yeoman life, was further inhibiting. Thus a great deal of useful social history went begging for a perspective.

Owsley's work on the "plain folk" absorbed him during the 1940s. His decision to abandon polemics served him well, for he steadily rose in the graces of his fellow professionals. In 1940, he was president of the recently formed Southern Historical Association, the "white hope of the South," as he, not inappropriately, called it in 1938.[55] He was well launched upon becoming one of the elder statesmen of a flourishing Southern historical profession. His friends and former students were numerous and affectionate towards a man who breathed more daunting fire in his prose than in his good-natured presence. His *Plain Folk of the Old South* was, with important exceptions, well received both in and out of the South. In 1948, he retired to a generously endowed chair in American History at Tuscaloosa in his native state and so took a final step away from the Vanderbilt of his embattled agrarianism.[56]

With age and seniority came a growing conservatism. By the early 1940s, anticommunism had usurped pride of place in his thinking. Even in 1938, he had been mildly encouraging to an American fascist who had sought his advice, because he saw fascism as a possible counterpoise to communism. By 1944, he had switched his national allegiances to the Republican Party, a long step for a man whose political perspectives had been nurtured on the legend of Reconstruction. What tipped him away from the Democrats was, by a devious logic, the wartime activities of John L. Lewis and the United Mine Workers. During 1943, Lewis had staged two strikes in defiance of the War Labor Board and threatened a third to stop a government move to draft miners. Owsley's reaction showed how the categories of South, anticommunism and American patriotism had jumbled in his mind. In November of 1943, he wrote to Tate in a bantering spirit that did not conceal his seriousness: "Behold in me, sir, not even a *Conservative* but a *reactionary*. On race and on the 'dictatorship of the proletariat' I stand where my friend John C. Calhoun stood one hundred years ago. If I must choose between 'big business' and 'big labor'—a choice I'd always hoped never to be compelled to make—I must choose big business. . . . Carnegie, Rockefeller and Guggenheim were civilized crooks, but John L. Lewis is a Neanderthal cannibal, and his entire union and many of the other labor unions are in his image. God help this country, for it is losing at home what the soldiers are being sent abroad to fight for: *the sovereignty of the people as against the sovereignty of government.*'[57]

The logic of switching political allegiance, as Thomas B. Alexander later observed in a letter, was curious when one recalled that Lewis himself was voting Republican and the Republicans were themselves striving to recover the black vote from the Democrats. But one infers that Owsley was concerned over the Roosevelt administrations's wartime improvement of the position of blacks and saw the Democrats now standing where the Republicans had stood during Reconstruction. It had become more important for Owsley to register his protest against the movement of the times than to be tidily logical about the appropriateness of his vehicle of protest. It is well to remember that Owsley's faith in the common man had never extended to the very common man, not the poor whites below his "plain folk" nor the English working class. His ideal was a property-owning democracy, and his reaction to unionism in the 1940s demonstrated that, at the last, property weighed more heavily with him than the abuses of corporate capitalism.[58]

As the 1940s wore into the 1950s, he became more belligerent in his anticommunism, until he became almost indistinguishable from the new Radical Right. We have, as painful evidence, an undated manuscript entitled "The Chief Stakes of the South in World Affairs Today." His old weakness for the conspiracy theory found new vent. "The tactics of the Kremlin," he wrote, "are to plant its cells and agitators in every area where there is any kind of tension between social and economic and racial groups, and to increase this tension by constant agitation of grievances, until violence, disorder and chaos result." He railed at "communist agents, and their fellow travellers, and soft headed dupes." The South, he thought, had been a special target of "agents of the Politburo" for thirty years.[59]

He became wilder in his views but, beyond the perfunctory gesture of switching his vote in presidential elections, he held to his old resolve to refrain from active political polemics. Unlike Donald Davidson, he held his public peace when the crisis of desegregation broke. He might speak in private against the views of his old friend Robert Penn Warren and lace a lecture with scowls at the Supreme Court, but he preferred the discretion of silence. When Davidson taxed him with the need for action, Owsley was to wave it aside with the remark, "Well, I'm just going to brighten my own little corner." In the event, he was spared the growing intensity of the racial situation in Tuscaloosa, for he died unexpectedly of a heart attack in Winchester, England, in 1956.[60]

nine:
Donald Davidson: "The Creed of Memory"

The career of Donald Davidson was dogged by the feeling, amounting almost to resentment, that he had started life with meagre advantage and never quite made up the difference. Ransom had drawn upon the largesse of the Rhodes trustees, Wade had been pampered by his uncle's fortune, Lytle had a rich family past, Tate and Warren had been prodigies. For Davidson, there had been a slow and laborious grind in small Tennessee towns, where he had taught in schools to pay for his education. At an age when Tate was a figure in New York, Davidson had not finished his first degree. Where Ransom was urbane, Wade witty, Warren fecund, and Tate brashly assured, Davidson seemed to find his way to the lecture room of intellectual opinion always a little too late and with his audience a few hours dispersed. Although at the heart of Agrarian counsels, he was never quite one with them. Speaking now to the survivors of the group, one finds them loud in his praises. He was, they will say, the finest of men, the gentlest, the kindest. But praise is preface to doubts about his poetry and deprecations of his politics. Even Davidson's biographers are half-apologetic: they pass over his opinions with neutral vagueness and stake his claim upon his prose style, the last resort of the embarrassed critic.[1]

Twenty-four years old before he received his B.A. from Vanderbilt University, life for Davidson was further complicated by his being drafted for the First World War and involvement in action on the western front. In 1941, on the eve of a fresh war, he recalled: "I was in the last war, over two years of it, in France and all that, and then the post-war which was even worse—and from which I've never really recovered, because I had to start under a handicap and never have 'caught up.'" For he came back to Vanderbilt in 1919 for a teaching position and was turned sadly away. He beat a retreat to the less formidable Kentucky Wesleyan College, equipped with a new wife, a new daughter, an indistinct promise from Edwin Mims that he would be summoned back, and a most melancholy disposition.[2]

Wartime experience seems to have given him no taste for either travel or Europe. Waiting in France for demobilization, he delivered severe judgment on the factious Europeans who had dragged him across the Atlantic and were deliberating at Versailles: "I believe that the Allied diplomats are using the same old methods that they clung to before the war, that, in fact, partly brought on the war in all probability, while in opposition to this is the American, idealistic, but thoroughly common-sense diplomacy of Wilson. It is my guess that it has been the European statesmen who have caused the delay. Europe is a hundred years behind

the United States, I would say." There is little evidence that he ever
deflected the drift of that opinion. While his friends went off regularly to
England, France, and Italy, Davidson did not bother to return until
three years before his death in 1968. Even then the trip was not his own
idea.[3]

In 1943, Davidson was asked if, granted the prerogative, he would
have allowed Joyce's *Ulysses* to be published. He returned an emphatic
"NO," and added, apropos an indelicate passage in a Warren poem—"piss
in his pants" was the offending passage—"All of you boys have been
corrupted by Europe." An old student was to remember Davidson's
expression of pain and disgust, when asked for a Rhodes scholarship
testimonial, and the exclamation, "Oxford—why in the world do you
want to go to Oxford." In the years before the outbreak of the Second
World War, Davidson was a supporter of America First. In 1937, he
resisted an editorial effort by Warren and Brooks to amend his anti-
Europeanism. "I insist," he told them, "on the uniqueness of the American establishment and on its separateness from Europe."[4]

This suspicion of a decadent Old World put him at odds with both
Ransom and Tate, though in sympathy with Frank Owsley. When Tate
was preaching the new gospel of Eliot, Davidson stayed unconvinced. In
his insecurity, he sometimes put it down to his own dullness. He told
Tate in 1922 that "for reasons of ignorance I find myself floundering
about and not quite understanding either your poems or Eliot's.... I
am such a poor philosopher and psychologist." Nonetheless he would
chaff Eliot's Anglicized hauteur, in a review of *For Lancelot Andrewes*.
Eliot, he alleged, "is not writing for us hungry sheep, swollen with the
wind of temporal doctrines, but for posterity. With troubled heart, one
surmises that Mr. Eliot would regard the possibility of writing on Sinclair
Lewis with exactly the same revulsion that he would contemplate a visit
to his mother country." Crucially, Davidson cared little for the emphasis
of Tate and Ransom upon religion. When Tate, in Paris, began to think
well of Roman Catholicism, Davidson observed: "I, too, am attracted
somewhat toward Catholicism, as toward High Church Episcopalianism.
But I like better to be tied up with no church at all. I find myself more
repelled than attracted by all clergymen and priests. If it were not for
them, possibly I could become something-or-other in a religious way. As
matters stand, I seem to be bothered less by religious matters than by
anything else. Maybe I'm just an animal after all."[5]

As a Fugitive poet, Davidson adopted a markedly less modern tone
than either Tate or Ransom. His verses were lusher, more Romantic,
looking backwards towards a fading bardic tradition rather than inward
to a faltering capacity for religious or philosophic coherence. Himself
an accomplished guitarist and singer, Davidson was wont to insist that

poetry, like folk song, should be available to the common man and convey the traditions of a people. In this, he was at one with the Howard Odum who was gathering up the white and black songs of the South. As Davidson put it in a later poem, "Happy the land where men hold dear/ Myth that is truest memory/Prophecy that is poetry."[6] And he was to stay closest, in instinct, to the "people." When Ransom was roused by the Dayton trial, Davidson too looked again at his Southernism; but the difference in tone is instructive. Ransom was annoyed to see a worthy, albeit untutored, position under fire and went like a lawyer to defend the fundamentalist case in language that the court of intellectual opinion might understand. Davidson, more simply, felt close to the men of the Tennessee hills. For him, it was not a position under attack, it was almost himself.

One says "almost," because the Davidson of the mid-1920s had not begun the alienation from the intellectual community that was to embitter his later years. He had achieved some distinction in his poetry. Restored to Vanderbilt, he seemed set for orderly academic promotion. From 1924, he was to run a book review page for the *Nashville Tennessean.* And part of his first impulse in writing about the South was, ironically, of the New South. His middle name was Grady, in honor of the editor of the *Atlanta Constitution.* Later, when he knew what that implied, he dropped its usage. But, in his youth, he knew little about the New South. The political education of his boyhood had been Confederate. He had been regaled by his grandparents with tales of the war, and by his father with reminiscences of seeing Andrew Johnson speak and the Klan ride. For hours he had sat outside the country store in Mulberry, Tennessee, and talked to the war veterans. At school, his friends used futilely to hunt their building for the blood stain which was said to mark the spot of General Van Dorn's death.[7]

Indeed, the New South had meant little to him until he went to university and had to read Edwin Mims's textbook, *Southern Prose and Poetry,* which was generously sprinkled with industrialist perorations. And Davidson was never to be free entirely of the influence of Edwin Mims. On Mims, his department chairman and an autocrat, rested Davidson's hopes of the academic security he desperately wanted and needed. As a teacher, Mims had given Davidson his first critique of the South's place in the modern world.[8] When Tate poured scorn on Mims's *The Advancing South,* Davidson came to the defense: "I agree that Mims on all aesthetic matters is not the man for you or me.... But, as I see it, his book and his industrious dissemination of ideas (which in a direct form wouldn't get far) make the South a little more habitable. What looks very bad ('vulgar' you say) in New York, looks perhaps 'vulgar' in a sense, but also hopeful, down here."[9]

When one turns to his first sustained commentary on the cultural politics of the South in 1928, one finds a mixed bag of emerging agrarianism and fading New South liberalism. The coming Davidson was foreshadowed in an emphasis upon the vitality of the frontier tradition in the South, the call for noninterference in Southern affairs, the defense of provincialism as "a refuge against the cruel conformity ordered by our always accelerating, standardizing civilization," the horror of the ugly artifacts of industry. But one also finds sentiments almost straight from *The Advancing South*. There was a defense of the recent progressive administration of the Tennessee governor Austin Peay, and a keenness to explain that the Dayton trial and fundamentalism would not retard the "progress" of the South. Educational growth was held to be encouraging, for universities were "nuclei from which ideas work outward, impregnating the commonwealth of social thought." In teachers like Ransom, Mims, and Paul Green, the universities were offering "resident spiritual forces that outweigh all the statistics of literacy and illiteracy." At the center of Mims's 1926 analysis had been the development of a more self-critical Southern public opinion, and Davidson stressed that point. Most astonishingly, he even smiled upon the Southern business community. While he regretted their loss of contact with the nineteenth-century paternalistic tradition, he saw them as the key to the situation. With their help, intellectual progress might come. Without it, Southern thought might be stifled.[10]

Davidson's role as a book page editor was important in this sympathy for the New South in its "educational" phase. Unlike his elitist friends, he bore a direct responsibility for addressing a substantial chunk of the Southern public. Welcoming the task of popularization, he wanted to ease the masses into rediscovering themselves and to help them sort out the wheat from the chaff of modern literature. "It may be true," he wrote in 1928, "as some of our critics have said, that the Southern audience has long been provincial in a bad sense, and needs to be scolded and admonished out of its obstinate wicked habits. But I cannot altogether agree, for the greater need seems to be that the South should explore its own mind and rediscover itself." Thus Davidson had put himself in the Mims-like role of a cultural missionary. But in 1928, he was far from clear about the nature of his mission.[11]

The task of Southern "rediscovery" was as much a personal quest as a public intention. In 1926, he had begun to speculate that perhaps the South offered prospects for the writer. Indeed, he had started his minor epic, *The Tall Men*. But until then, he had not much read Southern literature. Over the next several years he looked at the likes of William Wirt, William Byrd of Westover, Thomas Jefferson, and John Pendleton Kennedy. Davidson wanted to "define, as significantly as possible for the present and with all the critical soundness I can muster, the Southern Tradition as it has manifested itself in literature." But it is striking how tentative the venture seemed to him in the years before *I'll Take My Stand.* In 1926, he wondered if his feeling that the South offered a mode for the writer wasn't a delusion. In 1927, reading Southern literature, he was wary: "I have not yet gone far enough to say what I may be able to do or whether indeed the undertaking will prove ultimately worth while."[12]

"The undertaking" was a projected history of Southern literature. In the wake of the interest stirred by *The Advancing South,* Oxford University Press had asked Ransom to write such a book. Absorbed in philosophy, he declined. Thereupon they turned to Davidson. As a book page editor, Davidson had been facing the steady succession of new Southern literature —Cabell, Glasgow, Heyward, Stribling—and the fresh wave of historical writing on the region from Phillips, Beard, Claude Bowers. For perhaps the only period in his life, he was strictly *au courant.* By dint of his reading in eighteenth- and nineteenth-century Southern literature, he was ready by the summer of 1929 to produce a significant book. In that year, there were available only the scattered evaluations of New South critics and a few superficial surveys. It was an opportunity, and one he failed to grasp, despite a long summer of trying to turn out the book at Yaddo, the writers' colony. Ransom told Tate: "He's been steadily losing his power of productivity. Last summer, at some sacrifice, he went away to Yaddo to write a book; but after a month the book hadn't come, not begun to come. That impaired his morale, I think; it was a tragic experience." Davidson was very depressed about his life. He felt crowded out by the inexorable pressures of teaching, editing, and trying to write poetry and criticism.[13] This mood was the background to his involvement in the 1930 symposium. But for several years, he was to strike a bad patch. The time between *The Tall Men* in 1927 and the summer of 1932 was remarkably barren. It was the good fortune of Tate and Ransom to hit the stride of their commitment to the South around the moment of *I'll Take My Stand.* In 1930, Davidson was confused in his thinking. It was his tragedy that, when he did find his own voice, the debate and his friends had moved on.

In fact, his 1930 essay in the symposium and a piece on "Southern literature" for *Culture in the South* (published in 1934, but written in 1930) can be taken as the shadow of the book that never was. In "A Mirror for Artists," Davidson discoursed for twenty-four pages on the invalidity of an industrial theory of the arts, on the mutilating futility of industry trying to play the Maecenas. Only then did he come to the South. The essay did represent a repudiation of Mims and the New South, but it was not yet the mature Davidson. For it was heavy with borrowings from Ransom and Tate that were internally inconsistent with his own line of thought. For instance, he took Tate's idea of a dissociation between the artist and society, Ransom's emphasis on the futility of a humanist education in a technical world and the ex-Rhodes scholar's view of the Old South as a European civilization. These perspectives joined oddly with Davidson's lack of patience with artistic elitism and distrust of democracy. "Art in its great periods," he wrote, "has rarely been purely aristocratic. It has generally been also 'popular' art in a good sense and has been widely diffused." When he turned to the South, he pointed to folk crafts as its chief glory, "ballads, country songs and dances, in hymns and spirituals, in folk tales, in the folk crafts of weaving, quilting, furniture-making." And he was reluctant to identify the South with a conservative squirearchy. In the Old South, as he saw it, there had been "a fair balance between aristocratic and democratic elements. Plantation affected frontier; frontier affected plantation." Moreover, Davidson was very careful to separate the suspicious congruence in the growth of democracy and industrialism. "Democracy did not... disturb society unduly," he said. "It was a slow growth, it had some continuity with the past, and in an agrarian country like pre-Civil War America it permitted and favored a balanced life."

Nonetheless, and in distinction from his later views, Davidson was still reluctant to put too much weight upon the South as a concrete entity. He was scathing towards the "specious theory" that an independent country should produce an independent art, the thinking that had produced the silly demand for a great American novel. "For many reasons the Southern tradition deserves rehabilitation," he suggested, "but not among them is the reason that it would thus enable Southern artists to be strictly Southern artists." What did seem clear to him was that it was artistic folly to write across the grain of one's social background. This had weakened much New South literature: Glasgow, Stribling, and the rest had tried to become surrogate Northerners, because the Southern tradition had become inaccessible.[14]

For all this, the reader of "A Mirror for Artists" and "The Trend of Literature: A Partisan View" was left with a muddy impression of just what Davidson thought the South to be. He had vacillated uncomfortably between the South as a "nation within a nation," the universality of art and the provincialism of literary sources, the Southern-cum-European equation of Ransom and his own isolationism. In truth, he could not have it all ways. He could not be John Ransom, Allen Tate, and Donald Davidson all at the same time. It was to be several years before he had the courage to be himself.

That he was released from their influence to find his own way, later embodied in *The Attack Upon Leviathan,* was due to a certain deterioration in his relations with Tate and Ransom. The two had become irritated with Davidson's reluctance to commit himself to "practical" agrarianism, his dallying failure to secure a contract for *I'll Take My Stand* in 1930, his refusal to act over the Harlan strike or the idea of asking the Guggenheim Foundation to fund an agrarian newspaper. Ransom commiserated with

Tate from England: "I'm afraid Don's going to get, not less, but more incapable of action. His trouble is pretty deep. He can't be jollied out of his melancholy, and as for intimidation, Don is like a large Tennessee knob of limestone."[15] Tate's return to live in Tennessee cooled the warm relations that had flourished in their Fugitive days and been sustained in the remoteness of correspondence. Davidson came to be suspected of too rigidly provincial leanings. In early 1932, the editor of the *Hound and Horn* suggested that Davidson might be commissioned to write a piece on sectionalism. Tate responded coolly: "Alas, my editorial connection with you will force me to betray our secrets! Don, I should say, is the least clear-headed person in Tennessee.... He would not do you a good article on Sectionalism in general, but he would surely write a paper in which the philosophy of *Southern* sectionalism received a stirring defense. Of all our people, Don is the great Literalist in doctrine, and probably our finest character, but sheer, realistic intelligence—no."[16]

Intellectual differences were strengthened by social habits. Davidson was something of a Puritan, who frowned at the bootleg whiskey that often turned Agrarian gatherings a shade noisy. Friends were seldom invited to his home, partly because his Ohio-born wife felt little sympathy for them. Many years later, a student remembered an evening at the Davidson residence, when the after-dinner entertainment consisted of listening to Wagner with scores set solemnly before the guests. In 1936, Tate explained the social gulf between them like this: "What I have felt at times is this: some mild resentment for your withdrawing from us, for your difficulty of access, for your refusal to take any part in the simple social pleasures that not only give us relaxation from the difficulties of a special kind of life, but actually strengthen the more serious ties that hold us together....you have put such a dense barrier between your friends and your private life that we cannot penetrate it.... I cite all this to explain my own behavior in the last few years—behavior that can best be described as motivated by a feeling that it is futile to seek you out and to attempt to continue our social life with you." Harriet Owsley could not recall ever going to the Davidsons for dinner. And, when Andrew Lytle returned from California in the late 1930s with a new bride, he was surprised to be invited over by Davidson and scandalized when the latter remarked: "I've got Coca-Cola. But if you want beer, I'll have to get it." Lytle was appalled at the insensitive suggestion. "Beer," he later recalled, "I never drink beer. I drink whiskey!"[17]

The emotional separation between Davidson and some of his friends, a separation to which Wade formed an important exception, had a striking simultaneity with his shift towards a more literal sectionalism. It would be idle to speculate on which came first, for they fed each other. Tate and Ransom, when their involvement with agrarianism drove them away from Southernism, saw an opposite tendency in Davidson. In particular, they saw a polemical intention in some of his poetry. Davidson, following his own honest intellectual logic, saw their increasing remoteness. This fed his melancholy and solitary temperament, and drove him further into dependence upon the emotional group loyalty of Southernism. It was a gradual and uneven process. Arguments over the title of *I'll Take My Stand,* the Guggenheim application, and the Harlan strike coincided with Davidson's failure to write his history of Southern literature, the collapse of his book page in late 1930, and the death of his father. In between were the episodes where the group was driven together by common enterprise: the planning of the 1930 symposium and, later, the launching of the *American Review.* At these moments, Davidson could be found in optimistic mood. In March 1931, he could surmise that the Agrarians "feel pretty strongly that the current of the times is in our favor." In March 1933, he enthused about the new magazine: "I am terrifically optimistic about the prospects, where I was gloomy a week ago. My head already boils with ideas."[18]

During and after 1935, several incidents seemed to confirm his growing isolation within the group: a row over the tenth anniversary issue of the *Virginia Quarterly Review,* the planning of *Who Owns America?,* the editorial policy of the new *Southern Review,* and, much later, Ransom's attitude when editor of the *Kenyon Review.*

When in 1934 the editors of the *Virginia Quarterly Review* decided to have a special anniversary issue of the journal deal with Southern matters, they issued invitations to various Southerners to contribute essays, poems, and short stories. Davidson was pained to discover that, unlike Ransom, Tate, Warren, and Wade, he was not asked to contribute. While in Vermont, James Southall Wilson tactlessly read Davidson excerpts from a letter of Allen Tate, making suggestions of possible contributors but not mentioning Davidson. Though hurt, Davidson kept his silence. Eventually a belated invitation did turn up, and he decided to write an article on the genesis of *I'll Take My Stand* that might clear away misconceptions about the book's intentions. Meanwhile, in January 1935, the *Virgina Quarterly Review* carried an essay by H. L. Mencken that took the Agrarians, especially Davidson, soundly and rudely to task. Davidson remonstrated with the editor, Lambert Davis, that a friendly Southern journal had no business publishing the inaccurate fulminations of Mencken. Davis countered with a temperate and apologetic letter, which seemed to satisfy.[19]

Soon after, Davis found to his embarrassment that his anniversary issue threatened to become an Agrarian symposium. The Agrarians had been prompt and efficient in accepting his invitations, while Southerners of other ideological persuasions had been dilatory. Wishing to maintain a balance of opinion, he decided to reject Davidson's article.[20] At this, Davidson saw the faint shade of a plot to keep him out. Unwisely, he confided his fears to John Gould Fletcher, at a time when the poet was undergoing one of his periodic bouts of mental instability. At the conference in Baton Rouge in April to launch the *Southern Review,* Fletcher was to be at his most belligerent; on his way home to Little Rock, he was to collapse in Memphis.[21] In such a mood, he had decided to rush to Davidson's defense. The Arkansan hurled insulting scrawls to all the Agrarians who had contributed to the anniversary issue, to demand that they withdraw their articles or else he would "resign" from the group. Astonished at the violence of the outburst, Davidson found himself caught between his friends and Fletcher's ostensible defense. When the dust settled, he found himself a little more isolated.[22]

After *I'll Take My Stand* was published, there had been loose talk of producing a second symposium. In 1932, the idea had gained headway after discussions between Fletcher and Ransom in New Mexico. The business of approaching publishers was delegated to Davidson. Through no particular fault of his own, he was unable to interest anyone in the idea and the project languished.[23] In 1935, Tate and Herbert Agar revived the plan with distinctly nonsectional intentions. Like Frank Owsley, Davidson was on the sidelines. When the idea of an Agrarian-Distributist conference was broached, Davidson suggested a preliminary Agrarian parley. With a quiet despondency, he added to Tate: "But that is just my opinion. I defer on the question of policy and practical steps to you and Agar, who are now clearly the Generals-in-Chief." Later he remarked: "Well, it all sounds mighty exhilarating, after all these years of biting our nails in impotence. I only wish it were possible to hang out a Confederate flag when we meet next week." He well knew that the Stars and Bars was becoming un-fashionable.[24]

The *Southern Review* put Davidson a little further out in the cold. Warren was not his closest friend. In 1935, Davidson felt it just to remark that "Warren . . . has not seemed to me to be particularly keen for anything from me." If one one looks at a statement of editorial policy by Warren like this: "The SOUTHERN REVIEW is attempting to provide a kind of focus for literary activity in the South, but holds that its purpose can best be served by maintaining the highest standard possible, rather than by publishing something merely because its author happens to be a Southerner," one finds a sentiment intellectually palatable to Davidson, but emotionally distasteful. In the case of the *Kenyon Review,* Ransom's break with agrarianism and dislike of Davidson's "polemical" poetry was more brutally obvious. Only once did he ask Davidson to do even a review. One finds this in a Ransom letter to Tate in 1939: "Don is a real problem to me. I haven't been able yet to write about his book of selected poems, and I simply couldn't touch them in a published review; nor do I dare send them out to any good reviewer. Don just stopped growing before the rest of us did. . . . Don's case is partly private but partly, I'm afraid, the effect of ideology."[25]

So he came to realize through the 1930s that the most prominent intellectuals among his friends did not respect his work. The lonely feeling of rejection came to haunt and embitter him. In 1936, he felt moved to write that he had "become an outsider, and the state of my feelings is so confused and irritated that I cannot tell to my own satisfaction whether I have just stepped outside or been kicked outside." In 1937, he came to refer to himself as "a lone guerilla" and "Banquo's Ghost."[26]

To this estrangement, John Wade had proved an exception. Davidson and the Georgian had been friendly in 1930, when Wade's lack of polemical zeal had drawn criticism. Events in 1932 were to intensify this unlikely alliance of the patrician who liked irony to do service for commitment and the earnest English professor, who cast himself in the role of a prophet without honor. Davidson had lived for many years in Wesley Hall, a rambling dormitory on the Vanderbilt campus. In the spring of 1932, it burned to the ground. Neither Davidson nor his family were injured, but the blaze carried off most of their possessions. Books, correspondence, a First World War diary, back numbers of the *Fugitive* were consumed. Added to other setbacks, the incident badly jolted Davidson and, to recover his poise, he asked for and received a year's leave of absence. Generously, Wade offered to let Davidson stay in a cottage on his Marshallville estate. Thus, after a summer in Vermont, the Davidsons went as "refugees" to middle Georgia.[27]

The Marshallville year marked a turning point, at which Davidson began to climb out his slough of noncreativity. His time was free of book pages and teaching, he received a commission to write a major article on sectionalism for the *Hound and Horn,* the *American Review* was founded, his first look at life in Vermont had offered fresh perspectives. Even more important, the area around Marshallville was a revelation to him. Davidson's South had been the semifrontier regions of middle Tennessee. The plantation culture of Macon County surprised and pleased him with its reminiscence of the Old South. The grace of the Wade household, presided over by the forceful Ida, impressed him. "Marshallville is a grand place to rusticate," he told Lytle. "I lead a quiet life—cultivate a garden, wander about, read and (I hope) write, enjoy the people and the landscape. This is a really agrarian section—quite the Old South in tone and in deed. There are horses, mules, wagons, negroes, plantations, good soil, good people, good manners—and there *used to be* money. I like it all tremendously."[28]

Marshallville gave one precious commodity to a man deep in self-doubt —respect. It must have contrasted agreeably with the tangled intellectual relationships of Nashville. The "villagers" did not look upon him as a man who had failed to write his magnum opus, or a poet tinged fatally with "ideology." They saw only a courteous young professor, friend to the local squire, who joined in their community activities without condescension. He went along to their Sacred Harp meetings and lent his pleasant tenor voice. He gave a paper to the local discussion group and was applauded for putting the village radical in his place. On Confederate Memorial Day, he attended services at the local graveyard. Not a man to stand at the gate and ponder the dissociation of the modern sensibility, he sang their Civil War songs and listened, with growing emotion, to the roll of the honored dead. At the end, as the guest of the village, he was introduced to the gathering and read them his poem on "The Army of the Tennessee."[29]

All this helped to restore his confidence, both in himself and in the integrity of the ordinary Southerner. So he wrote of his new experiences in Georgia and Vermont, and started to refine his attitude towards the New South heritage. While his friends had so often found themselves held by the agrarian side of the Southern/agrarian equation, Davidson grew more fascinated by the Southern aspect. It seemed time to undertake a serious analysis of the place of sectionalism in American life. For he had read Parrington and knew that the redefinition of literature to include "political literature" had put new responsibilities upon the critic. He had pondered Beard's writings in 1930, with some distaste. In early 1933, after he had begun the new venture, he became aware of Turner's *The Significance of Sections in American History*. Exuberantly, he had written to Tate: "Have you seen . . . Turner's posthumous book.   I have not yet seen a copy, but the reviews indicate that it sustains powerfully *all* my major contentions as to the nature and importance of sectionalism . . . our ideas rest on a foundation which not even the most 'advanced' historians can lightly reject .
. . . I feel somewhat exultant that I had, without prompting, worked out something of what Turner concluded."[30]

From late 1933 to 1937, he composed and assembled the essays that form *The Attack on Leviathan: Regionalism and Nationalism in the United States*. It was published in 1938 by the University of North Carolina Press to a resounding silence. Not to Davidson's surprise, it sold very badly.[31] Overshadowed by the simultaneous publication of Jonathan Daniels's cheerful and journalistic *A Southerner Discovers the South,* Davidson reflected with characteristic gloom and defiance: "I am not, however, bothered so much on my own personal account, having long been used to rough and casual treatment and having ceased, long before this, to expect very much of the world."[32] This neglect has not been remedied since then. And yet, it was one of the most impressive analyses of sectionalism and the South to be offered in the 1930s, a decade peculiarly concerned with that problem. Indeed, with the exception of Odum's work, it was the *only* sustained examination of the problem, which proved both its strength and its weakness.[33]

Davidson finished *The Attack on Leviathan* at a time when the reputation of sectional analysis was deceptively high. In Parrington, Turner, Odum, wherever he turned, Davidson seemed to find authoritative voices to tell him that sectionalism was "an effective reality, amounting almost to a commonplace, to be accepted and dealt with entirely aside from its status as a political and social problem."[34] As a literary critic and poet, he well knew that he was in the midst of a "Southern Renaissance." Aware that he was an amateur in fields that mattered deeply for his analysis, it was a comfort to Davidson to be reassured.

Although he had seen that he disagreed with Odum over the weight to be attached to the words, "sectionalism" and "regionalism," when the latter had approached him during his fracas with Benjamin Kendrick, they had parted friends. Davidson had refused Odum's absolute distinction, but understood his motives: "The terms *section* and *sectionalism* seem to him too schismatic and contentious for complete acceptance. The scientist wants a scientific term. . . . The words *region* and *regionalism* suit his purpose better." As Davidson saw it: "I can't conceive of our country as offering a fixed hierarchy of values: 1. Something called a nation, of which you must think first; 2. Something called a region, of which you are privileged to think, if you are careful to give it second place. . . . I should say, rather that regionalism or sectionalism thinks of the nation in its proper place and of the region or section in its place, without elevating one above the other. I have no abstract devotion to some entity called the nation, but I am loyal to a loose historic entity called the United States, whose government, with some important exceptions, has acted as arbiter between sections." Nonetheless, with every statistic that Odum piled up about the "Southern Regions," Davidson felt secure that sectionalism was solid enough to put analytical weight upon. "Sociology," he observed in *The Attack on Leviathan,* "is indeed in many ways the friend of differentiation, and it has been led by its allies, the geographers, the demographers, and the anthropologists, to make new and broad extensions of its studies of the varying cultures existing within the general pattern of American life."[35]

So the early pages of the book were spent in drawing up his, occasionally unwilling, allies. Turner and Beard were arbitrated, to the disparagement of the latter. Like Turner and Owsley, Davidson saw American history as the ebb and flow of sectional imperialism. Although Davidson owed much to the Beardian concept of the Civil War as a "Second American Revolution," he could not accept Beard's view of sectionalism as a transient phenomenon that would pass with the nationalizing force of industrialization. To Davidson, Turner represented the Jeffersonian democratic tradition, "which takes into consideration old and well established American preferences, emanating both from inheritance and environment," while Beard betrayed a "late-European, anti-traditional view of all society": Turner was the historian of continuity, Beard the prophet of discontinuity.[36] Then, to Turner, Davidson added the authority of an Odum, purged of the "regional" interpretation. Shrewdly, Davidson struck at the two fundamental weaknesses of the Chapel Hill position: the improbability of social decisions being made by social scientists and the incongruity of manifestly local spokesmen attempting to "defuse" regional passions. As Davidson envisaged it, Chapel Hill was caught in a vicious circle. To move and act upon the region, it was necessary to arouse its communal feelings. But sectional emotions, once summoned from the vasty deep, were hard to control. "Can the social science regionalists achieve a unified effort without unleashing the sectional antagonisms that they disclaim?" he asked. And, reading these pages, one's mind goes forward to an old Howard Odum, hurriedly convening his friends to consider the 1954 Brown decision, and seeing his delicate straddling of the race question placed under intolerable strain.[37]

From sociology and history, Davidson turned to the arts. He traced the "cosmopolitan" phase of American literature from 1912 and the establishment of *Poetry* in Chicago, to the "regional" literature of the 1930s. This seemed a movement from a "European" phase, "an adventure paralleling . . . the adventure in internationalism represented by American participation in the World War and in European post-war economics" to a rediscovery of indigenous American materials. But he was careful to grant a place for both European and regional influences in the interplay that produced a worthwhile American literature. In this, he was repeating all of the strictures of a Tate and Warren against a too self-conscious regionalism. Nonetheless, his version of recent literary history paralleled his vision of political and economic sectionalism to a degree that would have discomfited his friends. The ebbing and flowing of literary preeminence—Boston at the time of Emerson, Chicago in 1912, New York in the 1920s, the South in the 1930s —matched his Turnerian idea of sectional imperialism.[38]

Running through Davidson's analysis was a distinctly Romantic thread, the idea of *genius loci*. As he wrote of American literature, "the indigenous materials will derive some of their shape and force from the *genius loci*—the region itself—and thus become a foreign influence pervading other regions, and giving as well as receiving. . . . The regions will develop their arts as they develop their people and ways of life." This made *The Attack on Leviathan* a historicist book, a part of the great if problematical tradition that started indistinctly with Giambattista Vico in Naples, flowered more coherently with Herder in Germany, and found expression in the analytical achievements of German historical writing in the nineteenth century, the tradition that held that men were necessarily gathered into and understood through organic groups, which leave evidence of themselves through the human institutions of language, customs, religion, legends, myths, moral and legal systems, literature, and the arts.[39]

But Davidson wished to arrogate historicism to individual American regions, not to the United States as a nation. His book was about American, not merely Southern, regionalism. As such, it was incumbent upon him to define how people and social life varied from region to region. Thus, in four chapters, he sketched his impression of regional "types" in the South, New England, New York, the Southwest and Old Northwest, and the Great Plains. It had been suggested by an editor that completeness required a chapter on the Far West, but Davidson eventually demurred because his personal experience did not extend so far. Although he was modern enough to be diffident about it, the crucial sentence ran like this: "Although I do not hold very devotedly to the economic determinism of modern historians, it was a temptation to say that the people were a great deal like the land."[40]

Vermont was taken as a metaphor for New England: here one found frugal Calvinists taught prudence by the severity of winter and the brevity of summer. John Wade's middle Georgia was seen as the South, lazy, gracious, flattered by a lush but intimidating environment that proffered rich crops, rattlesnakes, and the mixed benefits of the Negro race, "a cheerful grinning barnacle tucked away in all the tender spots of Southern life, not to be removed without pain, not to be cherished without tragedy." As for New York, its great port had made it the entrepreneur of European ideas and the eclectic sponge of émigré Americans from the hinterland. The Middle West was portrayed as a New England extended over vast but manageable prairies, easy of access, "where 'planning' rather than ruggedly individualistic growth fitted the topographical situation." The Old Southwest of Tennessee and Kentucky had a separate logic: "The genius of this land was in its great irregularity and variety, which both invited and repelled in its changing profile of mountain, plateau, hill, valley, plain and swamp. It more or less enforced self-sufficiency and isolation upon settlers and settlements that were secluded by the very contours of the land." As for the Great Plains, Davidson deferred in his characterization to the contemporary work of Walter Prescott Webb.[41]

In these crude blocks of analysis, Davidson did his best to weave a subtle portrait of the interaction between environment, historical factors like immigration, slavery, and the presence of Indians. But his brush strokes were too clumsy and willing, his units of analysis too large while being based on too small a range of experience. The farm of Homer Noble in Middlebury, Vermont, and the plantation of John Wade in Marshallville were not synonyms for New England and the South. It is doubtful that they even worked as metaphors. In this, Davidson had all the difficulties of Howard Odum in *American Regionalism,* with the advantages that the needs of social planning did not wreak havoc with regional groupings and Davidson could write well. Nonetheless, for all their vulnerability to intellectual atomism, these chapters offered a valuable insight into the conventional wisdom of American regionalism. Davidson may not have been right enough to satisfy the relativistic patchwork of the historical sociologists, but he faithfully mirrored what many Americans thought was right. As such, he was documenting a significant chunk of American psychological reality and, with imprecision, fragments of an American social reality always crucially out of focus. Thus, when dealing directly with social psychology, as in a chapter on "American Heroes," a study in the localized perception of hero worship, he was at his most convincing.[42]

Davidson was conscious of mounting an attack on the notion of an American national literature. He had, in effect, to put Madame de Staël to work for the South, not for the whole country. He was convinced that the pursuit of a distinctive "American" genre had been based upon a mistaken analogy with Europe. Thus he tried to trace the development of the concept of nationality from the Renaissance to the nineteenth century, when literature came to be defined as "the expression, attained by slow accretion and ingrained habit, of a character that might be described as national." As Davidson saw it, each traditional European national literature had required certain conditions: "one language, one race, a definite cultural homogeneity —or at least no heterogeneity fixed by inner geographic conditions; a definite intellectual leadership associated with the centralizing presence of a capital like Paris or London; and besides, a long period of growth under aristocratic and learned guidance, and a second period, no less important from the modern standpoint, of critical and retrospective exploration of the cultural tradition." As Davidson had spent much time explaining, the United States had only one of these conditions, language. Thus there was no American national literature, but only the accumulation of regional literatures. To Davidson, this offered an exhilarating prospect, because American writing could be constantly cross-fertilized by local influences: "No other great literature has ever enjoyed the prospect open to us, of an almost indefinite enrichment from provincial sources that are not, in the usual sense of the word, provincial at all, for our provinces are more like nations than provinces."[43]

It was as quasi nations that Davidson moved to arrogate to the regions some of the prerogatives of nationality. Unsurprisingly, he echoed the call of Owsley for regional governments. And, by reprinting an address to the college section of the National Council of Teachers of English, he called for the regionalization of educational institutions and textbooks. Concerned that students were obliged to read books that reflected, not their own regional perspectives, but those of the publishing center of New York, he insisted a "good regional theory of education would call for our institutions to exercise a dual function": to inculcate the universal body of knowledge, and to preserve the texture of the students' regional background. Textbooks should thus fall into two categories: the "national," which should pay just and equal attention to the diverse regions, and the "regional," which should be produced by and for a particular locality. In this way, Davidson hoped to mitigate the cultural implications of sectional imperialism at the grass roots and thereby stabilize regional mores.[44]

The bulk of *The Attack on Leviathan* was a general analysis of American regionalism. Davidson was keen to insist that he was not merely riding a Southern hobby horse. And his comments to an editor twenty years later on the publication of *Still Rebels, Still Yankees* can serve as a pertinent commentary to the earlier book: "The general theme that binds the essays...is the conflict between tradition and anti-tradition that characterizes modern society, with tradition viewed as the living continuum that makes society and civilization possible and anti-tradition as the disintegrative principle that destroys society and civilization in the name of science and progress.... The South, which has suffered most in its devoted defense of tradition, naturally offers me examples for consideration; but this is not a book about the South as such."[45] Nonetheless, four essays were grouped under the heading "Southern Essays," and it was proper, given his general regional theory, that as a Southerner he should have attempted to define his own relationship to the Southern tradition.

One theme was binding and familiar, the attack upon the New South. This led to curious alliances. In trying to rewrite the postbellum history of the South, Davidson had joined, not only Wade, but a younger historian, C. Vann Woodward. To Woodward was to fall the primary responsibility for supplanting the versions of Virginius Dabney and Edwin Mims. In odd ways, the analysis of Woodward and Davidson ran similar courses, channels dictated by the needs of demolishing a common enemy. Their ideological standpoints were very different, in that Woodward was deeply interested in the utility of class analyses. On this, he and Davidson were to dispute publicly in 1939. But both had a deep commitment to the inherent rationality of the Southern people, especially its agrarian tradition. In Woodward's case, the faith had taken a Populist turn. And Davidson reported to Tate that Woodward, in a letter to Davidson, had been anxious "to be put down in the right category, insists he is not a Marxian, wants us to think of him as an agrarian sympathizer." Indeed, there is virtue in regarding Woodward's later achievement as a historian, with its distinctive blend of the Southern conservative's feeling for the tragic aspects of the Southern past and the liberal's passion for social advance, as a synthesis of strands lying around separately in the debates of the 1930s.[46]

Davidson himself had not completely shed his ambivalence about liberalism. When he had sent a copy of an article on "The Dilemma of the Southern Liberals" to Edwin Mims in 1934, he had ended his letter: "May I then subscribe myself, a liberal of some sort, I know not what."[47] He was willing to grant that liberalism had delivered on some of its promises, with better roads, schools, libraries, and hospitals. But he was writing in the full knowledge of the Depression and with increasing, though confused, unease about the New Deal.[48] In this mood, he pointed to the failure of even the semblance of New South prosperity and the real challenge posed to the laissez-faire assumptions of nineteenth-century liberalism. The liberals, Davidson wrote, "will have to be a little more specific in their descriptions of the civilization which, they have long claimed, is so much nobler and more beneficent than the kind of civilization the South has traditionally preferred." With the 1930s in mind, he was more severe towards younger liberals than the generation of Walter Hines Page. As he wrote to Mims, the likes of Virginius Dabney and Gerald Johnson "have had an opportunity that Page did not have for making a fresh estimate of the social and political history of the South. They have shown themselves singularly unmalleable, almost incapable of receiving new points of view."[49]

What interested Davidson was an intensified search for a usable Southern past among the liberals. He singled out Dabney's *Liberalism in the South* as the most ambitious effort to "equip modern liberalism with precedents and sanctions." He noted their attempt to claim Jefferson as the apostle of educational reform, egalitarian democracy, and the separation of church and state. For Davidson, the intervening fact of industrialism was more than enough to cut off modern liberals from the philosopher of Monticello. Instead, he gave them a separate genealogy: "It can hardly be said that the Southern liberals have any ancestors in the South. Their intellectual pedigree, so far as it is American, must be traced out on the Northern side of the Potomac. They will discover their family portraits among the New England humanitarians."[50]

Against this, Davidson defined the essential Southern tradition as Jeffersonian and agrarian. Under the exigencies of the slavery controversy, Jeffersonian egalitarianism had been trimmed by Calhoun. The Civil War had been a struggle between two liberalisms, in which the romantic nationalist vision of the North had triumphed over the more traditional and realistic South. The abolition of slavery, he thought, had left a mess that Southerners combined to clear up during Reconstruction. Beginning well as exponents of honest and frugal government, the Bourbon regimes seemed to Davidson to have degenerated into cliques, drifting from agrarian support to industrial interests. For this, they paid with the Populist revolt. Davidson granted the valid agrarianism of the Populists, but he was at pains to deny their Jeffersonianism. Their program seemed too mixed, with the call for government ownership of railroads, free silver, the graduated income tax, the eight-hour day, the popular election of senators, the initiative, and the referendum.[51]

As Davidson sketched the scenario, the agrarian revolt dispossessed the Bourbons of the trappings of power but not the reality. They ruled agrarian legislatures by swapping economic concessions for humanitarian improvements: "Where their private interests were involved, they have ruled; where they were indifferent, they have let their bought legislatures flounder." Innocently, the New South liberal like Walter Hines Page provided a screen for this. In a surprisingly sympathetic portrait, Davidson dwelled upon Page's role in the counsels of Southern liberalism. He firmly identified the North Carolinian with the tradition of nineteenth-century liberalism, "which praised Arnold's 'sweetness and light' without much understanding, and looked to science and culture as the deliverers of mankind, perfectly certain that industrial prosperity would be the foundation of a great, a strenuous democratic civilization." But Davidson charged Page with a cavalier naivety about Southern traditions. It seemed to him foolhardy to think, as Page did, that the three "ghosts" of Southern life—the Confederacy, Negro subjection, and religious orthodoxy—could be dismissed by a mere educational system and a few good roads.[52]

Against the ready arguments of a Page, the inarticulate culture of the conservative South had floundered. As Davidson saw it, "Offstage the liberals and the chambers of commerce shook hands over the prostrate body of the Old South; and out in front the political Punch and Judy show went on to the old tune of 'Let the people rule.'" This state of affairs had continued until the Depression had forced retrenchments, especially in the pride of the humanitarian New South, its educational system. Thus the 1930s, by placing the old alliances under intolerable strains, had presented the liberals with their dilemma. Squeezed between recalcitrant rural legislatures and the New Deal, they had to choose. If they should decide for the New Deal, "they must favor a Federal Union more gigantically centralized than ever and more forbidding in its attitude toward private initiative...a dispensation that will enforce tenets of a decidedly socialistic cast: science to the limit, antagonism to all but the most diluted forms of religion, and equality for the Negro." In doing this, the liberals would cut themselves off from the mass of the Southern people. For the three ghosts were still too powerful to be flaunted, especially by a liberalism shorn of its alliance with the chambers of commerce. In an uncomfortable prophecy of the "massive resistance" movement of the 1950s, Davidson added that the Southern people would need little encouragement to turn those ghosts into "the hard actualities of a period of violence."[53]

One feeble ray of hope seemed apparent to Davidson. The simultaneous facts of a growing tide of Northern criticism of the South during the 1920s, a vociferous indigenous Southern industrialism, and the extension of government power had had an unexpected consequence: the revival of sectional consciousness. In this debate about the South, he saw a hope of establishing and applying coherent principles of action; and these principles had to be Jeffersonian, the tradition embodied by Jefferson himself and modified by John Taylor. On this, Davidson was unsure. At times, he retained the residual feeling that Southerners had just enough of the old ways in them to decide their own fate. At other moments, he cheerlessly faced the prospect, already conceded by John Wade, of the South "becoming the most inert and passive section of the United States, or else falling into blind and violent divisions whose pent-up force will hurl us at each other's throats. Then will Jefferson's prophetic vision come true. We shall take to eating one another, as they do in Europe."[54]

Even in his special role as a poet, he felt that industrialism would erode the Southern literary tradition. Admitting that the literary heritage of the South was not rich, he took some solace in such value as Parrington had uncovered. Like Ransom, he felt that too much of the South's creative effort had been channelled into "the eighteenth century arts of dress, conversation, manners...of architecture, handicraft, oratory, anecdote." If left undisturbed, the South would develop an effective artistic tradition. Being disturbed, the results were ambivalent. On the one hand, progressive centers of education like Chapel Hill had joined in the call for regional literary spokesmen. On the other, such calls, rooted in industrial modernity, placed the Southern artist at odds with himself, and the larger conflict of agrarian and industrial in American society would be etched in the writer's self-consciousness. As a poet, this was intimately pertinent to Davidson. He felt only the forlorn hope that poetry was now so unnoticed and unpromoted an art form that it might, through indifference, escape such pressures.[55]

This was the broad outline of *The Attack on Leviathan,* a systematic attempt to annex the social, cultural, and political life of the United States to regionalism. Forty years later, it reads less convincingly than it did, written in a crescendo of interest in sectionalism. The atomism of social psychology has dismembered Davidson's bedrock sense of regional types. Howard Odum, who seemed so massively the wave of the future in "Southern sociology," has long since lost his preeminence. Davidson's pioneer but impressionistic sketches of postbellum Southern history would be regarded as inadequate, though suggestive, by historians. Turner's sectional hypothesis has never been accorded the importance of his frontier thesis, and the latter has been savaged. To Davidson, it represented the measured judgment of the greatest of American historians; to a Richard Hofstadter, it was the undeveloped rumination of a man looking "backward to the post-Darwinian nineteenth century frame of mind...locked into the grand spatial metaphor that had dominated the first phase of his work."[56] Regionalism in the arts has weakened perceptibly since the 1930s. Writing at a very special moment in the history of American sectional consciousness, Davidson assumed that he was living in and describing the regional norms of American society. In fact, *The Attack on Leviathan* was the last flowering of the sectional intellectual tradition. In it, one can trace its virtues and its final bankruptcy.

One manner of approach to Davidson's writing must be weighed. As in much debate about Southern ideology, Davidson has been often dismissed, not for the logical validity of what he said, but for what he was. A conservative and racist, an opponent of conventional American liberalism and a philosopher of sectionalism, he was everything that most American historians have not been. He was painfully aware of this. As he wrote in *The Attack on Leviathan,* the "Southerner is always pleading a sectional case before a court that insists upon ruling sectional issues irrelevant."[57] The Whiggery of conventional American historiography has never served well those who have resisted progress, and Davidson has been a victim of this. Whatever the philosophical objections to this Whiggery, and they are considerable, one practical difficulty is apparent: it incapacitates the historian from dealing sympathetically with a very great deal of the Southern tradition. For seen from within the Southern tradition, *The Attack on Leviathan* was a desperate gesture of compromise. Davidson offered to split the difference between the South and the nation: America should be regional, and the regions should be American. He was taking up a middle position between his Confederate heritage and the New South school. He offered a cultural renewal of the Compromise of 1877, which he judged had been broken in the 1920s.

Nonetheless, problems remain. Davidson had come to the issue of regionalism through the filter of literature, and his units of social analysis bore the mark of this passage. "New York" stood as his metaphor for modernist change in the United States, not because it was the head office of much of American corporate industry, but because it contained the publishing houses, at whose products he had groaned in the 1920s. His "spatial metaphor" of regionalism did not allow him to cope with the dispersal of manufacturing outside the Northeast, any more than it allowed him to digest the presence of most Americans in urban areas. As significant as his inability to deal with Detroit, was his failure to assimilate Washington, D.C. Although the federal government made fleeting appearances as the manifestation of Leviathan, it was jammed awkwardly into the mêlée of sections and too readily viewed as the toy of a particular section. Both these faults stemmed from a single root: Davidson was not the historian of the American polity so much as the registrar of opinion about it. And it is as a record of subjectivity in American experience that his book is most valuable. Thus he gave great space to literary, sociological, and historical critiques. Like many a New South intellectual, he was prone to exaggerate grossly the importance of his own breed.

The difficulty with the book was precisely its coherence. Davidson had gathered together, with literal efficiency, the assumptions that had lain scattered through the rhetoric of politicians, the analyses of historians, sociologists, and critics. He raised to explicitness the validity of looking at American life through regional eyes. And he took the only tack those half-buried assumptions had given him: he regarded the region as a kind of nation, regionalism as a kind of nationalism. If one looks at Turner on sections, one finds this: "The significance of the section in American history is that it is the faint image of a European nation . . . . Our politics and our society have been shaped by sectional complexity and interplay not unlike what goes on between European nations." The later work of Wilbur Cash has this: "The peculiar history of the South has so greatly modified it from the general American norm that, when viewed as a whole, it decisively justifies the notion that the country is—not quite a nation within a nation, but the next thing to it."[58] Equally, John Ransom and Allen Tate deployed the South in a series of equations between national cultures, American and European. Although many had added to the phrase, "nation," hedging phrases to indicate that the South was "not quite, but almost," the qualification had and has made little functional difference to the manner of writing about the South. The assumption of distinctiveness has led to an analytical tradition indistinguishable from the formats of European and American nationalist writing. Davidson's problem was not that his perspective was different, but that he took it so ruthlessly to heart. Here was the quasi-nationalist interpretation of the South, extended to the other regions and exhaustively exploited.

A crucial aspect of the modern theory of nationalism has been its moral dimension. As David Potter has put it: "Where a body of people contests the exercise of authority by another body over it . . ., the crucial question is fundamentally whether the two are parts of a single community, or, more specifically, a single nation, in which case the exercise is valid; or whether they belong to separate communities, or nations, in which case it is not valid. In such a case, the determination of nationalism ceases to be a merely descriptive matter; it becomes an evaluative matter, for the attribution of nationality sanctions the acts of the group claiming autonomous powers." It is clear that this moral autonomy was the central claim, and difficulty, of *The Attack on Leviathan*. Within Davidson's regional definition of America was a regionalization of social morality. It seemed proper to exclude criticism on the grounds that it emanated from outside the region. And this, it must be said, was not an idea confined to Davidson. It marked Southern liberals as well, and was an important consequence of the translation of historicism to the South.[59]

The assumption of the prerogatives of nationality for an area that was not a nation put a dynamic into Davidson's arguments, just as it had into the less sweeping case of Howard Odum. Nations require institutions of exclusivity to enforce their norms. Half-aware of this need, Davidson was forced into demands for these institutions; hence his endorsement of regional governments, regional education and textbooks, tariffs between the regions, regional self-sufficiency, and the cultivation of regional cultural traditions. Nothing, in fact, betrayed the inaccuracy of his regional diagnosis of American society more than this impulse to give institutional reality to the sections.[60]

This same desire to give coherence to a South not notably coherent, made it necessary for him to readjust the Southern past to conservative, agrarian ends. Jefferson had to be poached back from the liberal, and the liberals themselves read out of the Southern tradition. For to grant industrial liberalism as an indigenous tradition would be to jeopardize the survival of an agrarian South, even with the erection of an institutional *cordon sanitaire*. The spirit of place could not tolerate too much diversity.

Obviously, Davidson's sense of the rigidity of sections was not unrelated to his Southern origins. Like Odum, he was led by the richness of the Southern sense of identity, a richness stronger in the South than anywhere else, to extend his case to the rest of the United States. But, as his attitude to Europe showed, the desire to be both Southern and American was deeply important to him. This influenced one important element in the analysis of Southern regionalism, the problem of race. Clearly racial hegemony was a crucial element in Southern identity, and it formed an element in Davidson's perspective. But it was not—and this contradicts received opinion about both Davidson and most Southern intellectuals—*the* element. Davidson's root explanation for regional differentiation was environmental. As such, he could not use Ulrich Phillips's argument. To have done so would have left him unable to extend the regional case to non-Southern areas. Without that extension, neither he, Owsley, nor Odum would have been able to spread the weight of resistance to the industrialist Northeast and able to hold on to their Americanism.

Nonetheless, white supremacy was important to Davidson. It was his tragedy that race gradually came to overwhelm the delicate balance he achieved in the 1930s. *The Attack on Leviathan* was written only just in time. A few years later, he could not, one feels, have kept race as a minor theme in his analysis. External events were moving to thrust the issue upon him. The failure of his book, his regrettable knack for saying the right things at the wrong time to the wrong audience, his deepening alienation from Tate and Ransom, his melancholy sense of estrangement, all lowered his capacity to withstand the challenge to his intellectual equilibrium. He came to need a fresh sense of social involvement to replace the intellectual comradeship that vexatious literary metaphysics and social inadequacies had taken away from him. Driven back upon himself and his South, he came to lose the distinction between the two. When the South's central social institution came under attack, the blow was personal and required a personal response.

At first, the strains were minor. Several of the new sociological studies of Southern race relations came his way during the 1930s for review. In 1936, it was Arthur Raper's study of Macon and Greene counties in Georgia, *Preface to Peasantry*. In 1937, it was John Dollard's *Caste and Class in a Southern Town*. The predominant tone of Davidson's comments was mingled anger and puzzlement, for he was genuinely surprised at books that asked him to repudiate the inferiority of the Negro. And he felt secure enough in the solidity of the Southern biracial system to poke fun at Dollard's Freudian and class analysis. As Davidson saw, Dollard's "grand assumption is that Southerntown [Dollard's pseudonym for Indianola, Mississippi] is abnormal and queer—otherwise he would not be investigating it. He, the sociologist, is not queer, and sociology is not queer. And what is queer about Southerntown? There are two races in it, white and black, that live together and yet are separate in certain fundamental relationships." The insistence that class, rather than race, was the fundamental fact in the social relations of Indianola elicited amusement from Davidson. Dollard's Freudian analysis of sexual relations between the races appalled his Puritanism, as well as his racism: here there was genuine anger. Still, Davidson felt that, on sexual and social equality, he had the whole South behind him. Miscegenation laws, he wrote, "represent the traditional will of white society to preserve its racial integrity. Southern dissent to this view is so slight as to be negligible. Even those Southern Liberals who go so far as to advocate greater economic and political privileges for the Negro do not dare, and probably do not wish, to challenge the biracial sexual code." Likewise, when he considered Arthur Raper's claims of racial exploitation in Macon County—the same Macon County that contained Marshallville and benign memories for Davidson—he was adamant on the virtues of segregation. But in 1936 and 1937, it seemed that biracialism, despite scattered troubles like Scottsboro, remained sound.[61]

By 1945, things had grown palpably insecure. The Second World War had advanced the Negro cause by significant notches. There had been the movement of the March on Washington, and the establishment of the Committee on Fair Employment Practices. The black community itself had begun to stir. In December 1942, the Durham conference had issued its demands for the ballot, civil rights, employment opportunity, and access to public services. More impelling than actual advance was the spiral of rumor about a fresh push for equality and black willingness to fight for democracy on the home front, to which a severely agitated Howard Odum addressed himself in *Race and Rumors of Race* during 1943. Southern conservatives and liberals alike were forced to appraise where they stood on segregation. To Davidson, it was only the fulfillment of the prophecy of *The Attack on Leviathan* and it required no somersaults to define his position. But this was ceasing to be shadow boxing. A little heavy-handed irony at the expense of Yale sociologists was no longer in order. It was now serious business, deeply serious.[62]

In the summer of 1945, Davidson published "Preface to Decision" in Allen Tate's *Sewanee Review,* and presented the segregationist case with brutal frankness. After sketching the development of reform sociology on race relations and discussing volumes like Charles S. Johnson's *Patterns of Negro Segregation,* and the symposium, *What the Negro Wants,* he pointed to federal legislation as the necessary lever of change. "The ground for decision," he wrote, ". . . is clear. Whatever steps are taken to solve the Negro problem will be taken within the context described. It will be considered in terms of welfare as sociology defines welfare and of democracy as democracy is represented by the Wagner Labor Act, the War Labor Board, the FEPC, and the judgements of the New Deal Supreme Court. . . . sooner or later, there will be direct legislative attack upon the segregation practiced in Southern states." To Davidson, segregation was a necessary device to harmonize relations between two races who were ineradicably opposed and to prevent the social relations that led to "biological mingling." Admitting its occasional "inconvenience" and violence, he insisted that the regime when unchallenged was "mild. . .and even indulgent." And he pointed to discrimination in the North. Most fundamentally, he charged that reform would both lead to violence and it would fail. "What reason," he asked, "has anybody—and most of all the Negro—to suppose that an unwilling populace will not again contrive means of evading or nullifying laws that cynically ignore the social will of the white majority."[63]

He was to prove as good as his word. In 1950, he joined the Tennessee States Rights Committee with the observation, "My criticism of the States Rights activities, particularly in Tennessee, is that they are not vigorous enough, not as hard-hitting, intense, and continuous as the circumstances require." In 1952, he seemed thoroughly a part of the McCarthyite ethos and was urging Tate to read Whittaker Chambers's *Witness.* In 1953, he drafted a telegram to President Eisenhower that read: "Respectfully urge that your foreign and domestic program cannot possibly succeed unless as Senator McCarthy urges your administration ceases to follow the Truman-Acheson policies which we voted against when we voted for you in 1952. We strongly urge Sen. McCarthy's views." In 1955, he became chairman of the Tennessee Federation for Constitutional Government, a "massive resistance" organization. In brief, the positions of anti-Marxism, anti-Europeanism, "Southernness," and white supremacy, which he had taken up with considerable thought and subtlety in the 1930s, had become iron reflexes by the 1950s. He had long since lost the emotional and intellectual reserves that might have preserved a measure of detachment: ideas had become slogans. The modest and uncertain Davidson of the *Fugitive* had become an old man galvanized by fear into political action.[64]

There is scattered evidence that the tangibility of the crisis came as a relief. At last, he could do more than fester in a "constant state of impotent indignation." He seemed to relax. Friends, to their amazement, found him willing to take a glass of whiskey. But the organization failed. Although it had some claim to statewide support, the Tennessee Federation had little grassroots influence. By 1960, even Vanderbilt itself had started a reluctant desegregation. He sent his old Agrarian friends memoranda on the race problem, but the rapport was vanished. Wade was sympathetic but reserved, Tate was now a puzzled liberal, Warren an active proponent of desegregation, contact with Ransom had long ceased, and Owsley was dead.[65]

Unwise critics have, too readily, dubbed Donald Davidson a "spokesman" for the South. He himself hated the term. In 1940, he protested to Tate: "You say I conceive myself as the 'spokesman' for a culture & a people! What foolishness!" It is true that his papers contain more letters from ordinary Southerners, echoing his political positions and his instinctive love for the region, than those of any other Agrarian.[66] And he was the only one, at the last, to mount the barricades on the side of the majority. But, like any intellectual, he was trapped in a certain isolation and, at best, he moved in sympathy with other Southerners. His idea of the South had been rooted in an uncomplicated perception. He had come to terms with his South by no elaborate route, from no critique of poetry or religion, but simply. The pattern of intellectualism he wove around his patriotism was beyond the reach of the average Southerner, but it remained anchored in a straightforward emotional need. The intellectual who defended the South was not uncommon, but the intellectual who defended it on its own terms was rare. John Gould Fletcher's memory of Davidson can be left as an obituary: "He was more interested in the South on the emotional side than on the intellectual. . . . He was capable of an unstudied frankness in regard to his ideals and beliefs, on many occasions, where Ransom would have employed all his resources of mental reserve; and for just this reason, Davidson was . . . far more discontented and unhappy at bottom than Ransom. He was, indeed, more or less lost amid the confused sophistications of modernity."[67]

part four:
The Survival of Southern Identity

ten:
The Idea of the South: An Interpretation

In February 1941, the house of Knopf, after much travail with an overwrought, dilatory and ill-organized author, published a book called *The Mind of the South*. Before coming to any conclusions about the nature of the Southern idea, one must dwell a little on this volume. For it was the last substantial contribution to the ideological disputes of the interwar years over the South, and the link between those debates and the present interest in Southern mythology.[1]

Wilbur Cash was a journalist, a rhetorician of no mean accomplishment, a disciple of the anticlerical Mencken and a student of the cotton mills. Like others, his views on the South were impelled by accidents of time and place. A child of Piedmont, North Carolina, with a love-hate relationship to the ordinary Southerner, he dwelled much upon the sins and strengths of the plain folk of the Appalachian foothills and saw in them a microcosm of the South.[2] In this, he was following a well-worn path: Odum and Davidson, like many others, had jumped from a rural Georgia or Tennessee to the region. Cash was knowledgeable and shrewd, making many useful suggestions about the race problem, industrialization, war and Reconstruction, but his achievement lay chiefly in a strategic decision about the proper subject matter for a book about the South. He chose to study, not the South, but the mind of the South. In fragmentary fashion, this had been done before him. But no one had isolated the topic with his severity, or attempted to use it as the fulcrum upon which to make Southern history turn.

In so doing, Cash was flying in the face of the traditional positivist approach to the region. For a William Dodd, Ulrich Phillips, or Frank Owsley, the logic had been to use the Southern mind as the janitor of social and economic history: it came to tidy up and rationalize the compulsions of plantation and farm, war and poverty. With boldness, Cash reversed this logic. Awareness, according to Cash, was the master of social history and not its servant. *The Mind of the South* claimed, by dint of an unwonted Hegelian phenomenology, that the Southern zeitgeist had had the ability to create and transform both the perception of the individual and socioeconomic realities. Wilbur Cash, by instinct rather than philosophical training, was an idealist historian, not only in the crude sense of believing that ideas were motive forces in the historical process, but also in a more specific dialectical sense. His book had buried in it the movement of thesis, antithesis, and synthesis.

The original thesis of Southern history, for Cash, had been the agricultural conditions of antebellum society. The climate, the lushness and friendliness of the land had been "itself a sort of cosmic conspiracy against reality in favor of romance." The frontier had discouraged intellectuality and loosened social bonds by creating an individualism, free of the "close-pressing throng . . . rigid class distinctions, the yoke of law and government, economic imperatives." Thus the early South had been disunited: the plantation had been "an independent social unit," farmers and crackers had been "in their own way self sufficient." In this way, the Southerner's world had been "an aggregation of human units, of self-contained and self-sufficient entities."[3]

To this thesis of an atomized, unself-aware society, Cash proffered the antithesis: the race problem, slavery, and the dispute with the North. From such tensions had come the synthesis of Southern self-consciousness. "It was," Cash asserted, "the conflict with the Yankee which really created the concept of the South as something more than a matter of geography, as an object of patriotism, in the minds of the Southerners." Under its pressure, the South had drawn together around the tenets of racial loyalty, a paternalistic myth, and a more severe Calvinistic religion. Cash's name for this synthesis was "the savage ideal," "that ideal whereunder dissent and variety are completely suppressed and men become, in all their attitudes, professions and actions, virtual replicas of one another."[4]

It is well to be clear on this point. Cash was asserting that, in his own words, the image of the planter "actually came to be" the planter. An atomized society, by the act of perceiving unity, had come to be unified. Thus "the delicate implication that this Southerner was somehow any Southerner at random" had been internalized, and the Southerner had "so absolutely identified his ego with the thing called the South as to become, so to say, a perambulating South in little."[5] This synthesis of perception and social reality was for Cash the central issue of continuity between Old and New South: the perception generated by an agricultural society had survived to influence the younger industrial society.

A central example in Cash's argument was the relationship between the "savage ideal" and class consciousness. Cash assumed that class loyalty was the natural product of an industrializing society. Logically, Southern industrialization ought to have created such a sentiment. From his vantage point among the cotton mills of Charlotte, it seemed that this had occurred only imperfectly. Cash's explanation was the transforming power of the "savage ideal," which correlated race, Southern patriotism, and religion against the issue of unionization. Discrete social issues had become so intertwined in the ideology of Southernism that to touch one aspect of Southern society was to set up a chain reaction that touched all issues. Thus, although Cash had thought to detect in the 1920s "powerful forces . . . toward the development of class consciousness," the Southern myth had proved too powerful at Gastonia. Such an analysis betokened a frustration: Cash felt sure that the South ought to have developed in a certain way, but stubbornly refused. Time and again, Cash dragged his readers and his historical Southerners to the brink of a breakthrough, time and again his mill workers seemed about to break into "The Red Flag," and time and again he had to shake his head and let them sing "Dixie" after all.[6]

In this idealist analysis, Cash was not quite alone among Southern intellectuals. One can find scattered moments elsewhere. Ransom had written *God Without Thunder* as an exercise in the manipulation of myth and by 1934 come to feel that the South was as much myth as reality; with his usual idiosyncrasy of language, he had called it "the aesthetic of regionalism," but ended by "marvelling at the power of that interregional but sympathetic symbol, the South." Almost casually, as he did all things, Wade was to come around to the mythic view of the South. In 1954, he declared quietly to Davidson that the South was "one of the really great abstractions of our race." Odum, though he believed his statistics when they told him that the region was empirically coherent, had nonetheless been interested in the social psychology of intersectional perception in *An American Epoch*. Such views were, indeed, refractions of the migration of intellectual modernism into the South. For, as H. Stuart Hughes has observed of the modernist canon of thought, it had come "to the conclusion that 'the former conceptions of a rational reality' were insufficient, and that human thought would have to make 'concessions' to a reality that could no longer be conceived as an orderly system. In this process of concession and adaptation, the 'activity of human consciousness' for the first time became of paramount importance. For consciousness seemed to offer the only link between man and the world of society and history."[7]

But Cash had gone much further than his contemporaries. Having given perception an active role in Southern history, he had allowed it to wreak havoc. Perception was not a footnote to positivist reality, but reality a footnote to perception. Southerners had not merely perceived the savage ideal and been dialectically influenced by it; they had become the savage ideal. If Donald Davidson was the Herder of modern Southern thought, Cash came close to being its Hegel. Finally he stumbled into being its Fichte.[8]

Nonetheless, the phenomenological problem of Southern history had been given its first significant airing, and the groundwork laid for the interest in mythology that followed the Second World War. Cash had been convinced that the Southern myth had been hard and unyielding, set in an unreasoning concrete. In fact, the years in which he had struggled to write *The Mind of the South* had indicated otherwise. The debate had thrown up a wide range of options. Cash himself had challenged the racial orthodoxy of the savage ideal. Tate had tried to swing the Southern idea away from Calvinism to Roman Catholicism and T. S. Eliot. Owsley had attempted to dilute the planter legacy and, with Odum, celebrate the

"plain folk." The Agrarians had wanted to hold the line against modernization, while Odum had striven mightily to bring the region into a rationalized
modern "mainstream." The myth was clearly negotiable, the dialectic was
free and complex. Even the impulse towards Southern identity was optional.
One could hold to it as a fundamental tool in understanding the world, like
Davidson; let it drift into vagueness, like Wade; forget it, like Ransom. In
nibbling ways, the idea of the South had come under pressure. But it had
not cracked. To understand why, one must probe a little further into the
nature of the Southern idea and construct a phenomenology for Southern
identity less totalitarian than that of Wilbur Cash.

❁ The problem can be approached at three related levels: at that of
"social reality," the institutional structure of Southern cultural nationalism;
at that of perception, the intellectual structures of Romanticism and
modernism; at that of myth. The first helps to define the empirical impulse
towards Southern identity, the second defines the analytical tools with
which such an impulse could be understood, and the third was the
dialectical product, the Southern idea. But the interchange between these
three levels was complicated and devious: none was finitely separable from
the others, each influenced the others and was, in turn, influenced by
them. It is the historian who, for sanity's sake, needs to still this Bacchanalian
whirl.

First, one must ask the old question again. What are the positivist
evidences for the existence of a coherent Southern culture? What binding
social institutions have existed to make the concept plausible? To answer
this, it helps to examine the most thoroughgoing functional definition of
nationalism available, that of Karl Deutsch. For the assumption behind this
question is functional; it presupposes that Southern identity is explicable as
a mirror image of a unified culture. Its inadequacies may help to indicate
why the second question, about the structure of perception, may be
necessary.

Deutsch has argued that a nation is a community, in which people
communicate with one another in more ways than just the physical interchange of goods. If community depends upon social communications, it
follows that the community-as-nation can be judged by the completeness
of its system of social communications. As Deutsch sees it, "The communi-
cative facilities of a society include a socially standardised system of
symbols, which is a language, and any number of auxiliary codes, such as
alphabets, systems of writing, painting, calculating, etc. They include
information stored in the living memories, associations, habits, and preferences of its members, and in its material facilities for the storage of

information, such as libraries, statues, signposts . . . . Some of these facilities, individual and social, also deal with the treatment of information, its recall from storage and memory, its transmission and recombination to new patterns. If these elements are in fact sufficiently complementary, they will add up to an integrated pattern or configuration of communicating, remembering and acting, that is, to a culture . . . and the individuals who have these complementary habits, vocabularies and facilities are what we call a people." Thus nationalism is the mode and methods by which social groups communicate more effectively with one another than with "out-siders"; national consciousness is the process by which "secondary symbols of nationality" are attached to primary items of information moving through channels of social communications or the mind of an individual. To be most effective, this must influence social decision making. "On a simple level," Deutsch writes, "they may secure for the items to which they are attached quicker or preferred attention, more frequent or speedier recall, greater weight in the process of decision. On another level, they may change some of the decision-making system's operating rules for whole classes of items—and thus, in a sense, its operating 'values'—with effects on the general behavior of the system, and even on the pursuit of its goals or on their change for new ones." The more precise the correlation between primary facts and secondary symbols, the more accurate the resemblance between reality and image, the more effective will be the nationality.[9]

On this logic, is there a Southern system of social communications? The answer must be a cautious affirmative. There are universities, which draw their constituency from predominantly Southern sources; magazines, that sell to a Southern audience; railroads and airlines, structured to serve the region; corporate organizations, with headquarters and distribution net-works bent to the South; party political alliances and caucuses, both in Washington and gatherings like the Southern Governors Conference; local organizations of intellectuals, such as the Southern Historical Association. Equally, there seems to be a discernible tendency for Southerners to be granted preference by Southern employers.[10] What is oddly neglected in the impressionistic literature on the South is that such institutions are not the shipwrecked remnants of the Old South, but the offsprings of economic and cultural modernization. Industry, far from destroying the South, has had a central responsibility for sustaining and deepening its hold on men's lives. The need of modern society for centers of organization has given more force to the Southern idea than ever did the decentralized, pre-industrial Old South, which was notoriously resistant to the pleas of Southern nationalists and reluctant to subscribe to an internalized system of social communications.[11]

In helping this bureaucratization, the generation of the 1920s and 1930s had a hand. Howard Odum was the most industrious promoter of such

an infrastructure, by creating an Institute for Research in Social Science
devoted to Southern problems, organizing the Southern Regional Committee of the Social Science Research Council, heading the Southern
Interracial Commission, administering funds for Southern higher education,
and periodically convening Southern intellectuals in a search for solutions
to problems deemed to be common. But the Agrarians too played their
part. They too turned up at conferences of the Southern Policy Committee.
At Ellen Glasgow's behest, they attended a meeting of Southern writers in
Charlottesville and later patronized a similar gathering in Charleston. They
were eager to support Southern periodicals and presses, such as the
Southern Review—which they founded—the *Virginia Quarterly Review*
and the *Sewanee Review.* Moreover, they were keen to bring national
periodicals, like the *American Review* and *Free America,* to be edited in
the region. Despite both Odum's and the Agrarians' caveats against
parochialism, they depended upon and created a Southern system of social
communications unimaginable to the Old South and luxurious by the
standards of 1890.

All this molded a South oddly reminiscent of Herder's vision of a
unauthoritarian nationalism. But this only half answers the question of
whether there is a coherent Southern culture. For the lines of social
communication were very crossed. One might, as an Odum or a Tate, grow
up in towns that gave you Southern magazines to read, took you to cheer
Confederate reunion parades, or delivered you into the hands of pedagogues
who used the South as a fundamental premise in social discourse. But the
South was not a nation-state. There were the norms of the American
nation to influence and overlap its own system of social communications.
The South shared a language with the rest of country, though many might
lay claim to a Southern accent.[12] Its political institutions, though bent to the
needs of white supremacy, were broadly similar; governors, state legislatures, presidential electors, federal and state courts molded social and
political life in comparable fashion. For most of the ordinary pattern of life,
the Southerner shared assumptions and habits with his counterpart in New
York, munched the same brand of corn flakes in the morning, watched or
listened to the same baseball and football games, bought the same automobiles from Detroit, drove upon highways made by the same machines.
In short, there was a strong case for David Potter's statement: "If historians
had not been captives to the idea that nationality equates with culture, and
that where there is separate nationalism there must be culture of equivalent
separateness, they would probably have been far quicker to recognize how
very thin the historical evidences of a separate Southern culture really
are."[13] There was a strong case, but not an overwhelming one, for there
were those Southern institutions to muddy the clarity of that assertion.

Such crossed lines left the Southern intellectual poised between the overlapping categories of region and nation, and the options for reconciling them were bewilderingly complex. They were the more devious, because an ex-colonial society felt the need to mingle the problem of Europe into the equations. Implicit in the intellectual history of nationalism, as in its political record, has been the notion of cultural contrast. Nationalism has been a negative, as well as a positive proposition. Madame de Staël's *De L'Allemagne* was haunted by the question, what is it in Germany that is not French? American nationalism, however, has had several points of reference: the internal sectional contrasts of North and South, East and West, and the image of Europe. It is true, as David Potter has cogently argued, that group loyalties need not be mutually exclusive. A man can be for his South and his America, and have his fondness for Provence all at once. But, as Potter further suggested, the need for action sometimes impels the subjection of one loyalty to another. In 1861, a man could not be for the South and the Union simultaneously and act.[14] For the intellectuals, however, thought *was* action and the disposition of their world views did not wait entirely upon the clamor of public dispute.

Thus one can trace the metaphysics of reconciling the South, the United States, and Europe differently for each of these figures. For Davidson, Owsley, and Odum, there was an indifference to Europe and so their problem resolved itself into reconciling the South and the nation. All claimed to be loyal Americans and devoted Southerners, but Davidson and Owsley sensed a contradiction in this which led to a devaluation of the federal government, a historiography of sectional imperialism, and a focusing of their loyalties upon the South. For Odum, there seemed no contradiction; he was content to run South and nation in a harmonious tandem. Nonetheless, for all three the loyalty to the South led to a doctrine of regional differentiation that was, in effect, a subjection of the vision of the United States to that of the South. John Wade deepened the confusion by expressing a doubt that Southernism was too abstract; as a particularist Georgian, he gave an uncomfortable reminder that the individual state was not a negligible factor in the adjustment of these metaphysics of identity. For Tate and Ransom, however, the problem deeply concerned the issue of Europe. As they saw it, the real difference lay, not between North and South, but between a traditional European culture and an industrialized America; their feeling for Europe controlled their sense of Southern identity. It was significant that Ransom's English experience in 1931 weakened his Southernism, while Owsley's visits to France and England only deepened his faith in a Southern democracy untrammeled by a deadening past. One can sense a proper unease in Allen Tate's remarks upon his friend's hostility to the French, for it endangered Tate's "European" sense of Southern identity: "There is something wrong with us. All these things are connected. It is a bad sign when our folks can't take Europe simply and naturally, and not like a crowd of self-improving Yankees."[15]

In these ways, the pattern of social communications created a context that suggested and impelled a Southern identity, but was so far from being authoritarian that men retained a great latitude. It is this that makes important the second question, What perception did men bring to the issue?

The easiest answer is the individual one, that each had different personalities and social experience. Odum had a determined optimism, while Davidson was a melancholy pessimist. Wade had an affluent background, and Tate a family history of genteel incompetence with money. Ransom travelled to England in comfort and at the benign behest of the Rhodes trust, while Davidson was dragged there unwillingly by the scarring necessity of war. The subtleties of individuality are endless and crucial.

The answer hardest to discipline is that of intellectual traditions of perception. It is complicated because the two main traditions, relevant to an understanding of the problem of Southern identity between the world wars, Romantic social theory and modernism, were not unrelated but, in fact, not too distant relatives. Modernism was, in many ways, the mangled and fragmented stepchild of Romanticism. The organicism of Romantic theory, embodied in the cultural theory of nationalism, had within it an awareness of diversity that could, with the collapse of self-confidence that the twentieth century impelled, break the theory itself.[16] M. H. Abrams has given the best coherent statement of Romantic philosophy. "After Kant and Schiller," Abrams has suggested, "it became a standard procedure for the major German philosophers to show that the secular history and destiny of mankind is congruent with the Biblical story of the loss and future recovery of paradise; to interpret that story as a mythical representation of man's departure from the happiness of ignorance and self-unity into the multiple self-divisions and conflicts attendant upon the emergence of self-consciousness, free decision, and the analytical intellect; to equate the fall, so interpreted, with the beginning of speculative philosophy itself; and to evaluate the fall as a fortunate self-division, because it was the necessary first step upon the educational journey by which thinking and striving man wins his way back toward his lost integrity, along a road which looks like a reversion but is in fact a progression."[17]

This vision had many siblings. For literature, it gave primacy to the spiritual and psychological autobiography. At its best, this was a tradition that saw literature as a way to move towards reintegration by a probing understanding of alienation; at its least edifying, it encouraged an indiscriminate fascination with emotions. For philosophy, it bred the concept of the dialectic, whether understood through the phenomenology of Hegel or the materialism of Marx. For Herder, both cause and effect of the Romantic theory, it gave the *Volk* an important place in the stand against fragmentation: man became himself by his relationship to the nation around him.[18]

Abrams and Frank Kermode have shown how this vision is the direct ancestor of the modernism that, distrustful of the Romantic's faith in an eventual reintegration of mind, body, and faith, was left to dwell despondently upon the theme of alienation. This vision came eventually to Eliot's *Waste Land*, Tate's self-consciousness before the Confederate dead, Ransom's Kantian dualism and sense of irony, and Wade's loss of confidence in the power of intellectuality.

What is important to understand, however, is that the Romantic argument was broken into many pieces by the nineteenth century. The phenomenology of Hegel passed to a Marx whose adaptations were positivist and unconcerned with self-consciousness, save as a footnote to economic relations. Frank Owsley was an unwilling heir to this tradition, when he chose to define the South by its social and economic proportions of yeoman farmer and planter. Comte had taken over the emphasis on progress, implicit in the chiliasm of Romanticism, and transmitted it to the sociology that Odum learned as a student: a faith in progress, intimately tied up with the destiny of the *Volk*. The Symbolist poets had adapted the introspective genre of Goethe and Wordsworth by converting it into a poetic that stressed the autonomy of knowledge gained during the poetic act. For them, the immediate predecessors of Eliot, Tate, and Ransom, the poem did not merely translate an external reality, but had become a special insight which existed only within the art form. On their logic, the poet was a special sage who used the image as a way of bringing together the broken pieces of the world. In time, this doctrine reemerged as a historical theory in the idea, given by Eliot to Tate, of a "dissociation of sensibility." As Kermode has suggested, Ezra Pound, Yeats, and Eliot sought "a historical period possessing the qualities they postulate for the Image: unity, indissociability; qualities which, though passionately desired, are, they say, uniquely hard to come by in the modern world."[19]

These fragments of the old argument—the positivist historical philosophy of an Owsley, the sociology of an Odum, the literary aestheticism of a Tate or Ransom—had been rendered fragments by many forces. Not least of these was the drive of modernization to specialize intellectual disciplines. Goethe and Coleridge, even Carlyle, had lived in an intellectual ambience that drew no sharp lines between philosophy, literature, and society; it was natural that they should have tried to keep them in an equilibrium. But the dizzying accumulation of knowledge in the nineteenth and early twentieth centuries, both cause and effect of professionalization, made intellectuals captives of specialized assumptions. When they emerged from the cocoons of their private worlds, they spoke in tongues unintelligible to one another.

For Frank Owsley, the child of a Rankean tradition of historical objectivity, it was obvious beyond argument that there were real facts in the world. Words, though agreeable if neatly turned, were an uncomplicated vehicle to allow the historian to transcribe the hard truths of an external reality. He came from a profession largely uninterested in philosophy, and only intermittently perplexed by relativism.

For Tate and Ransom, the world began in the individual consciousness, and words, in poetry, were a devious and autonomous force in bringing a Kantian dualism into relationship. They came from a profession deeply worried by the instability of thought, and obsessed with debilitating doubts about the fixity of values.

For Odum, steeped in the traditions of American academic sociology, values were still fairly stable and the conviction that progress was a necessary part of the social process was ingrained.

For Davidson, the Symbolist aesthetics of Tate were unpalatable. While Tate and Ransom saw poetry as a complex metaphorical exercise at odds with mundane social reality, Davidson was sure that poetry should be accessible to the common man: it should distill folk wisdom. Heretically for the Symbolists, Davidson defended the long narrative poem and saw nothing offensive in transcribing the raw subject matter of social reality. One recalls his remark upon the "Ode to the Confederate Dead": "And where, O Allen Tate, are the dead?"[20]

For Wade, standing skeptically aside from the professional intellect, thought, although it might be unstable, could still elicit an intermittent commitment.

None of these private debates would matter but for a slumbering factor peculiarly important for the student of the Southern idea. One aspect of the old Romantic argument, the cultural theory of nationalism, had grown inarticulate and forgotten as the theory it indubitably was. The tendency of the nineteenth century to institutionalize the theory in the South, to create the system of Southern social communications, had left Southerners the victims of its logic. Nothing is more striking in the range of discussion in the South about the South than the lack of interest in nationalism as an intellectually respectable way of organizing reality; it was merely assumed.

But the debate over Southern identity was not localized in any particular intellectual discipline. It called upon its participants to integrate many issues otherwise broken into special compartments. For the South was deemed to be an organism, and its definition required the integration of facts across time, space, and social divisions. Somehow 1830 and 1930, North Carolina and Louisiana, sharecropper and industrialist, black and white were to be brought into harmony. The lines were very long and exposed. All too often, they broke.

What is interesting is that they usually broke for oblique reasons. Modernism, though its principles were at variance with the organicism of Romantic nationalism, was so fragmented that its attack was not frontal, but indirect. The best example of this is the dispute between Tate and Davidson over the South. The argument between them over poetry, between the Symbolist and the bardic traditions, had begun to crystallize in their Fugitive days. For Davidson, the Confederate dead were the issue; for Tate, his awareness of the dead was central. For Davidson, art was the tool of life; for Tate, art was the highest loyalty. Both, when they became Agrarians, found that the compulsions of studying the South took them far beyond the confines of the individual poem. Tate became a historian, and sometime economist. Davidson likewise, though his interests were similarly "literary and critical" followed them into "historical, political, economic, social interpretations,"[21] into the pages of *The Attack Upon Leviathan*. But Tate's fear of polemic and propaganda, ingrained in his theory of art, pulled him short. He shifted his contribution to the debate from explicit social philosophy to the metaphor of *The Fathers*. Davidson, without such a commitment, saw no contradiction. Thus the lines held for Davidson, but broke for Tate.

Similarly, for Odum the strains that told upon his *Völkerpsychologie* were indirect. To a neo-Hegelian social psychology, he added a sociology of statistics. While he remained unaware of any possible contradiction, his peers came to think otherwise. The intellectual atomism of modern sociology broke his regionalism, just as the divergent demands of a complicated Southern social scene had frustrated his vision of an administrative structure for the region.

For Owsley, the breaking of the lines was more partial. His profession left unchallenged the utility of analyzing the history of a South. Indeed, the growth of courses in Southern history and the entrenchment of the Southern historical profession made the impulse very respectable. But the ethics of Rankean objectivity made one extension of the lines, into contemporary political discussion, imprudent. The introspection of modernization and professionalism was his difficulty.

Thus each individual brought to the confused pattern of social communications the texture of his own temperament and intellectual training. Each shed a light through the prism of the South, saw it emerge refracted and took comfort or not in its dispersed hues. The Southern idea was but the prism itself, flickering and mobile, both defined by the lights and changing with them: periodically, its facets would be recut and its rays differently disposed.

The function of the myth was complicated.[22] Its ability to absorb many rays was its strength, even though rendering it enigmatic. Men did not come to it whole and unhealed. Precisely its value lay in its organic counterpoint to a confusing and accelerating society. Southerners were collectively and individually many things: poets, social critics and activists, heirs of farm or plantation or city, sociologists or historians, Christians or agnostics, Americans or Southerners or surrogate Europeans, fugitives from or enthusiasts for bureaucratization. The idea of the South did not only express function, but was a way of integrating disparate functions.

It is no surprise that for each who used its language the most vivid complaint was the vanishing "wholeness" of human experience. Conversely, it seemed to serve those best for whom no single social role offered adequate compensation. Allen Tate and John Ransom wobbled uncomfortably in the late 1920s about the character of their careers; both, in time, came to define themselves more severely as literary critics and teachers. The New Criticism was, after all, the intellectual equivalent of professionalization for the student of literature. For John Wade, the crisis of social mobility had been incomplete; granted the birthright of Marshallville, he could stand aside from the profession of intellectual. Frank Owsley found a secure social role as a historian, once he had abandoned social "polemic" and recovered the esteem of his peers. Moreover, like Howard Odum, he had helped to create a subsection of his trade that, as Southern history or Southern sociology, posited no contradiction between belief and society. In all this, Donald Davidson was the chief victim. Like Ransom, he had been uncomfortable in the institutional world of the university. Unlike Ransom, he was never to make his peace with the university. Nor did his poetry secure him respect. Alienated from friendship and intellectual sympathy, his need for the Southern idea hardened *pari passu.* Feeling the shock of modernity without composure, he did not bend with the times but dug in his heels. And the gap yawned wider and wider. When Warren in 1947 asked him to contribute to a special issue of the *Sewanee Review* in honor of Ransom, Davidson refused: "Don't ask me to join in the public profession...," he replied. "I seem to be in another line, going another way, but I don't know how I got there, since I have simply stayed put, or so I thought."[23]

On this level, the idea of the South helped individuals through moments of personal strain. It contributed towards reconciling Tate to his tangled family past, Ransom to his aesthetic and pedagogical difficulties, Wade to his exile from Marshallville, Odum to the fundamentalist onslaught on his chosen sociological career, and Davidson to nearly everything. It could help to locate a place in society and history. It could also be a burden. Too often Southerners were to echo the sentiments of Joyce's Stephen Dedalus that history was a nightmare from which one was trying to awake. The myth, as Tate and Ransom found, did not always work. Tate moved on to an older framework, the Roman Catholic Church, to make sense of things. Robert Penn Warren, skeptical about its utility even in the 1930s, was to chose a more existential path. In his novel, *Flood,* the chief character was to speak of the South as "his country." But the sentiment was modified by the atomism of the admission, "There is no country but the heart."[74]

These individual impulses merged with the public character of the myth. One's relationship was not merely with the prism, but with those other figures who stood, absorbed, around it. The idea of the South was an indigenous mode of social discourse, a species of political and social thought. By subscription to it, social groups recognized the right of mutual criticism. Allen Tate, writing about religion in the Old South, was attempting historical analysis. With more force, but obliquely, he was pleading with his fellow Southerners that a traditional religion was a compelling social need. In this way, an autonomous point of social commentary was blended into the fabric of the historical myth. This added vitality to the discussion, at the price of provincializing it. By adopting the language of the Southern idea, Odum cut himself off from sociologists outside the region. An important figure inside the tradition of Southern social thought, he has been ignored outside it and one looks in vain for his name in histories of sociology. The Agrarians constantly complained that they were misunderstood by non-Southerners, for their social thought was buried in the language of the Southern idea. In 1932, Tate said to C. Hartley Grattan: "It has puzzled me exceedingly in the last two years that the left-wing critics should not have welcomed our *criticism* of the industrial regime." In 1931, he had likewise protested to Edmund Wilson that the latter had grasped nothing of Southern Agrarianism but an idea of "wistful boys mooning over the past." During their reunion of 1955, much discussion among the ex-Agrarians centered not on a repudiation of their social beliefs, but on their language in the 1930s. Many insisted that the mode of Southernism had weakened their effectiveness.[25]

As a system of social analysis, "Southernness" had the weakness which Wilbur Cash had indicated. It was so integrated that to touch one aspect was to lead one, willy-nilly, into many of its ramifications. A poet could end up writing about Robert E. Lee, a literary critic discoursing on economics, a historian dwelling on ethics, a sociologist pondering aesthetics. It became difficult to talk about anything without defining everything. As a historicist doctrine, moreover, it made it difficult for social analysis to cope with conflict. Its core was the desire to bring elements into harmony. Here the social consequences of the idea of the South were most incestuous. The belief had, since its inception in the early nineteenth century, both masked and diminished social conflict within the region. The claim of an Owsley or a Davidson that class conflict had no place in a discussion of the South, or the hope of Odum that regionalism would halt the slide into class divisions, was distortion of a society rich in social conflict; but it was an accurate mirror of the social belief of organicism that had influenced social division in the region.

In these interwar years, the assumptions of Romantic nationalism were mutating under the pressures of modernization. But they did not break. The phenomenology of the Southern idea had made that difficult. For the myth had come to bear the burden of community itself, in dialectical partnership with its younger cousin, the channels of Southern social communications. In the nineteenth century, the myth of Southern unity had bred the form of a Southern culture. In turn, the form preserved the myth even against the decline of intellectual faith. By a quirk of history, the fragmenting pressures of modernization bred an argument with the elder tradition of holism that, in bulk, only served to preserve the value of the old ways of social analysis. "The South" had become so ingrained into the language of society that even to dissociate oneself from the tradition was to confirm that system of language. The observation of the American linguist Benjamin Lee Whorf is a useful commentary on the fate of the Southern idea: "We dissect nature along lines laid down by our native languages. The categories and types that we isolate from the world of phenomena we do not find there because they stare every observer in the face; on the contrary, the world is presented in a kaleidoscopic flux of impressions which has to be organized in our minds—and this means largely by the linguistic systems in our minds. We cut nature up, organize into concepts, and ascribe significances as we do, largely because we are parties to an agreement to organize it in this way—an agreement that holds throughout our speech community and is codified in the patterns of our language. The agreement is, of course, an implicit and unstated one, BUT ITS TERMS ARE ABSOLUTELY OBLIGATORY; we cannot talk at all except by subscribing to the organization and classification of data which the agreement subscribes."[26]

The categories of section and nation have been less authoritarian. But they have been compelling, and their pressures can be read in the mental gymnastics forced upon intellectuals. To look at figures like Odum and Ransom is to be struck with the reflection that, as both admitted, Southernism was less than a full-blooded nationalism, but there was no shorthand way of talking about it save as a complete nationalism. The multiplicity of burdens on the idea of the South—its role for historical inquiry, social criticism, the healing of private and social tensions, the mirroring of personal identity in public facts—bred the confusion in which the individual could seem to find himself. The principle of integration existed in defiance of, and ironically because of, formidable evidence of fragmentation. Yet the idea of the South was a common property, on whose broad back one could rear the details of one's particular vision. So the debate was rooted in a paradox. It was assumed that the South was definable, discrete, and shared, while the "reality" was broken. No man's South was the same as another's. Thus, ironically, a community was in fact created, for men could talk about different things while imagining that they discussed the same entity. Thus, for those who made the effort of self-awareness, the center could hold.

notes

Introduction

Parts of this introduction and the following chapter have been developed in articles: see Michael O'Brien, "Thomas Wolfe and the Problem of Southern Identity: An English Perspective," *South Atlantic Quarterly* 70 (Winter 1971): 102-11; "Edwin Mims: An Aspect of the Mind of the New South Considered: I," *South Atlantic Quarterly* 73 (Spring 1974): 198-212; "C. Vann Woodward and the Burden of Southern Liberalism," *American Historical Review* 78 (June 1973): 589-604.

1. C. Vann Woodward, "The Search for Southern Identity," in *The Burden of Southern History,* rev. ed. (Baton Rouge, 1968), pp. 3-25; Ulrich B. Phillips, "The Central Theme of Southern History," in *The Course of the South to Secession,* ed. E. Merton Coulter (Washington, 1939), pp. 151-65; Howard Zinn, *The Southern Mystique* (New York, 1964), esp. pp. 217-63.

2. Dewey W. Grantham, "The Southern Bourbons Revisited," *South Atlantic Quarterly* 60 (Summer 1961): 293; see also Grantham, *The Democratic South* (Athens, Ga., 1963).

3. Charles G. Sellers, ed., *The Southerner as American* (Chapel Hill, 1960): Grantham's chapter, "An American Politics for the South," (p. 149) quotes Hartz, *The Liberal Tradition in America: An Interpretation of American Political Thought Since the Revolution* (New York, 1955) directly; on the "consensus" school, see Richard Hofstadter, *The Progressive Historians: Turner, Beard, Parrington* (New York, 1968), 437-66, and J. R. Pole, "The American Past: Is It Still Usable?" *Journal of American Studies* 1 (1967): 63-78.

4. William C. Havard, ed., *The Changing Politics of the South* (Baton Rouge, 1972), offers an image even more fragmented than that of its mentor, V. O. Key, Jr., *Southern Politics in State and Nation* (New York, 1949).

5. George B. Tindall, "Mythology: A New Frontier in Southern History," in *The Idea of the South: Pursuit of a Central Theme,* ed. Frank E. Vandiver (Chicago, 1964), p. 15; see, for example, Paul M. Gaston, *The New South Creed: A Study in Southern Mythmaking* (New York, 1970); David L. Smiley, "The Quest for the Central Theme in Southern History," *South Atlantic Quarterly* 71 (Summer 1972): 307-25; Ray Mathis, "Mythology and the Mind of the New South," *Georgia Historical Quarterly* 60 (Fall 1976): 228-38.

6. I have attempted to address this problem more directly in "W. J. Cash, Hegel and the South," *Journal of Southern History* 44 (August 1978): 379-98.

7. Vandiver, *The Idea of the South,* p. viii; Clement Eaton, review of *The Idea of the South,* in *Mississippi Quarterly* 18 (Spring 1965): 105.

8. See, for example, Harry Ashmore, *An Epitaph for Dixie* (New York, 1958); Woodward, "The Search for Southern Identity," begins, "The time is coming, if indeed it has not already arrived, when the Southerner will begin to ask himself whether there is really any longer very much point in calling himself a Southerner."

9. A useful survey is George B. Tindall, "Southerners Rediscover the South," in *The Emergence of the New South, 1913-1945* (Baton Rouge, 1967), 575-606.

10. Arthur O. Lovejoy, *The Great Chain of Being: A Study of the History of an Idea* (Cambridge, Mass., 1936) is the classic text of such an approach; for a sensible critique of Lovejoy and the methodological problems of intellectual history, see Quentin Skinner, "Meaning and Understanding in the History of Ideas," *History and Theory* 8 (1969): 3-53.

11. This definition relies partly on the discussion in Malcolm Bradbury, *The Social Context of Modern English Literature* (New York, 1971), pp. 3-19.

Part I: The Legacy. 1: On the Idea of the South: Origins, Mutation, and Fragmentation.

1. John R. Alden, *The First South* (Baton Rouge, 1961), pp. 17-18.
2. Peter Gay, *The Enlightenment: An Interpretation, II, The Science of Freedom*

(New York, 1969), pp. 319-23.

3. David Hume, *An Enquiry concerning Human Understanding*, in *Essays*, ed. T. H. Green and T. H. Grose (London, 1875), II: 68.

4. This is distilled from the following studies: F. M. Barnard, ed., *J. G. Herder on Social and Political Culture* (Cambridge, 1969); Isaiah Berlin, *Vico and Herder: Two Studies in the History of Ideas* (New York, 1976); W. H. Bruford, *Culture and Society in Classical Weimar, 1775-1806* (Cambridge, 1962); M. H. Abrams, *Natural Supernaturalism: Tradition and Revolution in Romantic Literature* (London, 1971); Frank Kermode, *Romantic Image* (London, 1957); Elie Kedourie, *Nationalism*, rev. ed. (New York, 1961). Naturally, the shift from the Enlightenment to Romanticism was neither total nor abrupt. Herder, for example, was a borderline figure. As Peter Gay reminds one, Hume's statements about the uniformity of human nature were not quite borne out by his practice: see Gay, *Voltaire's Politics: The Poet as Realist* (Princeton, 1959), p. 11, n. 20. Much evidence can be adduced that the Enlightenment comprehended and used relativistic perspectives. The question is, however, one of emphasis: the quantity of shifting emphases became, in time, a qualitative change. For a defense of the usefulness of Romanticism as an analytical tool in intellectual history, see René Wellek, *Concepts of Criticism* (New Haven, 1963), 128-221.

5. Rollin G. Osterweis, *Romanticism and Nationalism in the Old South* (New Haven, 1949), pp. 24-40, 151-52; Clement Eaton, *The Mind of the Old South*, rev. ed. (Baton Rouge, 1967); John T. Krumpelmann, *Southern Scholars in Goethe's Germany* (Chapel Hill, 1965); René Wellek, *Confrontations: Studies in the Intellectual and Literary Relations Between Germany, England, and the United States during the Nineteenth Century* (Princeton, 1965); Edmund Wilson, *Axel's Castle: A Study in the Imaginative Literature of 1870-1930* (New York, 1931), pp. 17-22.

6. William R. Taylor, *Cavalier and Yankee: The Old South and American National Character* (New York, 1961), unlike Osterweis, relies entirely on an "indigenous" reading of the sources of Southern mythology.

7. On Calhoun, see Louis Hartz, "South Carolina vs. the United States," in *America in Crisis*, ed. Daniel Aaron (New York, 1952), pp. 73-88; Thomas B. Alexander, "Persistent Whiggery in the Confederate South, 1860-1877," *Journal of Southern History* 27 (August 1961): 324-25; Ella Lonn, *Desertion during the Civil War* (New York, 1928); Carl Degler, *The Other South: Southern Dissenters in the Nineteenth Century* (New York, 1974); David M. Potter, "The Nature of Southern Separatism," in *The Impending Crisis, 1848-1861* (New York, 1976), pp. 448-84.

8. F. M. Barnard, *Herder's Social and Political Thought: From Enlightenment to Nationalism* (Oxford, 1965), pp. 59-66; Hartz, "South Carolina vs. the United States," observes that "if the pure metaphysical passion is to be found in American political thought at all, where would we place it if not in the men who have struggled so heroically with the categories of state and nation?"

9. Joel Chandler Harris, *Life of Henry W. Grady, Including His Writings and Speeches: A Memorial Volume* (New York, 1890), p. 129, quotes Grady thus: "I know that the ideal status is that every state should vote without regard for sectional lines. . . . I would to God that status could be reached!"

10. Quoted in Gaston, *New South Creed*, pp. 95-96.

11. C. Vann Woodward, *Origins of the New South 1877-1913* (Baton Rouge, 1951), pp. 154-74.

12. Gaston, *New South Creed*, pp. 187-214.

13. Edwin Mims, *Sidney Lanier* (Boston, 1905), esp. Chaps. 10 and 11; Thomas Nelson Page, *The Old South: Essays Social and Political* (New York, 1892); Raymond B. Nixon, *Henry W. Grady, Spokesman of the New South* (New York, 1943); on Gordon, see Woodward, *Tom Watson: Agrarian Rebel* (New York, 1938), pp. 61-63.

14. William P. Trent to H. B. Adams, 8 January 1898, in *Historical Scholarship in the United States, 1876-1901, As Revealed in the Correspondence of Herbert B. Adams,* ed. W. Stull Holt (Baltimore, 1938), p. 249; the only general guide to this generation of Southern intellectuals is Bruce L. Clayton, *The Savage Ideal: Intolerance and Intellectual Leadership in the South, 1890-1914* (Baltimore, 1972), and, unfortunately, it concentrates too much on the race problem.

15. See, for example, Edwin Alderman, "Charles Brantley Aycock: Epic Builder of Education," in *Southern Pioneers in Social Interpretation* ed. Howard W. Odum (Chapel Hill, 1925); Aycock to Edwin Mims, 6 November 1903, Edwin Mims Papers, Joint University Library, Nashville; on the Bassett Affair, see Richard Hofstadter and Walter P. Metzger, *The Development of Academic Freedom in the United States* (New York, 1955), pp. 445-50.

16. Louis R. Harlan, *Separate and Unequal: Public School Campaigns and Racism in the Southern Seaboard States, 1901-15* (Chapel Hill, 1958).

17. Walter Hines Page to Mims, 6 October 1911, Mims Papers; in this, little had changed since the ancien régime. Southern nationalists had constantly called for "Southern" books, only to be little heeded by the public; see John Ezell, "A Southern Education for Southrons," *Journal of Southern History* 17 (August 1951): 303-27.

18. Louis D. Rubin, Jr., *George W. Cable: The Life and Times of a Southern Heretic* (New York, 1969), p. 154; Mims to Clara Puryear, 7 February 1896, Mims Papers; Gaston, *New South Creed,* p. 88.

19. Virginius Dabney, *Liberalism in the South* (Chapel Hill, 1932), p. 416; William E. Dodd, *Statesmen of the Old South; or, From Radicalism to Conservative Revolt* (New York, 1911). In fact, Dodd had serious doubts about industrialization and the New South, though he approved of its educational initiatives. He took the agrarian content of Jeffersonianism as seriously as its civil libertarian side. It is some evidence of the strength of this schema of the Southern past that it could absorb perceptions like Dodd's and Thomas Nelson Page's without undue strain; on Dodd, see Robert Dallek, *Democrat and Diplomat: The Life of William E. Dodd* (New York, 1968), pp. 54-69.

20. Woodrow Wilson, "States Rights (1850-60)," in *The Cambridge Modern History,* VII, ed. A. W. Ward (New York, 1903-12), p. 442.

21. See, for example, Woodrow Wilson, *Robert E. Lee: An Interpretation* (Chapel Hill, 1924); Edwin Mims, "General Lee's Place in History," *Outlook* 84 (1906): 978-82; William P. Trent, *Robert E. Lee* (Boston, 1899); D. S. Freeman, *R. E. Lee, A Biography,* 4 vols. (New York, 1934-35), *Lee's Lieutenants: A Study in Command,* 3 vols. (New York, 1944), and *George Washington: A Biography* 6 vols. (New York, 1948-54). On the use of "Virginian" and "Southern" as synonyms, it is instructive to note a letter from Edwin Mims to Ellen Glasgow, upon the publication of *Vein of Iron,* in which the former observed: "You have completed the Virginia—and therefore Southern—Saga"; Mims to Glasgow, 18 July 1935, Ellen Glasgow Papers, University of Virginia, Charlottesville.

22. John Spencer Bassett, "The Industrial Decay of the Southern Planter," *South Atlantic Quarterly* 2 (1903): 112; Edwin Mims, *The Advancing South: Stories of Progress and Reaction* (New York, 1926).

23. Dabney, *Liberalism in the South,* p. 206.

24. George B. Tindall, *The Pursuit of Southern History: Presidential Addresses of the Southern Historical Association* (Baton Rouge, 1964), pp. xi, 21.

25. Guy A. Cardwell, Jr., "On Scholarship and Southern Literature," *South Atlantic Quarterly* 40 (1941): 60-72; J. B. Henneman, "English Studies in the South," in *The South in the Building of the Nation,* ed. Julian A. C. Chandler et al., 12 vols. (Richmond, 1909-13), *History of the Literary and Intellectual Life of the South,* ed. Henneman, pp. 115-34.

26. Edwin Mims, "Introduction," in *The South in the Building of the Nation,* VIII,

History of Southern Fiction, ed. Mims, p. xlvii. William P. Trent, *William Gilmore Simms* (Boston, 1892), esp. chap. 6, "Romantic Dreams and Political Nightmares."

27. Mims, "Introduction," in *History of Southern Fiction,* ed. Mims, p. lxiv; Trent, "Introduction," in *History of the Literary and Intellectual Life of the South,* pp. xxvii-xxviii.

28. Trent, "Introduction," in *History of the Literary and Intellectual Life of the South,* ed. Henneman, pp. xviii, xxviii-xxix; Arthur S. Link, "Woodrow Wilson: The American as Southerner," *Journal of Southern History* 36 (February 1970): 7-8.

29. Cf. Allen Tate's observation that Mims "was a Southern William Lyon Phelps"; Tate to the author, 26 May 1971.

30. Gunnar Myrdal et al., *An American Dilemma: The Negro Problem and American Democracy* (New York, 1944), pp. 466-73.

31. Page to Mims, 8 January 1900, Mims Papers: "We have a writer of criticism in the South who is a clever man and I suppose a well read man, but who seems to me totally unfitted for a critic. He is either so afraid of the error of provinciality—which is indeed a great danger to us—or else is so in love with what he conceives to be the cold criticalness of the North that he never wrote a sympathetic line in his life, and his praise is as insolent as his censure. You may know that I am speaking of Trent—and I am speaking of him I believe correctly. I started to read his book on Simms with the friendliest of feeling for him, but I ended satisfied that he was as ignorant of the art of criticism as he was of the spirit of the South. Because your Father believed in slavery you don't have to pillory him for a fool and a knave."

32. Mims, "Southern Magazines," in *History of the Literary and Intellectual Life of the South,* pp. 463-65.

33. Woodward, *Origins of the New South,* p. 156; the U.D.C. was founded in Atlanta in 1895.

34. I have found H. Stuart Hughes, *Consciousness and Society: The Reorientation of European Social Thought 1890-1930* (New York, 1958), the most useful guide to this.

35. Charles Beard, ed., *Toward Civilization* (New York, 1930), p. 298.

36. Twelve Southerners, *I'll Take My Stand: The South and the Agrarian Tradition* (New York, 1930), pp. xxii-xxiii (hereinafter cited as *ITMS*).

37. *ITMS,* pp. xxiii-xxiv.

38. Howard W. Odum, "Notes on the Technicways in Contemporary Society," *American Sociological Review* 2 (June 1937): 336-46; Odum to H. L. Mencken, 3 November 1930, Howard Washington Odum Papers, Southern Historical Collection, University of North Carolina, Chapel Hill, box 12, file 240 (hereinafter cited as Odum/box no./file no.).

39. For a contemporary reaction to the shift, see Stringfellow Barr to Virginius Dabney, 16 March 1936, *Virginia Quarterly Review* Papers, 2d ser., Alderman Library, University of Virginia, Charlottesville.

40. Grantham, *Democratic South,* p. 53; Tindall, *Emergence of the New South,* pp. 219-53.

41. Tindall, *Emergence of the New South,* pp. 160, 540-74; it is instructive that C. Vann Woodward, addressing a Virginian audience in 1954 on the history of segregation, felt obliged to emphasize that Jim Crow was not immemorial, but recent: Woodward, *The Strange Career of Jim Crow,* 2d rev. ed. (New York, 1966), p. xi.

42. Interview with Robert Penn Warren, Yale University, 10 September 1973; Warren suggested that one reason the essay lacked urgency was his feeling then that Southern history had "stopped," it was something that *had* happened, but wasn't happening anymore.

43. Donald Davidson to Allen Tate, 21 July 1930, Allen Tate Papers, Firestone Library, Princeton University, Princeton, N.J.; Davidson to Tate, 23 July 1930, Tate Papers; Davidson to Tate, "Saturday" [July 1930], Tate Papers.

44. Davidson to Will Alexander, 22 September 1929, Commission on Interracial Cooperation Papers, Trevor Arnett Library, Atlanta University, Atlanta.

45. Alexander to Davidson, 31 October 1929, Interracial Commission Papers.

46. Odum, *Social and Mental Traits of the Negro* (New York, 1910); Odum to Edwin L. Clarke, 21 March 1922, Odum/1/13; Odum to D. L. Chambers, 7 November 1930, Odum/12/241.

47. Odum, "A Program of Research on the Negro in the South over a Period of Years," 1 May 1926, Rockefeller Foundation Archives, Pocantico Hills, Tarrytown, N. Y., 3d ser., box 103, folder 1040.

48. Interview with Mary Frances Schinhan, November 1976, Chapel Hill; Wayne D. Brazil, "Howard W. Odum: The Building Years, 1884-1930" (Ph.D. diss., Harvard University, 1975), pp. 11-12, 18-26, 466-67; Brazil's dissertation is much the best history of Odum's early years.

49. Tate, *Memoirs and Opinions, 1926-1974* (Chicago, 1975), p. 30.

50. Irving Babbitt, *Rousseau and Romanticism* (New York, 1919). As will become clear later in this analysis, I have been impressed by and relied upon two books for my understanding of the literary and intellectual heritage of Romanticism: M. H. Abrams, *Natural Supernaturalism: Tradition and Revolution in Romantic Literature,* and Frank Kermode, *Romantic Image.*

51. Babbitt, *Literature and the American College: Essays in Defence of the Humanities* (New York, 1908); Norman Foerster, ed., *Humanism and America: Essays on the Outlook of Modern Civilization* (New York, 1930), p. 37; Tate, "The Fallacy of Humanism," *Criterion* 8 (July 1929): 661-81; *ITMS,* p. xxvi.

52. John Ransom, *God Without Thunder: An Unorthodox Defense of Orthodoxy* (New York, 1930); John Wade, *The Marshallville Methodist Church from Its Beginnings to 1950* (Marshallville, Ga., 1952).

53. This discussion of personal and social backgrounds has been pieced together from the following sources: interviews with Harriet Chappell Owsley, Anne Wade Rittenbury, Robert Penn Warren, Andrew Lytle, E. Merton Coulter, and Theresa Sherrer Davidson; Radcliffe Squires, *Allen Tate: A Literary Biography* (New York, 1971); Tate, *Memoirs and Opinions,* pp. 3-23; T. D. Young and M. Thomas Inge, *Donald Davidson* (New York, 1971); Brazil, "Howard Odum"; and my own manuscript research.

54. Dallek, *Democrat and Diplomat,* p. 28.

55. Leslie Fiedler, *Waiting for the End: The American Literary Scene from Hemingway to Baldwin* (New York, 1964), p. 152, speaks of the university relationship as "the truly distinguishing characteristic of the generation of the Forties-Fifties."

56. Davidson to Tate, 5 February 1929, Tate Papers.

57. The free-lance and the teacher did not always understand each other's difficulties. See Davidson to Wade, 7 July 1932, John Donald Wade Papers, University of Georgia, Athens: "Tate is bound to no routine as we are in our academic arrangements. If it pleases him to write something, whether for a newspaper or a quarterly, he has only to sit down and do it; but you and I have students to meet, classes to teach, papers to grade. If Tate wants to go to Europe or to Washington, to libraries or battlefields, for writing purposes, he has only to jump in his Ford and light out." Cf. Tate to Davidson, 4 December 1942, Donald Davidson Papers, Joint University Library, Nashville, box 11, file 1 (hereinafter cited as Davidson/box no./file no.): "You have always had a steady job and security, and of late a considerable royalty income; and I have had temporary jobs and insecurity, and right now I face great difficulties."

58. Ransom to Mims, 27 September 1926, Mims Papers; Davidson to Tate, 5 February 1929, Tate Papers; Fred C. Hobson, Jr., *Serpent in Eden: H. L. Mencken and the South* (Chapel Hill, 1974).

59. George H. Calcott, *History in the United States, 1800-1860: Its Practice and Purpose* (Baltimore, 1970), points to a remarkable lack of interest in antebellum Southern historiography about regional distinctiveness.

60. Davidson, *The Attack on Leviathan: Regionalism and Nationalism in the United States* (Chapel Hill, 1938), pp. 322-23.

61. Tate to John Gould Fletcher, 3 December 1930, John Gould Fletcher Papers, University of Arkansas, Fayetteville.

62. *ITMS*, p. xx: "Nobody now proposes for the South, or for any other community in this country, an independent political destiny."

63. Andrew Lytle, "John Taylor and the Political Economy of Agriculture," *American Review* 3 (September 1934): 443.

64. Charles Beard, *The Rise of American Civilization* (New York, 1927), part II, pp. 1-121; Parrington, *Romantic Revolution;* Frederick Jackson Turner, *The Significance of Sections in American History* (New York, 1932); Frank Owsley, "The Historical Philosophy of Frederick Jackson Turner," *American Review* 5 (Summer 1935): 371-72, comments on Dodd's Chicago lectures on sectionalism.

65. A typical review of *I'll Take My Stand* was that of Gerald Johnson, "The South Faces Itself," *Virginia Quarterly Review* 6 (January 1931): 157: "That the Twelve should turn to agrarianism as a remedy would seem to indicate that their sole knowledge of the South has been gleaned from the pages of Joel Chandler Harris and Thomas Nelson Page."

66. On Jefferson, cf. Davidson, *Attack on Leviathan,* pp. 328-30, with Tate to Davidson, 10 August 1929, Davidson/10/43; and Odum, *Southern Regions of the United States* (Chapel Hill, 1936), p. 225; on Jackson, cf. Owsley, "The Making of Andrew Jackson," *American Review* 1 (May 1933): 220-25, with Lytle, "John Taylor," *American Review* 4 (November 1934): 97; Lytle's view of Jackson anticipates that of Richard Hofstadter in *The American Political Tradition and the Men Who Made It* (New York, 1948), pp. 45-67.

67. Odum, *An American Epoch: Southern Portraiture in the National Picture* (New York, 1930): pp., 50-52; Lytle, "John Taylor," p. 439.

68. On these matters, see the following chapters on Tate, Owsley, and Davidson.

69. On the Dunning school, see Wendell H. Stephenson, *The South Lives in History: Southern Historians and Their Legacy* (Baton Rouge, 1955); Odum, *American Epoch,* pp. 41-42; Ransom, "Hearts and Heads," *American Review* 2 (March 1934): 559; Lytle, *Nathan Bedford Forrest and His Critter Company* (New York, 1931), pp. 378-88.

70. Interview with Rupert Vance, November 1973, Chapel Hill; Brazil, "Howard Odum," pp. 2, 5; Interview with Lytle.

71. Brazil, "Howard Odum," pp. 73-82; Louis R. Wilson, *The University of North Carolina, 1900-1930: The Making of a Modern University* (Chapel Hill, 1957), pp. 209, 220; Brazil, "Howard Odum," pp. 241-89.

72. Tate, *Essays of Four Decades* (New York, 1968), p. 520; Tate, "A Southern Romantic," *New Republic* 76 (30 August 1933): 67-70; Robert Penn Warren, "The Blind Poet: Sidney Lanier," *American Review* 2 (November 1933); Ransom, "Hearts and Heads."

73. Cleanth Brooks, *Modern Poetry and the Tradition* (Chapel Hill, 1939), passim.

Part II: The Sociological Vision: Odum. 2: Sociology in the South

1. Edwin Embree to Odum, 22 April 1936, Odum/18/391.

2. Odum, *Rainbow Round My Shoulder: The Blue Trail of Black Ulysses* (Indianapolis, 1928); *Wings on My Feet: Black Ulysses at the Wars* (Indianapolis, 1929); *Cold Blue Moon: Black Ulysses Afar Off* (Indianapolis, 1931). In fairness, it must be said that many have liked his prose style, including Ulrich Phillips: "Preface," *Life and Labor in the Old South* (Boston, 1929).

3. Wayne D. Brazil, "Howard W. Odum: The Building Years, 1884-1930" (Ph.D. diss., Harvard University, 1975), pp. 1-37.

4. *Ibid.*, pp. 38-60; C. Vann Woodward, *Origins of the New South 1877-1913* (Baton Rouge, 1951), p. 445; Odum to Rev. L. D. Gillespie, 22 January 1924, Odum/2/29; "I am myself an old Emory man and a great admirer of old Dr. Sledd."

5. Brazil, "Howard Odum," pp. 61-119; Odum, "G. Stanley Hall: Pioneer in Scientific Social Exploration," *Social Forces* 3 (November 1924): 141.

6. Odum, "G. Stanley Hall," p. 144; Hall, *Life and Confessions of a Psychologist* (New York, 1923), pp. 436, 521. Hall was further in the vanguard of the 'culture of professionalism'; see Burton J. Bledstein, *The Culture of Professionalism: The Middle Class and the Development of Higher Education in America* (New York, 1976).

7. Hall, "Wilhelm Wundt," in *Founders of Modern Psychology* (New York, 1912), p. 337; Jean B. Quandt, *From the Small Town to the Great Community: The Social Thought of Progressive Intellectuals* (New Brunswick, N.J., 1970), p. 29; Hall, *Life and Confessions*, pp. 476, 438.

8. Interview with Rupert Vance; Vance, "Howard W. Odum and the Case for the South" (paper delivered to the Southeastern meeting of the American Studies Association, Chapel Hill, 11 April 1970; copy in the possession of Mary Frances Schinhan); Odum, *Understanding Society: The Principles of Dynamic Sociology* (New York, 1947), chap. 14, reprinted in *Folk, Region and Society: Selected Papers of Howard W. Odum* ed. Katherine Jocher et al. (Chapel Hill, 1964), p. 230; *International Encyclopedia of the Social Sciences,* ed. David L. Sills, XVI (New York, 1968), pp. 581-86.

9. Walter A. Jessup to Odum, 13 April 1936, Odum/18/390; Louis R. Wilson, *The University of North Carolina, 1900-1930: The Making of a Modern University* (Chapel Hill, 1957), p. 474.

10. Ronald Fletcher, *The Making of Sociology. A Study of Sociological Theory* (London, 1971), I, *Beginnings and Foundations*, pp. 538-75.

11. William Graham Sumner, *Folkways: A Study of the Sociological Importance of Usages, Manners, Customs, Mores and Morals* (Boston, 1907), pp. 1-75, 77-78; on Sumner's relationship to Social Darwinism, see Richard Hofstadter, *Social Darwinism in American Thought* (Philadelphia, 1944), pp. 51-66. It must be stressed that Sumner was unsympathetic to Wundt's neo-Hegelianism: see Sumner, *Folkways*, p. 20; equally, it is unwise to identify Wundt too closely with Hegel: see Wundt, *Elements of Folk Psychology: Outlines of a Psychological History of the Development of Mankind,* trans. E. L. Schaub (London, 1916), pp. 520-21, which is distinctly Hegelian in its approach to history, but ends by criticizing Hegel's lack of empirical data.

12. Brazil, "Howard Odum," pp. 197-224.

13. *Ibid.,* pp. 225-30, 250, 282-89.

14. *Ibid.,* pp. 310-17.

15. Odum, "Part of the Opening Address of the first official meeting of 'The Educational Association of the Methodist Episcopal Church, South,' Memphis, Tennessee, March 4-6, 1919," Odum/1/1.

16. Brazil, "Howard Odum," pp. 310-37.

17. Odum to Bruce Payne, 10 September 1912, Odum/1/unmarked (first) folder; Odum to A. B. Hart, 20 March 1920, Odum/1/2.

18. Roy Lubove, *The Professional Altruist: The Emergence of Social Work as a Career, 1880-1930* (Cambridge, Mass., 1965), p. 142; Wilson, *University of North Carolina, 1900-1930,* pp. 446-49.

19. Lubove, *Professional Altruist,* esp. chap. 5, "In-Group and Out-Group: The Molding of a Professional Subculture," pp. 118-56; Odum fits most of the characterizations in Clarke A. Chambers, *Seedtime of Reform: American Social Service and Social Action, 1918-1933* (Minneapolis, 1963), esp. chap. 4; for example, he was in favor of women's

suffrage; cf. Odum, "Educational Notes," *Social Forces* 1 (November 1922): 60.

20. Odum to the editor, *The Survey,* n.d. [1920], Odum/1/7.

21. Odum, "Editorial Notes," *Social Forces* 1 (November 1922): 56-61.

22. *Ibid.,* 1 (January 1923): 181, 182.

23. *Ibid.,* 1 (November 1922): 56; Odum, "G. Stanley Hall," p. 145 (It may be significant that this observation on the South is abruptly interpolated).

24. Brazil, "Howard Odum," pp. 408-67; Harry Elmer Barnes, "Sociology and Ethics: A Genetic View of the Theory of Conduct," *Social Forces* 3 (January 1925), pp. 212-31; Willard B. Gatewood, Jr., *Preachers, Pedagogues and Politicians: The Evolution Controversy in North Carolina, 1920-1927* (Chapel Hill, 1966), pp. 114-20, 128.

25. Brazil, "Howard Odum," p. 325; Odum to Harry W. Chase, 7 January 1924, Odum/2/28; for his "invitations," see Odum to A. S. Johnson, 2 March 1925, Odum/3/61, and William P. McCorkle to Odum, 19 September 1925, Odum/4/74; Odum, letter marked "To the Editor", 20 February 1925, Odum/3/59; Odum to Rev. J. S. Foster, 7 March 1925, Odum/3/61.

26. Odum, "Editorial Notes," *Social Forces* 1 (March 1923): 318-20; David Chalmers, *Hooded Americanism: The History of the Ku Klux Klan* (New York, 1965), pp. 92-97.

27. Odum, "A More Articulate South," *Social Forces* 2 (September 1924): 730-35; Odum, "A Southern Promise," in *Southern Pioneers in Social Interpretation,* ed. Odum (Chapel Hill, 1925), pp. 3-27.

28. On Ransom and Davidson, see individual chapters; Mims, "The South Pleads for Just Criticism," *Independent* 117 (20 November 1926): 589-90, 599, and "Why the South is Anti-Evolution," *World's Work* 50 (September 1925): 548-52; Mencken to Odum (ca. 28 June 1925), Odum/4/69.

29. Odum, "The Duel to the Death," *Social Forces* 4 (September 1925): 189-94.

30. Brazil, "Howard Odum," p. 183.

31. Odum to Chase, 3 May 1920, Odum/1/2; Wilson, *University of North Carolina, 1900-1930,* p. 448.

32. Odum to Joseph H. Willits, 30 March 1954, Odum/30/621; Beardsley Ruml to Odum, 10 December 1929, Odum/9/198; Interview with Rupert Vance.

33. One must note that the foundation executive was a wily bird, constantly bombarded by men like Odum, and one occasionally finds annotations on Odum's various letters to New York that indicate skepticism; thus Odum to Sydnor Walker, 27 March 1925, Rockefeller Foundation Papers, 3d ser., box 109, folder 1106, contains the pencilled observation, presumably by Walker, "Very toading!!"; thus, much later, a report of a visit to Chapel Hill by a member of the General Education Board, 11 April 1952, General Education Board Papers, Rockefeller Foundations Archives, Pocantico Hills, Tarrytown, N.Y., 1st ser., 3d subser., box 459, folder 950, has this: "he never misses a chance when he has a foundation representative in tow."

34. Cameron Morrison to Odum, 7 June 1921, Odum/1/9; O. Max Gardner to Odum, 3 March 1930, Odum/10/209.

35. Brazil, "Howard Odum," pp. 350, 352, 518; Beardsley Ruml to Harry Chase, 16 June 1924, Rockefeller Foundation Papers, 3d ser., box 74, folder 781.

36. Brazil, "Howard Odum," pp. 338-84.

37. Odum to Jesse F. Steiner, 12 April 1927, Odum/6/132; Odum to Steiner, 21 April 1927, Odum/6/133.

38. Brazil, "Howard Odum," pp. 508-14.

39. Odum to Steiner, 16 May 1927, Odum/7/136.

40. Odum to Steiner, 23 May 1927, Odum/7/136.

41. Gerald Johnson to Odum, 25 November 1922, Odum/1/20; Odum to Johnson, 28 November 1922, Odum/1/20; Odum to George W. Ochs Oakes, 11 June 1926, Odum/5/101.

42. There is a map of his travels in Odum to Edmund Day, 5 November 1929, Rockefeller Foundation Papers, ser. 236, box 9, folder 113.

43. Odum to Gerald Johnson, 8 June 1929, Odum/9/184; Odum to William T. Couch, 1 July 1929, University of North Carolina Press Papers, Southern Historical Collection, file marked "Hibbard-Southern Series."

44. Will Alexander to Odum, 8 July 1929, Odum/9/185; Odum to Alexander, 10 July 1929, Odum/9/185; Alexander to Odum, 1 August 1929, Odum/9/187.

45. William F. Ogburn to Odum, 19 April 1929, Odum/9/183 (this includes a memo by Odum on regional plans); Odum to Ogburn, 9 September 1929, Odum/9/189.

46. French Strother to Odum, 10 April 1929, Odum/9/183; on Hoover and Strother, see Harris G. Warren, *Herbert Hoover and the Great Depression* (New York, 1959), p. 57; Odum to R. H. Thornton, 17 August 1929, Odum/9/188; Strother to Odum, 22 August 1929, Odum/9/188; Strother to Odum, 5 September 1929, Odum/9/189; Odum to Ogburn, 9 September 1929, Odum/9/189; Odum to Strother, 21 September 1929, Odum/9/190.

47. Report of the President's Research Committee on Social Trends, *Recent Social Trends in the United States*, 2 vols. (New York, 1933); Strother to Odum, 23 September 1929, Odum/9/191.

48. Odum had a signed photograph of Hoover in his study; Odum to Strother, 30 September 1929, Odum/9/191; Odum to Gerald Johnson, 9 November 1929, Odum/9/195; interview with Mary Frances Schinhan; Benjamin Kendrick to Odum, 9 November 1932, Odum/14/297. Subsequently, Odum was to exchange Christmas gifts with Hoover and visit the ex-president in California.

49. The correspondence between the Rockefeller Foundation, President Frank Graham, and Odum can be followed in the Rockefeller Foundation Papers, ser. 236, box 10, folder 118.

50. Odum to Gerald Johnson, 18 July 1931, Odum/12/256.

51. Alexander to Odum, 5 August 1931, Odum/12/257; Jackson Davis to Odum, 3 December 1931, Odum/13/263; Odum to Edmund Day, 19 December 1931, Odum/13/263.

52. Odum to Frank Graham, 23 December 1931, Odum/13/263.

53. Robert H. Bremner, *American Philanthropy* (Chicago, 1960), p. 155.

3: Odum: Southern Sociology

1. Rupert Vance, *Human Factors in Cotton Culture* (Chapel Hill, 1929); Harriet Herring, *Welfare Work in Mill Villages: The Story of Extra-Mill Activities in North Carolina* (Chapel Hill, 1929); Jennings J. Rhyne, *Some Cotton Mill Workers and Their Villages* (Chapel Hill, 1930); Roy M. Brown and Jesse F. Steiner, *The North Carolina Chain Gang* (Chapel Hill, 1927); Clarence Heer, *Income and Wages in the South* (Chapel Hill, 1930); Guy B. Johnson, *Folk Culture on St. Helena Island* (Chapel Hill, 1930); Claudius Murchison, *King Cotton is Sick* (Chapel Hill, 1930).

2. Wayne D. Brazil, "Howard W. Odum: The Building Years, 1884-1930" (Ph.D. diss., Harvard University, 1975), pp. 567-68; Mencken to Odum, 3 June 1928, Odum/8/177; Odum to D. L. Chambers, 29 May 1928, Odum/8/176; D. L. Chambers to Odum, 26 October 1931, Odum/13/261, gives the following sales figures: for *Rainbow Round My Shoulder,* 9317 copies, for *Wings on My Feet,* 3152 copies, for *Cold Blue Moon,* 1745 copies.

3. Odum, *An American Epoch: Southern Portraiture in the National Picture* (New York, 1930), pp. 3-16, 30-52.

4. *Ibid.,* pp. 53-65, 118, 180-218, 163-79.

5. *Ibid.,* p. 68.

6. *Ibid.,* pp. 66-116.

7. Odum to Benjamin Kendrick, 13 March 1930, Odum/10/210; Odum, "Dependable Theory and Social Change," *Social Forces* 2 (January 1924): 286; Odum, *American Epoch,* p. 112; Kendrick had dissented from Odum's adverse assessment of Tom Watson, and Odum reiterated with the observation, "I cannot quite see your viewpoint on Tom Watson . . . . I studied Watson for a long time and went from an admirer to a critic. I read faithfully year in and year out his *Jeffersonian,* and I am convinced that Tom Watson and Bishop Candler more than any other two sources have kept Georgia in the 'anti,' 'agin' mood": Odum to Kendrick, 13 March 1930, Odum/10/210.

8. Odum, *American Epoch,* pp. 330, 337-38.

9. Odum to Mencken, 3 November 1930, Odum/12/240; Odum to Sydnor Walker, 24 October 1930, Odum/12/238.

10. Davidson to W. T. Couch, 15 May 1932, University of North Carolina Press Papers, Southern Historical Collection, file marked "Culture Below the Potomac"; Couch to Davidson, 21 May 1932, Davidson/4/25.

11. Odum to Harriet Herring, 2 July 1924, Odum/2/39; Odum to Worth M. Tippy, 20 September 1926, Odum/6/109.

12. Kendrick's critique can be found in Odum/10/208; Odum to William F. Ogburn, 9 September 1929, Odum/9/189, said of Kendrick: "He is good and always has ideas and also is a good back field man to help us play safe."

13. Kendrick to Odum, 27 January 1934, Odum/16/339.

14. Kendrick, "A Southern Confederation of Learning: Higher Education and the New Regionalism in the South," *Southwest Review* 19 (Winter 1934): 182-95.

15. B. B. Kendrick and Alex Arnett, *The South Looks At Its Past* (Chapel Hill, 1935).

16. Odum to Kendrick, 29 January 1934, Odum/16/339.

17. *Ibid.*; Kendrick to Odum, 31 January 1934, Odum/16/339.

18. Odum to John Wade, 15 February 1934, Odum/16/341; Wade to Davidson, 6 March 1934, Davidson/11/27; Davidson to Wade, 3 March 1934, Odum/16/342; George F. Milton to Odum, 7 February 1934, Odum/16/340; Milton to Odum, 6 February 1934, Odum/16/340; the Odum files also contain letters to and from Frank Graham, Lambert Davis, Will Alexander, Stringfellow Barr, Louis R. Wilson, and Jackson Davis on this subject.

19. Odum to Sydnor Walker, 7 February 1934, Odum/16/340; Odum to Will Alexander, 8 February 1934, Odum/16/340; Odum to Walker, 19 February 1934, Odum/16/341.

20. Kendrick to Odum, 16 February 1934, Odum/16/341; Davidson to Wade, 3 March 1934, Odum/16/342.

21. Milton to Odum, 2 February 1934, Odum/16/340; Sydnor Walker to Odum, 9 February 1934, Odum/16/340; Walker to Odum, 26 March 1934, Odum/16/345.

22. Odum to Edmund Day, 30 January 1934, Odum/16/339; Odum to Robert T. Crane, 31 January 1934, Odum/16/339; Odum to Jackson Davis, 31 January 1934, Odum/16/339; Odum to Harry Chase, 7 February 1934, Odum/16/340; Kendrick to Odum, 11 May 1934, Odum/16/348: all Kendrick could secure was $500.

23. Davidson to Wade, 3 March 1934, Odum/16/342; Odum to Edmund Day, 27 January 1934, Odum/16/339.

24. Odum to Sydnor Walker, 20 May 1933, Odum/15/318; on the Hoover veto, see Preston J. Hubbard, *Origins of the TVA: The Muscle Shoals Controversy 1920-1932* (Nashville, 1961), p. 292.

25. Odum to Sydnor Walker, 19 May 1933, Odum/15/318; Odum to Robert T. Crane, 25 May 1933, Odum/15/319; Crane to Odum, 16 June 1933, Odum/15/321; Report of the Institute for Research in Social Science, 22 January 1934, Odum/16/338; on farm tenancy, see Wilma Dykeman and James Stokely, *Seeds of Southern Change: The Life of Will Alexander* (Chicago, 1962), pp. 202-47, George B. Tindall, *The Emergence of the New South, 1913-1945* (Baton Rouge, 1967), pp. 416, 598.

26. Odum to Harry Chase, 20 August 1934, Odum/16/354.

27. Odum, *Southern Regions of the United States* (Chapel Hill, 1936), pp. 4, 1-205.

28. Gerald Johnson to Odum, 10 May 1938, Odum/20/438; Odum to Gerald Johnson, 12 May 1938, Odum/20/439; interview with Rupert Vance; Odum, *Southern Regions,* p. 9.

29. Odum, *Southern Regions,* pp. 275-77.

30. Gerald Johnson, *The Wasted Land* (Chapel Hill, 1937), p. 25.

31. Odum to G.W. Forster, 21 April 1936, Odum/18/391; Odum, *Southern Regions,* p. 27.

32. Odum, *Southern Regions,* pp. 11-12, 624-25; Odum to Kendrick, 15 July 1932, Odum/14/287; Odum to Kendrick, 3 January 1933, Odum/14/302.

33. Odum, *Southern Regions,* pp. 57-59, 587, 209; one might note that, in his dealings with Harry Hopkins when Odum was chairman of the North Carolina Civil Works Administration, he had urged upon Washington a concentration of relief upon the middle class: see Odum to Hopkins (telegram), 17 September 1933, Odum/15/327.

34. Odum, *Southern Regions,* p. 481.

35. *Ibid.,* pp. 477-87.

36. Odum was annoyed when Myrdal, backed by the Carnegie Foundation, began his study because it thus spoiled his own plan for a similar Chapel Hill/Rockefeller Foundation project. Rather reluctantly, he allowed Johnson to help Myrdal. When Myrdal gave a none too enthusiastic account of the Interracial Commission, of which Odum was president, Odum was bitterly critical; see Odum to Edwin Embree, 3 May 1939, Odum/21/460; Odum to Frank Graham, 4 May 1939, Odum/21/460; Odum to Myrdal (telegram), 7 August 1942, plus an annotated criticism of a Myrdal manuscript, Odum/24/unmerged folder.

37. Only Rupert Vance may be said to have paid an informed attention to both politics and history, and was later commissioned by the Louisiana State University Press to write a volume on the contemporary South for the "History of the South" series: later, the task was assumed by George Tindall. In the 1930s, Vance planned a study of Southern political demagogues: interview with Rupert Vance.

38. Odum, *Southern Regions,* p. 57; Kendrick to Odum, 31 January 1934, Odum/16/339; Odum, *Southern Regions,* p. 507.

39. Odum, *Southern Regions,* pp. 428-29, repudiated the agrarian charge against science.

40. Odum, "Folk and Regional Conflict as a Field of Sociological Study," *Publications of the American Sociological Society* 25 (May 1931): 1-17.

41. Odum, "Notes on the Technicways in Contemporary Society," *American Sociological Review* 2 (June 1937): 336-46.

42. Odum, "Orderly Transitional Democracy," *Annals of the American Academy of Political and Social Science* 19 (March-April 1935): 303-13.

43. Odum, *Southern Regions,* p. 428.

44. *Ibid.,* pp. 227-28; on Odum and Spengler, see Odum, *Folk, Region and Society: Selected Papers of Howard W. Odum,* ed. Katherine Jocher et al. (Chapel Hill, 1964), pp. 232-34.

45. Odum, "Memorandum for President Chase" [February? 1926], Odum/5/89.

46. Odum, "Folk and Regional Conflict," pp. 9, 10.

47. Odum, *Southern Regions,* pp. 91, 261.

48. *Ibid.,* pp. 576-603.

49. *Ibid.*

50. These letters can be found in boxes 18 and 19 of the Odum Papers, but see especially Louis Brandeis to Odum, 12 May 1936, Odum/18/392; Stephen Early to Odum, 23 May 1936, Odum/18/392; M. A. LeHand to George Foster Peabody, 1 July 1936, Odum/18/395.

51. Davidson, "Howard Odum and the Sociological Proteus," *American Review* 8

(February 1937), 385-417; Broadus Mitchell, reviews in *American Economic Review* 26 (December 1936): 734-36, and *New Republic* 88 (26 August 1936): 81; for evidence of trepidation in "handling" such a complicated book, see Gerald Johnson to Odum, 23 April 1936, Odum/18/391.

4: Odum: The Failure of Regionalism

1. Raymond B. Fosdick, *The Story of the Rockefeller Foundation* (New York, 1952), p. 200; written on Odum to Beardsley Ruml, 26 March 1925, Rockefeller Foundation Papers, 3d ser., box 109, folder 1106.

2. Fosdick, *Rockefeller Foundation,* pp. 200-201.

3. *Ibid.,* p. 207.

4. Odum to Sydnor Walker, 25 February 1935, Odum/17/367. A further consideration was the usual reluctance of a foundation to be the permanent bankroll of an institution.

5. Odum to L. R. Wilson, 12 November 1932, Odum/14/297; Odum to Clarence Heer, 22 May 1933, Odum/15/318; Odum to Edmund Day, 22 May 1933, Odum/15/318.

6. Odum to L. R. Wilson, 22 January 1934, Odum/16/338; Odum to C. W. Eliot, 25 January 1934, Odum/16/339; Edmund Day to Odum, 23 January 1934, Odum/16/339; Odum to Edmund Day, 27 January 1934, Odum/16/339.

7. Program, "Institute on Regional Development," 17 June 1936, Odum/18/394; Odum to Frank Graham, 27 April 1936, Odum/18/391.

8. Odum to Will Alexander, 2 October 1937, Odum/19/418; Alexander to Odum, 7 October 1937, Odum/19/418.

9. Odum to Jackson Davis, 1 November 1937, Odum/19/420.

10. Margaret Simon to Odum, 22 November 1937, Odum/19/421; Jackson Davis to Odum, 13 December 1937, Odum/19/423; "Preliminary Statement and Tentative Agenda" [Atlanta, 15 January 1938], Odum/20/426.

11. "Notes on the Proceedings of the Southeastern Regional Advisory Committee" [23 February 1938], Odum/20/431.

12. "Preliminary Statement and Tentative Agenda," Odum/20/426; Odum to Will Alexander, 17 January 1938, Odum/20/426; the letters of acceptance are to be found in General Education Board Papers, 1st ser., 3d subser., box 412, folder 950.

13. Will Alexander to Odum, 3 June 1938, Odum/20/441.

14. "Notes on the Proceedings of the Southeastern Regional Advisory Committee," Odum/20/431.

15. "Tentative Program of Activities and Objectives," Southern States Industrial Council [22 February 1938], Odum/20/430; George B. Tindall, *The Emergence of the New South, 1913-1945* (Baton Rouge, 1967), pp. 444-45; Odum to Arthur Mann, 25 February 1938, Odum/20/431.

16. Tindall, *Emergence of the New South,* pp. 598-99; Mark Ethridge to Odum, 1 November 1938, Odum/21/447, observed, "If Southern leadership did not produce some program before about February 1st [1939], the New Dealers will put a Southern program into Congress. Both Barry [Bingham, editor of the *Louisville Courier-Journal*] and I are fearful of the reaction to that."

17. Odum to Arthur Mann, 20 August 1938, Odum/20/444; Odum to Emily Clay, 15 August 1938, Odum/20/444.

18. Thomas A. Krueger, *And Promises to Keep: The Southern Conference for Human Welfare, 1938-1948* (Nashville, 1967), p. 22; Charles S. Johnson to Odum, 6 September 1938, Odum/21/445; Odum to Francis Miller, 16 September 1938, Odum/21/445.

19. H. C. Nixon to Odum, 5 October 1938, Odum/21/446; Odum to Wilson Gee, 6 October 1938, Odum/21/446; Odum to Nixon, 8 October 1938, Odum/21/446; Wilson Gee to Odum, 11 October 1938, Odum/21/446; "Notes on the Proceedings of the Southeastern Regional Advisory Committee," p. 18, Odum/20/431.

20. Odum to Will Alexander, 24 October 1938, Odum/21/446; Alexander to Odum, 25 October 1938, Odum/21/446; Odum to Mark Ethridge, 14 November 1938, Odum/21/447.

21. Krueger, *And Promises to Keep,* pp. 20-39; Charles S. Johnson to Odum, 25 November 1938, and Mark Ethridge to Odum, 25 November 1938, Odum/21/448; Odum to Ethridge, 6 December 1938, Odum/21/449; Odum to Alexander, 6 December 1938, Odum/21/449.

22. Alexander to Odum, 4 March 1939, Odum/21/457.

23. Interviews with Will Alexander (3 March 1939, Washington), A. W. Dent (Superintendent of the Flint-Goodridge Hospital, Dillard University, 21 March 1939), Dr. T. Lynn Smith (22 March 1939, Louisiana State University), Alexander Fitzhugh (24 March 1939, Vicksburg), Brooks Hays (25 March 1939, Little Rock), Dr. T. S. Staples (25 March 1939, Hendrix College, Conway, Ark.), Wilson Gee, Dean Thomas Cooper of the University of Kentucky, Dr. W. I. Myers of Cornell University (25-26 March 1939, Washington), Paul Magnus Gross (13 April 1939, Duke University), President John L. Newcomb (17 April 1939, University of Virginia), Dr. Lynn Smith (27 April 1939, Louisiana State University), Dr. H. A. Dawson (Division of Rural Education of the N.E.A.), Dr. Nolen M. Irby (University of Georgia), Ed McCuiston (state agent for Negro schools in Arkansas), H. L. Caswell and F. B. O'Rear (Teachers College, Columbia University), President L. N. Duncan (Alabama Polytechnic Institute), H. C. Nixon (27 April 1939, New Orleans), Edgar B. Stern (27 April 1939, New Orleans), Dean S. Campbell (George Peabody College for Teachers, Nashville), Dean Calvin Hoover (Duke University); all these in General Education Board Papers, 1st ser., 3d subser., box 412, folder 950.

24. Interview with Odum, 11 May 1938, *ibid.;* "Preliminary Application: Council on Southern Regional Development," 7 March 1939, *ibid.;* interviews with Gee, Grossman, and Newcomb, *ibid.*

25. "Preliminary Application," 7 March 1939, *ibid.*

26. Odum to Alexander, 9 May 1939, Odum/21/462; Tindall, *Emergence of the New South,* p. 719; Odum to Arthur Mann, 31 May 1939, Odum/21/462.

27. Odum to Alexander, 21 September 1939, Odum/22/467; Gerald Johnson to Odum, 15 March 1939, Odum/21/458; Odum to Gerald Johnson, 21 March 1939, *ibid.*

28. Howard W. Odum and Harry E. Moore, *American Regionalism: A Cultural-Historical Approach to National Integration* (New York, 1939), pp. 3-4.

29. *Ibid.,* pp. 109-35, 188-212.

30. *Ibid.,* pp. 206-12.

31. *Ibid.,* p. 639.

32. *Ibid.,* pp. 277, 277-419.

33. *Ibid.,* p. 318; Moore to R. D. McKenzie, 21 June 1937, Odum/19/unmerged folder; Moore to Odum, 15 February 1937, Odum/19/409; Odum and Moore, *American Regionalism,* p. 320.

34. R. S. Woodworth and Mary S. Sheehan, *Contemporary Schools of Psychology* (London, 1964), pp. 214-50.

35. Max Wertheimer, *Productive Thinking* (New York, 1945), p. 199, quoted in Woodworth and Sheehan, *Contemporary Schools of Psychology,* p. 238; Kurt Koffka, *Principles of Gestalt Psychology* (London, 1935), p. 684.

36. Odum to Moore, 27 December 1937, Odum/19/unmerged folder: "Now as for your grand revision on gestalt, I am very appreciative. I have not changed a word in it.... It strengthens the chapter immensely. My only mild objection, if any at all, to the gestalt

would be that it might seem an imitation of the psychologist. As a matter of fact, you have eliminated all of this hazard and have made a real contribution"; Moore to Odum, "Thursday" [December 1937?], Odum/20/425: "I really think we have something worthwhile in the idea. And it as much yours as mine"; Moore to Odum, "Friday afternoon," Odum/20/425: "About the gestalt idea, I am pretty well convinced that it will be used more and more in the future and would like to get in on the ground floor of the movement."

37. Odum and Moore, *American Regionalism,* p. 414; cf. Moore to Odum, "Friday afternoon," Odum/20/425: "I have also re-inserted a couple of pages dealing with the ideas of cultural determinism and gestalt. It seems to me that the whole work leads up to these two ideas and that it would be a pity not to label them so that no one would be in doubt as to how we stand."

38. Odum and Moore, *American Regionalism,* pp. 421-617.

39. Odum, "A Sociological Approach to the Study and Practice of American Regionalism: A Factorial Syllabus," *Social Forces* 20 (May 1942): 425-36; Odum to Ellsworth Faris, 27 July 1942, Odum/24/522. To save disruption of the narrative, the correspondents with Odum are listed and identified here; unless otherwise stated, they are members of a department of sociology: Ellsworth Faris, University of Chicago; George T. Renner, Teachers' College, Columbia University; Read Bain, managing editor, *American Sociological Review;* Otis D. Duncan, Oklahoma A.&M. College; Maurice Davie, Yale University; C. Arnold Anderson, Iowa State College; Floyd N. House, University of Virginia; Logan Wilson, Tulane University; John F. Cuber, Kent State University; Robert Faris, Bryn Mawr College; Frederick E. Lumley, Ohio State University; Lawrence K. Frank, vice-president, Josiah Macy, Jr., Foundation (formerly of the Rockefeller Foundation); Edgar A. Schuler, Louisiana State University; Robert E. Park, University of Chicago; Edwin H. Sutherland, University of Washington; Pitrim Sorokin, Harvard University; Raymond F. Bellamy, Florida State College for Women; H. C. Brearley, George Peabody College for Teachers; W. Russell Tylor, University of Illinois; F. Stuart Chapin, University of Minnesota; Wayland Hayes, Vanderbilt University; George A. Lundberg, National Resources Planning Board, Washington; Irwin T. Sanders, University of Kentucky; Thomas D. Eliot, Northwestern University; Raymond Bowers, University of Rochester; Cecil C. North, Ohio State University.

40. Renner to Odum, 13 March 1942, Odum/24/515; Bain to Odum, 15 June 1942, Odum/24/518; Duncan to Odum, 29 June 1942, Odum/24/520.

41. Renner to Odum, 13 March 1942, Odum/24/515; Bain to Odum, 15 June 1942, Odum/24/518.

42. Davie to Odum, 24 June 1942, Odum/24/519; Anderson to Odum, 3 August 1942, Odum/24/523; House to Odum, 17 June 1942, Odum/24/518; Wilson to Odum, 21 June 1942, Odum/24/518.

43. Cuber to Odum, 26 June 1942, Odum/24/518; Svend Reimer, "Theoretical Aspects of Regionalism," *Social Forces* 21 (March 1943): 279 (cf. Harry Moore to Odum, 17 November 1937, Odum/19/420: "To make the argument stand up that regionalism is an outgrowth of actual experiences in dealing with social data in various disciplines, the definition should follow rather than precede the discussion of these disciplines. If the order is reversed and the concepts are defined to begin with, the discussion of their uses in other disciplines become a demonstration of what we have decided *a priori.* . . . Of course, it *is* partly true that . . . the idea preceded the evidence"); Duncan to Odum, 29 June 1942, Odum/24/520.

44. Odum, "A Sociological Approach to the Study and Practice of American Regionalism," pp. 435-36.

45. R. Faris to Odum, 23 June 1942, Odum/24/519; Lumley to Odum, 27 June 1942, Odum/24/520.

46. Frank to Odum, 23 July 1942, Odum/24/522; Schuler to Odum, 3 August 1942, Odum/24/523.

47. Lumley to Odum, 27 June 1942, Odum/24/520; Park to Odum, 21 August 1942, Odum/24/524.

48. Davie to Odum, 24 June 1942, Odum/24/519; Sutherland to Odum, 27 June 1942, Odum/24/520; Schuler to Odum, 3 August 1942, Odum/24/523.

49. Duncan to Odum, 29 June 1942, Odum/24/520; Sutherland to Odum, 27 June 1942, Odum/24/520; E. Faris to Odum, 21 July 1942, Odum/24/522.

50. Wilson to Odum, 21 June 1942, Odum/24/518.

51. R. Faris to Odum, 23 June 1942, Odum/24/519; Duncan to Odum, 29 June 1942, Odum/24/520; Sorokin to Odum, 1 July 1942, Odum/24/521.

52. Brearley to Odum, 24 June 1942, Odum/24/519; Cuber to Odum, 26 June 1942, Odum/24/520; Frank to Odum, 23 July 1942, Odum/24/522.

53. Duncan to Odum, 29 June 1942, 1942, Odum/24/520; Wilson to Odum, 21 June 1942, Odum/24/518; R. Faris to Odum, 23 June 1942, Odum/24/519.

54. Bellamy to Odum, 2 July 1942, Odum/24/521; Bellamy to Odum, 12 August 1942, Odum/24/523.

55. John B. Lansing to Odum, 6 July 1942, Odum/24/521.

56. Brearley to Odum, 24 June 1942, Odum/24/519; Bellamy to Odum, 2 July 1942, Odum/24/521; Anderson to Odum, 3 August 1942, Odum/24/523.

57. Memorandum, 9 March 1949, General Education Board Papers, 1st ser., 3d subser., box 510, folder 950; conversation with Mrs. Elizabeth Fink, assistant director, Institute for Research in Social Science, November 1976; John Shelton Reed, *The Enduring South: Subcultural Persistence in Mass Society* (Lexington, Mass., 1972).

John Wade. 5: A Turning Inward

1. On Southerners and "place," see C. Vann Woodward, *The Burden of Southern History,* rev. ed. (Baton Rouge, 1968), pp. 22-24; Caroline Tate to Wade [18 April 1939], Wade Papers.

2. Wade, First World War Diary, p. 124, Wade Papers.

3. Interview with E. Merton Coulter, Athens, Ga., 27 November 1973; on Ida Wade and the Florida land boom, see Wade to Ida Wade, 24 January 1926, Wade Papers, in which he attempted to press her into liquidating her holdings; see also D. E. Frederick to Ida Wade, 7 September 1927, Wade Papers, in which Frederick observed, "You can be perfectly happy without a million dollars."

4. First World War Diary, p. 5, Wade Papers; D. E. Frederick to Ida Wade, 15 February 1908.

5. Wade, Harvard Diary, 1914-1915, 3 October and 13 October 1914, Wade Papers; on Perry, see Bliss Perry, *And Gladly Teach: Reminiscences* (Boston, 1935); on Wendell, see M. A. DeWolfe Howe, *Barrett Wendell and His Letters* (Boston, 1924).

6. Wade to Ida Wade, 24 September 1914, Wade Papers; Harvard Diary, 17 May 1915, Wade Papers.

7. John Donald Wade, *Selected Essays and Other Writings of John Donald Wade,* ed. Donald Davidson (Athens, Ga., 1966), p. 166; Fred Lewis Pattee, quoted in Jay B. Hubbell, *The South in American Literature, 1607-1900* (Durham, N.C., 1954), p. 548.

8. Notebook marked "Van Doren American Lit. II," Wade Papers.

9. First World War Diary, p. 1, Wade Papers; cf. William Alexander Percy, *Lanterns on the Levee: Recollections of a Planter's Son* (New York, 1941), pp. 156-224.

10. First World War Diary, pp. 139, 66, 182-87, Wade Papers.

11. *Ibid.*, pp. 29, 20, 195-96, 19-20; cf. Percy, *Lanterns on the Levee*, 263-69, for a similar, and equally misplaced, confidence in the ability of the patrician Southerner to control the Negro.

12. First World War Diary, pp. 145, 155, 258, 17-19, Wade Papers.

13. *Ibid.*, pp. 263, 203, 24, 232.

14. *Ibid.*, pp. 290-92.

15. Wade, *Augustus Baldwin Longstreet: A Study in the Development of Culture in the South* (New York, 1924), pp. 115, 114, 55.

16. Quoted in Lester Hargrett to Wade, 31 December [1924], Wade Papers; Wade, *Longstreet*, pp. 244, 272.

17. Wade, *Longstreet*, p. 32. A list of books on the back flyleaf of his First World War Diary, probably dating from late 1918 or early 1919, has *The Education of Henry Adams* as its first item. The list also includes Lytton Strachey's *Eminent Victorians*, Julia Harris's *Life and Letters of Joel Chandler Harris*, Mencken's *The American Language*, Ulrich Phillips's *American Negro Slavery* and *Life of Robert Toombs*, and Maeterlinck's *The Burgomaster of Stilemonde*. Some have their prices marked, so it might have been a shopping list. The works by Adams, Harris, Mencken, and Strachey have been checked.

18. *Greensboro* (N.C.) *Daily News*, 27 April 1924, quoted in Wade, *Longstreet* (reprint ed., Athens, Ga., 1969), p. xvii.

19. Interview with E. Merton Coulter.

20. Odum to Wade, 31 March 1924, Odum/2/33; Odum to Wade, 30 April 1924, Odum/2/35.

21. Wade to Odum, 21 July 1924, Odum/2/40; Wade to Odum, 10 October 1924, Odum/3/45. The use of the word "anti-Klucker" is intriguing, and suggests that the Ku Klux Klan may have been an issue. Marshallville was in Macon County, where there had been a rash of Klan floggings in 1923, and Andrew Erwin, editor of the *Athens Banner-Herald* was active in anti-Klan campaigns. Wade had friends on the staff of Julian Harris's *Columbus Enquirer-Sun*, which was also opposed to the Klan. It would be surprising if a man of genteel upbringing like Wade did not dislike the Klan. However, it would be unwise to put too much weight upon a single ambiguous phrase, as no other evidence directly supports the inference. In this context, "anti-Klucker" may mean no more than "anti-cabal." On the Klan in Georgia, see David Chalmers, *Hooded Americanism: The History of the Ku Klux Klan* (New York, 1965), pp. 70-77.

22. There is a folder of clippings on the events of 1927 in the Wade Papers; on the *Iconoclast*, see Henry Fuller to William Couch, 14 December 1927, William T. Couch Papers, Southern Historical Collection, University of North Carolina, box 1, folder marked "1927b", (hereinafter cited as Couch/box no./folder no.); Wade to Odum, 5 June 1927, Odum/7/138.

23. Wade to Odum, 5 June 1927, Odum/7/138.

24. Interview with E. Merton Coulter; Wade to "Cousin Georgia," 20 June 1927, Wade Papers.

25. Wade to Ida Wade, 28 September 1927, Wade Papers.

26. On the coupling of Wade's name with Strachey, see Tate to Bernard Bandler, 23 October 1932, *Hound and Horn* Papers, Beinecke Library, Yale University, Allen Tate File; Davidson to Wade, 7 July 1932, Wade Papers; and Tate, "Beautiful Prose," *New Republic* 65 (10 December 1930): 113.

27. Wade, "Timothy Bloodworth," in *Dictionary of American Biography*, ed. Allen Johnson and Dumas Malone (New York, 1924-44), II: 385.

28. Wade, "Robert Lewis Dabney," *Dictionary of American Biography*, V: 20-21; Wade, "Virginius Dabney," *Dictionary of American Biography*, V: 22; Wade to Ida Wade, 3 January 1928, Wade Papers.

29. Three doctoral theses on Southern literary figures were done under Wade's supervision and subsequently published; see Edd Winfield Parks, *Charles Egbert Craddock (Mary Noailles Murfree)* (Chapel Hill, 1941); Linda Rhea, *Hugh Swinton Legaré: A Charleston Intellectual* (Chapel Hill, 1934); Richmond C. Beatty, *William Byrd of Westover* (New York, 1932).

30. Odum to Edmund Day, 4 April 1931, Rockefeller Foundation Papers, ser. 236, box 10, folder 118.

31. The friend was Roosevelt Walker; interview with E. Merton Coulter; Wade, *John Wesley* (New York, 1930), pp. xiii-xiv, viii.

32. Interview with E. Merton Coulter; Warren to Tate [November 1932], Tate Papers; Lytle to Tate, 23 October 1932, Tate Papers.

33. Lyle Lanier to Tate, 21 July [1930], Tate Papers (it seems that Wade suggested the title, *I'll Take My Stand,* which may give irony to an intention hitherto opaque); Wade to Barr, 31 October 1930, *Virginia Quarterly Review* Papers, 1st ser.

34. Gerald J. Smith, "Augustus Baldwin Longstreet and John Wade's 'Cousin Lucius,'" *Georgia Historical Quarterly* 61 (Summer 1972): 276-81; Tate to Fletcher, 4 November 1930, Fletcher Papers; Tate to Fletcher, 3 December 1930, Fletcher Papers.

35. *New York Times,* 14 February 1932.

36. Wade, "Southern Humor," in *Culture in the South,* ed. William Couch (Chapel Hill, 1934), p. 617, reprinted in Wade, *Essays,* p. 48.

37. Clipping, *Macon Telegraph,* May 1931, Wade Papers; "All of his days, he [Longstreet] was never able to go gentle into anything, and least of all did he go gentle into [the] War of the Sixties, during all of which he raged against what he felt sure was the slow dying of all proper Light," in Wade, "Georgia Scenes," *Georgia Review* 14 (Winter 1960): 444-47, reprinted in Wade, *Essays,* p. 168; clipping, *Macon Telegraph,* May 1931, Wade Papers.

38. Wade, "What the South Figured: 1865-1914," *Southern Review* (Autumn 1937): 360-67, reprinted in Wade, *Essays,* p. 83.

39. *Ibid.,*; Wade, "Old Wine in a New Bottle," *Virginia Quarterly Review* 11 (April 1935): 239-52, reprinted in Wade, *Essays,* p. 152.

40. *Ibid.,* pp. 157-58.

41. Wade, "Profits and Losses in the Life of Joel Chandler Harris," *American Review* 1 (April 1933); 17-35, reprinted in Wade, *Essays,* pp. 98-102; Wade, "Henry W. Grady," *Southern Review* 3 (Winter 1938): 479-509, reprinted in Wade, *Essays,* p. 134; cf. Woodward, *Origins of the New South 1877-1913* (Baton Rouge, 1951), pp. 142-74, esp. the footnote on p. 174, which credits a Wade essay.

42. Wade, "Jefferson: New Style," *American Mercury* 18 (September-December 1929): 293-300, reprinted in Wade, *Essays,* pp. 116, 117, 119.

43. Wade, *Essays,* pp. 159, 82.

44. *Ibid.,* p. 48.

45. Wade, "Southern Humor," in *Essays,* pp. 47-60; on the idea that Southern writing is predicated on a conversation with a listener, cf. Allen Tate, "A Southern Mode of the Imagination," in *Essays of Four Decades* (New York, 1968), pp. 583-84.

46. Wade, "Of the Mean and Sure Estate," in *Who Owns America? A New Declaration of Independence,* ed. Herbert Agar and Allen Tate (Boston, 1936), p. 263.

47. Wade to Odum, 8 March 1934, Odum/16/343. It is interesting to speculate whether Wade included Nashville among the "better-type communities," and the Agrarians amongst its victims.

48. Wade to Davidson, 8 November 1932, Davidson/11/25; interview with E. Merton Coulter; Wade to Davidson, 5 October 1938, Davidson/11/30.

49. Wade, *The Marshallville Methodist Church,* Wade Papers; Wade, "Culture," in John Cassius Meadows, *Contemporary Georgia* (Athens, Ga., 1942), pp. 1-43; the MS of

the novel is in Marshallville: it was submitted to various publishers, unsuccessfully, in the 1950s.

50. Wade to L. S. Doughty, 28 May 1948, Wade Papers; editorial announcement, quoted in Wade, *Essays*, p. 17.

51. Wade to Davidson, 8 August 1954, Davidson/11/37.

Part III: The Reaction to Modernism: The Southern Agrarians. 6: John Ransom: The Cycle of Commitment

1. On the Fugitive group, the best history is Louise Cowan, *The Fugitive Group: A Literary History* (Baton Rouge, 1959).

2. Ransom to Davidson, 23 June 1930, Davidson/8/34; *ITMS*, p. 3.

3. Dorothy Bethurum, in *Fugitives' Reunion: Conversations at Vanderbilt: May 3-5, 1956*, ed. Rob Roy Purdy (Nashville, 1959), p. 93.

4. *Ibid.*

5. When Ransom returned to England in 1931, he delayed his visit to Oxford until the following summer. As he explained to Cleanth Brooks, another Rhodes Scholar, "I've been waiting to see Oxford at its best, as I don't want to spoil some fixed impressions." See Ransom to Brooks, 25 May 1932, Cleanth Brooks Papers, Beinecke Library, Yale University.

6. Ransom to mother, 8 May 1912, Ransom Family Papers, Tennessee State Archives, Nashville, box 7, folder 9; Ransom to mother, 4 November 1911, Ransom/7/8; Ransom to mother, 12 August 1912, Ransom/7/9.

7. Ransom to mother, 14 November 1911, Ransom/7/8; Ransom to father, 29 October 1911, Ransom/7/8.

8. Ransom, *"Conservatism*, by Lord Hugh Cecil," longhand MS, Ransom/18/6 (the Home University Library had offered a prize for the best essay on Cecil's book, and this was Ransom's unsuccessful effort, in draft); Ransom to mother, 26 December 1911, Ransom/7/8; Ransom to father, 2 February 1913, Ransom/8/1.

9. Ransom to mother, 26 February 1913, Ransom/8/1; Ransom to father, 3 November 1913, Ransom/8/2.

10. Ransom, "The Question of Justice," *Yale Review* 4 (July 1915): 684-98.

11. Ransom to Mims, 1 December 1917, Mims Papers; Ransom to (Mims?), 5 March 1918, reprinted in *Vanderbilt Alumnus* 3 (April 1918): 178; Ransom to mother, 24 July 1912, Ransom/7/9 (this kind of admiration for Germany was fairly common among progressives: cf. Carl Resek, ed., *The Progressives* (Indianapolis, 1967), pp. xxii-xxiii); Ransom to Annie Ransom, 11 September [1912], Ransom/7/8.

12. Ransom to father, 30 May 1917, Ransom/8/4. It is worth observing that in neither Ransom's nor Davidson's letters from their training camps is the Spanish-American War mentioned as the first occasion that Southerners and Northerners had united in a common military venture after the war. They seemed to be starting from scratch. Cf. Paul H. Buck, *The Road to Reunion, 1865-1900* (Boston, 1937), p. 306.

13. Davidson, *Southern Writers in the Modern World* (Athens, Ga., 1958), p. 14; one of the few extant pieces of evidence about Ransom's view of public affairs in these years is in a letter to Mims from shortly before the presidential election of 1924: "The poor old Democratic party at this writing seems bent on extinguishing itself. I've had a half-hearted attachment for McAdoo as a Liberal. But now I could hardly vote for him if nominated—an utterly self-seeking man as I see him. Davis too, judging from the character of his support. Underwood has falsified, since he announced he could not by conviction consent to be a candidate unless the Klan were mentioned by name. Rolston [Senator from Indiana] I see nothing for except that he seems to have a sense

of decent modesty rather than a passionate ambition to be the nominee. [Newton D.] Baker and Walsh (Montana) are I think my favorites at this moment—either of them would be a case of the office seeking the man, and either is able and honest. I rather prefer Baker. But I think Coolidge will be the next President now without a doubt": Ransom to Mims, 6 July [1924], Mims Papers.

14. Thomas D. Young, ed., *John Crowe Ransom: Critical Essays and a Bibliography* (Baton Rouge, 1968), pp. 231-40.

15. Ransom to James Southall Wilson, 3 November 1926, *Virginia Quarterly Review* Papers; "Foreword," *The Fugitive* (April 1922).

16. Tate, "The Eighteenth Century South," *Nation* 124 (30 March 1927): 346; Ransom to Tate, 20 February 1927, Tate Papers.

17. Ransom to Tate, 3 (and 13) April 1927, Tate Papers.

18. Ransom, *The World's Body* (New York, 1938), pp. vii, viii.

19. Ransom to Tate, "Tuesday" [1927], Tate Papers.

20. Ransom to Tate, 25 June [1927], Tate Papers; Ransom to Tate, 13 September [1927], Tate Papers.

21. Ransom to Tate, 3 (and 13) April, 1927, Tate Papers; Ransom to Tate, 25 June 1927, Tate Papers; Ransom, "The South— Old or New," *Sewanee Review* 36 (April 1928): 139-47; "The South Defends Its Heritage," *Harper's* 159 (June 1929): 108-18; "Reconstructed but Unregenerate," in *ITMS*, pp. 1-27.

22. "Reconstructed but Unregenerate," passim.

23. Cf. Tate's remark on Ransom's history, in Tate, "Remarks on the Southern Religion," *ITMS*, p. 167: "A distinguished contributor to this symposium argues that the Southern population were originally much less rebellious against European stability than were the Northern. It is doubtful if history will support this, though I should personally like to do so, for it is the myth-making tendency of the mind in one of its most valuable forms."

24. Tate to Fletcher, 5 March 1929, Fletcher Papers.

25. Ransom to Tate, 5 September [1926], Tate Papers.

26. See, for example, Ransom, "Flux and Blur in Contemporary Art," *Sewanee Review* 37 (June 1929): 353-66, a review of Wyndham Lewis, *Time and Western Man*, which reads like a prospectus for Eliot's *Four Quartets*; cf. Tate's suggestion that "John's thought and Eliot's run along the same line; in fact, if John's book [*God Without Thunder*] is what I think it is, it leads right up to religion, whither Eliot has been bound all the time. Ransom and Eliot are more alike than any other two people alive; I have always suspected this, now I am convinced": Tate to Davidson, 18 February 1929, Davidson/10/55.

27. Ransom to Tate, 5 January 1930 (this letter is, in fact, dated 1929, but this is a New Year mistake), Tate Papers; Alice Stockell to George Fort Milton, 27 November 1930, George Fort Milton Papers, Library of Congress.

28. Ransom to Tate, 5 January 1930, Tate Papers; Ransom and Davidson to Tate, Warren, and Lytle, 5 September 1930, Tate Papers.

29. Ransom to Tate, 5 January 1930, Tate Papers; MS entitled "Articles of an Agrarian Reform," Davidson/18/22.

30. Ransom, "Humanists and Schoolmasters," p. 3 (MS enclosed in Ransom to Tate, 25 January 1930, Tate Papers).

31. *Ibid.,* p. 7.

32. Interview with Andrew Lytle.

33. Ransom to Davidson, 13 December [1931], Davidson/8/36.

34. Ransom to Tate, 25 October 1932, Tate Papers; Ransom also wrote an article, based upon a diary he had kept in England, that was apparently unwontedly dull and rejected by the *Hound and Horn:* see Ransom to Tate, 23 November 1931, Tate Papers; Tate to Davidson, 1 May 1932, Davidson/10/50; Bernard Bandler to Tate, 2 May 1932,

Hound and Horn Papers, Tate File. It is some reflection upon Ransom's lack of interest in history, even his own, that he usually destroyed old manuscripts and correspondence; this is in marked contrast to Tate and Davidson.

35. Ransom, "Land! An Answer to the Unemployment Problem," *Harper's* 165 (July 1932): 216-24; "Happy Farmers," *American Review* 1 (October 1933): 513-35.

36. Ransom, "A Capital for the New Deal," *American Review* 2 (December 1933): 141. The Nashville friend was Sidney Mttron Hirsch, at whose home many Fugitive meetings had been held.

37. Ransom, "Shall We Complete the Trade?" *Sewanee Review* 41 (April 1933): 187.

38. Haynes Johnson and Bernard M. Gwertzman, *Fulbright the Dissenter* (London, 1969), pp. 107-15, on the origins of the Fulbright-Hays Act; *The Times* (London), 22 June 1932, p. 13e; Tate to Warren, 9 December 1932, Robert Penn Warren Papers, Beinecke Library, Yale University; Warren to Tate [November 1932], Tate Papers.

39. Ransom to Tate, 25 October [1932], Tate Papers; Ransom to Davidson, 18 December [1932], Davidson/8/34.

40. Ransom, "The Aesthetic of Regionalism," *American Review* 2 (January 1934): 290-310.

41. Ransom to Tate, "Tuesday" [late winter 1933], Tate Papers; Ransom, "Hearts and Heads," *American Review* 2 (March 1934): 559.

42. Ransom to Fletcher, 7 March 1934, Fletcher Papers.

43. Ransom, "Modern With the Southern Accent," *Virginia Quarterly Review* 11 (April 1935): 184-200.

44. Ransom, "Shakespeare at Sonnets," *Southern Review* 2 (Winter 1938): 531-53; Davidson to Tate, 10 March 1938, Tate Papers; cf. Tate, *Memoirs and Opinions: 1926-1974* (Chicago, 1975), p. 40: "Logic was the mode of his thought and sensibility."

45. Louis Rubin has made the interesting, and, I think, accurate, suggestion that Ransom's description of Milton in the article, "A Poem Nearly Anonymous," is much more a description of Ransom's own withdrawal from politics than of Milton: Rubin, "A Critic Almost Anonymous, John Crowe Ransom Goes North," in *The New Criticism and After* ed. Thomas D. Young (Charlottesville, 1976), pp. 8-15.

46. Ransom, "What the South Wants," in *Who Owns America? A New Declaration of Independence,* ed. Herbert Agar and Allen Tate (Boston, 1936), p. 178; "The South is a Bulwark," *Scribners* 5 (May 1936), p. 300; Ransom to Lambert Davis, 5 July 1936, *Virginia Quarterly Review* Papers, 2d ser.

47. Ransom to Warren, 15 February [1935], *Southern Review* Papers, Ransom File, Beinecke Library, Yale University.

48. Ransom to Tate, 17 September [1936], Tate Papers; Ransom to Tate [September 1936], Tate Papers.

49. Ransom to Tate, 6 April 1937, Tate Papers; Ransom, "Art and the Human Economy," *Kenyon Review* 7 (Autumn 1945): pp. 683-88; Davidson to Tate, 27 March 1937, Tate Papers.

50. Ransom to Tate, 29 March 1939, Tate Papers; Tate to Lytle, 22 March 1939, Andrew Nelson Lytle Papers, Joint University Library, Nashville, box 5 file 5 (hereinafter cited as Lytle/box no./file no.).

7: Allen Tate: "The Punctilious Abyss"

1. Louise Cowan, *The Fugitive Group: A Literary History* (Baton Rouge), 1959), p. 104; Malcolm Cowley, *Exile's Return: A Literary Odyssey of the 1920s,* rev. ed. (New York, 1951), p. 309.

2. Tate, *Memoirs and Opinions, 1926-1974* (Chicago, 1975), p. 30; Tate to Davidson, 17 August 1922, Davidson/10/18; Rob Roy Purdy, ed., *Fugitives' Reunion: Conversations at Vanderbilt: May 3-5, 1956* (Nashville, 1959), p. 92; Tate to Davidson, 21 July 1922, Davidson/10/18; Tate to Davidson, 29 June 1923, Davidson/10/18.

3. Tate to Davidson, 17 December 1924, Davidson/10/28; Tate to Davidson, 8 June 1924, Davidson/8/24.

4. Tate, "Last Days of the Charming Lady," *Nation* 121 (28 October 1925): 485-86. In the light of his later views, it is as well to point out that Tate in 1925 saw the Old South as distinctly secular: "The South, before the Civil War, probably had little more than incidental commerce with the name of deity."

5. Tate to Davidson, 27 May 1925, Davidson/10/30; Tate to Davidson, 3 March 1926, Davidson/10/32.

6. Tate to Davidson, 26 June 1926, Davidson/10/33; Tate to Davidson, 29 July 1926, Davidson/10/34.

7. Tate, "One Escape from the Dilemma," *Fugitive* 3 (April 1924): 35; Eliot, "The Metaphysical Poets", quoted in Frank Kermode, *Romantic Image* (London, 1957), p. 154.

8. Tate, "A Poetry of Ideas," *New Republic* 47 (30 June 1926), pp. 173, 172. By this time, Tate had established personal contact with Eliot. In July 1926, Eliot had, after a lapse of ten months, declined to publish any of Tate's poetry in the *Criterion,* but given it some very thorough criticism. Eliot had hazarded the unwelcome opinion that Tate had greater talents as a critic than as a poet. See Tate to Davidson, 29 July 1926, Davidson/10/34.

9. Davidson to Tate, 15 February 1927, Tate Papers; Tate to Davidson, 20 February 1927, Davidson/10/37.

10. Tate to Davidson [12 April 1928], Davidson/10/41; Tate, *Memoirs and Opinions,* pp. 3-23.

11. Tate to Davidson, 1 March 1927, Davidson/10/37; Tate to Lytle, 15 March 1927, Lytle/5/1; Tate to James Southall Wilson, 23 May 1927, *Virginia Quarterly Review* Papers; Tate to Davidson, 28 April 1927, Davidson/10/37.

12. Tate to Davidson, 26 February 1928, Davidson 10/40; Cowley, *Exile's Return,* p. 223; Tate to Davidson, 28 April 1927, Davidson/10/37.

13. Tate to Fletcher, 11 June 1927, Fletcher Papers; Tate to Davidson, 11 June 1927, Davidson/10/37.

14. Tate to Davidson, 5 May 1927, Davidson/10/37; Tate to Davidson, 17 July 1927, Davidson/10/38; Cowan, *The Fugitive Group,* p. 36.

15. Tate to Fletcher, 27 August 1927, Fletcher Papers.

16. Christopher Hollis, *The American Heresy* (London, 1927), pp. 13, 168; Hollis, *The Seven Ages: Their Exits and Their Entrances* (London, 1974), pp. 1-100.

17. Tate to Fletcher, 24 December 1927, Fletcher Papers; Tate, *Jefferson Davis: His Rise and Fall* (New York, 1929), p. 303.

18. Tate to Fletcher, 21 November 1928, Fletcher Papers.

19. Tate, *Jefferson Davis,* pp. 96-97.

20. Tate, *Stonewall Jackson: The Good Soldier* (New York, 1928), pp. 59-62; Tate, *Jefferson Davis,* pp. 18-19, 188, 87, 300-302.

21. Tate to Fletcher, 5 March 1929, Fletcher Papers; Tate to Fletcher, 3 December 1930, Fletcher Papers; Tate to Lytle, 4 May 1929, Lytle/5/2.

22. Eliot, "The Humanism of Irving Babbitt," in *Selected Essays: 1917-1932* (London, 1932), pp. 419-28; on Tate's meeting with Eliot, see Tate to Davidson, 24 October 1928, Davidson/10/53, and Tate to Davidson, 18 February 1929, Davidson/10/55.

23. Tate to Fletcher, 19 October 1928, Fletcher Papers.

24. Tate to Fletcher, 21 November 1928, Fletcher Papers; Tate to Davidson, 18 February 1929, Davidson/10/55.

25. Tate to James Southall Wilson, 25 April 1929, *Virginia Quarterly Review* Papers; Tate to Davidson, 18 February 1929, Davidson/10/55; Tate to Lytle, 16 June 1929, Lytle/5/2: "Have you seen John Ransom's essay in Harper's? It is a great piece of work. The whole thing is so brilliant and profound that the editor had to put it in the back of the magazine; I am amazed that he ever accepted it. I am sending you a piece that I wrote last winter, now in the Criterion. It is nowhere so fine as John's, and it doesn't touch the political and social question, but it argues for much the same views from a more general position;" cf. Tate, "The Fallacy of Humanism," *Criterion* 8 (July 1929), pp. 661-81.

26. Tate to Ransom, 27 July 1929, Davidson/10/43.

27. Tate to Davidson, 10 August 1929, Davidson/10/43; Tate to Ransom, 27 July 1929, Davidson/10/43.

28. Tate to Fletcher, 21 November 1928, Fletcher Papers; Tate to Davidson, 9 November 1929, Davidson/10/44.

29. Tate to Fletcher, 19 October 1928, Fletcher Papers; Tate to Davidson, 10 August 1929, Davidson/10/43; Tate, "Mistaken Beauty," *New Republic* 59 (29 May 1929): 51.

30. Tate, "Mr. Cabell's Farewell," *New Republic* 61 (8 January 1930): 201-2.

31. *Ibid.*; Tate to Davidson, 12 December 1929, Davidson/10/44.

32. Radcliffe Squires, *Allen Tate: A Literary Biography* (New York, 1971), pp. 100-101.

33. Tate to Davidson, 9 February 1930, Davidson/10/46; *ITMS,* p. 155.

34. *ITMS,* pp. 155-75.

35. Cf. *ITMS,* p. 155, with the same essay, revised and reprinted in Tate, *Essays of Four Decades* (New York, 1968), p. 558.

36. *ITMS,* pp. 171-72.

37. Tate to Fletcher, 3 December 1930, Fletcher Papers.

38. Tate to Fletcher, 21 November 1928, Fletcher Papers: an intimation of the paradox of liberalism and conservatism in Tate can be gained from his remarks on the 1928 elections, "If I had been at home I should certainly [have] voted for Smith, both because he is a Democrat and because he was personally promising. But if any other Democrat had been running, I should have voted for [Norman] Thomas [the Socialist]. In that case the vote would have been merely the register of an opinion, and Thomas stands for it, as things are, better than any one else"; Fletcher, *Life is My Song* (New York, 1937), p. 344.

39. Tate to Davidson, 16 April 1931, Davidson/10/49; Tate to Davidson, 14 July 1931, Davidson/10/49.

40. Tate to Lytle, 16 July 1931, Lytle/5/2; Interview with Lytle.

41. Tate, unpublished MS of a life of Lee, p. 31, Tate Papers; Tate to Lytle, 16 July 1931, Lytle/5/2; Lytle, "Robert E. Lee," *Southern Review* (1935-36), repr. in *The Hero With the Private Parts: Essays by Andrew Lytle* (Baton Rouge, 1966), pp. 227-39.

42. Interview with Lytle; Lytle, *Nathan Bedford Forrest and his Critter Company* (New York, 1931); Tate to Davidson, 12 December 1929, Davidson/10/44; Tate to Fletcher, 4 November 1930, Fletcher Papers.

43. Tate, MS "Lee," p. 3: "The profits, for a few, were great at the very start, but these profits were invariably, and after the manner of the landed tradition, necessarily conceived in terms of keeping up the physical establishment of life, the home, the family, and finally that almost mystical entity that lies back of the mere sound of a family name. This, I believe, is the true meaning of aristocracy, and all those prejudices of class that the Virginians in time acquired were but the outward defenses of a great social idea. This idea was a great one because it contained in it probably as high a degree of political and moral disinterestedness as any society in the world has ever achieved"; Lytle, *Hero With the Private Parts,* p. 237; Tate, MS "Lee," p. 30.

44. Tate to James Southall Wilson, 4 September 1931, Southern Writers Conference Papers, Alderman Library, University of Virginia; Interview with Lambert Davis, Chapel Hill, 19 November 1973; Tate to J. S. Wilson, 29 October 1931, Southern Writers Conference Papers.

45. Tate, "Regionalism and Sectionalism," *New Republic* 69 (23 November 1931): 158-61.

46. Malcolm Cowley to Tate, 18 November 1931, Tate Papers; Tate to Edmund Wilson, 28 July 1931, Lytle/5/2; Tate to Ellen Glasgow, 30 March 1933, Ellen Glasgow Papers, Alderman Library, University of Virginia.

47. Tate to Davidson, 9 December 1930, Davidson/10/49; Tate and Lytle to Davidson, Ransom and Lyle Lanier, 11 December 1930, Davidson/7/9; Tate to Davidson, 13 December 1930, Davidson/10/49.

48. George B. Tindall, *The Emergence of the New South, 1913-1945* (Baton Rouge, 1967), pp. 383-85, on the Harlan Strike; Tate to Davidson and Warren, 10 December 1931, Warren Papers; Tate to Ransom, 17 December 1931, Tate Papers.

49. Tate to Bernard Bandler, 14 November 1931, *Hound and Horn* Papers, Tate File; Tate to Davidson, 17 December 1931, Davidson/10/49.

50. See *Hound and Horn* Papers, Tate file; on the publication of "To the Lacedaemonians," see Davidson to Wade, 5 July 1932, Wade Papers: this poem trod closer on the line between art and propaganda, much insisted upon by Tate, than he might have liked, if one takes at face value Davidson's observation, "There's so much in it of the doctrine that you and I have talked over."

51. Tate to Doris Levine, 27 May 1933, *Hound and Horn* Papers, Tate file, refers to it as "a study, based upon the genealogy of two families, of the forces that have disrupted all settled forms of life in America."

52. Tate to Lytle, 22 August 1932, Lytle/5/3; Tate to Davidson, 9 October 1932, Davidson/10/51.

53. Tate to Davidson, 10 December 1932, Davidson/10/51; Tate to Lytle, 4 November 1932, Lytle/5/3.

54. Tate to Davidson, 28 December 1932, Davidson/10/51; Tate to Warren, 9 December 1932, Warren Papers; Tate to Warren, 17 October 1933, Warren Papers.

55. Tate, "A View of the Whole South," *American Review* 2 (February 1934): 411-32, passim.

56. *Ibid.*, pp. 413, 430, Tate to Herbert Agar, 17 November 1933, Tate Papers; Tate to R. P. Blackmur, 18 December 1933, *Hound and Horn* papers, Tate file.

57. Tate to Warren, 15 December 1934, Warren Papers.

58. Tate to Lincoln Kirstein, 9 September 1933, *Hound and Horn* Papers, Tate file; Tate, "Where Are the People?" *American Review* 2 (December 1933): 231-37; Tate to Agar, 9 September 1933, Tate Papers. It is pertinent to note that Agar was heavily influenced by Oswald Spengler: see Agar, *Land of the Free* (Boston, 1935), especially chap. 1, "Culture or Colonialism?" Tate had read Spengler in the 1920s and there are occasional echoes of the German in his writings.

59. Tate to Lytle, 19 February 1935, Lytle/5/4.

60. Chard Smith to Agar, 8 April 1936, and Agar to Chard Smith, 13 April 1936, Tate Papers; Interview with Lytle.

61. Tate to Agar, 7 January 1937, Tate Papers.

62. Tate to E. F. Saxton, 17 November 1933, Davidson/10/52 (the prospectus is reprinted in *The Literary Correspondence of Donald Davidson and Allen Tate* ed. J. T. Fain and T. D. Young (Athens, Ga., 1974), pp. 409-11); Tate to Ellen Glasgow, 22 September 1935, Glasgow Papers.

63. Tate to Lambert Davis, 24 October 1934, *Virginia Quarterly Review* Papers.

64. Tate, "The Profession of Letters in the South," *Virginia Quarterly Review* 11 (April 1935): 161-76.

65. *Ibid.*, p. 173.

66. See, especially, his comments on the good manners of the French peasantry and those at the Southern Writers' Conference, in Tate to Lytle, 22 August 1932, Lytle/5/3, and Tate to James Southall Wilson, 29 October 1931, Southern Writers' Conference Papers.

67. Tate, in *Shenandoah* 3 (Summer 1952): 29.

8: Frank Owsley: "The Immoderate Past"

1. Interview with Lytle; interview with Harriet Chappell Owsley, Atlanta, November 1973; John Prebble, *Glencoe: The Story of the Massacre* (London, 1966), pp. 45-46. The importance of Scottish tradition on the formulation of myths about the South is not to be slighted, not alone for the novels of Walter Scott. In the immediate postbellum period, frequent analogies were made between the Lost Cause of the Confederacy and the "Auld Cause" of the Jacobites. A prime example of the Lost Cause genre, Thomas Dixon's *The Clansman,* was dedicated to a "Scotch-Irish leader of the South, my Uncle, Colonel LeRoy McAfee, Grand Titan of the invisible Empire of the Ku Klux Klan." See Rollin Osterweis, *The Myth of the Lost Cause, 1865-1900* (Hamden, Conn., 1973), pp. 25-26.

2. Interview with Harriet Owsley; on the tale of Uncle Dink, see Robert Penn Warren, "Afterword" to Lytle, *The Long Night* (paperback reprint, New York, 1973): however, Warren has mistakenly displaced the story of visiting Uncle Dink from Owsley's father to Owsley himself.

3. Interview with Harriet Owsley.

4. *Ibid.*; Wendell H. Stephenson, *Southern History in the Making* (Baton Rouge, 1964), pp. 132-43, on Petrie. As sometimes happens to graduate students, Owsley was the victim of a faculty squabble and obliged to retake his oral examinations; the dispute was between the liberal, Dodd and the conservative, Andrew McLaughlin, over the possibility of the former succeeding McLaughlin as head of the history department: see J. Fred Rippy, *Bygones I Cannot Help Recalling: The Memoirs of a Mobile Scholar* (Austin, 1966), pp. 123-25.

5. Interview with Harriet Owsley.

6. A. C. McLaughlin to Owsley, 12 March 1921, Frank Lawrence Owsley Papers, box 3, folder 20 (hereinafter cited as Owsley/box no./folder no.); Owsley, *States Rights in the Confederacy* (Chicago, 1925), pp. 1-2.

7. Interview with Lytle; Owsley to Davidson, 24 February 1927, Davidson/8/10.

8. Interview with Harriet Owsley.

9. *Ibid.*; Owsley, "My Impressions of England," MS in Owsley/8/22; Caroline Gordon to Lytle, 27 October 1928, Lytle/5/9.

10. Tate to Davidson, 10 December 1932, Davidson/10/51; Owsley to Davidson, 24 February 1927, Davidson/8/10.

11. Owsley, *King Cotton Diplomacy: Foreign Relations of the Confederate States of America,* rev. ed. (Chicago, 1959), pp. 542-58; the "war profits" conspiracy theory began during the argument over entry into the war in 1917 and remained widely held during the 1920s and 1930s: see Selig Adler, *The Isolationist Impulse: Its Twentieth Century Reaction* (New York, 1957), pp. 256-58.

12. Owsley, "My Impressions of England," p. 78, Owsley/8/22; cf. Mary Ellison, *Support for Secession: Lancashire and the American Civil War* (Chicago, 1972) p. 212, which criticizes Owsley's view of the English working classes, and H. Donaldson Jordan, review

of *King Cotton Diplomacy,* in *American Historical Review* 38 (October 1932): 135-37; a more benign view is taken by Bernard Cresap, "Frank L. Owsley and *King Cotton Diplomacy,"Alabama Review* (October 1973): 235-51.

13. Tate to Owsley, 2 July 1928, Owsley/5/10.

14. Owsley to Lytle, 7 March 1930, Lytle/4/2; *ITMS,* pp. 61-69; the notion of a second American Revolution was more susceptible to a pro-Confederate reading than Beard might have liked, in that hostility to untrammelled capitalism was too easily translatable into approval for those who opposed its rise: see Thomas J. Pressley, *Americans Interpret Their Civil War* (Princeton, 1954), pp. 242, 280-82.

15. *ITMS,* pp. 69-91.

16. Pressley, *Americans Interpret Their Civil War,* pp. 166-81; *ITMS,* pp. 77, 62, 79; Avery Craven to Owsley, 15 August 1934, Owsley/3/36; Thomas P. Abernethy to Owsley, 17 September 1933, Owsley/1/1.

17. Owsley to Davidson, 8 April 1931, Davidson/8/10; Owsley to Tate, 29 February 1932, Tate Papers.

18. Warren to Owsley, 22 February 1938, Owsley/5/19; Owsley to Warren, 24 February 1938, *Southern Review* Papers, Owsley file.

19. Brooks to Davidson, 18 March [1931], Davidson/3/36.

20. Interview with Harriet Owsley; Owsley, "The Chief Stakes of the South in World Affairs Today," unpublished MS, Owsley/8/15.

21. Dan T. Carter, *Scottsboro: A Tragedy of the American South* (Baton Rouge, 1969); Owsley, "Scottsboro: The Third Crusade," *American Review* 1 (Summer 1933): 259.

22. Owsley, "Scottsboro," pp. 257-85.

23. "48th Annual Meeting, Urbana, Illinois," *American Historical Review* 39 (April 1934): 434; Davidson to Wade, 15 January 1934, Wade Papers.

24. Fletcher to Owsley, 1 December 1933, Owsley/2/20.

25. Owsley to Fletcher, [December 1933], Fletcher Papers.

26. *Ibid.;* Owsley to Warren, 24 February 1938, *Southern Review* Papers, Owsley file.

27. Owsley to Fletcher, 11 March 1934, Fletcher Papers; Davidson to Wade, 25 March 1934, Wade Papers.

28. Davidson to Wade, 25 March 1934, Wade Papers; Davidson to Fletcher, 26 March 1934, Fletcher Papers; Owsley to Wade, 17 October 1934, Wade Papers; see also, "Secret Society Pledges Itself to Preserve Southern Culture and Traditions: Is Called Phalanx," *Vanderbilt Hustler* (23 March 1934), copy enclosed in Odum to A. R. Mann, 23 May 1938, General Education Board Papers, 1st ser., 2d subser., box 216, folder 333.1.

29. Owsley to James H. Kirkland, 20 January 1936, Owsley/6/15. Owsley had spent a good deal of his time in reviews, fending off neoabolitionist historians; see Owsley, "The War of the Sections," review of A. C. Cole, *The Irrepressible Conflict* and Gerald Johnson, *The Secession of the Southern States,* in *Virginia Quarterly Review* 10 (October 1934): 630-35, and "The American Triangle," review of James T. Adams, *America's Tragedy,* and George F. Milton, *The Eve of Conflict,* in *Virginia Quarterly Review* 11 (January 1935): 113-19.

30. Interview with Harriet Owsley; Owsley to Davidson, 8 April 1931, Davidson/8/10.

31. Owsley to Davidson, 24 August 1932, Davidson/8/10; Owsley to Davidson, 5 August 1933, Davidson/8/10.

32. Owsley, "The Pillars of Agrariansim," *American Review* 4 (March 1935): 529-47, reprinted in *The South, Old and New Frontiers: Selected Essays of Frank Lawrence Owsley* ed. Harriet C. Owsley (Athens, Ga., 1969), pp. 177-89.

33. Cf. Edgar W. Knight, *Among the Danes* (Chapel Hill, 1927); Rupert Vance had plans to visit Ireland and study its economy in the late 1930s: Odum to Jackson Davis, 14 January 1934, Odum/17/364.

34. Owsley, *The South: Selected Essays,* pp. 177-89; cf. William Yandell Elliott, *The Need for Constitutional Reform* (New York, 1935); Cowan, *The Fugitive Group,* pp. 3, 17-19, 76-77, 112, 197, on Elliott and the Fugitives.

35. On conservation and progressivism, see Samuel P. Hays, *Conservation and the Gospel of Efficiency: The Progressive Conservation Movement, 1890-1920* (Cambridge, Mass., 1959).

36. On the Southern Policy Committee, see George B. Tindall, *The Emergence of the New South, 1913-1945* (Baton Rouge, 1967), 592-93, and Francis P. Miller, *Man From the Valley: Memoirs of a Twentieth Century Virginian* (Chapel Hill, 1971), pp. 78-88; Francis P. Miller to Owsley, 23 and 30 January 1935, Owsley/4/1.

37. John H. Bankhead to Owsley, 12 March 1935, Owsley/1/7; Sidney Baldwin, *Poverty and Politics: The Rise and Decline of the Farm Security Administration* (Chapel Hill, 1938), pp. 129, 146-48. Bankhead introduced his bill on 11 February 1935, more than a month before he wrote to Owsley, and hearings before the Senate Committee on Agriculture and Forestry were held on 5 March. It is interesting that Henry Wallace, in his testimony, used the same anticommunist argument in pleading for the measure as Owsley.

38. William Dodd to Owsley, 26 March 1935, and 4 May 1935. Owsley/2/12; Hugo Black to Owsley, 26 March 1935, Owsley/1/11.

39. Owsley to William Couch, 11 March 1935, Couch/1/"1935."

40. Vance to Owsley, 29 March 1935, Owsley/5/13; Vance was acting in an advisory role for the Alexander/Tannenbaum group and the Department of Agriculture: Baldwin, *Poverty and Politics,* pp. 128, n.2, 131, n.5; according to Tate, Vance voted with the Agrarians on every issue during the Southern Policy Conference in Chattanooga: Tate to Davidson, 11 May 1936, Davidson/10/55.

41. William Couch, "An Agrarian Program for the South," *American Review* 3 (Summer 1934): 313-26.

42. Owsley to Couch, 18 March 1935 and 11 March 1935, Couch/1/"1935."

43. Owsley to Agar, 26 September 1935, Lytle/13/51; Owsley to Tate, 26 September 1935, Lytle/13/51; Agar to Owsley, 29 September 1935, Owsley/1/2; Owsley to Agar, 1 October 1935, Tate Papers.

44. E. D. Stewart, S.J., to Owsley, 15 November 1936, Owsley/5/5; Ralph Borsodi to E. D. Stewart, S.J., 25 January 1937, Owsley/1/11; J. C. Rawe, S.J., to E. D. Stewart, S.J., 7 February 1937, Owsley/4/16.

45. Agar to Owsley, 29 September 1935, Owsley/1/2; Owsley to Agar, 1 October 1935, Tate Papers.

46. Owsley, "The Foundations of Democracy," in *Who Owns America? A New Declaration of Independence,* ed. Herbert Agar and Allen Tate (Boston, 1936), pp. 52-67; Owsley's hostility to government by the Supreme Court was to become particularly apposite after the Brown Decision of 1954; cf. Owsley, "Democracy Unlimited," in Owsley, *The South: Selected Essays,* pp. 194-202, a lecture given at the University of Kentucky in 1955.

47. Owsley, "The Historical Philosophy of Frederick Jackson Turner," *American Review* 5 (Summer 1935):371-72; Turner, *The Significance of Sections in American History* (New York, 1932), p. 51.

48. Owsley, "A Key to Southern Liberalism," *Southern Review* 3 (Summer 1937): 28-38; "The Making of Andrew Jackson," *American Review* 1 (May 1933): 220-25; "The Soldier Who Walked with God," review of Freeman's *Lee,* in *American Review* 4 (February 1935): 435-39, and 5 (April 1935): 62-74; see also Douglas Southall Freeman to Owsley, 19 January 1935, Owsley/2/21.

49. Interview with Harriet Owsley.

50. On the poor whites, see A. J. Den Hollander, "The Tradition of the 'Poor Whites'" in *Culture in the South,* ed. William Couch (Chapel Hill, 1934), pp. 403-31; Fabian Linden, "Economic Democracy in the Slave South: An Appraisal of Some Recent Views," *Journal*

of Negro History 31 (April 1946): 140-89, and Owsley's brief rejoinder, "Letter to the Editor," *American Historical Review* 52 (July 1947): 845-49.

51. Owsley, *Plain Folk of the Old South* (Baton Rouge, 1949), pp. 90-91.

52. Roger W. Shugg, *Origins of Class Struggle in Louisiana: A Social History of White Farmers and Laborers during Slavery and After, 1840-1875* (Baton Rouge, 1939); see Owsley to Cleanth Brooks, 5 November 1939, *Southern Review* Papers, Owsley file: "I have not read Shugg's book, but I located much of his statistical ante bellum material for him and told him how to use it; but his Marxian title gives me the impression that he has misused the material"; later Owsley reviewed Shugg's book in *Journal of Southern History* 6 (February 1940): 116-17.

53. Richard Hofstadter, "U.B. Phillips and the Plantation Leged," *Journal of Negro History* 29 (April 1944): 109-24; Eugene Genovese, *In Red and Black: Marxian Explorations in Southern and Afro-American History* (New York, 1971), pp. 264-67, defends Phillips's position. The whole problem of the relationship, cultural and political, between plantation and farm remains unresolved, although there are a very few suggestive microcosmic studies: Randolph B. Campbell, "Planters and Plain Folk: Harrison County, Texas, as a Test Case, 1850-1860," *Journal of Southern History* 40 (August 1974): 369-98, comes out cautiously for the Phillips-Genovese planter dominance theory.

54. Owsley, *Plain Folk,* pp. 93, 133, 134, 139; Isaiah Berlin, *Vico and Herder: Two Studies in the History of Ideas* (New York, 1976), p. 196.

55. Owsley to Warren, 18 October 1938, *Southern Review* Papers, Owsley file.

56. Owsley had grown increasingly disenchanted with Vanderbilt, as the Agrarians had, one by one, severed their links with it. Moreover, he was frustrated with the difficulties of running a graduate program at a university with few manuscript holdings and little inclination to alter the situation. In retrospect, he came to look upon his Agrarian phase with nostalgia, as a "lost utopia": Owsley to Warren, 25 August 1946, Owsley/6/14, and Owsley to "Carter," 14 March 1952, Owsley/6/17.

57. Owsley to Geoffrey Stone, 24 May 1938, Owsley/6/16, Owsley to Tate, 14 November 1943, Tate Papers.

58. Thomas B. Alexander to Owsley, 17 October 1944, Owsley/1/3; see also Glover Moore to Owsley, 24 December 1943, Owsley/4/8.

59. Owsley, "The Chief States of the South in World Affairs Today," unpublished MS, Owsley/8/15.

60. Interview with Harriet Owsley; Owsley to Lytle, 28 February 1956, Lytle/4/2: "Our negro trouble here is unending. The Supreme Court has handed the Negro a privilege—or right—that one searches the Constitution in vain to find. It is a mighty stride toward the monolithic State that our Yankee Liberals are creating.... I believe that ultimately the negroes will be admitted in limited numbers to state universities—very limited. Personally, while I cringe at the idea, yet I am of the opinion that our professional schools—medicine, dentistry, law, and theology—should train the Southern negro doctors, lawyers, and preachers. There would be such a relatively few, no problem would be created—at least no major problem. But public schools—I am convinced that integration at this level and of a mass proportion would be the last word in disaster to the white South and to the U.S. The schools would be ruined—as they have been in Washington—and endless strife would follow. Furthermore, schools are *social* institutions. This would end in a lot of race mixture."

9: Donald Davidson: "The Creed of Memory"

1. Interviews with Lytle and Warren; T. D. Young and M. Thomas Inge, *Donald Davidson* (New York, 1971), p. 148.

2. Davidson to Fletcher, 22 May 1941, Davidson/2/5; Interview with Theresa Sherrer Davidson, Middlebury, Vt., 15 September 1973.

3. Davidson to father, 4 May 1919, Davidson/1/1; interview with Theresa Davidson; the brief tour of 1965 to Ireland, England, Italy, and Greece, was paid for by Richard Dodd, a wealthy friend from Marshallville; Davidson did toy briefly with visiting Europe in the early 1930s, but not too seriously: see Davidson to Wade, 20 June 1932, Wade Papers.

4. Richmond Beatty to Brainerd Cheney, 28 December [1943], Brainerd Cheney Papers, Joint University Library, Nashville, box 4, file 3; Bernard Breyer to Davidson, 17 January 1954, Davidson/3/34; Senator Robert R. Reynolds to Davidson, 7 February 1939, Davidson/8/39; Senator McKellar to Davidson, 4 February 1939, Davidson/7/14; Davidson to Warren and Brooks, 6 February 1937, *Southern Review* Papers, Davidson file. During the Spanish Civil War, Davidson protested to the university authorities when pro-Loyalist circulars were distributed in Vanderbilt mailboxes: "I wish to make it plain, however," he wrote, "that neither the Fascist cause, the Communist cause, nor any other European cause is among the causes in which I have an interest. I am against them all, without exception: Russia, Italy, Germany, France and England—and I am especially against any or all of them in so far as they endeavor in any way to enlist American support and embroil us in their troubles." See Davidson to O. C. Carmichael, 14 December 1938, Davidson/1/44.

5. Davidson to Tate, 13 August 1922, Davidson/1/3; Davidson, "Critic's Almanac," *Nashville Tennessean,* 23 June 1929, reprinted in Davidson, *The Spyglass: Views and Reviews, 1924-1930,* ed. J. T. Fain (Nashville, 1963), p. 140; Davidson to Tate, 29 July 1929, Tate Papers.

6. Lewis Simpson, "Introduction: Donald Davidson and the Southern Defense of Poetry," to Davidson, *Still Rebels, Still Yankees and Other Essays* (Baton Rouge, 1972); Davidson, "Meditation on Literary Fame," in *The Long Street: Poems* (Nashville, 1961), p. 37.

7. Davidson to John Mebane, 19 September 1960, Davidson/2/54; Davidson to Louis Rubin, 24 January 1954, Davidson/2/39; Davidson to Louis Rubin, 10 May 1955, Davidson/2/47.

8. On Mims and Davidson, see Michael O'Brien (ed.), "Edwin Mims and Donald Davidson: A Correspondence, 1923-1958," *Southern Review* 10 (Autumn 1974): 904-6; Davidson to Rubin, 24 January 1954, Davidson/2/39.

9. Davidson to Tate, 15 August 1926, Tate Papers.

10. Davidson, "First Fruits of Dayton: The Intellectual Evolution in Dixie," *Forum* 89 (June 1928): 896-907.

11. Davidson, *The Spyglass,* pp. 5-6.

12. Davidson to Tate, 22 June 1927, Tate Papers; Davidson to Fletcher, 13 June 1927, Davidson/1/10; Davidson to Fletcher, 21 March 1926, Davidson/1/8.

13. Ransom to Mims, 27 September 1926, Mims Papers; Davidson to Ransom, 5 July 1929, Davidson/1/12; Ransom to Tate, 22 February [1930], Tate Papers; Davidson to Tate, 5 February 1929, Tate Papers.

14. *ITMS,* pp. 28-50; Davidson, "The Trend of Literature: A Partisan View," in *Culture in the South,* ed. Couch, pp. 183-210.

15. Interview with Lytle; Ransom to Tate, 3 January [1932], Tate Papers.

16. Tate to Bernard Bandler, 24 February 1932, *Hound and Horn* papers, Tate file.

17. Conversation with Robert Buffington, Atlanta, November 1973 (Wagner was Davidson's favorite composer); Tate to Davidson, 27 March 1936, Davidson/10/54; interview with Harriet Owsley; interview with Lytle.

18. Davidson to Fletcher, 23 March 1931, Davidson/1/18; Davidson to Tate, 16 March 1933, Tate Papers.

19. Davidson to Tate, 17 March 1935, Davidson/1/27; Davidson to Lambert Davis, 9 January 1935, Davidson/1/26; Lambert Davis to Davidson, 17 January 1935, Davidson/4/37; Davidson to Lambert Davis, 23 January 1935, Davidson/1/26; Davidson to Lambert Davis, 28 January 1935, *Virginia Quarterly Review* Papers.

20. Lambert Davis to Ellen Glasgow, 31 December 1934, *Virginia Quarterly Review* Papers.

21. Davidson to Fletcher, 6 March 1935, Davidson/1/26; Davidson to Fletcher, 12 March 1935, Davidson/1/27; Charlie May Fletcher to Davidson, n.d. [1951], contains this: "I don't suppose any of the group with whom he [Fletcher] quarreled so bitterly in 1935 knew that it was at the beginning of one of his periods of illness. He managed to get as far as Memphis, on his way from New Orleans, then he had to telephone his sister to come for him while he waited in the railway station. I have come across an hour by hour report of the trained nurse who took care of him, and he was evidently far worse than in his last illness [Fletcher committed suicide in 1950]. But I am convinced that he wrote letters, previous to that, without knowing what he was saying. Only one with him twenty-four hours a day, as I was, could see the approach of the cycles."

22. See, for example, Fletcher to Warren, 11 March 1935, Warren Papers; Ransom to Fletcher, 13 March 1935, Tate Papers (apparently not sent); Fletcher to Tate, 13 March [1935], Tate Papers; Fletcher to Tate, 14 March 1935, Tate Papers; Ransom to Fletcher, 15 March [1935], Fletcher Papers; Davidson's account of the affair can be seen in Davidson to Tate, 17 March 1935, Davidson/1/27.

23. Ransom to Fletcher, 18 July 1933, Fletcher Papers; Davidson to Macmillans, 5 January 1934, Tate Papers; Davidson to Macmillans, 13 March 1934, Davidson/1/25.

24. Davidson to Tate, 24 April 1936, Tate Papers.

25. Davidson to Fletcher, 6 March 1935, Davidson/1/26; Warren to Catherine Wilds, 25 May 1936, Tate Papers; Ransom to Tate, 29 March 1939, Tate Papers.

26. Davidson to Warren, 21 October 1936, *Southern Review* Papers, Davidson file; Davidson to Tate, 27 March 1937, Tate Papers.

27. Davidson to Mims, 29 March 1932, and 30 March 1932, Davidson/1/19; Davidson to Wade, 20 June 1932, Wade Papers.

28. Davidson to Lytle, 27 October 1932, Lytle/1/19.

29. Davidson to Wade, 25 January 1933, Wade Papers; Davidson to Wade, 17 May 1933, Wade Papers; Davidson, "The Sacred Harp in the Land of Eden," *Virginia Quarterly Review* 10 (April 1934): 203-17; this poem is reprinted in *The Literary Correspondence of Donald Davidson and Allen Tate*, ed. T. D. Young and J. T. Fain (Athens, Ga., 1974), pp. 412-16.

30. Davidson to William Couch, 8 March 1931, Davidson/1/18; Davidson to Fletcher, 26 July 1930, Davidson/1/15; Davidson to Tate, 19 February 1933, Tate Papers.

31. Lambert Davis to Davidson, 4 January 1949, Davidson/4/39, gives the following sales figures:

1937-38	206	1941-42	7	1945-46	10
1938-39	204	1942-43	9	1946-47	29
1939-40	75	1943-44	8	1947-48	16
1940-41	6	1944-45	12	1948-49	3

In 1948, the University of North Carolina Press pulped unbound copies and allowed *The Attack on Leviathan* to go out of print. Davidson was furious. Lambert Davis, editor of the press, had to go on a peace mission to Nashville to prevent Davidson from suing the press. In a subsequent memorandum, Davis shrewdly observed: "The core of Mr. Davidson's dissatisfaction, I am sure, is the feeling that the Press exercised some kind of censorship on his work. He is almost the only surviving member of the Nashville group of the '20s whose southernism has been intensified rather than modified by the passage of time. He has parted company, one by one, with nearly all the members of that group, and he very definitely has the feeling that the world is against him, and that there are sinister machinations against his expression of his opinions": "Memorandum on Conversation with Donald Davidson," 23 February 1949, University of North Carolina Press Papers, *Attack on Leviathan* file.

32. Davidson to Couch, 19 June 1938, Davidson/1/41.

33. Only Russell Kirk and Francis B. Simkins subsequently gave it any attention: see Simkins, "The South," in *Regionalism in America,* ed. Merrill Jensen (Madison, 1952), pp. 148, 155, 156, 168, and Simkins to Fletcher, n.d. [1949?], Davidson/8/34; and Russell Kirk, "The Poet as Guardian: Donald Davidson," in *Confessions of a Bohemian Tory: Episodes and Reflections of a Vagrant Career* (New York, 1963), p. 154.

34. Davidson, *The Attack on Leviathan: Regionalism and Nationalism in the United States* (Chapel Hill, 1938), p. 4.

35. *Ibid.,* p. 41; Davidson to Wade, 3 March 1934, Odum/16/342; Davidson, *Attack on Leviathan,* p. 40.

36. Davidson, *Attack on Leviathan,* pp. 13-38.

37. *Ibid.,* pp. 39-64, 285-311; clipping, *Raleigh News and Observer,* 10 November 1954, Odum/30/Obituary file.

38. Davidson, *Attack on Leviathan,* pp. 65-101.

39. *Ibid.,* p. 96; Isaiah Berlin, *Vico and Herder: Two Studies in the History of Ideas* (New York, 1976), passim; Hayden White, *Metahistory: The Historical Imagination in Nineteenth Century Europe* (Baltimore, 1973), pp. 43-264.

40. Davidson to Ferris Greenslet, 31 October 1933, Davidson/1/22 (note that Davidson had started serious planning for the book as early as 1933); Davidson, *Attack on Leviathan,* p. 137.

41. Davidson, *Attack on Leviathan,* pp. 131-211; cf. Walter P. Webb, *The Great Plains* (New York, 1931).

42. Davidson, *Attack on Leviathan,* pp. 212-27.

43. *Ibid.,* pp. 228-39.

44. *Ibid.,* pp. 240-57.

45. Quoted in Simpson, "Introduction," to Davidson, *Still Rebels, Still Yankees,* p. xvi.

46. C. Vann Woodward, "Hillbilly Realism," *Southern Review* 4 (Spring 1939): 676-81; Davidson, "The Class Approach to Southern Problems," *Southern Review* 5 (Autumn 1939): 261-72; Davidson to Tate, 28 November 1939, Tate Papers.

47. Davidson to Mims, 24 January 1934, Mims Papers.

48. Davidson to Stringfellow Barr, 3 June 1933, *Virginia Quarterly Review* Papers: "and please will somebody tell me what to expect of the New Deal!"; Davidson to Tate, 7 June 1933, Tate Papers: "I am more at sea, when it comes to judging the trend of affairs, than I was a year ago. Sometimes I think we are about to enter on a new period of commercial & industrial vulgarity that will eclipse the Hoover regime completely; sometimes I think things will may not be so bad, after all. There is no doubt, however, that Roosevelt is either putting on a revolution or doing the things that will inevitably produce one at last."; Davidson to William Watts Ball, 10 January 1937, William Watts Ball Papers, Duke University: "The Rooseveltians seem to me to have given the South a rake-off, which was coming to us, but they have done so at a price which I don't like to contemplate. They have done nothing to end permanently our condition of colonial dependency. We are still tied and helpless, disgorging most of our money and material wealth at the will of the eastern exploitative mechanism. The only difference under the New Deal is that we are given a little more money to disgorge and don't, so to speak, have to cough up our lifeblood every moment."

49. Davidson, *Attack on Leviathan,* p. 262; Davidson to Mims, 24 January 1934, Mims Papers.

50. Davidson, *Attack on Leviathan,* pp. 265, 267.

51. *Ibid.,* pp. 267-72.

52. *Ibid.,* pp. 272-78.

53. *Ibid.,* pp. 279-84.

54. *Ibid.,* pp. 312-38.

55. *Ibid.,* pp. 339-46.

56. Richard Hofstadter, *The Progressive Historians: Turner, Beard, Parrington* (New York, 1968), p. 100.

57. Davidson, *Attack on Leviathan,* p. 323: on this "Whiggery", see J. R. Pole, "The American Past: Is It Still Usable?" *Journal of American Studies* 1 (1967): 63-78, and "The New History and the Sense of Social Purpose in American Historical Writing," *Transactions of the Royal Historical Society* 23 (1973): 221-42.

58. Turner, *The Significance of Sections in American History* (New York, 1932), p. 50; Wilbur J. Cash, *The Mind of the South,* (New York, 1941), p. viii.

59. David Potter, "The Historian's Use of Nationalism, and Vice Versa," in *The South and the Sectional Conflict* (Baton Rouge, 1968), p. 39; cf. Claudius Murchison, "Captains of Southern Industry," *Virginia Quarterly Review* 7 (July 1931): 379: "If a correct ethical judgement of the Southern business man is sought, he must be viewed not in relation to that which is foreign to him, but in relation to the surroundings and circumstances which produced him. If he is to be tested, it must be through his success or failure in meeting the requirements which are unique to his own environment."

60. Davidson, *Attack on Leviathan,* p. 6: "The states and the Federal government represent conceptions or organizations rather than organisms. The government (or governments) cannot take formal notice, is in fact specifically forbidden in certain instances to take formal notice, of the actual geographic divisions—the sections or regions. The real and concrete thing does not express itself overtly in the abstract conception. The organizations do not coincide with the organisms."

61. Davidson, "Gulliver with Hay Fever," *American Review* 9 (Summer 1937): 153, 164-65; Davidson, "A Sociologist in Eden," *American Review* 8 (December 1936): 177-204; Davidson persistently distinguished between the sociology of Raper, on the one hand, and Odum and Vance, on the other, mainly because, one feels, Raper (whose *The Tragedy of Lynching* had been published in 1933) dealt more directly with race relations; Raper himself regarded the distinction as artificial: see Raper to Lillian Smith, 19 April 1938, enclosed in Raper to William Couch, 20 April 1938, University of North Carolina Press Papers, *Attack on Leviathan* file.

62. George B. Tindall, *The Emergence of the New South: 1913-1945* (Baton Rouge, 1967) pp. 711-21; Odum, *Race and Rumors of Race: Challenge to American Crisis* (Chapel Hill, 1943).

63. Davidson, "Preface to Decision," *Sewanee Review* 53 (Summer 1945): 394-412; Tate mildly dissented in the next issue, but observed that "any responsible leader who ignores Mr. Davidson's central argument ignores it at the peril of the South and the country": Tate, "Mr. Davidson and the Race Problem," *Sewanee Review* 53 (Autumn 1945): 659-60.

64. Davidson to James W. Perkins, 7 June 1950, Davidson/2/31; Davidson to Tate, 4 May 1952, Davidson/2/32; Davidson to Dwight Eisenhower, draft of a telegram, written on the back of a bill, dated 3 December 1954, Davidson/2/71; Davidson to Russell Kirk, 24 August 1955, Davidson/2/48. I speak of Davidson as an old man. In fact, he was only fifty-seven in 1950, but it is interesting that his letters betray an old man's querulousness from as early as the 1930s. The psychologist might make much of this; untutored, I resist the temptation.

65. Numan V. Bartley, *The Rise of Massive Resistance: Race and Politics in the South During the 1950s* (Baton Rouge, 1969), pp. 99-100; Davidson to Lytle, 14 March 1960, Lytle/1/20.

66. Davidson to Tate, 23 February 1940, Tate Papers; see, for example, Hugh Gordon Porter to Davidson, 13 May 1935, Davidson/8/28, and Mary Chalmers Hood to Davidson, 16 May 1935, Davidson/6/14.

67. Fletcher, *Life is My Song* (New York, 1937), p. 343.

Part IV: The Survival of Southern Identity. 10: The Idea of the South: An Interpretation

1. See W. J. Cash file, Alfred A. Knopf editorial offices, 201 East 50th Street, New York.

2. Joseph L. Morrison, *W. J. Cash: Southern Prophet* (New York, 1967), pp. 3-106; C. Vann Woodward, "The Elusive Mind of the South," in *American Counterpoint: Slavery and Racism in the North-South Dialogue* (Boston, 1971), pp. 267-70.

3. Cash, *The Mind of the South* (New York, 1941), pp. 48, 32-36.

4. *Ibid.,* 68-70, 84, 93-94.

5. *Ibid.,* pp. 75, 70, 115.

6. *Ibid.,* pp. 290, 362.

7. Ransom, "The Aesthetic of Regionalism," *American Review* 2 (January 1934): 307; Wade to Davidson, 8 August 1954, Davidson/11/37; Odum, *An American Epoch: Southern Portraiture in the National Picture* (New York, 1930), 66-116; H. Stuart Hughes, *Consciousness and Society: The Reorientation of European Social Thought 1890-1930* (New York, 1958), p. 428.

8. On the difference between the use of dialectic by Hegel and Fichte, see J. N. Findlay, *Hegel: A Re-Examination* (London, 1958), pp. 69-70, and Walter Kaufmann, *Hegel: A Reinterpretation* (New York, 1965), pp. 102-11: roughly speaking, the difference is that Fichte saw the synthesis as uniting and abolishing the disparateness of the forces that made it up, while Hegel believed that the synthesis retained the forces, which continued to influence its development; for Hegel, the tensions were only reconciled in the mind of the philosophical observer.

9. Karl Deutsch, *Nationalism and Social Communication: An Inquiry into the Foundations of Nationality* (New York, 1953), pp. 65, 69, 70-71, 146-47.

10. Both Vanderbilt University and the University of North Carolina, both Davidson and Odum, concurred in such a policy.

11. John S. Ezell, "A Southern Education for Southrons," *Journal of Southern History* 17 (August 1951): 303-27; David M. Potter, *The Impending Crisis 1848-1861* (New York, 1976), pp. 448-84.

12. Linguists do not seem to take the idea of a Southern language seriously, nor is there a single Southern dialect. Rather there are a number of dialects that convention has chosen, for social and political reasons, to group together: see William Cabell Greet, "Southern Speech," in *Culture in the South,* ed. William Couch (Chapel Hill, 1934), pp. 594-615, which observes, "There were and are many varieties of speech in the South, all closely related to speech in other parts of the country."

13. Potter, *The South and the Sectional Conflict* (Baton Rouge, 1968), pp. 69-70.

14. *Ibid.,* pp. 49, 66-68.

15. Tate to Davidson, 10 December 1932, Davidson/10/51.

16. Frank Kermode, *Romantic Image* (London, 1957), passim, but especially 152-77, which includes a comment on Ransom and Tate: M. H. Abrams, *Natural Supernaturalism: Tradition and Revolution in Romantic Literature* (London, 1971), p. 427, comments directly on Kermode's ideas, agrees that there are continuities between Romanticism and modernism, but insists upon the earlier movement's elan. For a more idiosyncratic statement of

the continuity, see Morse Peckham, *Beyond the Tragic Vision: The Quest for Identity in the Nineteenth Century* (New York, 1962).

17. Abrams, *Natural Supernaturalism*, p. 217.

18. *Ibid.*, passim; Herbert Marcuse, *Reason and Revolution: Hegel and the Rise of Social Theory* (Oxford, 1941), pp. 251-374; F. M. Barnard, ed., *J. G. Herder on Social and Political Culture* (Cambridge, 1969), pp. 32-34.

19. Kermode, *Romantic Image*, p. 160.

20. Davidson to Tate, 15 February 1927, Tate Papers; one might note that Davidson thought both his own, Tate's, and Ransom's poems were children of the Romantic movement's diagnosis of alienation and was hurt to be accused by Tate of being "romantic," knowing how that was a term of abuse in Tate's critical vocabulary: see Davidson to Tate, 23 February 1940, Tate Papers.

21. Davidson to Ferris Greenslet, 18 October 1933, Davidson/1/22.

22. It will be seen that my sympathies among the proponent theories of myth lie with Bronislaw Malinowski's functionalism, rather than Claude Lévi-Strauss' structuralism, with the rider that a functionalism of disparate needs seems more apposite than one that expresses a single integrated need; without such a modification one is hard put to explain the existence of conflicting versions of the Southern idea. In other words, the social function of myth must be conjoined to its individual psychological usefulness. Structuralism does not seem very useful to the historian, since Lévi-Strauss identifies ahistoricity as the primary characteristic of myth; nonetheless, it might be interesting to see a structuralist interpretation of Southern mythology's tendency to cohere around polarities. See Henry Tudor, *Political Myth* (London, 1972), esp. chap. 2; Edmund Leach, *Lévi-Strauss* (London, 1971), esp. pp. 13-17; *The Structuralists from Marx to Lévi-Strauss* ed. Richard and Fernande DeGeorge (New York, 1972); Bronislaw Malinowski, *Sex, Culture and Myth* (London, 1963).

23. Davidson to Warren, 28 February 1947, Warren Papers.

24. Warren, *Flood: A Romance of Our Time* (New York, 1963), p. 440; see the observations on this novel in Lewis P. Simpson, *The Dispossessed Garden: Pastoral and History in Southern Literature* (Athens, Ga., 1975), pp. 91-94.

25. Tate to C. Hartley Grattan, 28 November 1932, Tate Papers; Tate to Edmund Wilson, 28 July 1931, Lytle/5/2; Purdy, ed., *Fugitives' Reunion: Conversations at Vanderbilt: May 3-5, 1956* (Nashville, 1959), pp. 177-223.

26. John B. Carroll, ed., *Language, Thought and Reality: Selected Writings of Benjamin Lee Whorf* (Cambridge, Mass, 1956), p. 213, quoted in Max Black, *The Labyrinth of Language* (London, 1970), p. 97.

bibliographical note

Manuscript Sources

William Watts Ball Papers, Duke University, Durham, N.C.
William C. Binkley Papers, Joint University Library, Nashville.
Eugene Cunningham Branson Papers, Southern Historical Collection, University of North Carolina, Chapel Hill.
Cleanth Brooks Papers, Yale University, New Haven.
Wilbur Cash Correspondence, Alfred A. Knopf editorial offices, New York.
Brainerd Cheney Papers, Joint University Library.
Commission on Interracial Cooperation Papers, Atlanta University.
William Terry Couch Papers, Southern Historical Collection.
Donald Davidson Papers, Joint University Library.
Robert England MSS, University of Virginia, Charlottesville.
John Gould Fletcher Papers, University of Arkansas, Fayetteville.
General Education Board Papers, Rockefeller Foundation Archives, Pocantico Hills, Tarrytown N.Y.
Ellen Glasgow Papers, University of Virginia.
Hound and Horn Papers, Yale University.
Institute for Research in Social Science Papers, Southern Historical Collection.
Alfred A. Knopf Correspondence, W. J. Cash file, New York Public Library.
Andrew Nelson Lytle Papers, Joint University Library.
H. L. Mencken Papers, W. J. Cash file, New York Public Library.
George Fort Milton Papers, Library of Congress, Washington, D.C.
Edwin Mims Papers, Joint University Library.
Howard Washington Odum Papers, Southern Historical Collection.
Howard Washington Odum MSS, in the possession of Mrs. Mary Frances (Odum) Schinhan, Chapel Hill.
Frank Lawrence Owsley Papers, Joint University Library.
Ransom Family Papers, 1833-1957, John Crowe Ransom file, Tennessee State Archives, Nashville.
Rockefeller Foundation Papers, Pocantico Hills, Tarrytown, N.Y.
Southern Review Papers, Yale University.
Allen Tate Papers, Princeton University.
University of North Carolina Press Papers, Southern Historical Collection.
Virginia Quarterly Review Papers, University of Virginia.
John Donald Wade Papers, University of Georgia, Athens.
Robert Penn Warren Papers, Yale University.
James Southall Wilson MSS, University of Virginia.
Yale Review Papers, Yale University.

Interviews

Cleanth Brooks, New Haven, September 1973.
William Terry Couch, Chapel Hill, November 1973.
E. Merton Coulter, Athens, Ga., November 1973.
Theresa Sherrer Davidson, Middlebury, Vt., September 1973.

Lambert Davis, Chapel Hill, November 1973.
Andrew Lytle, Monteagle, Tenn., August 1973.
Harriet Chappell Owsley, Atlanta, November 1973.
Anne Wade Rittenbury, Nashville, August 1973.
Mary Frances Schinhan, Chapel Hill, November 1976.
Charlie May Simon (Mrs. John Gould Fletcher), Little Rock, August 1973.
Rupert Vance, Chapel Hill, November 1973.
Robert Penn Warren, New Haven and Bridgeport, September 1973.

index

THE JOHNS HOPKINS UNIVERSITY PRESS

This book was composed in Alphatype Times Roman by David Lorton from a design by Charles West. It was printed on 50 lb. Publishers Eggshell Wove and bound by The Maple Press Company.